The BIG BOOK of VEGETARIAN RECIPES

The BIG BOOK of VEGETARIAN RECIPES

More Than 700 Easy Vegetarian Recipes for Healthy and Flavorful Meals

Rachel Rappaport, author of *The Big Book of Slow Cooker Recipes*

Avon, Massachusetts

Copyright © 2014 by F+W Media, Inc.

All rights reserved. This book, or parts thereof, may not be reproduced in any form without permission from the publisher; exceptions are made for brief excerpts used in published reviews.

Published by Adams Media, a division of F+W Media, Inc.
57 Littlefield Street, Avon, MA 02322. U.S.A.
www.adamsmedia.com

ISBN 10: 1-4405-7257-7
ISBN 13: 978-1-4405-7257-9
eISBN 10: 1-4405-7258-5
eISBN 13: 978-1-4405-7258-6

Printed in the United States of America.

10 9 8 7 6 5 4 3 2 1

Library of Congress Cataloging-in-Publication Data

Rappaport, Rachel.
  The big book of vegetarian recipes / Rachel Rappaport, author of The big book of slow cooker recipes.
      pages cm
   Includes bibliographical references and index.
   ISBN-13: 978-1-4405-7257-9 (paperback : alkaline paper)
   ISBN-10: 1-4405-7257-7 (paperback : alkaline paper)
   ISBN-13: 978-1-4405-7258-6 (epub)
   ISBN-10: 1-4405-7258-5 (epub)
   1. Vegetarian cooking. I. Title.
   TX837.R265 2013
   641.5'636--dc23
                                                                     2013030849

Contains material adapted and abridged from: *The Everything® Vegetarian Cookbook* by Jay Weinstein, copyright © 2002 by F+W Media, Inc., ISBN 10: 1-58062-640-8; ISBN 13: 978-1-58062-640-8; *The Everything® Vegetarian Slow Cooker Cookbook* by Amy Snyder and Justin Snyder, copyright © 2012 by F+W Media, Inc., ISBN 10: 1-4405-2858-6, ISBN 13: 978-1-4405-2858-3; and *The Everything® Vegetarian Pressure Cooker Cookbook* by Amy Snyder and Justin Snyder, copyright © 2010 by F+W Media, Inc., ISBN 10: 1-4405-0672-8, ISBN 13: 978-1-4405-0672-7.

Always follow safety and commonsense cooking protocol while using kitchen utensils, operating ovens and stoves, and handling uncooked food. If children are assisting in the preparation of any recipe, they should always be supervised by an adult.

Many of the designations used by manufacturers and sellers to distinguish their products are claimed as trademarks. Where those designations appear in this book and F+W Media was aware of a trademark claim, the designations have been printed with initial capital letters.

Cover image © Artur Synenko/123rf.com.

This book is available at quantity discounts for bulk purchases. For information, please call 1-800-289-0963.

CONTENTS

Introduction 21

1 Breakfast and Brunch 23

Home Fries 24
Granola 24
Stuffed Eggs 25
Scrambled Egg Burritos 25
Miso Eggs Benedict 26
Boursin Omelet 27
Scrambled Eggs Masala 28
Challah French Toast 29
Corny Polenta Breakfast Pancakes .. 30
Scones 31
Tofu Frittata 32
Sunrise Tofu Scramble 33
Garden Tofu Scramble 34
Spicy Tofu Scramble 35
Country Grits 36
Cheese Grits 36
Red Pepper Grits 37
Almond and Dried Cherry Granola ... 37
Breakfast Quinoa with Fruit 38
French Toast Casserole 38
Hash Browns 39
Onion, Pepper, and Potato Hash Browns 39
Pressure Cooker Hash Browns 40
Slow Cooker Spicy Tofu Scramble .. 41
Poblano Hash Browns 42
Tempeh Sausage Crumbles 42
Breakfast Tofu and Veggies 43
Easy Tofu "Eggs" 43
Grandma's Cornmeal Mush 44
Breakfast Casserole 44
Spicy Breakfast Burrito 45
Slow Cooker Tofu Ranchero 46
Huevos Rancheros 47
Roasted Vegetable Frittata 48
Spinach Quiche 49
Rosemary Home Fries 50
White Gravy 50
Pear Oatmeal 51
Banana Nut Bread Oatmeal 51
Steel-Cut Oats 52
Apple Streusel Oatmeal 53

Irish Oatmeal with Fruit..................54
Maple-Pecan Oatmeal 55
Three Pepper Vegan Frittata...........56
Yeasty Tofu and Veggies 57
Pressure Cooker Tofu Ranchero......58
Spinach and Portobello Benedict ...59

2 Sauces and Spreads 60

Basil Pesto 62
Red Garlic Mayonnaise (Rouille) 62
Tofu Sour Cream 63
Onion Jam..63
Aioli (Garlic Mayonnaise) 64
Maître d' Butter...............................64
Black Olive Butter 65
Garlic and Basil Butter 65
Rosemary-Lemon Butter 66
Chili-Orange Butter for
   Grilled Bread 66
Apple Butter.....................................67
Vanilla-Spice Pear Butter.................68
Cranberry Sauce..............................69
Slow-Roasted Garlic and
   Tomato Sauce...............................69
Basic Fresh Tomato Sauce...............70
Quick Tomato Sauce 71
Fresh Tomato Sauce........................72
Garden Marinara Sauce 73
Basic Marinara Sauce 74
Vegan Alfredo 74

White Bean Alfredo Sauce 75
Jalapeño-Tomatillo Sauce 76
Lemon Dill Sauce............................76
Creamy Dijon Sauce.......................77
Country White Gravy 77
Puttanesca Sauce 78
Barbecue Sauce 79
Country Barbecue Sauce................80
New Mexico Chili Sauce 81
Mole 81
Homemade Ketchup 82
Raspberry Coulis 83
Coconut Curry Sauce 83
White Wine–Garlic Sauce...............84
Three Pepper Sauce.......................84
Roasted Red Pepper Sauce 85
Easy Peanut Sauce 85
Spicy Peanut Sauce 86
Espagnole 87
Béchamel Sauce 88
Au Jus...88
Beurre Blanc...................................89
Vodka Sauce...................................90
Yellow Pepper Coulis 91
Cashew Cream Sauce.....................92
Plum Sauce.....................................93
Cranberry-Apple Chutney...............94
Fresh Tomato Chutney....................95
Green Tomato Chutney...................96

Sweet Onion Relish 97
Strawberry Jam 98
Dried Apricot Preserves 99
Mixed Citrus Marmalade 100
Rainbow Bell Pepper Marmalade ... 101
Blueberry Jam 102
Mincemeat 103
Peach and Toasted Almond
    Preserves 104
Caribbean Relish 105
Blackberry Jam 106
Peach Jam 107
Easy Grape Jelly 107

3 Salads 108

Southeast Asian Slaw 110
Warm Chickpea Salad 111
Edamame-Seaweed Salad 112
Three Bean Salad 113
Tomato and Bread Salad
    (Panzanella) 114
Salad of Celery Root and Pears 115
Winter Greens Salad with Green
    Beans and Roquefort Vinaigrette ... 116
Tatsoi Salad 117
Orange-Sesame Vinaigrette 118
Madras Curry Dressing 119
Classic American Potato Salad 120
Asian Cucumber Salad 120
Succotash Salad 121

Summer Vegetable Slaw 122
Caesar Salad 123
Quick Three Bean Salad 124
Insalata Caprese
    (Tomato-Mozzarella Salad) 125
Grilled Vegetable Antipasto 126
Roasted Peppers 127
Wild Rice Salad with Mushrooms
    and Almonds 128
Tabbouleh 129
Tofu Salad 130
Sweet White Salad with
    Shaved Asiago 131
Barley and Corn Salad 132
Mixed Baby Greens with
    Balsamic Vinaigrette 133
Lentil Salad 134
California Garden Salad with
    Avocado and Sprouts 135
Marinated Beet Salad 136
Basic Egg Salad 137
Warm Potato Salad with
    Balsamic Vinegar and Onions 138
Curried New Potato Salad 139
Dill Potato Salad 139
German Potato Salad 140
Sweet Potato Salad 141
Mediterranean Sweet Potato Salad 142
Warm Spinach Salad with
    Potatoes, Red Onions, and
    Kalamata Olives 143

Tomato, Garlic, and Parsley Quinoa Salad..................144
Wheat Berry Salad 145
Quinoa Artichoke Hearts Salad.....146
Olive and Pepper Couscous Salad ... 147
Greek Salad Tacos........................148
Ricotta and Goat Cheese Crespelle 149

4 Hors d'Oeuvres and Snacks..................150

Rancheros Salsa..........................152
Artichoke Dip 153
Cheese Fondue 154
Chinese Soy Sauce Eggs 155
Vegan Spinach and Artichoke Dip.... 156
Potato Pakoras (Fritters)...............157
Crudités with Three Dips 158
Curry Dip 159
Watercress Dip 160
Baba Ghanoush 161
Slow Cooker Baba Ghanoush 162
Stuffed Grape Leaves..................163
Chickpea-Parsley-Dill Dip.............164
Jalapeño Cheese Dip 165
Chili-Cheese Dip 166
Broccoli Dip................................167
Frijole Dip 168
Caramelized Onion Dip................169
Mixed Veggie Dip 170

Summer Fruit Dip........................171
Sun-Dried Tomato Pesto Dip 172
Eggplant Caviar..........................173
Texas Caviar 174
Fried Green Tomato Bruschetta....175
Guacamole 176
Hummus 177
Zesty Lemon Hummus.................178
Manchego-Potato Tacos with Pickled Jalapeños.............179
Mini Lentil-Scallion Pancakes with Cumin Cream 180
Mini Goat Cheese Pizzas.............181
Spicy Buffalo Strips 182
Teriyaki "Chicken" Strips.............183
Tomatillo Salsa...........................184
Roasted Garlic Spread 185
Steamed Spring Rolls..................186
Dhal 187
Sweet and Sour "Meatballs"........188
Barbecue "Meatballs"..................189
Vegetable Gado-Gado.................190
Stuffed Mushrooms.....................191
Sweet Fennel with Lemon and Shaved Parmigiano 192
Sweet Potato and Rosemary Pizza.....193
Tomato and Black Olive Bruschetta....194
Spicy White Bean–Citrus Dip 195
Black Bean Dip 196

Wild Mushroom Ragout in
   Puff Pastry Shells 197
Salsa Fresca (Pico de Gallo) 198
Cajun Peanuts 198
Cinnamon and Sugar Peanuts........ 199
Boiled Peanuts 200
Spiced Pecans 201
Cheese Soufflé 202
Artichoke and Cheese Squares 203
Two Cheese Strata 204
Fricos (Cheese Crisps) 205

5 Soups, Stews, and Chilies ... 206

Vegetable Stock 208
Pressure Cooker Vegetable
   Stock.. 209
Vegetable Broth 210
No-Beef Broth 210
Red Bean and Pasta Soup.............. 211
White Bean and Barley Soup 212
Red Lentil Soup 213
Black Bean Soup 214
Cream of Asparagus Soup 215
Tomato Soup 216
Tomato Basil Soup......................... 216
Wild Mushroom Soup
   with Thyme................................. 217
Mushroom Vegetable Stock.......... 218
Carrot Purée with Nutmeg............ 219

Smoky Black-Eyed Pea Soup
   with Sweet Potatoes and
   Mustard Greens.......................... 220
Pumpkin Soup with Caraway Seeds ... 221
Pumpkin-Ale Soup 222
Chilled Curry Potato-Fennel Soup.... 223
Smooth Cauliflower Soup
   with Coriander............................ 224
Gazpacho 225
Yellow Split Pea Soup with
   Cactus and Hominy 226
Vichyssoise (Potato and
   Leek Soup)................................... 227
Minestrone Soup 228
Minestrone with Basil Pesto 229
Lentil Soup with Cumin 230
Tuscan White Bean Soup 231
Cuban Black Bean Soup with
   Coriander Tofu Sour Cream 232
Corn and Potato Chowder............ 233
Mushroom, Barley, and
   Collard Greens Soup 234
Pinto Bean Soup with
   Salsa Fresca 235
Acorn Squash Soup with
   Anise and Carrots....................... 236
Miso Soup 237
Tofu Noodle Soup 238
Hot and Sour Soup........................ 239
Cauliflower Soup 240
French Onion Soup 241
Garden Vegetable Soup................ 242

Potato-Leek Soup 242
Beer-Cheese Soup 243
Butternut Squash Soup 244
Creamy Chickpea Soup 245
Mushroom Barley Soup 246
Summer Borscht 247
Simple Split Pea Soup 248
Tortilla Soup 249
Greek-Style Orzo and Spinach Soup 250
Pho 251
Wild Rice and Portobello Soup 252
Celery Root Soup 253
Brunswick Stew 254
Jamaican Red Bean Stew 255
Southwest Corn Chowder 256
Okra Gumbo 257
Mediterranean Vegetable Stew 258
White Bean and Tomato Stew 259
Seitan and Mushroom Stew 260
Curried Seitan Stew 261
Vegetable Dumpling Stew 262
Étouffée 263
Seitan and Cabbage Stew 264
Posole 265
Pumpkin Stew 266
Cauliflower Chowder 267
White Bean Cassoulet 268
Korean-Style Hot Pot 269
Seitan Bourguignonne 270

Super Greens Stew 271
Texas Stew 272
Mock Meatball Stew 273
Vegan Chili 274
Southwest Vegetable Chili 275
Cincinnati Chili 276
Chili con "Carne" 277
Shredded "Chicken" Chili 278
Five Pepper Chili 279
Sweet Potato Chili 280
Three Bean Chili 281
Fajita Chili 282
Black Bean, Corn, and Fresh Tomato Chili 283
Red Bean Chili 284
Lentil Chili 285
Garden Vegetable Chili 286
Black Bean and "Sausage" Chili 287
Acorn Squash Chili 288
Summer Chili 289

6 Root Vegetables 290
White Potato Pie 292
Basic Pie Dough 293
Roasted Yukon Gold Potatoes 294
Turnip and Potato Gratin 295
Parsnip Purée 296
Slow Cooker Parsnip Purée 297

Yuca con Mojo (Yuca with Garlic and Lime) 298
Roasted Beets 299
Citrusy Beets 300
French Fries 301
Carrot Timbales 302
Honey-Orange Beets 303
Buttered Beets 304
Rutabaga Oven Fries 305
Herb-Mixed Turnips 306
Curried Parsnips 307
"Steamed" Artichokes 308
Celery Root, Artichoke, and Potato Gratin 309
Celery Root Mash 310
Gingered Mashed Sweet Potatoes 311
Parsnip and Carrot Bake 312
Carrot and Mushroom Terrine 313
Carrots and Ginger 314
Creamed Carrots 315
Mashed Turnips 316
Braised Beet Greens 317
Turnip and Carrot Purée 318
Savory Turnip Greens 319
Parsnip Purée 320
Crisp Potato Pancakes 321
Rosemary New Potatoes 322
Roasted Garlic Mashed Potatoes 323
Moroccan Root Vegetables 324
Garlic Parsley Mashed Potatoes ... 325
Rosemary Mashed Potatoes 326
Twice-Baked Potatoes 327
Potato Messaround 328
Sweet Potato Casserole 329
Potatoes Paprikash 330
Rosemary-Garlic Mashed Potatoes 331
Southwestern Casserole 332
Cheesy Peasy Potatoes 333
Potato Risotto 334
Scalloped Potatoes 335
Potatoes Au Gratin 336
Rosemary Fingerling Potatoes 337
Braised Fingerling Potatoes 338
Dill Red Potatoes 339
Chipotle and Thyme Sweet Potatoes 340
Maple-Glazed Sweet Potatoes 341
Herbed Potatoes 342
Potato Piccata 343
Celery Root, Artichoke, and Potato Gratin 309
Chipotle and Thyme Mashed Sweet Potatoes 344
Mashed Sweet Potatoes 345
Pressure Cooker Maple-Glazed Sweet Potatoes 346
Mexican Spice Potatoes 347
Garlic-Parmesan Mashed Potatoes 348
Potato-Broccoli Casserole 349
Garlic-Parsley Potatoes 350
Old-Fashioned Glazed Carrots 351

7 Grains, Beans, and Legumes ... 352

Brown Rice 354
White Rice 354
Wild Rice 355
Quinoa 355
Couscous 356
Red Beans and Yellow Rice 357
Red Beans and Rice Pie with Oregano and Tomatoes 358
New Orleans Red Beans and Rice 359
Red Beans and Rice 360
Puerto Rican Gandules (Pigeon Peas) 361
Quinoa Salad with Tomatoes and Cilantro 362
Minted Sweet Peas 362
Sushi Rice 363
Avocado Kappa Maki Sushi Rolls 364
Chickpeas in Potato-Onion Curry 365
Indian Chapati Pan Bread 366
Avocado-Beet Wraps with Succotash 367
Kasha Varnishkes 368
Wheat and Corn Wraps with Tofu ... 369
Fried Rice with Green Peas and Egg 370
Tuscan White Bean Ragout 371
Raj's Chickpeas in Tomato Sauce .. 372
Wild Rice Vegetable Pancakes 373
Wild Rice with Apples and Almonds 374
Wild Rice with Mixed Vegetables 374
Egyptian Lentils and Rice 375
Mexican Rice 375
Cuban Black Beans and Rice (Moros y Cristianos) 376
Black Bean Burritos 377
Barley Risotto 378
Peppery Brown Rice Risotto 379
Pumpkin Risotto 380
Easy Saffron Vegetable Risotto 381
Wild Mushroom Risotto 382
Wild Mushroom Risotto with Truffles 383
Beet Risotto Cakes 384
Polenta with Butter and Cheese ... 385
Pan-Freid Polenta with Marinara ... 386
Creamy Thyme Polenta 387
Chinese Black Rice 387
Creole Jambalaya 388
Mexican Frijoles Refritos (Refried Beans) 389
Hummus bi Tahini with Sprouts and Cherry Tomatoes in a Pita Pocket 390
Couscous-Stuffed Red Peppers 391
Bulgur Stuffing 392
Three Grain Pilaf 393
Rice Pilaf 394

Vegetable Rice Pilaf	395
Cranberry-Pecan Pilaf	396
Green Rice Pilaf	396
Tomatillo Rice	397
Stuffed Peppers	398
Vegetable Fried Rice	399
Paella	400
Pressure Cooker Paella	401
Vegan Chorizo Paella	402
Eggplant "Lasagna"	403
Portobello Barley	404
Saffron Rice	405
Bulgur with Broccoli and Carrot	405
Mock Chicken and Rice	406
Spanish Rice	407
Brown Rice and Vegetables	408
Curried Rice	408
Chipotle Black Bean Salad	409
Mediterranean Chickpeas	410
Open-Faced Bean Burrito	411
Slow Cooker Refried Beans	412
Cuban Black Beans	413
Pressure Cooker Cuban Black Beans and Rice	414
Curried Lentils	415
Hoppin' John	416
Chipotle-Thyme Black Beans	417
Beer-Lime Black Beans	418
Black Bean–Cilantro Fritters	419
Boston-Style Baked Beans	420
Bourbon Baked Beans	421
Pinto Beans	422
Adzuki Beans	422
Lima Beans	423
Lima Beans and Dumplings	424
Black Beans	425
White Beans	426
Black-Eyed Peas	427
Lentils	428
Mexican Beer Black Beans	429
White Beans with Rosemary and Fresh Tomato	430
Wasabi-Barbecue Chickpeas	431
Lentils with Sautéed Spinach, White Wine, and Garlic	432
Chana Masala	433
Easy Edamame	434
Summer Vegetable Bean Salad	435
Black Bean Salsa	436
Spicy Black-Eyed Peas and Kale	437
Red Beans with Plantains	438
Red Bean Fritters	439
White Beans with Garlic and Fresh Tomato	440
White Beans and Rice	441
White Bean–Leek Purée	442
Pressure Cooker Wasabi-Barbecue Chickpeas	443
Chickpea "Tuna" Salad Sandwich	444
Pressure Cooker Hoppin' John	445
Lentil-Spinach Curry	446

Lentil Pâté 447
Red Lentil Curry 448
Pressure Cooker Chana Masala 449
Sea Salt Edamame 450
Dinner Loaf 451

8 Leafy Greens and Cruciferous Vegetables....452

Artichokes in Court Bouillon with Lemon Butter 454
Spinach and Tomato Sauté 455
Aloo Gobi (Cauliflower and Potato Curry) 456
Pressure Cooker Aloo Gobi 457
Curried Cauliflower 458
Stir-Fried Asian Greens 459
Shanghai Bok Choy with Garlic and Black Bean Sauce 460
Braised Swiss Chard 461
Cabbage Stewed in Tomato Sauce .. 462
Spinach with Pine Nuts (Pignoli) and Garlic 462
Vegan Creamed Spinach 463
Basic Buttered Brussels Sprouts 464
Pan-Seared Brussels Sprouts 465
Cranberry-Walnut Brussels Sprouts 466
Smoky Spiced Collard Greens with Turnip 466
Braised Red Cabbage (Chou Rouge à la Flamande) 467
Scented Escarole with Fennel 468
Broccoli Florets with Lemon Butter Sauce 469
Sautéed Broccoli Raab 470
Broccoli in Lemon Butter Sauce ... 471
Creamed Spinach 472
Stuffed Cabbage 473
Kimchi-Style Cabbage 474
Gai Lan (Chinese Broccoli) with Toasted Garlic 475
Swiss Chard Rolls with Root Vegetables 476
Spinach Pancakes with Cardamom . 477
Spinach-Stuffed Vegetables 478
Spinach and Feta Pie 479
Grilled Radicchio 480
Kale with Garlic and Thyme 481
Kale with Red Pepper Flakes and Cumin 482
Szechuan Stir-Fried Cabbage with Hot Peppers 483
Garlicky Broccoli Raab 484
Collard Greens with Tomatoes and Cheddar 485
Southern-Style Collards 486
Soy-Glazed Bok Choy 487
Baby Bok Choy 488
Homemade Sauerkraut 489

9 Tomatoes and Other Vegetables............................ 490

Tomato and Cheese Tart 492

Cumin-Roasted Butternut Squash 493
Mushroom-Stuffed Tomatoes......... 494
Herb-Stuffed Tomatoes 495
Stewed Tomatoes.......................... 495
Herbed Red and Yellow Tomatoes
  on Honey-Nut Bread 496
Fried Green Tomatoes with
  Rémoulade Sauce 497
Tomato Confit with Fine Herbs 498
Red and Yellow Plum Tomato
  Chutney 499
Chilaquiles (Tortilla Stew) 500
Avocado Sashimi with
  Miso Dressing 501
Ratatouille 502
Quick Tomato and Oregano Sauté .. 503
Zucchini "Lasagna" 504
Eggplant Rolatine 505
Simple Salsa 506
Stir-Fried Snow Peas with Cilantro .. 506
Eggplant Parmigiano 507
Pressure Cooker Ratatouille.......... 508
Eggplant Caponata 509
Mashed Eggplant and
  Tomato Salad............................ 510
Steamed Asparagus with
  Hollandaise Sauce 511
Pressure Cooker Asparagus with
  Vegan Hollandaise Sauce 512
Eggplant and Tomato Sauté 513
Meatless Moussaka 514

Spiced "Baked" Eggplant............. 515
Stuffed Eggplant 516
Zucchini Ragout 517
Asparagus-Shallot Sauté 518
Roasted Vegetables 519
Chinese Wrinkled String Beans..... 520
Green Beans and Pine Nut Sauté . 521
Fresh Green Beans with Toasted
  Sesame 522
Rosemary-Thyme Green Beans 522
Fennel Cooked in White Wine 523
Butternut Squash 524
Stewed Squash............................. 525
Spaghetti Squash 525
Winter Vegetable Medley 526
Corn on the Cob 527
Cilantro-Lime Corn on the Cob........ 528
Creamed Corn.............................. 529
Corn and Pepper Pudding 530
Pressure Cooker Creamed Corn ... 531
Okra with Corn and Tomato.......... 532
Succotash 533
Corn Maque Choux....................... 534
Cheesy Poblano Peppers.............. 535
Roasted Red Bell Pepper Purée.... 536
Brie Timbales with Roasted Red
  Pepper Sauce 537

10 Onions, Mushrooms, and Truffles 538

Jumbo Beer-Battered Onion Rings 540
Stuffed Onions 541
Braised Leeks 542
Grilled Leeks with Tarragon and Lemon 543
Scallion Pancakes 544
Leek Tart 545
Caramelized Pearl Onions 546
Slow Cooker Caramelized Onions 547
Onion Tart 548
Roasted Sweet Onions 549
Roasted Shallots 550
Grilled Onions with Balsamic Glaze .551
Grilled Scallions 552
Leek Potato Cakes 553
Garlic Bread 554
Baked Peppers and Onions 555
Vidalia Onion Salad 556
Chive Dumplings 557
Pissaladière 558
Pickled Red Onions 559
Duxelles 560
Risotto with Portobello Mushrooms, Onions, and Garlic 561
Creamed Morels and Asparagus Tips in Vol-au-Vents 562
Fettuccine with Morels and Spring Onions 563
Polenta-Style Grits with Wild Mushroom Ragout 564
Josh's Mushroom Dip 565
Portobello Pita with Buckwheat and Beans 566
Grilled Marinated Portobello Mushrooms 567
Mushroom-Spelt Sauté 568
Chinese Three Slivers 569
Chinese Black Mushrooms with Jade Bok Choy 570
Taiwanese Mushroom Egg 571
Spring Mushroom Risotto with Morels and Asparagus 572
Mushroom Bruschetta 573
Mushroom-Barley "Risotto" 574
Oven-Roasted Mushrooms 575
Vegetable-Stuffed Portobello Mushrooms 576
Creamed Mushrooms 577
Mushroom-Tofu Stir-Fry 578
Mushroom Turnovers (Empanadas) 579
Pickled Mushrooms 580
Warm Oyster Mushroom Salad 580
Mushroom-Leek Tart 581
Mushroom Barley 582
Mushroom and Olive Blend 583

11 Pasta Dishes 584

Basic Pasta 586
Gemelli with Asparagus Tips, Lemon, and Butter 587
Pumpkin-Spinach Lasagna 588
Swiss Chard Ravioli 589
White Lasagna with Spinach and Mushrooms.................................. 590
Fusilli (Spirals) with Grilled Eggplant, Garlic, and Spicy Tomato Sauce ... 591
Farfalle (Bow-Ties) Fra Diavolo 592
Five-Minute Pasta Pesto 592
Fettuccine Alfredo 593
Ziti with Peppers and Marinated Mozzarella 594
Spaghetti with Asparagus, Parmesan, and Cream 595
Orecchiette with Roasted Peppers, Green Beans, and Pesto............. 596
The Best Pesto 597
Linguine with Olives, Capers, and Tomatoes 598
Polenta with Wild Mushrooms 599
Fettuccine with Shiitake Mushrooms and Brown Butter 600
Angel Hair with Broccoli Raab, Toasted Garlic, Fava Beans, and Pecorino Cheese 601
Spaghetti with Sweet Corn, Tomatoes, and Goat Cheese....... 602
Baked Ziti 603
Spinach Manicotti 603
Raw Veggie Pasta Toss.................. 604
Basic Pasta Salad.......................... 605
Roasted Vegetable Pasta 606
Small Shells with Grilled Vegetables, Olives, Oregano, and Tomatoes ... 607
Linguine with Gorgonzola, Asparagus, and Cream................ 608
Spaghetti Ai Pomodorini............... 609
Tagliatelle Aglio e Olio................. 609
Macaroni and Cheese 610
Pasta Primavera with Vegetables.......................... 611
Pasta Salad with Tomato, Arugula, and Feta 612
Gnocchi and Mushrooms in Rosemary Alfredo Sauce............................. 613
Vegetable Linguine in White Bean Alfredo Sauce............................. 614
Rotini with Red Wine Marinara........ 615
Pasta Fagiole................................615
Orzo-Stuffed Poblano Peppers.......... 616
Orzo-Stuffed Tomatoes 617
Pasta Puttanesca 618
Whole-Wheat Fettuccine with Mushroom Cream Sauce............ 619
Broccoli–Pine Nut Pasta Salad......... 620
Fresh Spinach–White Wine Angel Hair Pasta 621
Portobello Stroganoff 622
Bow-Tie Pasta in a Sage Beurre Blanc Sauce 623

12 Desserts, Baked Goods, and Beverages ... 624

Pumpkin Bread ... 626
Banana Bread ... 627
Banana Nut Bread ... 628
Tarte Tatin ... 629
Simple Cloverleaf Dinner Rolls ... 630
Chocolate Mousse ... 631
Noodle Pudding ... 632
Old-Fashioned Baked Apples ... 632
"Baked" Apples ... 633
Easy Applesauce ... 634
Special Occasion Chunky Applesauce ... 634
Cinnamon-Apple Cobbler with Rome Beauty Apples ... 635
Cranberry Applesauce ... 636
Pink McIntosh Applesauce with Cranberry Chutney ... 637
Cranberry Chutney ... 637
Golden Delicious Apple-Strawberry Crisp ... 638
Apple-Walnut Upside-Down Pie ... 639
Spicy Southwestern Cornbread ... 640
Tiramisu ... 641
Crème Caramel ... 642
Savory Sun-Dried Tomato Cheesecake ... 643
Carrot Cake ... 644
Chocolate Cake ... 645
Spiced Chocolate Cake ... 646
Red Velvet Cake ... 647
Sour Cream Butter Cake ... 648
Flourless Chocolate Cake ... 649
Banana Pudding Cake ... 650
Glazed Lemon Poppy Seed Cake ... 651
Cornmeal Cake ... 652
Basic Yellow Cake ... 652
Butter-Cream Frosting ... 653
Blondies ... 654
Pears Poached in White Wine with Strawberry Sauce ... 654
Spiced Peaches ... 655
Ginger Poached Pears ... 656
Cinnamon Poached Apples ... 656
Poached Mixed Berries ... 657
Port-Poached Figs ... 657
Dried Fruit Compote ... 658
Fruit Compote ... 659
Chocolate Chip Cookies ... 660
Crepes ... 660
Cottage Cheese Blintzes ... 661
Peanut Butter Cake ... 661
Coconut Rice Pudding ... 662
Hot Fudge Fondue ... 662
Chocolate-Almond Fondue ... 663
Chocolate-Cinnamon Fondue ... 663
Bananas Foster ... 664
Caramel Apples and Pears ... 664

Chocolate Almond Bars 665

Chocolate Coconut Bars 665

White Chocolate–Macadamia
   Nut Bars 666

Chocolate-Covered Pretzels 666

Chocolate-Berry Bread
   Pudding 667

Lemon Cheesecake 668

Creamy Coconut Rice Pudding 669

Molten Fudge Pudding Cake........670

Plum Pudding with
   Brandy Sauce.............................671

Peanut Butter and
   Fudge Cheesecake....................672

Date Pudding 673

Piña Colada Bread Pudding..........674

Tapioca Pudding 675

Steamed Dessert Bread 676

Vegan Flan.....................................677

Hot Cranberry-Pineapple Punch ...678

Ginger-Pear Punch 679

White Tea–Berry Fusion 679

Vanilla-Lavender Tea 680

Chai Tea...680

Café Mocha 681

Pumpkin Spice...............................681

Minty Hot Chocolate.....................682

Hot Buttered Rum 682

Hot Toddy 683

Spiked Apple Cider.......................683

Spiced Wine 684

Irish Coffee 684

Mixed Berry Punch 685

Peach Iced Tea 685

Southern-Style Sweet Tea 686

Mango-Mint Iced Tea 686

Sangria 687

Honey-Mint Green Tea..................687

Blackberry-Mint White Tea............688

Cherry and Lime Punch.................688

Raspberry Lemonade 689

Cherry Lemonade..........................689

Orange and Lime Punch 690

Passion Fruit Green Tea 690

Appendix: Standard U.S. / Metric
   Measurement Conversions 691

Index 692

INTRODUCTION

If you're looking for flavorful vegetarian meals you and your family will enjoy, look no further!

Millions of people all over the world are living the vegetarian lifestyle. There are many reasons people abstain from meat, ranging from the philosophical to the practical. Health-conscious people adopt the vegetarian diet for a variety of reasons. A vegetarian diet rich in whole grains and vitamin- and fiber-rich vegetables and fruit has been shown to dramatically decrease the risk of certain chronic diseases such as diabetes, obesity, heart disease, and high blood pressure. A vegetarian diet has been shown to reduce the risk of some cancers. Beyond the health benefits, eating a vegetarian diet is very cost-effective. By eliminating expensive meat from your diet, grocery bills will be drastically reduced.

Some new to the vegetarian lifestyle might wonder what exactly vegetarians eat. They will be happy to learn that vegetarians eat a wide variety of foods. Vegetarians refrain from eating meat and instead make up their diet with grains, legumes, fruits, vegetables, dairy, and eggs.

The basic vegetarian pantry includes canned or dried beans, sweeteners like sugar, agave nectar, honey, and maple syrup, lentils, various varieties of rice, canned tomatoes, pasta, oils such as olive and canola, vinegars, hot sauce, mustards, peanut butter, dried fruit, mayonnaise, spices, and whole grains like wheat berries, oats, and kasha. The vegetarian refrigerator is stocked with not only fresh fruits and vegetables but calcium-rich dairy like milk, yogurt, and cheese, soy or almond milk, tofu products, pickles, sun-dried tomatoes, salsa, and relishes as well.

Well-stocked pantries can include items from regions with a rich history of vegetarian cooking. Chinese condiments like soy sauce, hoisin sauce, tamari, and sesame oil; Indian ingredients such as mango chutney, red lentils, and garam masala; and Japanese ingredients like miso paste, rice vinegar, soba noodles, sushi rice, and wasabi all make international vegetarian cooking a breeze.

Now that you have all of these ingredients, what do you do with them? You're in luck. This cookbook is jam-packed with more than seven hundred recipes ranging from breakfast recipes to beverages, main dishes, and desserts. With so many recipes, it is simple to find one that meets your needs.

Use that Japanese miso in delicious Miso Eggs Benedict. Eliminate the need for bottled condiments with mysterious ingredients by making your own barbecue sauce, aioli, tofu sour cream, and flavored compound butters. Wow dinner guests by serving Mini Lentil-Scallion Pancakes with Cumin Cream or Wild Mushroom Risotto with Truffles. Feel like baking? Whip up some Golden Delicious Apple-Strawberry Crisp, Simple Cloverleaf Dinner Rolls, or Red Velvet Cake.

If you are a busy cook, you will appreciate that some of the recipes call for a slow cooker, so you can put up dinner in the morning and come home to a warm vegetarian meal, or a pressure cooker, which makes a full meal in a quarter of the usual time. Slow cooker and pressure cooker recipes are indicated with the following icons for easy reference.

- Slow Cooker: SC
- Pressure Cooker: PC

Use this book as your guide into the wonderful, flavorful world of vegetarian cooking.

CHAPTER 1
BREAKFAST AND BRUNCH

RECIPE LIST

HOME FRIES 24
GRANOLA 24
STUFFED EGGS 25
SCRAMBLED EGG BURRITOS 25
MISO EGGS BENEDICT 26
BOURSIN OMELET 27
SCRAMBLED EGGS MASALA 28
CHALLAH FRENCH TOAST 29
CORNY POLENTA BREAKFAST PANCAKES 30
SCONES 31
TOFU FRITTATA 32
SUNRISE TOFU SCRAMBLE 33
GARDEN TOFU SCRAMBLE 34
SPICY TOFU SCRAMBLE 35
COUNTRY GRITS 36
CHEESE GRITS 36
RED PEPPER GRITS 37
ALMOND AND DRIED CHERRY GRANOLA 37
BREAKFAST QUINOA WITH FRUIT 38
FRENCH TOAST CASSEROLE 38
HASH BROWNS 39
ONION, PEPPER, AND POTATO HASH BROWNS 39
PRESSURE COOKER HASH BROWNS 40

SLOW COOKER SPICY TOFU SCRAMBLE 41
POBLANO HASH BROWNS 42
TEMPEH SAUSAGE CRUMBLES 42
BREAKFAST TOFU AND VEGGIES 43
EASY TOFU "EGGS" 43
GRANDMA'S CORNMEAL MUSH 44
BREAKFAST CASSEROLE 44
SPICY BREAKFAST BURRITO 45
SLOW COOKER TOFU RANCHERO 46
HUEVOS RANCHEROS 47
ROASTED VEGETABLE FRITTATA 48
SPINACH QUICHE 49
ROSEMARY HOME FRIES 50
WHITE GRAVY 50
PEAR OATMEAL 51
BANANA NUT BREAD OATMEAL 51
STEEL-CUT OATS 52
APPLE STREUSEL OATMEAL 53
IRISH OATMEAL WITH FRUIT 54
MAPLE-PECAN OATMEAL 55
THREE PEPPER VEGAN FRITTATA 56
YEASTY TOFU AND VEGGIES 57
PRESSURE COOKER TOFU RANCHERO 58
SPINACH AND PORTOBELLO BENEDICT 59

HOME FRIES

Like hash browns, home fries can also be served with a variety of toppings or plain with a side of ketchup.

Serves 4

2 tablespoons olive oil

4 cups red potatoes, diced

1½ teaspoons paprika

1 teaspoon chili powder

1½ teaspoons salt

1 teaspoon black pepper

1. Bring the olive oil to medium heat in the pressure cooker. Add the potatoes and sauté for about 3 minutes.

2. Add all remaining ingredients and stir. Lock the lid in place and bring to high pressure; maintain pressure for 7 minutes. Remove from heat and quick-release the pressure.

GRANOLA

This crunchy, healthful cereal is a delicious snack, and travels well. Consider keeping some in your "emergency travel kit" for occasions where you might not be offered vegetarian foods.

Serves 8

3 cups rolled oats (such as Quaker Quick Oats)

1½ cups wheat germ

1 cup chopped walnuts, almonds, peanuts, or a combination

1 cup shredded coconut

½ cup sesame seeds

½ cup nonfat dry milk

¼ cup oil

½ cup honey

1 cup brown sugar

1 cup raisins

1. Heat oven to 350°F. Spread the oats onto a baking sheet; bake for 15 minutes. Lower oven to 325°F.

2. In a large mixing bowl, combine the toasted oats with wheat germ, nuts, coconut, sesame seeds, nonfat dry milk, oil, honey, and brown sugar. Mix well with your hands. Transfer to a baking sheet; spread into a single layer. Bake for 10 to 15 minutes, until lightly browned. Toss with raisins. Cool to room temperature before serving.

STUFFED EGGS

These filled eggs are a variation on deviled eggs, and are a great first course or garnish for a main-course salad. Their tops are attractively browned under the broiler.

Serves 8

8 hard-boiled eggs

¼ cup Dijon mustard

3 tablespoons heavy cream

2 tablespoons finely chopped shallot

1 tablespoon rice wine vinegar

1 tablespoon chopped chives

1 tablespoon chopped tarragon

Salt and white pepper to taste

Unsalted butter

1. Heat the broiler. Peel and halve the eggs. Take out the yolks and combine them with the mustard, cream, shallot, vinegar, chives, and tarragon. Season with salt and white pepper. Transfer mixture to a piping bag, and pipe it into the egg whites (you can also use a spoon).

2. Place the filled eggs in a baking dish or broiler pan. Dot the tops with a tiny nugget of butter, and broil them until lightly browned, about 5 minutes. Serve warm.

SCRAMBLED EGG BURRITOS

This innovative "wrap" adds some spice to breakfast or brunch!

Serves 4

1 tablespoon unsalted butter

1 medium onion, finely chopped (about 1 cup)

½ cup sliced Roasted Peppers (see Chapter 3)

9 extra-large eggs, beaten

½ cup cream

Few dashes of hot pepper sauce

2 cups shredded jalapeño jack cheese

Salt and pepper to taste

4 (12") flour tortillas

Salsa Fresca (see Chapter 4) or store-bought salsa

1. In a large skillet over medium heat, melt the butter; add the onions and sliced Roasted Peppers. Cook until the onions are soft and translucent, about 5 minutes. Combine the eggs and the cream, and add them to the pan. Cook, stirring constantly with a wooden spoon, until the eggs are about half cooked—still very runny; add the hot pepper sauce, cheese, salt, and pepper. Remove from heat. Eggs should be soft, creamy, and have small curds.

2. Soften the tortillas by placing them directly atop the stove burner on medium heat; a few black spots are okay. Spoon ¼ of the egg mixture slightly off center on a tortilla. Fold the sides in upon the egg and roll the tortilla away from yourself, folding the filling in and tucking with your fingers to keep even pressure. Repeat with remaining tortillas. Serve with salsa.

MISO EGGS BENEDICT

Miso has a salty flavor that replaces the Canadian bacon used in traditional eggs Benedict. Have all of the ingredients ready to go, and set the English muffins to toast at the same time as you put the eggs in to poach, so you can place freshly poached eggs onto freshly toasted muffins.

Serves 4

3 tablespoons white vinegar

1 teaspoon salt

4 extra-large eggs

2 English muffins, split

Butter

½ teaspoon miso paste

½ cup hollandaise sauce

Chives (optional)

Hot pepper sauce (optional)

1. Combine the vinegar and salt in a deep skillet with 2" of water. Crack each egg into its own cup. When water boils, lower flame as low as you can. Gently lower the eggs into the hot water, one by one, and pour them from the cups into the pan. Set the muffins to toast.

2. Poach the eggs for no more than 3 minutes, then remove them with a slotted spoon, allowing excess water to drain back into the skillet. Transfer poached eggs to a waiting plate. Mash together the butter and miso; spread this mixture onto the toasted muffins. Place 1 poached egg onto each. Spoon generous helpings of hollandaise sauce onto each, and serve immediately with a sprinkling of chives and hot pepper sauce on the side, if using.

Make in Advance

Note: Eggs can be poached up to a day in advance, and stored submerged in cold water. To reheat, gently place in fresh boiling water for a minute before using.

BOURSIN OMELET

An omelet, say the chefs at the Culinary Institute of America (CIA), is yellow, never browned, and cigar-shaped, not folded like a half-moon. Over the years, I've forgiven myself many times for my delicious, slightly brown, half-moon omelets, and occasionally jumped through the hoops necessary to make the ultimate CIA omelet.

Serves 1

3 large eggs

¼ cup half-and-half or milk

¼ teaspoon salt

Pinch of white pepper or a dash of hot pepper sauce

1 teaspoon unsalted butter

2 tablespoons Boursin or other creamy, tangy cheese, such as goat cheese

1 teaspoon chopped chives or scallions

1. Whisk together the eggs, half-and-half (or milk), salt, and pepper (or hot pepper sauce). Melt the butter in an 8", nonstick skillet over medium-low heat (this is a case where a truly nonstick skillet is really important). Swirl the pan to thoroughly coat it with butter; add the egg mixture. Allow the eggs to sizzle for a minute without disturbing them. Then, using a wooden implement or heatproof rubber spatula, scramble the still-liquidy eggs around in the pan; smooth out the top with your implement, and allow to cook, undisturbed, until the eggs are 90 percent set, but still glistening on top (residual heat will cook the egg the rest of the way when you fold it).

2. Crumble the cheese into the center of the omelet. Now, you have to make a choice: cigar-shaped or the easy way.

3. *For a cigar-shaped ("French rolled") omelet:* Strike the handle of the pan with the heel of your hand to loosen the omelet and move it to the tip of the pan; use an implement to fold the third of the omelet closest to you into the center, covering the cheese. Place a plate at a 90-degree angle to the tip of the pan. Gently tilt the pan to the plate, allowing the omelet to "roll" into a cigar shape. Sprinkle with chives; take a photograph of it before eating.

4. *For a simple omelet:* Fold the omelet in half, slide onto the plate, sprinkle with chives or scallions and enjoy.

SCRAMBLED EGGS MASALA

I don't know if these eggs were ever served in Mumbai, but authentic or no, they have a fragrant allure. Serve them with Indian breads for a special brunch.

Serves 2

2 tablespoons butter

¼ cup chopped onion

¼ teaspoon cumin seed, toasted in a dry pan and crushed (or very fresh cumin powder, toasted a minute in a dry pan)

¼ cup diced tomatoes

4 eggs, scrambled

Salt and white pepper to taste

4 teaspoons chopped fresh mint leaves

1. Melt the butter in a medium nonstick skillet over a moderate heat. Add the onions; cook 5–8 minutes, until soft. Add cumin and tomatoes; cook a minute more.

2. Stir in the eggs, salt, and pepper. Using a wooden spoon, constantly stir the eggs until they form soft, creamy curds; transfer to plates and serve immediately. Garnish with the mint.

CHALLAH FRENCH TOAST

Challah is a braided, egg-enriched bread, which is a traditional start to the Jewish Sabbath meal. Its richness and golden color make for the most luxurious French toast. The key here is to let the "royale" (egg mixture) soak all the way to the center of thick bread slices, and then cook slowly, so it gets cooked in the middle without overbrowning.

Serves 4

½ teaspoon ground cinnamon

3 cups milk

6 extra-large eggs, beaten

1 teaspoon vanilla extract

3 tablespoons sugar

1 teaspoon salt

8 thick slices (1" thick) challah or other bread

2 tablespoons unsalted butter

Pure maple syrup

1. In a mixing bowl, make a paste with the cinnamon and a drop of the milk. Whisk in the rest of the milk, the eggs, vanilla, sugar, and salt. Transfer to a wide, deep dish, and submerge the bread slices in the egg mixture. Allow to soak for at least 10 minutes, pressing the slices gently under with your fingertips to keep them submerged, and turning them halfway through.

2. Heat a large, heavy-bottomed skillet (the best is a cast-iron "Griswold") over a medium-low flame. A piece of butter should sizzle but not smoke when it is added. Melt ¼ of the butter, and fry the soaked bread 2 pieces at a time (it's important not to crowd the pan) on both sides until they bounce back when poked with a finger, about 4 minutes per side. Serve them as they come out of the pan, or keep them warm in the oven. Do not reuse butter—wipe the pan after each batch. Serve with pure maple syrup.

CORNY POLENTA BREAKFAST PANCAKES

If you have leftover polenta from another dish, you can omit the first step in this recipe, and substitute 3 cups of cooked polenta.

Serves 8

1 cup coarse yellow cornmeal

2 cups boiling water

1¼ cups flour

1¼ teaspoons table salt

2½ tablespoons sugar

4½ tablespoons baking powder

¾ cup milk

2 eggs plus 1 egg white, beaten

5 ounces (1¼ sticks) melted butter

Pure maple syrup

1. Make the polenta by whisking the cornmeal directly into the boiling water. It should quickly thicken to a paste. Transfer immediately to a platter or pan to cool.

2. Sift together flour, salt, sugar, and baking powder. In a separate bowl, whisk together milk, eggs, and melted butter. Whisk flour mixture into egg mixture, mixing only as much as is necessary to combine. Overmixing will toughen the cakes. Crumble the cooled polenta into the batter, breaking up large pieces between your fingers. Adjust consistency of the batter with additional milk, if necessary, to achieve the consistency of thick oatmeal.

3. Cook on a hot, buttered griddle, cast-iron skillet, or nonstick pan, forming 3–4" pancakes, cooking thoroughly on both sides. Serve with pure maple syrup.

SCONES

Tender and buttery, these delicate tinless muffins are traditionally served with fine marmalades and jams and thick English "clotted" cream at teatime. If you don't have cake flour, use 100 percent all-purpose flour.

Yields 12 scones

- 2 cups cake flour
- 2 cups all-purpose flour
- 1½ teaspoons baking powder
- 1 teaspoon salt
- ½ cup sugar
- 4 ounces (1 stick) butter, cut into pieces the size of a hazelnut
- 4 ounces (1 stick) margarine, cut into pieces the size of a hazelnut
- ¾ cup currants or raisins (optional)
- 2 eggs
- About ½ cup milk

1. Heat oven to 350°F. Whisk together the cake flour, all-purpose flour, baking powder, salt, and sugar in a bowl until fluffy. Add the butter and margarine; mix with your hands, pinching together the flour between your fingers to coat it. Continue mixing until the flour has taken on the color of the butter, and it clumps, but there should still be some nuggets of butter/margarine. Add currants or raisins, if using.

2. In a separate bowl, whisk together the eggs and milk. Add egg mixture to the flour mixture, and mix with your hands or a wooden spoon just until combined. Do not overmix, as it will make the batter tough. The consistency should be like oatmeal. Add additional milk if necessary.

3. Drop the batter into 12 scones on an oiled sheet pan. Bake until set, about 20 minutes, on top shelf of the oven. For extra color, flash under the broiler for a moment to brown the tops.

SC TOFU FRITTATA

Frittatas are traditionally made with eggs, but you can use tofu instead for a cholesterol-free breakfast dish.

Serves 4

2 tablespoons olive oil
1 cup red potatoes, peeled and diced
½ onion, diced
½ cup red pepper, diced
½ cup green pepper, diced
1 teaspoon jalapeño, minced
1 clove garlic, minced
¼ cup parsley
16 ounces firm tofu
½ cup unsweetened soymilk
4 teaspoons cornstarch
2 tablespoons nutritional yeast
1 teaspoon mustard
½ teaspoon turmeric
1 teaspoon salt
¼ teaspoon black pepper

1. Add the oil to a 4-quart slow cooker and sauté the potatoes, onion, peppers, jalapeño, and garlic on low heat for about 15–20 minutes.

2. Meanwhile, in a blender or food processor, combine the rest of the ingredients until smooth, then pour the mixture into the slow cooker with the potatoes.

3. Cover and cook on medium-high heat for 4 hours, or until the frittata has firmed.

Make It a Scramble
To shorten the preparation time for this meal while keeping all of the flavors, try making this dish into a scramble by preparing the entire recipe in the slow cooker. Skip the step of blending the tofu and omit the cornstarch. Add remaining ingredients, breaking apart tofu as you stir, and sauté until cooked through.

SUNRISE TOFU SCRAMBLE

This Sunrise Tofu Scramble is a great dish that will get your day started right!

Serves 4

16 ounces firm tofu, drained and crumbled
½ cup broccoli florets, chopped
½ cup button mushrooms, sliced
2 tablespoons olive oil
2 teaspoons turmeric
1 teaspoon cumin
¼ teaspoon garlic powder
⅛ teaspoon red pepper flakes
2 cloves garlic, minced
1 teaspoon salt
¼ teaspoon black pepper
½ cup tomato, diced
1 lemon, juiced
2 tablespoons fresh parsley, chopped

1. Add the tofu, broccoli, mushrooms, oil, turmeric, cumin, garlic powder, red pepper flakes, garlic, salt, and black pepper to a 4-quart slow cooker. Cover and cook on medium heat for 4 hours.

2. Add the tomato, lemon juice, and parsley to the scramble and serve.

PC GARDEN TOFU SCRAMBLE

Go gourmet with this tofu scramble by substituting shiitake mushrooms and Japanese eggplant instead of the broccoli and button mushrooms.

Serves 2–4

16 ounces firm tofu, drained and mashed
1 teaspoon fresh lemon juice
1 teaspoon salt
½ teaspoon black pepper
½ teaspoon turmeric
1 tablespoon olive oil
½ cup broccoli florets, blanched
½ cup button mushrooms, sliced
½ cup tomato, diced
1 clove garlic, minced
¼ cup water
2 tablespoons parsley, chopped

1. In a large bowl, mash the tofu with your hands or a fork, then stir in the lemon juice, salt, pepper, and turmeric.
2. Bring the olive oil to medium heat in the pressure cooker. Add the broccoli and mushrooms and sauté for 5 minutes. Add the tomato and garlic, and sauté for an additional 30 seconds.
3. Pour in the tofu mixture and water; stir, then lock the lid into place. Bring to medium pressure and maintain for 6 minutes. Remove from heat and allow pressure to release naturally.
4. Remove the lid and stir in the parsley before serving.

PC SPICY TOFU SCRAMBLE

Serve this spicy scramble on its own or rolled up in a flour tortilla to make a delicious breakfast burrito.

Serves 2–4

16 ounces firm tofu, drained and mashed

1 teaspoon fresh lemon juice

1 teaspoon salt

½ teaspoon black pepper

½ teaspoon turmeric

1 tablespoon olive oil

¼ cup onion, diced

¼ cup red bell pepper, diced

¼ cup tomato

1 clove garlic, minced

1 teaspoon cumin

½ teaspoon chipotle powder

½ teaspoon chili powder

¼ cup water

2 tablespoons cilantro, chopped

1. In a large bowl, mash the tofu with your hands or a fork, then stir in the lemon juice, salt, pepper, and turmeric.

2. Bring the olive oil to medium heat in the pressure cooker. Add the onion and bell pepper and sauté for 3 minutes. Add the tomato, garlic, cumin, chipotle powder, and chili powder and sauté for an additional 30 seconds.

3. Pour in the tofu mixture and water; stir, then lock the lid into place. Bring to medium pressure and maintain for 6 minutes. Remove from heat and allow pressure to release naturally.

4. Remove the lid and stir in the cilantro before serving.

SC COUNTRY GRITS

Start these simple grits in the evening and wake up to a delicious breakfast in the morning.

Serves 4

2 cups stone-ground grits

6 cups water

2 tablespoons butter or vegan margarine

1 teaspoon salt

¼ teaspoon black pepper

⅛ teaspoon cayenne pepper

Add all ingredients to a 4-quart slow cooker. Cover and cook on low heat for 6–9 hours.

SC CHEESE GRITS

Top each individual bowl of grits with cheese and place in the broiler until melted for an even tastier treat.

Serves 4

2 cups stone-ground grits

6 cups water

2 tablespoons butter or vegan margarine

1 cup shredded Cheddar or vegan cheese

1 teaspoon salt

¼ teaspoon black pepper

⅛ teaspoon cayenne pepper

Add all ingredients to a 4-quart slow cooker. Cover and cook on low heat for 6–9 hours.

PC RED PEPPER GRITS

Cooking grits in Vegetable Stock instead of water adds more depth to the flavor and makes them more appropriate for dinner or lunch.

Serves 4

4 cups Pressure Cooker Vegetable Stock (see Chapter 5)
1 teaspoon salt
¼ teaspoon dried thyme
1 cup stone-ground grits
½ tablespoon dried red pepper flakes

1. Bring the stock, salt, and thyme to a boil in the pressure cooker over high heat. Slowly stir in the grits.
2. Lock the lid into place. Bring to high pressure and maintain for 10 minutes. Remove from heat and allow pressure to release naturally.
3. Remove the lid and stir in the red pepper flakes before serving.

Grits

Grits are a Southern breakfast staple that are served topped with butter or margarine, salt, pepper, and sometimes cheese. They're very similar to polenta, especially when polenta is served creamy.

SC ALMOND AND DRIED CHERRY GRANOLA

Agave nectar is a natural sweetener that many vegans use in place of honey.

Serves 24

5 cups old-fashioned rolled oats
1 cup slivered almonds
¼ cup agave nectar
¼ cup canola oil
1 teaspoon vanilla
½ cup dried tart cherries
¼ cup unsweetened flaked coconut
½ cup sunflower seeds

1. Place the oats and almonds into a 4-quart slow cooker. Drizzle with agave nectar, oil, and vanilla. Stir the mixture to distribute the syrup evenly.
2. Cook on high, uncovered, for 1½ hours, stirring every 15–20 minutes.
3. Add the cherries, coconut, and sunflower seeds. Reduce heat to low. Cook for 4 hours, uncovered, stirring every 20 minutes.
4. Allow the granola to cool fully, and then store it in an airtight container for up to 1 month.

SC BREAKFAST QUINOA WITH FRUIT

Take a break from oatmeal and try this fruity quinoa instead!

Serves 4

1 cup quinoa

2 cups water

½ cup dried mixed berries

1 pear, thinly sliced

1 teaspoon dark brown sugar

½ teaspoon ground ginger

¼ teaspoon cinnamon

⅛ teaspoon cloves

⅛ teaspoon nutmeg

Place all ingredients into a 4-quart slow cooker. Cover and cook on low heat for 2–3 hours, or until the quinoa is fully cooked.

Quinoa

Quinoa, pronounced "keen-wah," is actually a seed, not a grain, closely related to spinach. It was originally cultivated by the Incas. It contains more high-quality protein than any other grain or cereal and is also high in iron, magnesium, phosphorus, and zinc, and a source of calcium, B vitamins, and fiber.

SC FRENCH TOAST CASSEROLE

This recipe is great for breakfast, and it's a wonderful way to use bread that is slightly stale.

Serves 8

12 slices whole-grain raisin bread

6 eggs

1 teaspoon vanilla

2 cups fat-free evaporated milk

2 tablespoons dark brown sugar

1 teaspoon cinnamon

¼ teaspoon nutmeg

1. Spray a 4-quart slow cooker with nonstick spray. Layer the bread in the slow cooker. In a small bowl, whisk the eggs, vanilla, evaporated milk, brown sugar, cinnamon, and nutmeg. Pour over the bread.

2. Cover and cook on low for 6–8 hours.

3. Remove the lid and cook uncovered for 30 minutes, or until the liquid has evaporated.

SC HASH BROWNS

Also called home fries, this home-style dish will serve 4 as a main dish or 6 if part of a hearty breakfast.

Serves 4

1 teaspoon canola oil

1 large onion, thinly sliced

1½ pounds red potatoes, thinly sliced

1. Heat oil in a nonstick skillet. Add the onions and potatoes and sauté until just browned, about 6 minutes. The potatoes should not be fully cooked.
2. Add mixture to a 2- or 4-quart slow cooker. Cook on low for 3–4 hours or on high for 1½ hours.

SC ONION, PEPPER, AND POTATO HASH BROWNS

Use a cheese grater to grate the potatoes for this dish.

Serves 4

2 tablespoons olive oil

4 cups russet potatoes, peeled and grated

½ onion, diced

1 poblano pepper, cored and diced

2 cloves garlic, minced

1 teaspoon chili powder

½ teaspoon paprika

½ teaspoon cumin

1 teaspoon salt

¼ teaspoon pepper

Add all ingredients to a 4-quart slow cooker. Cover and cook on medium heat for 4 hours.

PC PRESSURE COOKER HASH BROWNS

Feel free to serve these hash browns any way you'd like—scattered, covered, or smothered.

Serves 4

4 cups russet potatoes, peeled and grated

2 tablespoons olive oil

2 tablespoons butter or vegan margarine, such as Earth Balance

Salt and freshly ground pepper, to taste

1. Prepare the potatoes and set aside.
2. Add the oil and butter or margarine to the pressure cooker and bring to temperature over medium heat.
3. Add the hash brown potatoes; sauté for 5 minutes, stirring occasionally, until they are just beginning to brown. Season with the salt and pepper.
4. Use a wide metal spatula to press the potatoes down firmly in the pan.
5. Lock the lid in place and bring to low pressure; maintain pressure for 6 minutes. Remove from heat and quick-release the pressure.

Preparing the Potatoes

Rinsing and thoroughly drying the grated potatoes will help you achieve a delicious, crispy brown exterior on your hash browns. After grating the potatoes, pour them into a colander and let sit under running cold water for 1 minute to remove the extra starch. Once done, let the potatoes air dry or use a towel to remove excess water before cooking.

SC SLOW COOKER SPICY TOFU SCRAMBLE

Serve this spicy scramble on its own or rolled up in a flour tortilla to make a delicious breakfast burrito.

Serves 4

2 tablespoons olive oil

½ onion, diced

½ red pepper, diced

2 cloves garlic, minced

1 (16-ounce) package firm tofu, drained and crumbled

2 teaspoons turmeric

1 teaspoon cumin

½ teaspoon chipotle powder

½ teaspoon chili powder

1 teaspoon salt

¼ teaspoon black pepper

¼ cup tomato, diced

1 lemon, juiced

2 tablespoons fresh cilantro, chopped

1. Add the oil to a 4-quart slow cooker and sauté the onion, red pepper, and garlic on medium-high heat for about 3 minutes.

2. Mix in the tofu, turmeric, cumin, chipotle powder, chili powder, salt, and black pepper. Cover and cook on medium heat for 2–4 hours.

3. About 5 minutes before the scramble is finished, add the tomato, lemon juice, and cilantro.

PC POBLANO HASH BROWNS

Any type of pepper will do, such as poblano, jalapeño, or bell pepper, in these spicy hash browns.

Serves 4

4 cups russet potatoes, peeled and grated

2 tablespoons olive oil

2 tablespoons butter or vegan margarine, such as Earth Balance

¼ cup onion, diced

1 poblano pepper, cored and diced

1 clove garlic, minced

Salt and freshly ground pepper, to taste

1 teaspoon cumin

1. Prepare the grated potatoes by rinsing in a colander, then air drying or using a towel to remove excess water.
2. Add the oil and butter to the pressure cooker and bring to temperature over medium heat. Add the onion and poblano pepper and sauté until just soft, about 5 minutes.
3. Add the garlic and potatoes; sauté for an additional 5 minutes, stirring occasionally, until they are just beginning to brown. Season with the salt, pepper, and cumin.
4. Use a wide metal spatula to press the potatoes down firmly in the pan.
5. Lock the lid in place and bring to low pressure; maintain pressure for 6 minutes. Remove from heat and quick-release the pressure.

SC TEMPEH SAUSAGE CRUMBLES

Try this delicious and nutritious alternative to pork sausage.

Serves 4

1 (13-ounce) package tempeh, crumbled

1 teaspoon dried sage

2 teaspoons brown sugar

⅛ teaspoon red pepper flakes

⅛ teaspoon dried marjoram

1 cup vegetarian "chicken" broth

1 teaspoon salt

¼ teaspoon black pepper

1. In a medium bowl, mix all the ingredients together.
2. Add all ingredients to a 4-quart slow cooker. Cover and cook on medium heat for 4 hours.

SC BREAKFAST TOFU AND VEGGIES

Nutritional yeast has a cheesy flavor, and should not be replaced with other types of yeast.

Serves 4

¼ cup olive oil

1 (16-ounce) package extra-firm tofu, drained and cubed

½ onion, diced

1 cup broccoli, chopped

½ green bell pepper, chopped

½ zucchini, chopped

½ cup yellow squash, chopped

3 tablespoons soy sauce

¼ cup nutritional yeast

1. Add the oil to a 4-quart slow cooker and sauté the tofu for about 5–8 minutes on medium-high heat, stirring occasionally.
2. Add the vegetables and the soy sauce. Cover and cook on medium heat for 2–4 hours.
3. About 1 minute before the tofu and veggies are finished, stir in the nutritional yeast and serve.

SC EASY TOFU "EGGS"

Tofu "eggs" are a great form of protein and taste delicious. They contain very little fat and no cholesterol. Build upon this basic recipe to create a variety of tofu scrambles.

Serves 4

2 tablespoons olive oil

1 (16-ounce) package firm tofu, drained and crumbled

¼ cup onion, diced

2 cloves garlic, minced

1 teaspoon turmeric

1 teaspoon salt

¼ teaspoon black pepper

1 lemon, juiced

1. Add all ingredients, except for the lemon juice, to a 4-quart slow cooker. Cover and cook on medium heat for 2–4 hours.
2. About 3 minutes before the "eggs" are finished, stir in the lemon juice.

SC GRANDMA'S CORNMEAL MUSH

This recipe cooks into a thick cornmeal porridge. It makes for a tasty and inexpensive breakfast food.

Serves 4

2 cups yellow cornmeal

8 cups water

1 teaspoon salt

2 tablespoons butter or vegan margarine

1. Add all ingredients to a 4-quart slow cooker. Cover and cook on medium heat for 4 hours.
2. Allow the mush to cool for at least 30 minutes. Serve with maple syrup.

SC BREAKFAST CASSEROLE

To simplify this recipe, use Morningstar Farm Sausage Style Crumbles instead of the Tempeh Sausage Crumbles recipe in this book. Omit the cottage cheese to make this a vegan dish.

Serves 4

¼ cup olive oil

3 cups potatoes, peeled and grated

1 onion, diced

½ green bell pepper, chopped

2 cups Tempeh Sausage Crumbles (see recipe in this chapter)

6 eggs, beaten, or Easy Tofu "Eggs" (see recipe in this chapter)

1 cup cottage cheese

2 cups Cheddar cheese or vegan cheese

1 teaspoon salt

¼ teaspoon black pepper

Add all ingredients to a 4-quart slow cooker. Cover and cook on medium heat for 4 hours.

SC SPICY BREAKFAST BURRITO

To make this burrito vegan instead of vegetarian, use tofu instead of cooked eggs.

Serves 4

- ¼ cup olive oil
- 1 (16-ounce) package firm tofu, drained and crumbled
- ¼ cup red onion, diced
- 1 tablespoon jalapeño, minced
- ¼ cup red bell pepper, diced
- ¼ cup poblano pepper, diced
- 1 cup cooked black beans, drained
- 2 teaspoons turmeric
- 1 teaspoon cumin
- ½ teaspoon chili powder
- 1 teaspoon salt
- ¼ teaspoon black pepper
- 4 large flour tortillas
- 1 avocado, peeled and sliced
- ½ cup tomato, diced
- ¼ cup cilantro, chopped
- ½ cup chipotle salsa
- ½ cup shredded Cheddar cheese or vegan Cheddar cheese

1. Add olive oil, tofu, onion, jalapeño, red bell pepper, and poblano pepper to a 4-quart slow cooker and sauté on medium-high for 5–8 minutes.

2. Add the black beans, turmeric, cumin, chili powder, salt, and black pepper. Cover and cook on medium heat for 4 hours.

3. Scoop the filling onto the tortillas and add the avocado, tomato, cilantro, salsa, and cheese. Fold the sides of the tortilla in and roll up the burrito.

Steaming Tortillas

For best results, steam tortillas on the stovetop using a steamer basket. If you're in a hurry, throw the tortillas into the microwave one at a time and heat for about 30 seconds.

SC SLOW COOKER TOFU RANCHERO

Bring Mexican cuisine to the breakfast table with an easy Tofu Ranchero.

Serves 4

3 tablespoons olive oil

1 (16-ounce) package firm tofu, drained and crumbled

½ onion, diced

2 cloves garlic, minced

1 lemon, juiced

½ teaspoon turmeric

1 teaspoon salt

¼ teaspoon black pepper

1 cup cooked pinto beans, drained

8 corn tortillas

½ cup shredded Cheddar cheese or vegan Cheddar cheese

½ cup chipotle salsa

1. Add the olive oil, tofu, onion, garlic, lemon, turmeric, salt, black pepper, and pinto beans to a 4-quart slow cooker. Cover and cook on medium heat for 4 hours.

2. When the ranchero filling is nearly done, brown the tortillas on both sides using a small sauté pan.

3. Preheat the oven to 350°F.

4. Place the tortillas on a baking sheet and add the filling. Sprinkle the cheese over the rancheros and bake until the cheese has melted, about 5 minutes. Top with the chipotle salsa.

HUEVOS RANCHEROS

Rich and delicious, this Mexican ranch breakfast will fuel your whole morning, even if you're climbing Mt. Everest that day. While this recipe calls for scrambled eggs, it works equally well with any style of eggs.

Serves 4

1 can Mexican-style black beans in sauce or Cuban Black Beans (see Chapter 7)

2 cups Rancheros Salsa (see Chapter 4) or store-bought Mexican salsa

8 large eggs

½ cup half-and-half

½ teaspoon salt

Unsalted butter

8 soft corn tortillas (8" diameter)

1 cup shredded Monterey jack or mild Cheddar cheese

½ cup sour cream or Tofu Sour Cream (see Chapter 2)

Chopped cilantro

1. Heat the beans and Rancheros Salsa in separate pots over low flames. Scramble together the eggs, half-and-half, and salt. Melt the butter in a nonstick pan; cook the scrambled eggs over a low flame until soft and creamy, with small curds.

2. Soften the tortillas either by steaming or flash cooking over an open gas burner. Place 2 tortillas onto each plate. Divide the hot black beans evenly onto these tortillas. Spoon the eggs onto the beans, then sauce with a ladleful of Rancheros Salsa. Garnish with cheese, sour cream, and cilantro. Serve immediately.

ROASTED VEGETABLE FRITTATA

This perfect brunch main course can be made ahead and served at slightly above room temperature. It's a perfect way to utilize leftover vegetables of all sorts—any vegetables will work.

Serves 8

1 medium zucchini, quartered lengthwise

1 medium yellow squash, quartered lengthwise

1 cup small white mushrooms

1 small (Italian) eggplant, or ¼ of a regular eggplant, cut into large chunks

2 tablespoons olive oil

9 eggs, beaten

¾ cup half-and-half

½ teaspoon salt

2 tablespoons unsalted butter

1 baked potato, diced

1 medium onion, chopped

Chopped Italian parsley or cilantro

½ cup diced tomatoes (about 1 large)

1 cup shredded cheese (Monterey jack, Cheddar, or Havarti, for example)

Black pepper to taste

1. Heat oven to 400°F. Toss zucchini, yellow squash, mushrooms, and eggplant with olive oil; spread into a baking sheet or roasting pan. Roast until tender, about 20 minutes. (Note: This step can be done up to 2 days in advance.) Raise oven temperature to 450°F.

2. In a bowl, whisk together the eggs, half-and-half, and salt. In an oven-safe, 10" nonstick skillet, melt the butter over medium heat. Add the potatoes, onions, and parsley (or cilantro); cook until the onions are softened and the potatoes are slightly browned. Add the roasted vegetables and the egg mixture. Cook, stirring with a wooden spoon, until the mixture begins to thicken, but is still mostly liquid. Stir in the tomatoes and cheese. Season with pepper. Place pan on center rack of oven, and bake until frittata puffs slightly and begins to brown on top, about 15 minutes. Remove from oven and transfer frittata to a serving plate. Allow it to rest 5 minutes before cutting into 8 wedges and serving, garnished with additional parsley or cilantro.

SPINACH QUICHE

There's no yummier way to get the iron, calcium, and other goodness from spinach than this elegant, simple, savory pie.

Serves 6

1 batch Basic Pie Dough (see Chapter 6) or 1 store-bought, unsweetened 9" pie shell

¼ cup scallions, chopped

2 tablespoons unsalted butter

1 pound (1 package) fresh spinach, washed, stems removed, roughly chopped

Pinch of nutmeg

½ teaspoon salt

¼ teaspoon fresh ground black pepper

3 large eggs

6 ounces half-and-half or milk

¼ cup shredded Gruyère or Swiss cheese

1. Heat oven to 350°F. If using fresh pie dough, roll out a disk 11" in diameter and line it into an ungreased, 9" pie pan. Crimp edges, gently place wax paper over the unbaked crust, and fill the cavity with dried beans or pie beads. Bake until golden brown, 15–20 minutes (this is known as "blind baking" the crust). Cool on a rack; remove beans. If using a store-bought shell, bake according to package directions for "blind baking." Increase oven temperature to 375°F.

2. Heat the scallions and butter in a skillet until they sizzle. Add spinach, nutmeg, salt, and pepper; cook until spinach is wilted. Whisk together eggs and half-and-half in a bowl. Add the spinach mixture. Sprinkle half of the cheese into the prebaked pie crust; add the spinach-egg mixture. Top with remaining cheese; bake 35 minutes, until the top is domed and beginning to brown.

SC ROSEMARY HOME FRIES

Like hash browns, home fries can also be served with a variety of toppings or plain with a side of ketchup.

Serves 4

¼ cup olive oil

4 cups red potatoes, diced

½ red onion, diced

1 poblano pepper, diced

½ red bell pepper, diced

1 teaspoon salt

¼ teaspoon black pepper

2 tablespoons fresh rosemary, chopped

1. Add all ingredients, except for the rosemary, to a 4-quart slow cooker. Cover and cook on medium heat for 4 hours.

2. About 10 minutes before the potatoes are done, add the rosemary and cook for the remainder of the time.

SC WHITE GRAVY

For a delicious and filling breakfast, try this gravy over biscuits.

Serves 4

½ cup vegetable oil

¼ cup onion, minced

3 cloves garlic, minced

¼ cup flour

4 tablespoons soy sauce

2 cups water

½ teaspoon dried sage

⅛ teaspoon dried thyme

½ teaspoon salt

¼ teaspoon black pepper

1. Add the oil to the slow cooker and sauté the onion and garlic over medium heat for about 3–5 minutes. Slowly stir in the flour to create a roux.

2. Add the rest of the ingredients to the slow cooker. Cover and cook on medium heat for 1 hour, stirring occasionally.

SC PEAR OATMEAL

Cooking rolled oats overnight makes them so creamy they could be served as dessert. Cooking them with fruit is just the icing on the cake.

Serves 4

2 Bosc pears, cored and thinly sliced

2¼ cups pear cider

1½ cups old-fashioned rolled oats

1 tablespoon dark brown sugar

½ teaspoon cinnamon

Place all ingredients in a 4-quart slow cooker. Cook on low overnight, approximately 8–9 hours. Stir and serve.

PC BANANA NUT BREAD OATMEAL

Skip instant oatmeal packets, which can be high in sugar, and make this homemade version instead.

Serves 2

¾ cup water

1 cup milk or soymilk

1 cup quick-cooking oats

2 bananas, sliced

2 tablespoons brown sugar

2 teaspoons cinnamon

2 tablespoons chopped walnuts

1. Place all of the ingredients in the pressure cooker.
2. Lock the lid into place. Bring to high pressure and maintain for 5 minutes. Remove from heat and allow pressure to release naturally.
3. Remove the lid and stir the oatmeal, adding more milk or soymilk if desired.

PC STEEL-CUT OATS

Steel-cut oats, whole grain oats that have been cut into only 2–3 pieces, are sometimes referred to as Irish oatmeal. They are high in B vitamins, calcium, protein, and fiber.

Serves 2

4 cups water

1 cup steel-cut oats, toasted

1 tablespoon butter or vegan margarine, such as Earth Balance

Pinch salt

1. Place the rack in the pressure cooker; pour ½ cup water over the rack.

2. In a metal bowl that will fit inside the pressure cooker and rest on the rack, add the oats, butter or margarine, salt, and 3½ cups water. Lock the lid into place.

3. Bring to low pressure. For chewy oatmeal, maintain the pressure for 5 minutes. For creamy oatmeal, maintain pressure for 8 minutes.

4. Remove from heat and allow pressure to release naturally. Use tongs to lift the metal bowl out of the pressure cooker.

5. Spoon the cooked oats into bowls; season and serve as you would regular oatmeal.

Toasting Steel-Cut Oats

Preheat the oven to 300°F. Place the steel-cut oats on a baking sheet. Bake for 20 minutes. Store toasted steel-cut oats in a covered container in a cool place. Toasting steel-cut oats will enhance the flavor and allow them to cook in half the time.

PC APPLE STREUSEL OATMEAL

Get creative and turn any of your favorite desserts into a breakfast oatmeal.

Serves 2

¾ cup water

1 cup milk or soymilk

1 cup quick-cooking oats

2 apples, peeled, cored, and diced

2 tablespoons brown sugar

2 teaspoons cinnamon

2 tablespoons chopped pecans

1. Place all of the ingredients in the pressure cooker.

2. Lock the lid into place. Bring to high pressure and maintain for 5 minutes. Remove from heat and allow pressure to release naturally.

3. Remove the lid and stir the oatmeal, adding more milk or soymilk if desired.

PC IRISH OATMEAL WITH FRUIT

You can substitute other dried fruit according to your tastes. Try prunes, dates, and cherries for different flavors.

Serves 2

3 cups water

1 cup toasted steel-cut oats

2 teaspoons butter or vegan margarine, such as Earth Balance

1 cup apple juice

1 tablespoon dried cranberries

1 tablespoon golden raisins

1 tablespoon snipped dried apricots

1 tablespoon maple syrup

¼ teaspoon ground cinnamon

Pinch salt

1. Place the rack in the pressure cooker; pour ½ cup water over the rack.

2. In a metal bowl that will fit inside the pressure cooker and rest on the rack, add the 2½ cups water, oats, butter or margarine, apple juice, cranberries, raisins, apricots, maple syrup, cinnamon, and salt; stir to combine.

3. Lock the lid into place. Bring to low pressure. For chewy oatmeal, maintain the pressure for 5 minutes. For creamy oatmeal, maintain pressure for 8 minutes.

4. Remove from heat and allow pressure to release naturally. Use tongs to lift the metal bowl out of the pressure cooker.

Cooking Ahead

If you're not a morning person, you can make Irish Oatmeal with Fruit the night before. Once it's cooled, divide between two covered, microwave-safe containers and refrigerate overnight. The next morning, cover each bowl with a paper towel to catch any splatters and then microwave on high for 1–2 minutes or until heated through.

PC MAPLE-PECAN OATMEAL

Rolled oats or quick-cooking oats will work in this recipe. Just be sure to adjust the cooking time accordingly.

Serves 2

¾ cup water
1 cup milk or soymilk
1 cup quick-cooking oats
2 tablespoons maple syrup
2 tablespoons chopped pecans

1. Place all of the ingredients in the pressure cooker.
2. Lock the lid into place. Bring to high pressure and maintain for 5 minutes. Remove from heat and allow pressure to release naturally.
3. Remove the lid and stir the oatmeal, adding more milk if desired.

PC THREE PEPPER VEGAN FRITTATA

Frittatas are traditionally made with eggs, but you can use tofu for a cholesterol-free breakfast dish instead.

Serves 4

2 tablespoons olive oil
1 cup red potatoes, peeled and diced
½ cup onion, diced
½ cup red bell pepper, diced
½ cup green bell pepper, diced
1 teaspoon jalapeño, minced
1 clove garlic, minced
¼ cup chopped parsley
16 ounces firm tofu
½ cup unsweetened soymilk
4 teaspoons cornstarch
2 teaspoons nutritional yeast
1 teaspoon mustard
½ teaspoon turmeric
1 teaspoon salt

1. Preheat the oven to 400°F.
2. Bring the olive oil to medium heat in the pressure cooker. Add the potatoes, onion, peppers, garlic, and parsley, and sauté for 3 minutes. Lock the lid in place and bring to high pressure; maintain pressure for 6 minutes. Remove from heat and quick-release the pressure.
3. Combine the tofu, soymilk, cornstarch, nutritional yeast, mustard, turmeric, and salt in a blender or food processor until smooth, then pour the tofu mixture into the cooked potato mixture.
4. Spoon the mixture into an oiled quiche or pie pan. Bake for 45 minutes, or until the frittata is firm, then remove from heat and let stand before serving.

Make It a Scramble

To shorten the preparation time for this meal while keeping all of the flavors, try making this dish into a scramble by preparing the entire recipe in the pressure cooker. Skip the step of blending the tofu and omit the cornstarch. Add remaining ingredients, breaking apart tofu as you stir, and sauté until cooked through.

YEASTY TOFU AND VEGGIES

This delicious, cheesy-tasting recipe is perfect for breakfast!

Serves 4

1 16-ounce package extra-firm tofu
2 tablespoons vegetable oil
2 tablespoons soy sauce
1 cup water
½ onion, diced
1 cup broccoli, blanched and chopped
½ green bell pepper, chopped
½ zucchini, chopped
½ cup yellow squash, chopped
¼ cup nutritional yeast

1. Wrap the block of tofu in paper towels and press for 5 minutes by adding weight on top. Remove the paper towels and cut the tofu into ½"-thick pieces. Add 1 tablespoon of oil to the pressure cooker and sauté the tofu until it is light brown on all sides. Add 1 tablespoon of soy sauce and sauté for 10 seconds more. Remove the tofu.

2. Place the water in the pressure cooker along with the steamer tray. Place the tofu on top of the steamer tray. Lock the lid into place; bring to high pressure and maintain for 5 minutes. Remove from heat and allow pressure to release naturally.

3. Add 1 tablespoon of oil to a large pan and sauté the onions, broccoli, bell pepper, zucchini, and squash until tender. Add the tofu and 1 tablespoon soy sauce and sauté for 1 minute more. Sprinkle the nutritional yeast on top and serve.

PRESSURE COOKER TOFU RANCHERO

Bring Mexican cuisine to the breakfast table with this easy Tofu Ranchero.

Serves 4

16 ounces firm tofu, drained and mashed

1 teaspoon fresh lemon juice

1 teaspoon salt

½ teaspoon black pepper

½ teaspoon turmeric

2 tablespoons olive oil

¼ cup onion, diced

1 clove garlic, minced

8 corn tortillas

1 cup vegetarian refried beans, warmed

½ cup cheese or vegan cheese

½ cup chipotle salsa

1. Preheat the oven to 350°F. In a large bowl, mash the tofu with your hands or a fork, then stir in the lemon juice, salt, pepper, and turmeric.

2. Bring 1 tablespoon olive oil to medium heat in the pressure cooker. Add the onion and sauté for 3 minutes. Add the garlic and sauté for an additional 30 seconds.

3. Pour in the tofu mixture and stir, then lock the lid into place. Bring to medium pressure and maintain for 6 minutes. Remove from heat and allow pressure to release naturally.

4. Heat 1 tablespoon olive oil in a small sauté pan over medium heat. Cook the tortillas one at a time, until they begin to brown on each side.

5. Place all 8 of the tortillas on 1 or 2 baking sheets. Divide the refried beans evenly among the tortillas, then top with the cooked tofu mixture. Sprinkle cheese over each of the tortillas, then bake until the cheese begins to melt.

6. Remove from the oven and top with salsa before serving.

PC SPINACH AND PORTOBELLO BENEDICT

If making this recipe vegan, read the label before purchasing your English muffins. Some brands are not vegan.

Serves 2

½ cup silken tofu
1 tablespoon lemon juice
1 teaspoon Dijon mustard
⅛ teaspoon cayenne pepper
⅛ teaspoon turmeric
1 tablespoon vegetable oil
Salt, to taste
1 tablespoon olive oil
4 small portobello mushroom caps
2 cups fresh spinach
2 English muffins, toasted

1. Add the silken tofu to a food processor and purée until smooth. Add the lemon juice, mustard, cayenne, and turmeric. Blend until well combined. With the food processor still running, slowly add the vegetable oil and blend until combined. Season with salt, to taste, to complete the vegan hollandaise.

2. Pour the hollandaise into a small saucepan over low heat and cook until the sauce is warm. Keep warm until ready to serve.

3. Heat the olive oil in the pressure cooker over low heat. Add the mushroom caps and spinach and stir until coated with the oil.

4. Lock the lid into place. Bring to medium pressure and maintain for 3 minutes. Remove from heat and quick-release the pressure.

5. Place 2 open-faced English muffins on each plate and top each half with 1 portobello cap and sautéed spinach. Drizzle with a spoonful of the warm vegan hollandaise to finish.

CHAPTER 2
SAUCES AND SPREADS

RECIPE LIST

BASIL PESTO **62**

RED GARLIC MAYONNAISE (ROUILLE) **62**

TOFU SOUR CREAM **63**

ONION JAM **63**

AIOLI (GARLIC MAYONNAISE) **64**

MAÎTRE D' BUTTER **64**

BLACK OLIVE BUTTER **65**

GARLIC AND BASIL BUTTER **65**

ROSEMARY-LEMON BUTTER **66**

CHILI-ORANGE BUTTER FOR GRILLED BREAD **66**

APPLE BUTTER **67**

VANILLA-SPICE PEAR BUTTER **68**

CRANBERRY SAUCE **69**

SLOW-ROASTED GARLIC AND TOMATO SAUCE **69**

BASIC FRESH TOMATO SAUCE **70**

QUICK TOMATO SAUCE **71**

FRESH TOMATO SAUCE **72**

GARDEN MARINARA SAUCE **73**

BASIC MARINARA SAUCE **74**

VEGAN ALFREDO **74**

WHITE BEAN ALFREDO SAUCE **75**

JALAPEÑO-TOMATILLO SAUCE **76**

LEMON DILL SAUCE **76**

CREAMY DIJON SAUCE **77**

COUNTRY WHITE GRAVY **77**

PUTTANESCA SAUCE **78**

BARBECUE SAUCE **79**

COUNTRY BARBECUE SAUCE **80**

NEW MEXICO CHILI SAUCE **81**

MOLE **81**

HOMEMADE KETCHUP **82**

RASPBERRY COULIS **83**

COCONUT CURRY SAUCE **83**

WHITE WINE–GARLIC SAUCE **84**

THREE PEPPER SAUCE **84**

ROASTED RED PEPPER SAUCE **85**

EASY PEANUT SAUCE **85**

SPICY PEANUT SAUCE **86**

ESPAGNOLE **87**

BÉCHAMEL SAUCE **88**

AU JUS **88**

BEURRE BLANC **89**

VODKA SAUCE **90**

YELLOW PEPPER COULIS **91**

CASHEW CREAM SAUCE **92**

PLUM SAUCE **93**

CRANBERRY-APPLE CHUTNEY **94**

FRESH TOMATO CHUTNEY **95**

GREEN TOMATO CHUTNEY **96**

SWEET ONION RELISH **97**

STRAWBERRY JAM **98**

DRIED APRICOT PRESERVES **99**

MIXED CITRUS MARMALADE **100**

RAINBOW BELL PEPPER MARMALADE **101**

BLUEBERRY JAM **102**

MINCEMEAT **103**

PEACH AND TOASTED ALMOND PRESERVES **104**

CARIBBEAN RELISH **105**

BLACKBERRY JAM **106**

PEACH JAM **107**

EASY GRAPE JELLY **107**

BASIL PESTO

This is an exquisite sauce for pasta, vegetables, grilled items, and soup garnish.

Serves 8

5 cloves garlic, peeled

½ cup toasted pine nuts

1 large bunch basil, stems and veins removed, washed thoroughly

1½ cups extra-virgin olive oil

⅓ cup grated Parmesan cheese

Coarse salt and freshly ground black pepper

1. Pulse garlic in food processor until finely chopped. Add nuts and pulse a few times to give them a rough chop. Scrape the bowl to loosen anything stuck to the sides.

2. Pile in all of the basil. Drizzle half of the oil over the leaves, and pulse until basil is medium chopped, about the size of fresh thyme leaves. Remove from food processor to a mixing bowl.

3. Using a plastic spatula or a wooden spoon, fold in the Parmesan cheese, season with salt and pepper, and thin to sauce consistency with the remaining olive oil. Will keep in the refrigerator for 1 week, or in the freezer for up to 2 months. When using frozen pesto, do not thaw, but break off what you need from a frozen state.

RED GARLIC MAYONNAISE (ROUILLE)

This mayonnaise tastes great on any sandwich!

Yields 1½ cups

2 cloves garlic, chopped very fine

1 cup mayonnaise or soy mayo

1 small red pepper, roasted, peeled, and puréed

Salt to taste

½ lemon

Pinch of cayenne

Whisk together garlic, mayonnaise or soy mayo, and roasted pepper purée. Season with a pinch of salt, a squeeze of lemon, and cayenne.

TOFU SOUR CREAM

This delicious spread not only provides a vegan alternative to fat-rich sour cream, but also provides essential protein for vegetarians. It is important to include soy foods as a daily part of a vegetarian diet.

Yields about 1½ cups

1½ cups firm silken tofu, broken up

1 tablespoon extra-virgin olive oil

1 tablespoon vegetable oil

2 teaspoons fresh lemon juice

2 teaspoons apple cider vinegar

½ teaspoon sugar

½ teaspoon salt

Combine all ingredients in a blender or food processor. Process or blend until smooth. Chill. Keeps for up to 10 days.

ONION JAM

The concentrated sweetness and naturally complex flavor of this caramelized onion spread come from slow cooking, which breaks down the cell walls of the onions, releasing 100 percent of their flavor. Serve it with French bread slices or crackers as an hors d'oeuvre, or as a component of a dinner meal.

Serves 8

6–8 large onions

2 tablespoons olive oil

2 sprigs fresh thyme or ½ teaspoon dried (optional)

½ teaspoon salt

1. Halve the onions through the root end, peel them, and slice them very thinly across the grain.

2. Heat the olive oil in a large, heavy-bottomed Dutch oven over medium heat until it shimmers, but does not smoke. Add the thyme and the sliced onions. Sprinkle with salt. Lower heat; cook slowly to wilt the onions completely, stirring gently with a wooden spoon. As the onions begin to caramelize (turn brown), use the wooden spoon to scrape dried-on juices from the bottom of the pot; stir regularly to incorporate as much of these browned juices as possible. Cook this way until onions are dark brown, and mostly disintegrated into a thick spread, usually about 40 minutes, depending on the water content of your onions. Cool to room temperature, or serve warm.

AIOLI (GARLIC MAYONNAISE)

In Belgium, where "frites" (homemade French fries) are a national dish, ketchup is a rarity. Instead, the Belgians dip their fried potatoes in seasoned mayonnaises like aioli, flavored with fresh or roasted garlic. Once you've tried this luxurious flavor combination, you may never reach for ketchup again.

Serves 8

2 large cloves garlic, finely chopped, or pushed through a press

¼ teaspoon salt

2 large egg yolks

1 teaspoon Dijon mustard

Juice of 1 lemon (about ¼ cup), divided

1 cup extra-virgin olive oil

1. Mash together the garlic and salt in a large mixing bowl. Wet a cloth towel, wring it out, fold it in half, and set it onto a work surface (this will hold your bowl steady while you work). Set the mixing bowl on the towel, and mix in the yolks, mustard, and 2 teaspoons of the lemon juice.

2. Using a rapid whisking action, very gradually whisk ¼ of the olive oil into the yolk mixture. Add a few drops of room-temperature water in, to help incorporate the oil, then repeat with remaining oil, adding it in a slow, steady stream, while whisking vigorously. Season to taste with remaining lemon juice.

MAÎTRE D' BUTTER

To store this butter, chill it, then cut small "coins" of compound butter to use at any time. It can be frozen for up to 3 months.

Yields 8 1 tablespoon servings

4 ounces (1 stick) butter

1 tablespoon freshly squeezed lemon juice

2–3 tablespoons chopped parsley

1 tablespoon finely minced shallot or scallion

Salt and pepper

1. Beat the butter in a 2-quart mixing bowl with a wooden spoon, adding the lemon juice a little at a time until it is incorporated. Stir in the parsley, shallot or scallion, and salt and pepper to taste.

2. Spread or spoon-drop soft butter over each vegetable as it comes off the grill. Or shape it into a stick on a piece of plastic wrap, and roll it up for later use.

Mix It Up!

Mixing olives, herbs, and essences into whole butter is easy and will juice up your barbecue table this summer. Some butter-flavor combinations are classic, like Maître d' Butter with shallots, lemon, and parsley.

BLACK OLIVE BUTTER

The olives in this butter will give it the salty taste you crave!

Yields 8 1 tablespoon servings

⅓ cup Kalamata, Niçoise, or other black olives, pitted

8 ounces (2 sticks) unsalted butter, room temperature

1 tablespoon freshly squeezed lemon juice

Pinch of crushed red pepper flakes (optional)

1. In a food processor, pulse olives until they are finely chopped, but not puréed.
2. With the processor running, gradually add the butter, then the lemon juice and red pepper flakes. Scrape down the sides of the bowl with a rubber spatula and mix a little by hand.
3. Turn out onto a piece of plastic food wrap and roll into a log, about 1" in diameter, twisting the ends of the plastic wrap to tighten the roll. Chill or freeze, and cut crosswise into "coins" when needed.

GARLIC AND BASIL BUTTER

The fresh basil in this recipe is perfect in the summertime. Pick it right from your garden!

Yields 8 1 tablespoon servings

4 ounces (1 stick) butter, room temperature

2 cloves garlic, finely minced

Salt and pepper

½ cup fresh basil leaves, washed

1. Cream the butter in a 2-quart mixing bowl with a wooden spoon until smooth. Work in the minced garlic, and salt and pepper to taste.
2. With a very sharp knife, gently chop the basil leaves and stir them into the butter. Spread or spoon onto grilled polenta or vegetables as they come off the grill. This butter is best used the day it is made.

ROSEMARY-LEMON BUTTER

What's more refreshing than lemonade on a hot day? This Rosemary-Lemon Butter, that's what! It's perfect to serve at a picnic or just spread on bread whenever you need a taste of summertime.

Yields 8 1 tablespoon servings

3 lush sprigs fresh rosemary, leaves only

1 large lemon

8 ounces (2 sticks) butter, room temperature, cut into ½" slices

Salt and pepper

1. Chop the rosemary leaves finely.
2. Zest lemon with fine side of grater, then squeeze juice and reserve.
3. In a food processor or by hand, mix the butter until smooth. Work in the rosemary and lemon zest, then the juice, salt, and pepper.

CHILI-ORANGE BUTTER FOR GRILLED BREAD

The chili pepper in this recipe gives this butter a kick! It's great on grilled bread!

Yields 8 1 tablespoon servings

8 ounces butter, room temperature

1 teaspoon orange juice concentrate

2 teaspoons dark honey

2 teaspoons New Mexico chili powder, or other chili powder

Pinch of salt

1. Pulse butter in a food processor until smooth. With machine running, add orange juice concentrate, honey, chili powder, and salt.
2. Spread or spoon onto grilled country bread.

Added Char

Chefs have been melting flavored butters, called compound butters, over grilled items like portobello mushrooms for years, adding flavor and richness, while taking advantage of the savory natural juices cooked foods produce. They know that as the butter melts, it mixes with the intense char on the food's surface, making a sauce that capitalizes on the food's own unique character.

PC APPLE BUTTER

Serve on toast or as a sandwich spread.

Yields about 2 cups

1 cup apple juice or cider

12 medium apples (about 3 pounds)

1½ teaspoons ground cinnamon

½ teaspoon ground allspice

⅛ teaspoon ground cloves

1½ cups sugar

1–2 drops oil of cinnamon (optional)

1. Add the apple juice or cider to the pressure cooker. Wash, peel, core, and dice the apples. Lock the lid into place, bring to high pressure, and immediately remove from heat; let the pressure release naturally for 10 minutes. Quick-release any remaining pressure.

2. Press cooled apples through a fine sieve or food mill, or process in a food processor or blender. Return apples and liquids to pressure cooker, add the cinnamon, allspice, cloves, sugar, and oil of cinnamon, if using.

3. Return the pan to medium heat and bring to a simmer. Simmer uncovered and stir until the sugar is dissolved. Reduce heat, simmer, and stir for 1 hour. Note that it's important that you frequently stir the apple butter from the bottom of the pan to prevent it from burning.

PC VANILLA-SPICE PEAR BUTTER

Bartlett pears are light green and are especially prevalent in the Pacific Northwest. Serve on scones or toasted English muffins.

Yields about 2 cups

6 medium Bartlett pears
¼ cup dry white wine
1 tablespoon fresh lemon juice
¾ cup sugar
2 orange slices
1 lemon slice
2 whole cloves
1 vanilla bean, split lengthwise
1 cinnamon stick
¼ teaspoon ground cardamom
Pinch salt

1. Rinse, peel, and core the pears, and cut them into 1" dice. Add the pears, wine, and lemon juice to the pressure cooker. Lock the lid into place and bring to low pressure; maintain pressure for 8 minutes.

2. Remove from heat and allow pressure to release naturally for 10 minutes. Quick-release any remaining pressure and remove the lid. Transfer the fruit and juices to a blender or food processor and purée.

3. Return the purée to the pressure cooker. Add the sugar. Stir and cook over low heat until sugar dissolves. Stir in the remaining ingredients. Increase the heat to medium and boil gently, cooking and stirring for about 30 minutes or until mixture thickens and mounds slightly on a spoon.

4. Remove and discard the orange and lemon slices, cloves, and cinnamon stick. Remove the vanilla pod; use the back of a knife to scrape away any vanilla seeds still clinging to the pod and stir them into the pear butter. Cool and refrigerate covered for up to 10 days or freeze for up to 4 months.

PC CRANBERRY SAUCE

For additional flavor, stir in some orange liqueur, bourbon, or brandy.

Serves 6

1 (12-ounce) bag fresh cranberries

1 cup sugar

½ cup water, apple juice, or pineapple juice

Pinch salt

1 tablespoon frozen orange juice concentrate

Cinnamon and ground cloves, to taste (optional)

1. Rinse and drain the cranberries. Remove and discard any stems or blemished cranberries. Add to the pressure cooker along with the sugar, water or apple/pineapple juice, and salt. Lock the lid and bring to high pressure; maintain for 6 minutes.

2. Remove from heat and allow pressure to release naturally for 10 minutes. Remove the lid. Stir in the orange juice concentrate. Stir well, breaking the cranberries apart with a spoon.

3. Taste for seasoning, stirring in additional sugar and cinnamon and cloves if desired. Serve warm or chilled.

SC SLOW-ROASTED GARLIC AND TOMATO SAUCE

Canned, diced tomatoes are a good substitute for fresh, vine-ripened tomatoes when fresh tomatoes are not in season.

Yields 4 cups

2 tablespoons olive oil

2½ pounds fresh, vine-ripened tomatoes, peeled and diced

1 teaspoon dried parsley

1 teaspoon dried basil

1 tablespoon balsamic vinegar

½ teaspoon granulated cane sugar

Salt, to taste

Freshly ground black pepper, to taste

3 heads roasted garlic, cloves removed from peel

In a 4-quart slow cooker, add all ingredients. Cover and cook on low for 3–4 hours.

Roasting Garlic

Roast whole heads of garlic by cutting off the top ¼, drizzling with olive oil, and then wrapping in aluminum foil. Cook in an oven preheated to 400°F for about 45 minutes.

BASIC FRESH TOMATO SAUCE

August and September are tomato harvest season in the East, when thousands of cooks pack summer's bounty into jars of fruity tomato sauce to last them the whole year. This sauce freezes well, and can also be canned.

Yields 1 quart

4 pounds tomatoes, preferably Roma plum tomatoes, but any variety will do

2 tablespoons olive oil

1 large onion, roughly chopped

5 cloves garlic, chopped (about 2 tablespoons)

1 teaspoon sugar

2 tablespoons tomato paste

1 cup washed fresh basil leaves, stems removed (optional)

Salt and freshly ground black pepper

1. Halve the tomatoes and squeeze out as many seeds as you can. Dice the tomatoes. Heat the olive oil in a large saucepan or Dutch oven (pan should be enamel, steel, or glass-lined) over medium heat until hot enough to sizzle when a piece of onion is added. Add the onion; cook until soft and beginning to brown slightly, about 10 minutes. Stir in the garlic, sugar, and tomato paste; cook 2 minutes more, stirring constantly. Add the tomatoes; cook 10 minutes until mixture becomes brothy.

2. Uncover, lower flame to a slow simmer, and cook 30 minutes more, until all tomatoes are fully softened; season to taste. If you prefer chunky sauce, add the basil, if desired. For smooth sauce, purée and strain, then add the basil leaves at the end.

QUICK TOMATO SAUCE

This sauce can be assembled in 20 minutes from ingredients right in the house. It is an excellent all-purpose red sauce for pasta or any recipe calling for tomato sauce.

Yields 1 quart

2 tablespoons olive oil

1 medium onion, chopped

2 tablespoons chopped garlic (about 5 cloves)

1 teaspoon dried oregano (optional)

1 tablespoon tomato paste

1 teaspoon sugar

1 (28-ounce) can crushed tomatoes (use a domestic brand like Redpack, Progresso, Hunt's, or Muir Glen Organic—most imports in supermarkets are old and sour)

1 (14-ounce) can diced tomatoes in purée

Salt and freshly ground black pepper

Heat the oil in a medium saucepan for 1 minute over medium heat. Add onions, garlic, and oregano if using; cook 5 minutes, until onions are translucent. Stir in tomato paste and sugar; cook, stirring, 5 minutes more. Add crushed tomatoes, diced tomatoes, salt, and pepper. Simmer 10 minutes.

PC FRESH TOMATO SAUCE

You can use this sauce immediately, refrigerate it in a covered container for up to a week, or freeze it for 6 months.

Yields 4 cups

2 tablespoons olive oil
2 cloves garlic, peeled and minced
2½ pounds fresh, vine-ripened tomatoes
1 teaspoon dried parsley
1 teaspoon dried basil
1 tablespoon balsamic vinegar
½ teaspoon granulated cane sugar
Salt, to taste
Freshly ground black pepper, to taste

1. Add the oil to the pressure cooker and bring to temperature over medium heat. Add the garlic; sauté for 30 seconds.

2. Peel and dice the tomatoes. Add them to the pressure cooker along with any juice from the tomatoes. Add the remaining ingredients.

3. Lock the lid in place and bring to low pressure; maintain for 10 minutes. Remove from heat and allow pressure to release naturally.

4. Remove the lid and stir the sauce. If you prefer a thicker sauce, return to heat and simmer uncovered for 10 minutes or until it reaches the desired thickness.

Balancing the Acidity

When tasting your tomato sauce and thinking "what else do I need to add?" many cooks reach for additional salt, but that might not be the ingredient you need. To balance out the acidity, the taste you may be trying to omit, try adding sugar or even grated carrot to the sauce.

PC GARDEN MARINARA SAUCE

Serve warmed sauce over pasta, rice, or vegetables.

Serves 4–6

2 tablespoons olive oil

1 large sweet onion, diced

1 small red bell pepper, diced

1 large carrot, peeled and grated

4 cloves garlic, minced

1 tablespoon dried parsley

½ teaspoon dried ground fennel

1 teaspoon dried basil

1 bay leaf

Pinch dried red pepper flakes

¼ teaspoon salt

1 (14½-ounce) can diced tomatoes in sauce

½ cup Pressure Cooker Vegetable Stock (see Chapter 5)

1. Add the oil to the pressure cooker and bring to temperature over medium-high heat. Add the onion, bell pepper, and carrot; sauté for 3 minutes. Stir in the garlic and sauté an additional 30 seconds. Stir in the remaining ingredients.

2. Lock the lid into place. Bring the pressure cooker to low pressure; maintain for 10 minutes. Quick-release the pressure. Remove the lid. Stir the sauce. Remove and discard the bay leaf. If desired, use an immersion blender to purée the sauce.

PC BASIC MARINARA SAUCE

For a "meaty" marinara, add cooked Boca Ground Crumbles.

Serves 4–6

2 tablespoons olive oil
½ onion, diced
2 cloves garlic, minced
2 (14-ounce) cans diced tomatoes
½ teaspoons sugar
1 tablespoon tomato paste
⅓ cup water
1 tablespoon fresh lemon juice
2 tablespoons fresh basil, chopped
Salt and pepper, to taste

1. Add the oil to the pressure cooker and sauté the onion until golden brown. Add the garlic and sauté for an additional 30 seconds. Add the tomatoes, sugar, tomato paste, and water.

2. Lock the lid into place and bring to high pressure. Once the pressure is achieved, turn the heat to low and cook for about 5 minutes. Remove from heat and allow pressure to release naturally. Stir in the lemon juice and basil, and add salt and pepper to taste.

SC VEGAN ALFREDO

Top cooked fettuccine with this updated version of a classic sauce.

Serves 8

1 cup raw cashews
1 cup water
½ cup unsweetened soymilk
3 cups Vegetable Broth (see Chapter 5)
Juice of ½ lemon
½ cup nutritional yeast
1 teaspoon mustard
2 cloves garlic, minced
2 teaspoons salt
1 teaspoon pepper

1. In a blender, place the cashews, water, and soymilk. Process until very smooth.

2. In a 4-quart slow cooker, pour the blended cashew sauce and all remaining ingredients and stir well. Cover and cook over low heat for 1 hour.

Cooking with Cashews

Cashews are an excellent ingredient to use when you want to create a creamy vegan dish, but be sure to use raw cashews, not roasted or cooked in any other way. Also, remember that nuts are high in calories and fat, so they should be consumed in small quantities.

PC WHITE BEAN ALFREDO SAUCE

Using white beans as the base of a creamy sauce reduces the amount of dairy and fat in the recipe, and makes for a much healthier alternative.

Serves 4

1 cup dried cannellini beans

8 cups water

¼ cup butter or vegan margarine, such as Earth Balance

2 cloves garlic, minced

1 cup milk or unsweetened soymilk

1 teaspoon lemon juice

1½ teaspoons salt

½ teaspoon black pepper

1. Add the beans and 4 cups of water to the pressure cooker. Lock the lid into place; bring to high pressure for 1 minute. Remove from heat and quick-release the pressure. Drain beans and set aside.

2. Clean pressure cooker and add butter or margarine. Sauté the garlic for 2 minutes, stirring continuously. Add the drained beans and remaining 4 cups of water.

3. Lock the lid into place; bring to high pressure and maintain for 15 minutes. Quick-release the pressure.

4. Pour the beans into a blender or food processor in batches and purée. The mixture will be thick.

5. Return to the pressure cooker over low heat and slowly stir in the milk or soymilk until desired consistency is reached. Add lemon juice, salt, and pepper, and heat until warm. Serve with fresh herbs, such as parsley, if desired.

SC JALAPEÑO-TOMATILLO SAUCE

Serve this sauce over rice or in burritos or tacos.

Serves 4

1 teaspoon canola oil
2 cloves garlic, minced
1 onion, sliced
7 tomatillos, diced
2 jalapeños, minced
½ cup water

1. In a nonstick pan, heat the oil. Add the garlic, onion, tomatillos, and jalapeños and sauté about 5 minutes.
2. In a 4-quart slow cooker, place the mixture; add the water and stir. Cover and cook on low for 8 hours.

SC LEMON DILL SAUCE

Tofu, pasta, or crisp vegetables such as asparagus make a great vehicle for this sauce.

Serves 4

2 cups Vegetable Broth (see Chapter 5)
½ cup lemon juice
½ cup fresh dill, chopped
1 teaspoon salt
¼ teaspoon white pepper

In a 2- or 4-quart slow cooker, place all ingredients. Cook on high, uncovered, for 3 hours.

SC CREAMY DIJON SAUCE

Dijon mustard is best in this recipe, but other varieties of high-quality mustard will work well too.

Yields 2 cups

1 tablespoon butter or vegan margarine
1 tablespoon flour
1 cup unsweetened soymilk
½ cup white wine
½ cup Vegetable Broth (see Chapter 5)
2 tablespoons Dijon mustard
¼ cup chopped shallots
½ teaspoon salt
½ teaspoon pepper

1. In the bottom of a 2-quart slow cooker, melt the butter or margarine. Stir in the flour to form a roux.
2. Whisk in the soymilk, white wine, and Vegetable Broth and stir until there are no lumps and it is well combined.
3. Add all remaining ingredients. Cover and cook over low heat for 3 hours.

SC COUNTRY WHITE GRAVY

Kick this gravy up a notch by adding pieces of cooked vegetarian sausage crumbles just before serving.

Serves 8

½ cup vegetable oil
¼ cup onion, diced
3 cloves garlic, minced
½ cup flour
4 teaspoons nutritional yeast
4 tablespoons soy sauce
2 cups water
½ teaspoon dried sage
½ teaspoon salt
¼ teaspoon pepper

1. In a small saucepan, heat the oil over medium-low heat. Add the onion and garlic and sauté for 2 minutes.
2. Transfer the oil mixture to a 4-quart slow cooker over low heat.
3. Stir in the flour to make a roux, then gradually add the nutritional yeast, soy sauce, and water, stirring constantly.
4. Add the sage, salt, and pepper, then cover, and cook for 1 hour.

SC PUTTANESCA SAUCE

You can easily omit the anchovies found in the recipes for many puttanesca sauces and replace it with olive brine, the liquid that olives are packed in.

Serves 6

1 tablespoon olive oil

4 cloves garlic, minced

1 onion, diced

1 cup sliced black olives

1 tablespoon olive brine

1 (28-ounce) can crushed tomatoes

1 (15-ounce) can diced tomatoes

1 tablespoon crushed red pepper

2 tablespoons drained nonpareil-size capers

2 tablespoons fresh basil, chopped

1. In a large sauté pan, heat the olive oil over medium heat. Add the garlic and onion and sauté until soft, about 3–4 minutes.

2. In a 4-quart slow cooker, place the onion and garlic; add the remaining ingredients. Stir to distribute the ingredients evenly.

3. Cook on low for 4–6 hours. If the sauce looks very wet at the end of the cooking time, remove the lid and cook on high for 15–30 minutes before serving.

What Is Sautéing?
Sautéing is a method of cooking that uses a small amount of fat to cook food in a shallow pan over medium-high heat. The goal is to brown the food while preserving its color, moisture, and flavor.

SC BARBECUE SAUCE

Barbecue recipes vary greatly from region to region in the United States, so feel free to customize this one in order to please your taste buds.

Yields 5 cups

4 cups ketchup

¼ cup soy sauce

¼ cup maple syrup

¼ cup prepared mustard

2 tablespoons apple cider vinegar

1 tablespoon liquid smoke

2 teaspoons chipotle powder

1 teaspoon dried thyme

1 teaspoon sweet paprika

1 teaspoon garlic powder

1 teaspoon cumin

In a 4-quart slow cooker, add all ingredients and stir well. Cover and cook on low for 4–6 hours.

[PC] COUNTRY BARBECUE SAUCE

You can use this barbecue sauce as a sauce served on the side, a dipping sauce, or a grilling wet mop sauce.

Yields approximately 5 cups

4 cups ketchup

½ cup apple cider vinegar

½ cup vegetarian Worcestershire sauce

½ cup light brown sugar, firmly packed

¼ cup molasses

¼ cup prepared mustard

2 tablespoons barbecue seasoning

1 teaspoon freshly ground black pepper

1 tablespoon liquid smoke (optional)

2 tablespoons hot sauce, or to taste (optional)

Salt, to taste (optional)

Add all ingredients except optional seasonings to the pressure cooker. Stir to mix. Lock the lid into place. Bring to low pressure; maintain for 20 minutes. Remove from heat and quick-release the pressure. Taste for seasoning and add the desired amount of optional seasoning. Ladle into sterilized glass jars; cover and store in the refrigerator for up to 3 months.

Barbecue Seasoning

Barbecue seasoning is a blend of herbs and spices that can be found in the spice aisle of your local grocery store. To make your own, mix equal parts brown sugar, ground red pepper, salt, garlic powder, onion powder, paprika, and dried oregano.

NEW MEXICO CHILI SAUCE

This tomato-based Southwestern sauce is the ultimate salsa for Black Bean Burritos (see Chapter 7), a wonderful accompaniment to scrambled eggs or omelets, and the base for the sauce in Chilaquiles (see Chapter 9).

Yields 3 cups

- 1 teaspoon olive oil
- 1 medium onion, roughly chopped
- 5 New Mexico chilies, seeded, soaked, and puréed
- 1 (28-ounce) jar roasted-garlic-flavored marinara sauce
- ½ teaspoon ground cumin
- ½ teaspoon dried oregano

Heat the oil in a saucepan over a medium flame. Add onion; cook, stirring occasionally, until translucent, about 5 minutes. Add chili purée; cook 3 minutes more. Add the marinara sauce, cumin, and oregano. Simmer 10 minutes. Purée in a blender until very smooth.

SC MOLE

Just like barbecue sauce in the United States, mole sauce recipes vary greatly by region, and no two are exactly the same.

Yields 2 cups

- 2 tablespoons olive oil
- ½ onion, finely diced
- 3 garlic cloves, minced
- 1 teaspoon ground cumin
- ¼ teaspoon ground cinnamon
- ¼ teaspoon ground coriander
- 1 tablespoon chili powder
- 2 chipotles in adobo, seeded and minced
- 1 teaspoon salt
- 4 cups Vegetable Broth (see Chapter 5)
- 1 ounce vegan dark chocolate, chopped

1. In a sauté pan over medium heat, add the oil, onion, and garlic and sauté about 3 minutes. Add the cumin, cinnamon, and coriander and sauté for 1 minute.

2. Transfer the sautéed mixture to a 4-quart slow cooker. Add the chili powder, chipotles, and salt, then whisk in the Vegetable Broth. Finally, add the chocolate.

3. Cover and cook over medium heat for 2 hours.

SC HOMEMADE KETCHUP

Why buy bottled when homemade ketchup is this easy?

Serves 32

1 (15-ounce) can no-salt-added tomato sauce

2 teaspoons water

½ teaspoon onion powder

½ cup sugar

⅓ cup cider vinegar

¼ teaspoon sea salt

¼ teaspoon ground cinnamon

⅛ teaspoon ground cloves

Pinch ground allspice

Pinch nutmeg

Pinch freshly ground pepper

⅔ teaspoon sweet paprika

1. In a 2-quart slow cooker, add all ingredients except paprika. Cover and cook for 2–4 hours, or until ketchup reaches desired consistency, stirring occasionally.

2. Turn off the slow cooker or remove the crock from the slow cooker and stir in the paprika.

3. Allow mixture to cool, then put in a covered container (such as a recycled ketchup bottle). Store in the refrigerator until needed.

Ketchup with a Kick

If you like zesty ketchup, you can add crushed red peppers, cayenne pepper, or salt-free chili powder along with, or instead of, the cinnamon and other seasonings. Another alternative is to use hot paprika rather than sweet paprika.

SC RASPBERRY COULIS

A coulis is a thick sauce made from puréed fruits or vegetables. In this recipe, the slow cooking eliminates the need for puréeing because the fruit cooks down enough that straining is unnecessary.

Serves 8

12 ounces fresh or frozen raspberries

1 teaspoon balsamic vinegar

2 tablespoons sugar

1. In a 2-quart slow cooker, place all ingredients. Mash gently with a potato masher.
2. Cook on low for 4 hours, uncovered. Stir before serving.

Taste, Taste, Taste

When using fresh berries, it is important to taste them prior to sweetening. One batch of berries might be tart while the next might be very sweet. Reduce or eliminate extra sugar if using very ripe, sweet berries.

SC COCONUT CURRY SAUCE

Red curry paste is ideal for this recipe, but any variety will do.

Yields about 2 cups

1 (14-ounce) can coconut milk

1 cup Vegetable Broth (see Chapter 5)

1 teaspoon soy sauce

1 tablespoon curry paste

1 tablespoon lime juice

2 cloves garlic, minced

½ teaspoon salt

¼ cup chopped cilantro

1. In a 4-quart slow cooker, add all ingredients except cilantro. Cover and cook on low heat for 2 hours.
2. Add the chopped cilantro and cook for an additional 30 minutes.

SC WHITE WINE–GARLIC SAUCE

Not all alcohol is removed from a dish when cooked, so avoid this sauce if you abstain from drinking.

Yields 2 cups

6 tablespoons butter or vegan margarine

2 tablespoons shallot, minced

5 cloves garlic, minced

1 cup white wine

1 cup Vegetable Broth (see Chapter 5)

1½ teaspoons salt

1. In a sauté pan, melt the butter or margarine over medium heat. Add the shallot and garlic and sauté for 2 minutes.
2. Add the sautéed blend to a 4-quart slow cooker. Add all remaining ingredients, stir, and cook on low for 2 hours.

Which Wine?

As a general rule, if you wouldn't drink it, then don't cook with it, and remember to consider how the flavor of the wine will pair with other ingredients. If you are trying to achieve a rich, earthy sauce, then don't use a floral or fruity white. Instead, choose an oaky chardonnay.

SC THREE PEPPER SAUCE

Cayenne peppers are most commonly found dried and ground in the herbs and spices aisle of your grocery store.

Serves 4

1 (28-ounce) can diced tomatoes

2 tablespoons tomato paste

1 red bell pepper, finely diced

1 green bell pepper, finely diced

½ red onion, diced

3 cloves garlic, minced

1 teaspoon cayenne pepper

½ teaspoon sugar

½ teaspoon salt

In a 4-quart slow cooker, add all ingredients. Cover and cook on low heat for 6–8 hours.

PC ROASTED RED PEPPER SAUCE

Save time by using canned or jarred roasted red peppers instead of roasting them yourself.

Serves 4

2 cups roasted red peppers

2 cups Pressure Cooker Vegetable Stock (see Chapter 5)

2 tablespoons red wine vinegar

2 tablespoons extra-virgin olive oil

1 teaspoon garlic powder

½ cup fresh basil

Salt and pepper, to taste

1. Purée the red peppers, stock, vinegar, and oil in a food processor or blender. Pour the mixture into the pressure cooker and add the garlic powder.

2. Lock the lid into place and bring to high pressure. Once the pressure is achieved, turn the heat to low and cook for about 5 minutes. Remove from heat and allow pressure to release naturally.

3. Add the basil and season with salt and pepper, to taste, before serving.

SC EASY PEANUT SAUCE

Choose a peanut butter that is free of added flavors and is as natural as possible, so that it won't distort the flavors in your dish.

Yields 3 cups

1 cup smooth peanut butter

4 tablespoons maple syrup

½ cup sesame oil

1 teaspoon cayenne pepper

1½ teaspoons cumin

1 teaspoon garlic powder

1½ teaspoons salt

2 cups water

1. In a blender, add all ingredients except for the water. Blend as you slowly add the water until you reach the desired consistency.

2. Pour the sauce into a 2-quart slow cooker and cook over low heat for 1 hour.

Uses for Peanut Sauce

Peanut sauce can be used to dress Asian noodles such as udon or soba noodles. It may also be used as a dipping sauce for steamed broccoli or spring rolls.

PC SPICY PEANUT SAUCE

Use as a dipping sauce for broccoli or spring rolls.

Yields 1½ cups

½ cup smooth peanut butter
2 tablespoons maple syrup
2 cloves garlic, peeled
1" piece fresh ginger, peeled and chopped
¼ cup rice vinegar
¼ cup sesame oil
1 teaspoon cayenne pepper
1 teaspoon cumin
2 teaspoons dried red chili flakes
1 cup water
Salt and pepper, to taste

1. In a large blender, combine all the ingredients except salt and pepper, adding the water a little at a time to control the consistency.
2. Lock the lid into place and bring to high pressure. Once the pressure is achieved, turn the heat to low and cook for about 3 minutes. Remove from heat and allow pressure to release naturally.
3. Taste for seasoning, and add salt and pepper if needed.

ESPAGNOLE

Espagnole is one of the "mother sauces," and is used as the foundation for other sauces in this book.

Yields 3 cups

- 1 small carrot, chopped
- 1 medium white onion, chopped
- ¼ cup butter or vegan margarine, such as Earth Balance
- ¼ cup flour
- 4 cups hot Pressure Cooker Vegetable Stock (see Chapter 5)
- ¼ cup canned tomato purée
- 2 large garlic cloves, chopped
- 1 celery rib, chopped
- ½ teaspoon whole black peppercorns
- 1 bay leaf

1. Sauté the carrot and onion in the butter over medium-high heat in the pressure cooker until golden. Add the flour and whisk to form a roux. Continue to cook, stirring continuously, until the roux is medium brown, about 30 minutes. While whisking, add the hot stock, being sure to prevent lumps. Add the tomato purée, garlic, celery, peppercorns, and bay leaf.

2. Lock the lid into place and bring to high pressure. Once the pressure is achieved, turn the heat to low and cook for about 5 minutes. Remove from heat and allow pressure to release naturally.

3. Bring the sauce to a simmer; cook, uncovered, until reduced to 3 cups, stirring frequently. Remove the solids from the sauce before serving.

What Is a Roux?

A roux is a blend of equal parts fat, such as butter, margarine, or oil, and flour that is used to thicken sauces. It's cooked over various levels of heat and different lengths of time to achieve either a white, blond, or brown roux.

PC BÉCHAMEL SAUCE

Béchamel is one of the most commonly used "mother sauces," and is the foundation for an Alfredo sauce.

Yields 3 cups

½ cup butter or vegan margarine, such as Earth Balance

½ cup all-purpose flour

4 cups milk, heated, or unsweetened soymilk

1 teaspoon salt

1 teaspoon pepper

1. Soften the butter over medium heat in the pressure cooker. Add flour and stir to create a roux. Gradually whisk in the warm milk or soymilk until there are no lumps.

2. Lock the lid into place and bring to high pressure. Once the pressure is achieved, turn the heat to low and allow to cook for about 5 minutes, or until the sauce has thickened. Remove from heat and allow pressure to release naturally.

3. Season with salt and pepper.

PC AU JUS

Try Better Than Bouillon No Beef Base instead of plain Vegetable Stock in this rich sauce.

Yields 1½ cups

1 tablespoon butter or vegan margarine, such as Earth Balance

1 shallot, minced

1 tablespoon flour

2 cups faux-beef stock or Pressure Cooker Vegetable Stock (see Chapter 5)

1 cup red wine

¼ teaspoon liquid smoke

1 teaspoon salt

1 teaspoon pepper

1. Add the butter to the pressure cooker and sauté the shallot over medium-high heat until golden brown. Stir in the flour to create a roux. Add the stock, red wine, liquid smoke, salt, and pepper to the roux.

2. Lock the lid into place and bring to high pressure. Once the pressure is achieved, turn the heat to low and cook for about 5 minutes. Allow pressure to release naturally. Remove lid and continue to simmer over low heat until the sauce has reduced by half.

PC BEURRE BLANC

Try adding a variety of ingredients to this basic beurre blanc—herbs, spices, or even fruit!

Yields 1 cup

2 cups white wine

1 tablespoon shallot, minced

2 cups butter, cold, or vegan margarine, such as Earth Balance

1 teaspoon salt

1. Heat the wine and shallot in the pressure cooker and bring to a simmer. Let the wine reduce to half.

2. While the wine is reducing, begin cutting the butter or margarine into medium cubes. Once reduced, begin whisking the cubes of butter or margarine in a few at a time, in order to create an emulsion. Once all the butter or margarine has been whisked into the sauce, lock the lid into place and bring to high pressure. When pressure is achieved, turn the heat to low and cook for 5 minutes. Quick-release the pressure and remove the lid. Season with salt.

PC VODKA SAUCE

Cooking with alcohol helps bring out flavors in some foods, including tomatoes.

Serves 4–6

2 tablespoons olive oil

½ onion, diced

2 cloves garlic, minced

1 teaspoon dried red pepper flakes

1 cup vodka

2 (14-ounce) cans diced tomatoes

2 tablespoons tomato paste

⅓ cup water

1 cup heavy cream or unsweetened soymilk or unsweetened vegan cream, such as MimicCreme

2 tablespoons fresh parsley, chopped

2 tablespoons fresh basil, chopped

Salt and pepper, to taste

1. Add the olive oil to the pressure cooker; sauté the onions until golden brown. Add the garlic and red pepper flakes, and sauté an additional minute. Add the vodka and simmer for about 10 minutes. Add the diced tomatoes, tomato paste, and water.

2. Lock the lid into place and bring to high pressure. Once the pressure is achieved, turn the heat to low and cook for about 5 minutes. Remove from heat and allow pressure to release naturally.

3. Stir in the heavy cream, soymilk, or vegan cream and simmer for 2 minutes. Add the parsley and basil. Taste for seasoning, and add salt and pepper if needed.

PC YELLOW PEPPER COULIS

A coulis is a thick sauce often made from puréed fruit or vegetables.

Yields 1½ cups

2 tablespoons olive oil

4 yellow peppers, seeded and diced

4 shallots, minced

1 cup white wine

1 cup Pressure Cooker Vegetable Stock (see Chapter 5)

1 teaspoon salt

½ teaspoon black pepper

1. Add the olive oil to the pressure cooker and sauté the yellow peppers and shallots until they start to turn golden brown. Add the white wine and reduce by half. Add the Vegetable Stock.

2. Lock the lid into place and bring to high pressure. Once the pressure is achieved, turn the heat to low and cook for 5 minutes. Remove from heat and quick-release the pressure.

3. Season with salt and pepper.

PC CASHEW CREAM SAUCE

To make an alcohol-free sauce, double the amount of Vegetable Stock or water instead of including 1 cup wine.

Yields 2½ cups

1 cup of cashews

1 cup white wine

1 cup milk, or unsweetened soymilk

1 cup Pressure Cooker Vegetable Stock (see Chapter 5) or water

2 cups Béchamel Sauce (see recipe in this chapter)

Salt and pepper, to taste

1. Grind the cashews in a food processor or a coffee grinder. Set aside.

2. Add the white wine to the pressure cooker over medium heat and bring to a simmer. Allow the wine to reduce by half. Stir in the ground cashews, milk or soymilk, stock, and Béchamel Sauce.

3. Lock the lid into place and bring to low pressure. Maintain pressure for 5 minutes, then allow pressure to release naturally. Remove lid and continue to cook over low heat, until reduced by half.

4. Taste for seasoning, and add salt and pepper if needed.

Uses for Cashew Cream

In many recipes, cashew cream can be used in place of dairy. This savory version would be best suited to replace heavy cream or cheeses, but there are also plain versions of cashew cream that can be used in desserts.

PC PLUM SAUCE

Plum sauce is often served with egg rolls, but you can also use it as a glaze on tofu or vegetables.

Yields 4 cups

8 cups (about 3 pounds) plums, pitted and cut in half

1 small sweet onion, diced

1 cup water

1 teaspoon fresh ginger, peeled and minced

1 clove garlic, minced

¾ cup granulated sugar

½ cup rice vinegar or cider vinegar

1 teaspoon ground coriander

½ teaspoon salt

½ teaspoon cinnamon

¼ teaspoon cayenne pepper

¼ teaspoon ground cloves

1. Add the plums, onion, water, ginger, and garlic to the pressure cooker. Lock the lid into place and bring to low pressure; maintain for 5 minutes. Remove from heat and quick-release the pressure.

2. Use an immersion blender to pulverize the contents of the pressure cooker before straining it, or press the cooked plum mixture through a sieve.

3. Return the liquefied and strained plum mixture to the pressure cooker and stir in sugar, vinegar, coriander, salt, cinnamon, cayenne pepper, and cloves. Lock the lid into place and bring to low pressure; maintain for 5 minutes. Remove from heat and quick-release the pressure. Remove the lid and check the sauce; it should have the consistency of applesauce. If it isn't yet thick enough, place the uncovered pressure cooker over medium heat and simmer until desired consistency is achieved.

PC CRANBERRY-APPLE CHUTNEY

Chutney is an Indian dish that was introduced to the rest of the world by the British.

Serves 16

1 (12-ounce) bag cranberries

1 cup light brown sugar, packed

1 small sweet onion, peeled and diced

1 jalapeño pepper, seeded and minced

2 tablespoons fresh ginger, peeled and grated

1 clove garlic, minced

1 teaspoon yellow mustard seed

3" cinnamon stick

1 teaspoon lemon juice

¼ teaspoon salt

3 pounds tart cooking apples

Ground ginger, to taste (optional)

Ground cinnamon, to taste (optional)

1. Rinse and pick over the cranberries. Add the cranberries, brown sugar, onion, jalapeño, ginger, garlic, mustard, cinnamon stick, lemon juice, and salt to a 5- to 7-quart pressure cooker. Cook over medium heat until the sugar dissolves, stirring occasionally.

2. Peel and core the apples; cut into strips, 1" in length. Place the apples in a layer over the cranberry mixture in the pressure cooker. Do not stir the apples into the mixture.

3. Lock the lid in place and bring to high pressure. Cook on high pressure for 1 minute. Remove from heat and quick-release the pressure.

4. Remove the cinnamon stick. Taste for seasoning and add ground ginger and ground cinnamon if desired.

5. Store in a covered container in the refrigerator for up to 2 weeks. Serve heated or chilled.

For Best Results

Placing the apples over the cranberry mixture prevents the cranberries from foaming as they cook, which could clog the pressure cooker vent. Serve this chutney with roast pork or turkey. If you'd like to make cranberry-pear chutney, substitute 3 pounds of peeled and cored ripe Bartlett pears for the apples.

PC FRESH TOMATO CHUTNEY

For a change of pace, you can spread this chutney over Indian chapati bread, flatbread, or pizza crust; top with goat cheese or vegan mozzarella; and bake.

Yields 4 cups

4 pounds ripe tomatoes, peeled

1" piece fresh ginger

3 cloves garlic

1¾ cups white sugar

1 cup red wine vinegar

2 onions, diced

¼ cup golden raisins

¾ teaspoon ground cinnamon

½ teaspoon ground coriander

¼ teaspoon ground cloves

¼ teaspoon ground nutmeg

¼ teaspoon ground ginger

1 teaspoon chili powder

1 pinch paprika

1 tablespoon curry paste

1. Purée the peeled tomatoes and fresh ginger in a blender or food processor.
2. Pour the puréed tomato mixture into the pressure cooker. Stir in the remaining ingredients. Stir to mix, lock the lid into place, and cook at low pressure for 10 minutes. Remove from heat and allow pressure to release naturally. Refrigerate in a covered container until ready to use. Serve chilled or at room temperature.

Peeling Fresh, Vine-Ripened Tomatoes

Add enough water to a saucepan to cover the tomatoes; bring to a boil over medium-high heat. Use a slotted spoon to submerge the tomatoes in the boiling water for 1 minute, or until their skins begin to crack and peel. Use the slotted spoon to remove the tomatoes from the water and plunge them into ice water. The peelings will slip right off.

PC GREEN TOMATO CHUTNEY

If you prefer spicy chutney, you can substitute an Anaheim and 4 small red chili or jalapeño peppers for the red bell peppers.

Yields 5 cups

2 pounds green tomatoes, diced, with stems removed

1 white onion, quartered lengthwise, and thinly sliced

2 red bell peppers, diced

¼ cup dried currants

2 tablespoons fresh ginger, grated

¾ cup dark brown sugar, firmly packed

¾ cup white wine or white distilled vinegar

Pinch sea salt

1. Put all ingredients in the pressure cooker; stir to mix. Lock on the lid and bring to low pressure. Cook on low pressure for 10 minutes. Remove from heat and allow pressure to release naturally.

2. Cool and refrigerate overnight before serving. Can be stored in a covered container in the refrigerator for 2 months.

PC SWEET ONION RELISH

Use sweet onions like Vidalia, Candy, First Edition, Maui, or Walla Walla for this relish.

Yields 4 cups

4 medium sweet onions
Water, as needed
¾ cup golden raisins
1 cup agave nectar
1 tablespoon cider vinegar
Pinch salt

1. Peel and thinly slice onions. Add onions to the pressure cooker and pour in water to cover. Bring to a boil over high heat; drain immediately and discard water.

2. Return onions to pressure cooker; stir in raisins, agave nectar, vinegar, and salt until agave nectar is evenly distributed throughout onion slices.

3. Lock on lid, bring to high pressure, and cook for 5 minutes. Reduce heat and maintain low pressure for an additional 10 minutes. Remove from heat and allow pressure to release naturally.

4. Remove lid and stir relish. If relish needs thickening, return pan to heat; bring to a gentle boil for 5 minutes. Can be served warm or stored in a covered container in the refrigerator for up to 4 weeks.

PC STRAWBERRY JAM

In addition to the usual uses for fruit spread, this jam is the perfect addition to some plain yogurt or soy yogurt.

Yields 4 cups

4 cups strawberries

3 cups granulated cane sugar

¼ cup fresh lemon juice

1. Rinse and hull the strawberries, then quarter or halve them. Add to the pressure cooker. Stir in the sugar. Set aside for 1 hour or until the strawberries are juicy.

2. Use a potato masher to crush the fruit and mix in the sugar until the sugar is dissolved. Stir in the lemon juice.

3. Lock the lid in place. Bring the cooker to full pressure and cook for 7 minutes. Remove from heat and allow pressure to release naturally.

4. Remove the lid. Return to heat and bring to a full boil over medium-high heat. Boil for 3 minutes or until jam reaches the desired gel state.

5. Skim off and discard any foam. Ladle into hot, sterilized glass containers or jars, leaving ½" of headspace. Seal the containers or jars. Cool and refrigerate for a week or freeze. (If you prefer, you can follow the instructions that came with your canning jars and process the jam for shelf storage.)

PC DRIED APRICOT PRESERVES

Never fill the pressure cooker more than half full when making preserves, chutneys, or other fruit dishes.

Yields 7 cups

4 cups dried apricots, chopped

2 cups water

5 black peppercorns

5 cardamom pods

2 (3") cinnamon sticks

2 star anises

½ cup lemon juice

4 cups granulated cane sugar

1. Add the apricots to a bowl or to the pressure cooker. Pour in the water, cover, and let the apricots soak for 24 hours.

2. Wrap the peppercorns, cardamom pods, cinnamon sticks, and star anises in cheesecloth and secure with a string. Add to the pressure cooker along with the apricots, soaking water, and lemon juice. Lock the lid into place. Bring to pressure and cook on low pressure for 10 minutes. Remove from heat and allow pressure to release naturally.

3. Uncover the pressure cooker. Remove and discard the cheesecloth spice bag and stir in the sugar.

4. Return the pressure cooker to the heat and bring to a rapid boil over medium-high heat. Boil covered for 2 minutes and uncovered for 2 minutes or until the apricot mixture reaches the gel point.

5. Skim off and discard any foam. Ladle into hot, sterilized glass containers or jars, leaving ½" of headspace. Seal the containers or jars. Cool and refrigerate for a week or freeze. (If you prefer, you can follow the instructions that came with your canning jars and process the preserves for shelf storage.)

Determining the Gel Point

Test a small amount of preserves by spooning onto an ice-cold plate. The gel point is reached when the preserves are as thick as you desire. A softer set is ideal for use in sauces; if you prefer a firm, jam-like consistency, you may need to continue to boil the mixture for up to 20 minutes.

MIXED CITRUS MARMALADE

Jam sugar contains pectin, the soluble dietary fiber extracted from citrus fruits used as a gelling agent for jams, jellies, and marmalades.

Yields 4 cups

1 large orange

1 lime

2 lemons

2 clementines or satsumas

1 pink grapefruit

3 cups water

4 pounds jam sugar

1. Wash the fruit in hot water to remove any wax. Remove the zest from the orange, lime, and lemons; add to the pressure cooker. Quarter all fruit and place in a large (doubled) piece of cheesecloth; twist the cheesecloth to squeeze out the juice into the pressure cooker. Tie the cheesecloth over the fruit and seeds and add it to the pressure cooker along with half of the water. Lock the lid in place and bring the pressure cooker to high pressure; cook on high for 10 minutes. Remove from heat and allow pressure to release naturally.

2. Remove the lid from the pressure cooker. Place the cooker over medium heat and add the remaining water and sugar. Bring to a boil, stirring continuously until all the sugar has dissolved.

3. While the mixture continues to boil, place the lid back on the cooker (but do not lock it into place). Leave the lid in place for 2 minutes, remove it, and then continue to let the mixture boil for 8 minutes or until the desired gel point is reached.

4. Skim off and discard any foam. Ladle into hot, sterilized glass containers or jars, leaving ½" of head space. Seal the containers or jars. Cool and refrigerate for a week or freeze until needed. (If you prefer, you can follow the instructions that came with your canning jars and process the preserves for shelf storage.)

Sugar Crystals and the Gelling Process

After you've added sugar, putting the lid back on the pressure cooker once the mixture comes to a boil creates steam inside the cooker that will cause any sugar clinging to the sides of the pan to wash down into the mixture. Even one lone sugar crystal can set off a chain reaction that will cause the entire mixture to crystallize rather than remain in its gelled state.

RAINBOW BELL PEPPER MARMALADE

Serve Rainbow Bell Pepper Marmalade as a relish for tempeh or seitan, or on top of cheese on crackers.

Yields 2 cups

1 large green bell pepper

1 large red bell pepper

1 large yellow bell pepper

1 large purple or orange bell pepper

1 small yellow, white, or sweet onion

Water, as needed

2 cups granulated cane sugar

Pinch salt

2 tablespoons balsamic vinegar

1. Wash, quarter, and seed the bell peppers; cut them into thin slices or dice them. Peel, quarter, and thinly slice the onion. Add the peppers and onion to the pressure cooker.

2. Add enough water to the pressure cooker to cover the peppers and onion. Bring to a boil over high heat; drain immediately and discard the water.

3. Return the peppers and onion to the pressure cooker. Stir in the sugar, salt, and vinegar. Bring to high pressure and cook for 5 minutes. Remove pan from the heat and let sit for 5 minutes.

4. Quick-release any remaining pressure. Remove the lid and return the pan to the heat. Simmer briskly over medium-high heat for 6 minutes or until the mixture is thickened. Once cooled, store in a covered container in the refrigerator overnight before using.

PC BLUEBERRY JAM

You can substitute a 6-ounce bottle of pectin for the dry pectin.

Yields 4 cups

4 cups blueberries

4 cups granulated cane sugar

1 cup orange juice

1 teaspoon orange zest

Pinch freshly ground nutmeg

Pinch salt

1 (1¾-ounce) package dry pectin

1. Add the blueberries, sugar, orange juice, orange zest, nutmeg, and salt to the pressure cooker. Stir to combine.
2. Lock on the lid and bring to low pressure. Maintain pressure for 3 minutes. Remove from heat and allow pressure to release naturally.
3. Remove the lid. Either process in a food mill to separate the pulp from the skins or push the blueberry mixture through a strainer.
4. Return the pulp to the pressure cooker. Place over medium-high heat, stir in the pectin, and bring mixture to a rolling boil, stirring constantly. Continue to boil and stir for 1 minute.
5. Skim off and discard any foam. Ladle into hot, sterilized glass containers or jars, leaving 1" of headspace. Seal the containers or jars. Cool and refrigerate for up to 5 weeks or freeze for up to 8 months. (If you prefer, you can follow the instructions that came with your canning jars and process the preserves for shelf storage.)

PC MINCEMEAT

Use mincemeat as a condiment or in mincemeat pie.

Yields 5 cups

2½ pounds pears

1 tart green apple

1 lemon, juiced and zested

1 orange, juiced and zested

1 cup golden raisins

½ cup dried cranberries or dried currants

½ cup light brown sugar, firmly packed

1 teaspoon ground cinnamon

½ teaspoon ground ginger

¼ teaspoon ground cloves

¼ teaspoon ground nutmeg

Pinch salt

½ cup walnuts or pecans, chopped and toasted

½ cup brandy or Cognac

1. Peel, core, and dice the pears and apple. Wash the lemon and orange to remove any waxy coating. Add apples and pears to the pressure cooker along with lemon zest and juice, orange zest and juice, raisins, cranberries or currants, brown sugar, cinnamon, ginger, cloves, nutmeg, and salt. Stir to combine.

2. Lock the lid into place and bring to high pressure; maintain pressure for 10 minutes. Remove from heat and allow pressure to release naturally.

3. Return to heat and bring to a simmer. Simmer for 10 minutes or until mixture is very thick. Stir in the nuts and brandy or Cognac. Continue to simmer for an additional 5 minutes.

4. Ladle into hot, sterilized glass containers or jars, leaving ½" of headspace. Seal the containers or jars. Cool and then refrigerate for a week or freeze. (If you prefer, you can follow the instructions that came with your canning jars and process the preserves for shelf storage.)

Mincemeat Seasoning

Seasoning is an arbitrary thing. You'll want to add some of the spices to the mincemeat before you cook it, but if you prefer to taste for seasoning and then increase the spices according to your taste, use half of the spices during the cooking process, and add more later if desired.

PC PEACH AND TOASTED ALMOND PRESERVES

Toasting the almonds is an important step that enhances the rich flavor of these preserves.

Yields 4 cups

6 fresh ripe peaches

1 cup water

1 (8-ounce) package dried apricots, diced

½ cup toasted almonds

1¼ cups orange juice

¼ cup lemon juice

4½ cups granulated cane sugar

2 whole cloves

1 (3") cinnamon stick

Pinch salt

1 (1¾-ounce) package pectin powder

1. Use a skewer or toothpick to poke several holes in each of the peaches. Place the peaches in the pressure cooker and pour the water over them. Lock the lid on the pressure cooker. Bring to high pressure and maintain for 3 minutes.

2. Quick-release the pressure and remove the lid. Use a slotted spoon to move the peaches to a large bowl of ice water or to a bowl under cold running water. Peel the peaches and then cut them into small pieces, discarding the pits.

3. Add the peaches, apricots, almonds, orange juice, lemon juice, sugar, cloves, cinnamon stick, and salt to water remaining in the pressure cooker. Stir to combine. Lock on the lid and bring to high pressure; maintain pressure for 2 minutes.

4. Remove the pressure cooker from the heat. Quick-release the pressure and remove the lid. Remove the cloves and cinnamon stick; discard. Stir the pectin into the fruit mixture. Return to the heat and bring to a rolling boil over medium-high heat, stirring constantly.

5. Skim off and discard any foam. Ladle into hot, sterilized glass containers or jars, leaving 1" of headspace. Seal the containers or jars. Cool and then refrigerate for up to 5 weeks or freeze for up to 8 months. (If you prefer, you can follow the instructions that came with your canning jars and process the preserves for shelf storage.)

Toasting Nuts

Preheat oven to 350°F. Place nuts in a shallow baking pan. Stirring occasionally, bake for 8 minutes or until the nuts are fragrant and golden brown. You can also toast nuts in a frying pan over medium-high heat. Stir and shake the pan constantly for 5 minutes or until nuts are golden brown.

PC CARIBBEAN RELISH

Think of this relish as hummus with a Caribbean flair.

Serves 12

1½ cups red or white kidney beans

7 cups water

2 teaspoons vegetable oil

Salt, to taste

2 tablespoons tahini paste

¾ cup crushed pineapple, drained

4 cloves garlic, minced

¼ teaspoon dried cumin

¼ teaspoon ground ginger

¼ teaspoon freshly ground white pepper

½ cup fresh cilantro, minced

1. Add the beans to the pressure cooker and pour 3 cups water over them or enough to cover the beans completely. Cover and let soak overnight. Drain and return to the pressure cooker. Pour 4 cups water over the beans. Add the oil. Lock the lid into place. Bring to high pressure; maintain pressure for 10 minutes. Remove from heat and allow pressure to release naturally for 10 minutes.

2. Quick-release any remaining pressure. Remove the lid and, if the beans are cooked through, drain them. If additional cooking time is needed, lock the lid into place, return to high pressure, and cook for an additional 2–5 minutes.

3. Add the cooked beans, salt, tahini, pineapple, garlic, cumin, ginger, pepper, and cilantro to a blender or food processor. Pulse until mixed but still chunky. Transfer to a covered container and chill.

PC BLACKBERRY JAM

Experiment with the types of berries used to make homemade jam, or try a combination of a few.

Yields 4 cups

4 cups blackberries

4 cups granulated cane sugar

1 cup orange juice

1 teaspoon lemon juice

Pinch salt

1 (1¾-ounce) package dry pectin

1. Add the blackberries, sugar, orange juice, lemon juice, and salt to the pressure cooker. Stir to combine.

2. Lock on the lid and bring to low pressure. Maintain pressure for 3 minutes. Remove from heat and allow pressure to release naturally.

3. Remove the lid. Either process in a food mill to separate the pulp from the skins or push the blackberry mixture through a strainer.

4. Return the pulp to the pressure cooker. Place over medium-high heat, stir in the pectin, and bring mixture to a rolling boil, stirring constantly. Continue to boil and stir for 1 minute.

5. Skim off and discard any foam. Ladle into hot, sterilized glass containers or jars, leaving 1" of headspace. Seal the containers or jars. Cool and refrigerate for up to 5 weeks or freeze for up to 8 months. (If you prefer, you can follow the instructions that came with your canning jars and process the preserves for shelf storage.)

PC PEACH JAM

In most states, peach season takes place during the summer. Using in-season fruit will result in the best flavor for homemade jams.

Yields 4 cups

4 cups peaches, peeled and chopped

4 cups granulated sugar

1 teaspoon lemon juice

1 (1¾-ounce) package dry pectin

1. Add the peaches, sugar, and lemon juice to the pressure cooker. Stir to combine. Lock on the lid and bring to low pressure. Maintain for 3 minutes. Remove from heat and allow pressure to release naturally.

2. Remove the lid. Place over medium-high heat, stir in the pectin, and bring mixture to a rolling boil, stirring constantly. Continue to boil and stir for 1 minute. Skim off and discard any foam. Ladle into hot, sterilized glass containers, leaving 1" of headspace. Seal. Cool and refrigerate for up to 5 weeks or freeze for up to 8 months.

PC EASY GRAPE JELLY

A lunchbox staple can seem gourmet when you're making the jelly yourself.

Yields 5 cups

5 cups grape juice

2 (1¾-ounce) packages dry pectin

½ cup sugar

1. Add grape juice and pectin to the pressure cooker and bring to medium-high heat. Stir to combine. Lock on the lid and bring to high pressure. Maintain pressure for 1 minute. Remove from heat and quick-release the pressure. Remove the lid. Slowly stir in the sugar.

2. Skim off and discard any foam. Ladle into hot, sterilized glass containers, leaving 1" of headspace. Seal. Let cool at room temperature for 24 hours, then refrigerate for up to 5 weeks or freeze for up to 8 months.

Choosing Your Juice

For this recipe, avoid using any light or diet juices because they most likely have a higher water content or artificial sweeteners, and will result in less flavor.

CHAPTER 3
SALADS

RECIPE LIST

SOUTHEAST ASIAN SLAW 110

WARM CHICKPEA SALAD 111

EDAMAME-SEAWEED SALAD 112

THREE BEAN SALAD 113

TOMATO AND BREAD SALAD (PANZANELLA) 114

SALAD OF CELERY ROOT AND PEARS 115

WINTER GREENS SALAD WITH GREEN BEANS AND ROQUEFORT VINAIGRETTE 116

TATSOI SALAD 117

ORANGE-SESAME VINAIGRETTE 118

MADRAS CURRY DRESSING 119

CLASSIC AMERICAN POTATO SALAD 120

ASIAN CUCUMBER SALAD 120

SUCCOTASH SALAD 121

SUMMER VEGETABLE SLAW 122

CAESAR SALAD 123

QUICK THREE BEAN SALAD 124

INSALATA CAPRESE (TOMATO-MOZZARELLA SALAD) 125

GRILLED VEGETABLE ANTIPASTO 126

ROASTED PEPPERS 127

WILD RICE SALAD WITH MUSHROOMS AND ALMONDS 128

TABBOULEH 129

TOFU SALAD 130

SWEET WHITE SALAD WITH SHAVED ASIAGO 131

BARLEY AND CORN SALAD 132

MIXED BABY GREENS WITH BALSAMIC VINAIGRETTE 133

LENTIL SALAD 134

CALIFORNIA GARDEN SALAD WITH AVOCADO AND SPROUTS 135

MARINATED BEET SALAD 136

BASIC EGG SALAD 137

WARM POTATO SALAD WITH BALSAMIC VINEGAR AND ONIONS 138

CURRIED NEW POTATO SALAD 139

DILL POTATO SALAD 139

GERMAN POTATO SALAD 140

SWEET POTATO SALAD **141**

MEDITERRANEAN SWEET
POTATO SALAD **142**

WARM SPINACH SALAD WITH
POTATOES, RED ONIONS, AND
KALAMATA OLIVES **143**

TOMATO, GARLIC, AND PARSLEY
QUINOA SALAD **144**

WHEAT BERRY SALAD **145**

QUINOA ARTICHOKE HEARTS SALAD **146**

OLIVE AND PEPPER COUSCOUS SALAD **147**

GREEK SALAD TACOS **148**

RICOTTA AND GOAT CHEESE CRESPELLE **149**

SOUTHEAST ASIAN SLAW

This crisp, lightly spiced salad is fine enough to roll in Asian-inspired wraps, and combines beautifully with jasmine rice, cooked in coconut milk to make a unique taste.

Serves 4

¼ head (about ½ pound) Napa cabbage

½ carrot, grated

1 small red onion, julienne

1 small Thai "bird" chili or jalapeño pepper, finely chopped

¼ cup chopped cilantro

Juice of 1 lime

1 tablespoon rice wine vinegar

1 teaspoon sugar

1 teaspoon vegetable oil

A few drops sesame oil

½ teaspoon salt

1. Shred the cabbage as fine as you possibly can, using a knife, mandoline, or slicing machine. Combine with carrot, onion, chili pepper, and cilantro.

2. Dress with lime, rice vinegar, sugar, vegetable oil, sesame oil, and salt; toss thoroughly.

3. Refrigerate for at least 30 minutes before serving.

PC WARM CHICKPEA SALAD

In the summer, you can put the salad in an aluminum baking pan and cook it over indirect heat on a covered grill. Or skip the baking part entirely, chill the salad, and serve it cold.

Serves 12

1 pound dried chickpeas

10 cups water

1½ tablespoons vegetable oil

2 teaspoons salt

4 green onions, sliced

1 cup red onion, diced

1 small green bell pepper, diced

1 small red bell pepper, diced

½ cup fresh parsley, minced

1 large carrot, peeled and grated

¼ cup extra-virgin olive oil

2 teaspoons fresh lemon juice

2 teaspoons white wine vinegar

1 tablespoon mayonnaise or vegan mayonnaise, such as Vegenaise

1 clove garlic, minced

⅛ teaspoon freshly ground white pepper

½ teaspoon dried oregano

¼ cup Parmigiano-Reggiano and Romano cheese, grated, or vegan cheese, such as Daiya Mozzarella Style Shreds

1. Rinse and drain the chickpeas. Soak them in 6 cups of water for at least 4 hours or overnight. Drain. Add chickpeas to the pressure cooker along with 4 cups of water and the vegetable oil. Lock the lid in place and bring to high pressure; maintain pressure for 20 minutes. Remove from heat and allow pressure to release naturally. Drain the beans and transfer them to an ovenproof 9" × 13" casserole dish.

2. Add the salt, green onions, red onion, green and red bell peppers, parsley, and carrot to the casserole dish and toss with the beans.

3. Preheat the oven to 375°F.

4. To prepare the dressing, add the oil, lemon juice, vinegar, mayonnaise, garlic, pepper, and oregano to a small bowl or measuring cup. Whisk to mix. Pour the dressing over the bean mixture; stir to combine. Sprinkle the cheese over the dressed beans. Bake for 6 minutes. Stir before serving.

PC EDAMAME-SEAWEED SALAD

There are many types of edible seaweed. The most popular varieties include arame, hijiki, and wakame.

Serves 4

1 cup edamame, shelled

8 cups water, plus more as needed

1 tablespoon vegetable oil

½ cup dried arame, chopped

1 tablespoon sesame oil

1 clove garlic, minced

½ teaspoon fresh ginger, minced

1 teaspoon rice wine vinegar

1 teaspoon salt

1. Add the edamame and 4 cups water to the pressure cooker. Lock the lid into place; bring to high pressure for 1 minute. Remove from heat and quick-release the pressure.

2. Drain the water, rinse the edamame, and add to the pressure cooker again with the remaining 4 cups water. Soak for 1 hour.

3. Add the vegetable oil. Lock the lid into place; bring to high pressure and maintain for 11 minutes. Remove from heat and allow pressure to release naturally. Drain and set aside.

4. While the edamame is cooking, cover the arame with water in a small bowl and let sit for 7 minutes. Drain and set aside.

5. In a small sauté pan, heat the sesame oil over medium heat. Add the garlic and ginger and sauté for 30 seconds. Add the vinegar and salt, then the cooked edamame and arame.

6. Serve warm or chilled.

PC THREE BEAN SALAD

Cover and refrigerate this salad for at least 2 hours before serving. It can even be made a day in advance and left in the refrigerator overnight.

Serves 8–10

⅓ cup apple cider vinegar

¼ cup sugar

2½ teaspoons salt, plus more to taste

½ teaspoon pepper, plus more to taste

¼ cup olive oil

½ cup dried chickpeas

½ cup dried kidney beans

8 cups water

1 tablespoon vegetable oil

1 cup fresh or frozen green beans, cut into 1" pieces

1 cup flat leaf parsley, chopped

½ cup onion, diced

½ cup cucumber, diced

1. In a small bowl, whisk together the vinegar, sugar, 1½ teaspoons salt, and ½ teaspoon pepper. While whisking continuously, slowly add the olive oil. Once well combined, cover and refrigerate.

2. Add the chickpeas, kidney beans, and 4 cups water to the pressure cooker. Lock the lid into place; bring to high pressure for 1 minute. Remove from heat and quick-release the pressure.

3. Drain the water, rinse the beans, and add to the pressure cooker again with the remaining 4 cups water. Soak for 1 hour.

4. Add the vegetable oil and 1 teaspoon salt. Lock the lid into place; bring to high pressure and maintain for 20 minutes. Quick-release the pressure and open the lid. Add the green beans, lock the lid, and bring to high pressure for an additional 3 minutes. Remove from heat and allow the pressure to release naturally.

5. Drain the cooked beans and add to a large mixing bowl. Stir in all remaining ingredients and dressing. Cover and refrigerate for 2 hours before serving.

Bean Variations

Almost any combination of beans can be used to make a bean salad. Try black beans, pinto beans, and navy beans mixed with Mexican flavors, or adzuki beans, soybeans, and green beans with Japanese flavors.

TOMATO AND BREAD SALAD (PANZANELLA)

Panzanella (bread salad) is a favorite side dish in Italy, where it is served with sliced cheeses. Using both yellow and red tomatoes can make this a festive touch on your plate.

Serves 4 as an appetizer or side dish

2 cups diced (½") ripe red tomatoes, any variety

¼ cup finely chopped red onion

½ teaspoon salt

1½ tablespoons extra-virgin olive oil

2 teaspoons fresh lemon juice

2 cups day-old country bread, cut into ½" cubes, air-dried overnight or baked 20 minutes at 325°F

¼ cup roughly chopped Italian parsley

Black pepper to taste

1. Dress tomatoes and chopped onion with salt, olive oil, and lemon juice.
2. Toss gently with dried bread cubes and parsley.
3. Season with freshly ground black pepper.

SALAD OF CELERY ROOT AND PEARS

Wintertime in the Northeast brings basketfuls of celeriac (celery roots) to the produce markets. Their herby, vegetal flavor pairs perfectly with pears. Variations on this combination are popular all winter long.

Serves 6

1 medium celery root (about the size of a baseball), peeled

¼ cup mayonnaise (homemade is best, but any will do)

½ hard-boiled egg, chopped

1 tablespoon finely chopped Italian (flat-leaf) parsley

2 cornichons (little sour gherkins), finely chopped

2 tablespoons Dijon mustard

Juice of 1 lemon

2 tablespoons extra-virgin olive oil

Salt and freshly ground black pepper

2 ripe pears (Bartlett and Bosc are great, but choose your own variety)

1. Julienne (cut into very thin strips) the celery root. Combine mayonnaise, chopped egg, parsley, cornichons, mustard, lemon, and olive oil, and toss with celery root. Season with salt and pepper.

2. Peel pears and slice into 6 to 8 wedges each. Divide dressed celery root into 6 portions, and garnish with pear slices.

WINTER GREENS SALAD WITH GREEN BEANS AND ROQUEFORT VINAIGRETTE

This type of salad highlights the fruitiness of blue cheese and the sweetness of the vegetables with the lightness of a vinaigrette dressing.

Serves 4

SALAD

1 bunch watercress

2 heads Belgium endive

1 small red onion

½ pound green beans

DRESSING

⅓ cup balsamic vinegar

⅓ cup vegetable oil

⅓ cup extra-virgin olive oil

1 tablespoon chopped chives

¼ pound Roquefort or other quality blue cheese

Coarse (kosher) salt and freshly ground black pepper

1. Rinse watercress and break into bite-size pieces. Cut endives diagonally into 3 or 4 sections each, discarding cores. Slice red onion into thin rings.

2. In 3 quarts of rapidly boiling salted water, cook green beans in 2 separate batches until just tender, about 5 minutes, then plunge them into salted ice water to stop the cooking process. Combine with greens and onion.

3. Whisk together vinegar, vegetable oil, olive oil, and chives. Roughly break the blue cheese into dressing; stir with a spoon, leaving some large chunks. Season with salt and pepper. Dress salad with ⅓ cup of dressing. Remaining dressing will keep, refrigerated, for 2 weeks.

4. Arrange salad onto 4 plates, with onion rings and green beans displayed prominently on top.

TATSOI SALAD

Light, floral, and zesty, this salad pairs antioxidant-rich Japanese spinach (tatsoi) with springtime-fresh cross-cultural dressing. The salad works equally well with other types of spinach.

Serves 4

6 cups tatsoi (Japanese "baby" spinach leaves)

¼ cup Orange-Sesame Vinaigrette (see recipe in this chapter)

½ cup red Bermuda onion, sliced paper-thin

1. Wash and spin the tatsoi leaves, then toss gently with ½ of the dressing. Distribute onto 4 salad plates.

2. Arrange sliced onions atop each salad, and finish with a final spoonful of dressing.

ORANGE-SESAME VINAIGRETTE

This vinaigrette tastes great on the Tatsoi Salad found in this chapter.

Yields about 1¼ cups

Zest of ½ orange

Zest of ½ lime

1 pickled jalapeño pepper (usually found near the olives in supermarkets), chopped, and 1 tablespoon of the brine it came in

¼ cup Japanese rice wine vinegar

¼ cup orange juice concentrate

1½ teaspoons Dijon mustard

A few drops sesame oil (about ⅛ teaspoon)

¼ cup peanut oil

¼ cup olive oil

Salt and freshly ground black pepper

1. Combine zest, pickled jalapeño and brine, rice vinegar, orange concentrate, Dijon, and sesame oil in a blender.

2. Blend on medium speed, slowly drizzling in the peanut and olive oils. Season to taste with salt and pepper.

MADRAS CURRY DRESSING

Perfect as a dip for crudités or a spread on sandwiches, this dressing balances the sweetness of dried fruits with the complexity of Indian spices and light chili "heat."

Yields about 1¼ cups

1 tablespoon oil

1 small red onion, finely chopped

2 tablespoons chopped red bell pepper

1 teaspoon finely chopped and seeded jalapeño pepper

2 tablespoons Madras curry powder

1 teaspoon ground coriander

1 teaspoon ground turmeric

1 tablespoon raisins, soaked in ½ cup warm water

¼ teaspoon cayenne pepper (optional)

Juice of 1 lime (about 2 tablespoons)

1 cup mayonnaise

2 tablespoons chopped cilantro

Salt and pepper to taste

1. In a small skillet, heat oil over medium heat for 1 minute. Add onion, bell pepper, and jalapeño. Cook until onion is translucent, about 2 minutes; add curry powder, coriander, and turmeric. Cook 4 minutes more, stirring with a wooden spoon. Some of the spices may stick—this is not a problem. Remove from heat; allow to cool a few minutes. Drain the raisins.

2. In the bowl of a food processor, combine onion mixture, raisins, and cayenne pepper. Pulse until smooth, scraping sides of bowl frequently. Add half of lime juice and the mayonnaise. Pulse to combine, then stir in cilantro. Adjust seasoning with salt, pepper, and remaining lime juice. Can be made up to 1 week in advance.

CLASSIC AMERICAN POTATO SALAD

Fourth of July picnics wouldn't be the same without this favorite. For an interesting twist, try making it with specialty potatoes, like slim "fingerlings," from your produce market.

Serves 8

¾ cup mayonnaise

1 teaspoon sugar

2 teaspoons Dijon-style mustard

2 pounds potatoes (any variety), boiled, skinned, and cut into chunks

1 small carrot, peeled and grated

Salt and white pepper to taste

1 tablespoon roughly chopped Italian parsley

Whisk together the first 3 ingredients in a small bowl. Add potatoes and carrots; toss them gently to coat. Season to taste. Garnish with chopped parsley.

ASIAN CUCUMBER SALAD

This refreshing, crisp dish is the perfect counterbalance with grilled tempeh, spicy corn fritters, and other hearty fare..

Serves 4

¼ cup rice wine vinegar

1 teaspoon sugar

1 teaspoon chopped jalapeño pepper

1 European-style long cucumber or 1 large regular cucumber

Sesame oil

1. Whisk together vinegar, sugar, and chopped jalapeño. If using a European cuke, it is not necessary to peel, but if using an American cuke, peel it. Halve the cucumber lengthwise; remove seeds. Slice seeded cucumber very thinly into half-moons. Combine with dressing, drizzle in a few drops of sesame oil, and toss to coat.

2. Marinate for at least 10 minutes before serving.

SUCCOTASH SALAD

In summer, any excuse to use sweet corn is welcome. In New England, fresh cranberry beans are in the market in June and July, and they are delicious in this complete-protein salad. This is a variation on a recipe from New England chef Jasper White.

Serves 8

8 ears sweet corn, shucked (or 16 ounces top-quality frozen corn)

½ pound dried pinto or red kidney beans, cooked or 2 (16-ounce) cans, drained and rinsed

¼ cup champagne vinegar or rice wine vinegar

¼ cup extra-virgin olive oil

¼ cup chopped chives

Salt and pepper to taste

1. Shave corn kernels from cob, shearing them from the stem end to the tip with a knife. Cook in rapidly boiling salted water for 1 minute.

2. Toss with beans, vinegar, oil, and chives; season to taste.

SUMMER VEGETABLE SLAW

Bursting with summer's bounty, this slaw is a colorful fiesta. The best renditions of this summer harvest celebration, introduced to me by New England chef Jasper White, utilize whatever vegetables are freshest and best at the market—the more the better!

Serves 8

1 small head Napa cabbage or regular green cabbage (about 1 pound)

1 large "horse" carrot, or 2 regular carrots, peeled

¼ pound snow peas

1 each red, yellow, and green bell peppers, seeded

12 green beans

1 small red onion

2 ears fresh sweet corn, shucked

½ teaspoon sugar

¼ cup cider vinegar

1 tablespoon vegetable oil (preferably peanut oil)

Pinch of celery seeds

Salt and black pepper to taste

1. Quarter and core the cabbage; slice as thinly as possible. Using a swivel peeler, shave carrot into as many paper-thin curls as you can. Discard or save remaining carrot for another use. Cut carrot curls, snow peas, bell peppers, green beans, and onion into fine julienne. Cut corn kernels from the cob.

2. Combine all vegetables in a large mixing bowl; dress with sugar, vinegar, oil, celery seeds, salt, and pepper. Allow to sit at least 10 minutes before serving. This is an excellent accompaniment to crispy fried foods like beer-battered onion rings.

CAESAR SALAD

Vegetarian Worcestershire sauce is now available in health food stores, and may be added for an additional dimension if you wish, but this vegetarian version of America's favorite salad is authentic in taste as-is.

Serves 8

DRESSING:

1 egg yolk

1 tablespoon Dijon mustard

Juice of ½ lemon (about 2 tablespoons)

2 cloves garlic, finely chopped

½ cup vegetable oil (preferably peanut oil)

¼ cup grated Parmigiano-Reggiano cheese

Pinch of cayenne pepper (optional)

Salt and pepper

SALAD:

1 head romaine lettuce, washed, torn into bite-size pieces

1 cup croutons

1 small wedge Parmigiano-Reggiano cheese (optional)

1. Make the dressing: In a mixing bowl or food processor, combine the egg yolk, mustard, lemon juice, and garlic. Vigorously whisk or process in the oil, starting just a drop at a time, and gradually drizzling it in a small stream, until all is emulsified into a smooth mayonnaise. Stir in the cheese, cayenne, salt, and pepper, and a little extra lemon if desired.

2. Toss the lettuce and croutons with the dressing, and divide onto 8 plates, arranging croutons on top. If desired, shave curls of Parmigiano over each salad, using a vegetable peeler. Dressing may be made up to 1 week in advance.

QUICK THREE BEAN SALAD

When taken as part of a lunch buffet with some form of grain, salad bean dishes like this complete the amino acids necessary in our diet, forming complete proteins. And it's simply delicious!

Serves 6

1 (16-ounce) can green beans
1 (16-ounce) can yellow wax beans
1 (16-ounce) can red kidney beans
1 onion
½ cup sugar
⅔ cup vinegar
⅓ cup vegetable oil
½ teaspoon salt
⅛ teaspoon pepper

Drain the beans. Slice the onion thinly, then cut the slices into quarters. Whisk together the sugar, vinegar, oil, salt, and pepper. Combine the beans, onions, and dressing, mixing well. Chill at least 4 hours, or overnight, stirring occasionally. If desired, salad can be drained before serving.

INSALATA CAPRESE (TOMATO-MOZZARELLA SALAD)

Since the essence of this salad is its purity of flavors, only the highest quality of ingredients should be used. If you are unable to find fresh basil or good fresh kneaded mozzarella, make something else.

Serves 4

4 large, ripe red tomatoes

2 loaves fresh mozzarella or mozzarella di bufala

8 top sprigs of fresh basil

2 tablespoons very high quality extra-virgin olive oil

Coarse (kosher) salt and freshly ground black pepper

1. Slice each tomato into 4 thick slices, discarding the polar ends. Cut each mozzarella into 6 even slices. Shingle alternating tomato and mozzarella slices onto 4 plates, starting and ending with tomato slices.

2. Garnish with 2 sprigs basil each, and drizzle olive oil over all. Sprinkle with salt and a few grinds of black pepper. Serve immediately.

Shuffle Off to Buffalo Mozzarella

Mozzarella di bufala comes from the countryside surrounding Naples in southern Italy, and possesses a fresh, tangy, milky flavor. Unlike other fresh mozzarellas made from cow's milk, this regional delight is made from the milk of water buffalo. Retreating Nazis destroyed the buffalo herd that had lived in the region since the second century A.D., but the resourceful Italians imported new buffalo from India after the war. If you see this cheese, buy it. It is shipped daily from Rome, packed in eight-ounce kneaded balls suspended in their own whey. It's a perfect cheese for a Caprese salad, or simply to slice and serve all by itself.

GRILLED VEGETABLE ANTIPASTO

If a gas stove or grill is unavailable, the broiler element of an electric or gas oven will also work for Roasted Peppers (see recipe in this chapter). Arrange them 2" from the heating element, and follow same procedure as the stovetop method.

Serves 8

SALAD

1 medium eggplant, cut into 16 wedges, lightly salted

2 yellow squash, quartered lengthwise

2 zucchini, quartered lengthwise

4 plum tomatoes, halved lengthwise

2 each green and red bell peppers, roasted

2 tablespoons olive oil

Salt and pepper

Pinch of crushed red pepper (optional)

8 portobello mushrooms, stems removed

2 heads radicchio, core intact, quartered

DRESSING:

½ cup extra-virgin olive oil

1 tablespoon balsamic vinegar

Pinch of sugar (optional)

2 shallots, finely chopped

4 sprigs fresh thyme, leaves picked and chopped

Salt and pepper

8 sprigs parsley

1. Heat grill (or a stovetop grill pan) to medium-hot. In a large mixing bowl, toss eggplant, squash, zucchini, tomatoes, and peppers with 1 tablespoon olive oil, salt, pepper, and crushed red pepper. Use a pastry brush or your hands to brush remaining oil on tops of mushrooms and radicchio; season well.

2. Cook vegetables on the grill, without turning, until they are slightly more than halfway done. Eggplant and mushrooms will take longest, while the radicchio will take only a few moments. Cook the tomatoes skin-side down only. Turn the other vegetables to finish, then arrange on a serving platter.

3. Whisk together the extra-virgin olive oil, vinegar, sugar (if using), shallots, and chopped thyme. Season to taste, and drizzle over cooked vegetables while they're still warm. Marinate 20 minutes before serving, garnished with parsley sprigs.

ROASTED PEPPERS

The sweet vegetal flavor and silky texture of roasted pepper fillets breathe freshness into all they touch. There's a floral, garden-y aroma they convey that can't be duplicated. The process of roasting and peeling peppers over a gas stove or grill is simple:

Serves 4

2 green bell peppers

2 red bell peppers

1. Place bell peppers (any color or shape) directly onto the burner grate over a high flame. Allow the flames to lick the skin of the peppers, making them blister and turn black. Rotate the peppers using metal tongs or forks.

2. Once peppers are blackened all around, transfer them to an airtight container, sealed plastic bag, or plastic-wrap-covered bowl. Allow them to steam for 10 minutes.

3. Slip skins off from peppers with your fingers. Remove and discard stems and seeds, but try to keep the pieces of pepper as whole as possible. If desired, you may rinse the pepper fillets under cool water, but this washes away some of the flavorful natural juices. Enjoy.

Stovetop Grills

Cast-iron or alloy pans with a ridged cooking surface allow cooks to create a grilled taste and appearance in the kitchen. These "grill pans" are very popular in professional kitchens, where space considerations and ventilation issues prevent flame grilling. A 12"-diameter cast-iron grill pan is an inexpensive (about $20) item that can revolutionize your cooking. It allows quick, low-fat cooking year-round.

To grill on a grill pan without food sticking, heat it very hot, and season it with a few drops of oil. Also toss any vegetables or other foods you grill with a few drops of oil. The key to stick-free grilling here is to leave cooking foods undisturbed for the first few minutes of cooking, allowing them time to form a crust. Then, using a thin spatula and a pair of tongs or a roasting fork, gently loosen items and turn them.

Mushrooms, polenta, garden vegetables, and potatoes make wonderful antipasti (appetizers), simply tossed with a few drops of olive oil and salt and pepper, and seared on a stovetop grill. Drizzle them with fine balsamic vinegar for a taste of Mediterranean Italy anytime.

WILD RICE SALAD WITH MUSHROOMS AND ALMONDS

Pair grains like wild rice with beans and legumes for complete proteins, essential to the vegetarian diet, and a curiously good culinary combination!

Serves 8

8 ounces uncooked wild rice

1 cup whole almonds

1 tablespoon extra-virgin olive oil

8 ounces shiitake or other exotic mushrooms, sliced

Salt and pepper to taste

¼ cup yellow raisins, soaked in 1 cup warm water for 30 minutes up to overnight

2 scallions, chopped

Juice of 1 lemon (about ¼ cup)

1 teaspoon ground cumin, toasted in a dry pan until fragrant

1. Boil the wild rice in lightly salted water until tender, and most grains have burst open (about 35 minutes); drain. Lightly toast almonds in a dry skillet over medium heat until most have small browned spots and they attain an oily sheen; spread on a plate to cool to room temperature. Heat oil in a medium skillet over high heat for 1 minute, then cook the mushrooms until tender, about 5 minutes; season with salt and pepper.

2. In a mixing bowl, combine rice, almonds, mushrooms (with their cooking oil), raisins, and scallions. Dress with lemon and cumin, and season with salt and pepper. Toss well to coat. Serve chilled or at room temperature.

TABBOULEH

Middle Eastern bulgur wheat absorbs water quickly, giving it a pliable and chewy texture unlike anything else in the world. This is an everyday dish in Egypt. Perfect with stuffed grape leaves.

Serves 6

1 cup cracked (bulgur) wheat
1 small cucumber, chopped
3 scallions, finely chopped
2 ripe tomatoes, seeded and chopped
2 tablespoons chopped chives
1 cup chopped Italian parsley
½ cup extra-virgin olive oil
Juice of 2 lemons (about ½ cup)
Salt and pepper

1. Soak the wheat in 1 quart of water for 15 minutes (or overnight). Drain and squeeze out excess moisture by tying up in a cheesecloth or clean kitchen towel.

2. Combine with cucumber, scallions, tomatoes, chives, and parsley in a mixing bowl. Dress with olive oil, lemon, salt, and pepper.

3. Set aside to marinate for 2–3 hours before serving.

TOFU SALAD

Soy foods are a vegetarian's best way to get complete, natural proteins. Keeping delicious, snackable marinated tofu on hand for sandwiches and salads will ensure that you get these nutrients in a satisfying way. Marinated tofu will remain fresh in the fridge for 4–5 days. One of the best ways to store the cubes is in a zip-top bag with all the air squeezed out.

Serves 6

5 tofu cakes, cut into 1" cubes

MARINADE:

2 tablespoons water

Black pepper

2 teaspoons sugar

¼ cup dry sherry or Chinese cooking wine

¼ cup soy sauce

¼ cup white wine vinegar

1 clove garlic, chopped

Pinch of anise seed, toasted and ground

1 tablespoon sesame oil

1 tablespoon vegetable oil

SALAD:

1 carrot, julienne

¼ pound snow peas, julienne

1 cup finely chopped cabbage

5 cremini or white mushrooms, sliced

4 scallions, julienne

DRESSING:

½ teaspoon salt

2 teaspoons sesame oil

2 teaspoons tamari soy sauce

Juice of ½ lemon

Black pepper to taste

1 tablespoon sugar

1. Spread tofu into a single layer in a baking dish or sheet pan. Whisk together the ingredients for the marinade, and pour it over the tofu. Marinate for 3 hours or overnight in the refrigerator, turning occasionally.

2. Combine salad ingredients, toss with dressing, and place in the refrigerator to marinate 1 hour. Add tofu, and toss gently to combine just before serving.

SWEET WHITE SALAD WITH SHAVED ASIAGO

This recipe doesn't call for croutons, but feel free to add them on if you'd like more of a crunch.

Serves 4

4 ounces (about 2 heads) frisée or fine curly endive

4 heads Belgium endive, cut into 1" pieces

1 cup julienne of jicama

1 small sweet onion, sliced into paper-thin rings

Juice of ½ lemon (about 2 tablespoons)

1 tablespoon extra-virgin olive oil

1 teaspoon orange juice concentrate

Salt and pepper to taste

Wedge of Asiago cheese, Parmigiano-Reggiano, or other good "grana" cheese

1. Wash and dry the frisée; combine with Belgium endive, jicama, and onions. Whisk together the lemon juice, olive oil, orange juice concentrate, salt, and pepper; toss with salad to coat.

2. Arrange salad onto 4 plates, piling it as high as possible. Using a swivel peeler, gently shave 4 or 5 curls of Asiago cheese over each salad, and serve immediately.

BARLEY AND CORN SALAD

Whole grains like barley provide many of the B vitamins vegetarians need to fight off diseases, and are higher in protein, vitamin E, zinc, phosphorus, and other phytonutrients than refined grains.

Serves 8

1 cup barley

1 pound frozen sweet corn kernels

1 carrot, chopped finely

2 ribs celery, chopped finely

1 medium red onion, chopped finely

1 tablespoon red wine vinegar or cider vinegar

2 tablespoons extra-virgin olive oil

½ cup chopped fresh herbs, such as parsley, chives, basil, oregano, mint and/or cilantro

Salt and freshly ground black pepper to taste

1. Boil the barley in 2 quarts of lightly salted water until it is very tender, about 30 minutes. Drain and spread on a platter to cool. Heat a dry cast-iron pan or skillet over a high flame for 1 minute. Add the corn and cook without stirring until some kernels attain a slight char, and the corn has a smoky aroma, about 5 minutes.

2. Combine the barley, corn, carrot, celery, and onion in a mixing bowl. Add all remaining ingredients and toss well to coat.

MIXED BABY GREENS WITH BALSAMIC VINAIGRETTE

This is a nice, basic house salad.

Serves 6–8

8 ounces baby mixed greens (mesclun)

1 bunch chives, cut into 2" pieces

1 tablespoon good quality balsamic vinegar

2 tablespoons good quality extra-virgin olive oil

1 tablespoon finely chopped shallots

Salt and freshly ground pepper to taste

Wash greens and spin dry; combine with chives. Whisk together the vinegar, oil, and shallots. Season to taste.

Toasting Spices for Flavor and Aroma

You'd become bland, too, if you just sat on the shelf for months! You'd be glad if someone lit a fire under your seed casing. Spices lose their potency from the moment they go into the jar. The best way to bring out the most flavor and aroma in them is to "wake them up" with a light toasting. Usually, this simply enhances the power of the spice, so you get more flavor from less spice. Sometimes, as in the case of cumin and anise, it gives the spice a roundness and new dimension that the spice never would have had without toasting. For best flavor, buy spices in the most whole form you can find, whether it's seeds, like cumin, coriander, and anise; nuts, like nutmeg; or bark, like cinnamon sticks. I keep a small electric coffee grinder for grinding spices. Natural oils in spices are what give them flavor. These oils evaporate and dissipate with exposure to air. They remain much more intact inside the whole seeds, nuts, roots, or bark, and are unlocked by toasting and grinding. Even powdered spices can benefit greatly from a light toasting. The method is simple:

Sprinkle the spice into a small dry skillet, and heat it over a medium flame until the spice's aroma comes forth. If you're using a powdered spice, that's all you need to do. Go ahead and use the spice from there. For whole spices, you may choose to grind them after toasting. Usually, you don't seek to brown the spices at all, and you never want to turn any part of them black. But certain dishes call for lightly browned spices, which attain a greater degree of flavor complexity.

LENTIL SALAD

Lentils have been found among the remains of prehistoric communities and are mentioned in the earliest books of the Bible. They cook more quickly than other beans, and never require soaking.

Serves 8

1 pound dried lentils

2 medium onions, finely chopped

3 scallions, chopped

1 green pepper, finely chopped

1 tablespoon toasted cumin powder

Pinch of cayenne pepper

Juice of 1 lemon (about ¼ cup)

2 tablespoons extra-virgin olive oil

Salt and freshly ground black pepper

Wash lentils and pick through to take out any stones. Boil in 2 quarts of lightly salted water until tender but not broken up. Spread on a pan to cool. Combine with onions, scallions, and green pepper. Dress with remaining ingredients, and serve with a bed of dressed baby greens.

CALIFORNIA GARDEN SALAD WITH AVOCADO AND SPROUTS

The fruity taste of large, green Florida avocados gives this salad a lighter, more summery flavor, though the Hass is the more authentic California item.

Serves 4

DRESSING:

1 tablespoon fresh-squeezed lemon juice

3 tablespoons extra-virgin olive oil

1 tablespoon finely chopped shallot or chive

½ teaspoon salt

¼ teaspoon freshly ground black pepper

SALAD

2 heads Boston or Bibb lettuce

2 ripe tomatoes, cored, cut into 8 wedges each

1 ripe avocado

1 cup alfalfa sprouts

1. Make the dressing: Combine the lemon juice, olive oil, shallot or chive, salt, and pepper in a small bowl, mixing well.

2. Arrange lettuce leaves, stem-end in, onto 4 plates, making flower-petal pattern. Inner leaves will be too small, so reserve them for another use.

3. Toss tomatoes in 1 tablespoon dressing; place 4 onto each salad. Peel avocado, cut into 8 wedges, and toss with 1 tablespoon dressing. Place 2 wedges on each salad. Divide sprouts into 4 bunches, and place a bunch in the center of each salad. Drizzle salads with remaining dressing, or serve on the side.

MARINATED BEET SALAD

The natural sweetness and delicate texture of fresh beets seem to have been forgotten by many Americans, who have relegated this noble root vegetable to a curiosity in many places. This simple salad highlights these distinctive characteristics.

Serves 6

1 pound fresh beets, stem end trimmed

1 tablespoon red wine vinegar

6 large romaine lettuce leaves, washed

DRESSING:

1 tablespoon rice wine vinegar or white wine vinegar

2 tablespoons extra-virgin olive oil

¼ teaspoon dried oregano leaves

¼ teaspoon dried basil leaves

½ teaspoon freshly chopped parsley

1 teaspoon finely chopped shallots

Salt and pepper to taste

1. Boil beets in a small saucepan with red wine vinegar and enough water to cover. Cook until tender, about 30 minutes. Chill, then peel and cut into ¼" slices.

2. In a bowl, combine rice wine vinegar, olive oil, oregano, basil, parsley, and shallots. Season with salt and pepper. Add beets, and marinate 10–15 minutes. Place lettuce leaves on 6 plates, trimming stem end to fit inside rim. Arrange beets in an overlapping pattern atop lettuce leaves, and drizzle with remaining marinade.

Note: Beets can be cooked and marinated up to 2 days in advance.

BASIC EGG SALAD

You can't go wrong with this Basic Egg Salad!

Yields about ⅔ cup

1 tablespoon cream cheese

¼ cup salad dressing or mayonnaise

1 tablespoon finely minced onion

4 hard-boiled eggs, chopped (or 6 hard-boiled eggs chopped with 4 of the yolks removed for a lighter, healthier option)

1 tablespoon sweet pickle relish, slightly drained, or 1 tablespoon chopped sweet pickles

Salt and pepper to taste

Soften the cream cheese and combine well with the salad dressing or mayonnaise and onion. Combine dressing with the chopped egg and relish. Add salt and pepper. Chill before serving.

WARM POTATO SALAD WITH BALSAMIC VINEGAR AND ONIONS

This substantial main-course salad is highly adaptable. Serve it atop fresh spinach leaves in the springtime for a hearty lunch, or beside scrambled eggs for a winter breakfast.

Serves 8

2 tablespoons extra-virgin olive oil

2 medium onions, thinly sliced

1 tablespoon fresh thyme leaves (about 3 sprigs) or 1 teaspoon dried

½ teaspoon sugar (optional)

1 tablespoon balsamic vinegar

1 pound small white "boiling" potatoes (a.k.a. "creamer" potatoes), halved, boiled until very tender, and drained

Salt and pepper to taste

Pinch of fresh chopped Italian parsley

1. Heat olive oil over medium heat in a medium skillet for 1 minute; add onions, thyme, and sugar (if using). Cook slowly, stirring regularly with a wooden spoon, until onions are very soft and browned to the color of caramel, about 10 minutes.

2. Stir in balsamic vinegar; remove from heat. Toss gently with warm cooked potatoes, and season with salt and pepper. Allow to rest 10 minutes before serving, garnished with chopped parsley.

CURRIED NEW POTATO SALAD

Simple to make, but with a complex taste, this is a great, attractive buffet item for a picnic lunch.

Serves 8

2 pounds red new potatoes, cut into bite-size chunks

3 hard-boiled eggs, cut into bite-size chunks

1 recipe Madras Curry Dressing (see recipe in this chapter)

1 tablespoon chopped cilantro

Boil potatoes in lightly salted water until very tender, about 15 minutes; cool. Combine with eggs and curry dressing; toss to coat. Serve chilled, garnished with cilantro leaves.

PC DILL POTATO SALAD

Instead of—or in addition to—fresh dill, you can use minced dill pickles in this potato salad recipe.

Serves 6–8

1 cup water

2 pounds red potatoes, quartered

½ cup mayonnaise or vegan mayonnaise, such as Vegenaise

1 teaspoon yellow mustard

1 teaspoon cider vinegar

1 tablespoon fresh dill, chopped

Salt and pepper, to taste

½ cup red onion, chopped

½ cup celery, chopped

1. Add the water and the potatoes to the pressure cooker. Lock the lid into place and bring to high pressure. Once the pressure is achieved, turn the heat to low and cook for 3–4 minutes. Remove from heat and allow pressure to release naturally. Drain the potatoes and rinse with cold water.

2. Whisk together the mayonnaise, yellow mustard, cider vinegar, dill, salt, and pepper.

3. Combine the potatoes with the chopped onion and celery and then add the mayonnaise mixture.

4. Season with more salt and pepper, if necessary.

PC GERMAN POTATO SALAD

Making potato salad with warm potatoes will lead to a mushier product that has fewer large chunks. Rinsing the cooked potatoes with cold water will help cool them off, or you can refrigerate, or let stand at room temperature, for an hour before mixing with additional ingredients.

Serves 6–8

1 cup water

2 pounds red potatoes, quartered

½ cup olive oil

2 tablespoons Dijon mustard

2 tablespoons white wine vinegar

2 tablespoons mayonnaise or vegan mayonnaise, such as Vegenaise

1 teaspoon garlic powder

1½ teaspoons salt

½ cup red pepper, chopped

½ cup celery, chopped

⅓ cup red onion, chopped

1. Add the water and the potatoes to the pressure cooker. Lock the lid into place and bring to high pressure. Once the pressure is achieved, turn the heat to low and cook for 3–4 minutes. Remove from heat and allow pressure to release naturally. Drain the potatoes and rinse with cold water.

2. To make the dressing, whisk together the olive oil, mustard, vinegar, mayonnaise, garlic powder, and salt in a small bowl.

3. In a large bowl, combine the pepper, celery, onion, cooked potatoes, and the dressing. Toss to coat.

SC SWEET POTATO SALAD

This salad, like many others, can be served warm and straight out of the slow cooker or chilled before serving.

Serves 6

3 tablespoons extra-virgin olive oil

1 onion, chopped

3 cloves garlic, minced

1 pound sweet potatoes, peeled and cubed

½ teaspoon dried ginger

½ teaspoon paprika

1 teaspoon cumin

1 teaspoon salt

¼ teaspoon black pepper

1 tablespoon fresh lemon juice

¼ cup fresh parsley, chopped

1. Add the olive oil to the slow cooker and sauté the onion and garlic on high heat until they are golden brown, about 2–3 minutes.

2. Add the rest of the ingredients except for the lemon juice and parsley. Cover and cook on medium heat for 4 hours.

3. Mix the lemon juice and parsley into the sweet potato salad.

PC MEDITERRANEAN SWEET POTATO SALAD

Serve this salad at room temperature or chilled after refrigerating for a few hours.

Serves 4

¼ cup olive oil

1 onion, diced

2 cloves garlic, minced

1 teaspoon cumin

1 teaspoon paprika

¼ cup fresh lemon juice

1 cup water

3 cups sweet potatoes, peeled and cubed

¼ cup green olives

3 tablespoons parsley, chopped

Salt and pepper, to taste

1. Add olive oil to pressure cooker; sauté the onion until golden brown. Add the garlic, cumin, paprika, and lemon juice; cook for 2 minutes. Pour into a bowl. Set aside.

2. Add the water and the sweet potatoes to the pressure cooker. Lock the lid into place and bring to high pressure. Once achieved, turn the heat to low and cook for 5 minutes. Remove from heat; release pressure naturally.

3. Drain the sweet potatoes in a colander. In a large bowl, toss the onion mixture with the potatoes. Add the olives and parsley. Season with salt and pepper.

WARM SPINACH SALAD WITH POTATOES, RED ONIONS, AND KALAMATA OLIVES

Use this recipe as a master recipe—a starting point from which to make myriad variations of your own.

Serves 4

1 pound fresh curly-leaf spinach, washed, stems removed

¼ cup extra-virgin olive oil

1 pound small red potatoes, cut into ½" slices, boiled 10 minutes, and drained

1 medium red onion, halved, thinly sliced

20 Kalamata or other black olives, pitted

1 tablespoon balsamic vinegar

Salt and pepper to taste

1. Place spinach in a large mixing bowl. Heat olive oil in a large skillet over high heat for 1 minute; add potatoes and onion. Cook over high heat until lightly browned, about 5 minutes. Remove from heat; add olives, vinegar, salt, and pepper.

2. Pour potato mixture over spinach, and invert skillet over bowl to hold in heat. Allow to steam 1 minute, then divide onto 4 plates, arranging potatoes, onions, and olives on top. Serve warm.

PC TOMATO, GARLIC, AND PARSLEY QUINOA SALAD

The combination of tomato, garlic, and parsley goes well with just about any grain, so if you don't like quinoa, substitute couscous or rice instead.

Serves 4

1 cup quinoa

2 cups water

2 tablespoons olive oil

2 cloves garlic, minced

1 cup diced tomatoes

¼ cup chopped parsley

1 tablespoon lemon juice

1 teaspoon salt

1. Add the quinoa and water to the pressure cooker. Lock the lid into place; bring to high pressure and maintain for 6 minutes. Remove from heat and allow pressure to release naturally. Fluff with a fork.

2. In a small sauté pan, add the olive oil over medium heat. Sauté the garlic for 30 seconds, then add the tomatoes, parsley, and lemon juice. Sauté for 1 minute. Stir the tomato mixture and salt into the cooked quinoa. Season with additional salt, to taste.

PC WHEAT BERRY SALAD

For an elegant presentation, place a teaspoon of Wheat Berry Salad on individual sections of baby romaine hearts.

Serves 12

1½ tablespoons vegetable oil

6¾ cups water

1½ cups wheat berries

1½ teaspoons Dijon mustard

1 teaspoon sugar

1 teaspoon sea salt

½ teaspoon freshly ground black pepper

¼ cup white wine vinegar

½ cup extra-virgin olive oil

½ small red onion, peeled and diced

1⅓ cups frozen corn or peas, thawed

1 medium zucchini, peeled, grated, and drained

2 stalks celery, finely diced

1 red bell pepper, seeded and diced

4 green onions, diced

¼ cup sun-dried tomatoes, diced

¼ cup fresh parsley, chopped

1. Add the oil, water, and wheat berries to the pressure cooker. Lock the lid into place and bring to high pressure; maintain pressure for 50 minutes. Remove from heat and quick-release the pressure. Fluff with a fork. If the grains aren't yet as tender as you'd like, simmer and stir the mixture for a few minutes, adding more water if necessary. When done to your liking, drain and transfer to a large bowl.

2. Make the dressing by puréeing the mustard, sugar, salt, pepper, vinegar, olive oil, and red onion in a food processor or blender. Start by stirring ½ cup dressing into the cooled wheat berries. Toss the seasoned wheat berries with remaining ingredients. Taste for seasoning; add additional salt, pepper, or dressing if needed. Cover and refrigerate any leftover dressing for up to 3 days.

QUINOA ARTICHOKE HEARTS SALAD

The amount of dressing called for in this recipe is a suggestion. You may wish to use more or less dressing, depending on how strongly the dressing you're using is seasoned.

Serves 4

1 cup pecans

1 cup quinoa

2½ cups water

2 cups frozen artichoke hearts

2 cups cherry or grape tomatoes, halved

½ small red onion, thinly sliced

¼ cup Italian salad dressing

2 heads Belgian endive

1. Roughly chop the pecans and add them to the pressure cooker over medium heat. Dry roast for several minutes, stirring continuously to prevent the nuts from burning. The pecans are sufficiently toasted when they're fragrant and slightly brown. Transfer to a bowl and set aside to cool.

2. Add the quinoa and water to the pressure cooker. Lock the lid into place and bring to high pressure; maintain pressure for 2 minutes. Remove from heat and allow pressure to release naturally for 10 minutes. Quick-release any remaining pressure. Transfer to a colander; drain and rinse under cold water. Drain well and transfer to a large bowl.

3. While the quinoa is cooking, prepare the artichoke hearts according to package directions and then plunge into cold water to cool and stop the cooking process. When cooled, cut into quarters.

4. Stir the artichoke hearts into the quinoa along with the tomatoes and red onion. Toss with the salad dressing. At this point, the quinoa mixture can be covered and refrigerated until ready to serve. This allows the flavors to blend. However, if you'll be refrigerating the quinoa mixture for more than 1 hour, leave the cherry or grape tomatoes whole rather than halving them.

5. To prepare the salad, separate the endive leaves. Rinse, drain, and divide them between 4 plates. Top each with ¼ of the quinoa mixture. Sprinkle ¼ cup of the toasted pecans over the top of each salad.

Tasty Substitutions

Customize this dish to your liking by choosing your favorite dressing in place of Italian. A creamy dressing, such as a vegetarian Caesar or creamy dill, is a delicious option.

PC OLIVE AND PEPPER COUSCOUS SALAD

Kalamata olives are a type of black olive that will add a "meaty" flavor to this dish and are a recommended variety for your mixed olives.

Serves 4

1 cup couscous

2 cups water

½ cup mixed olives, pitted and chopped

1 red bell pepper, diced

1 clove garlic, minced

1 teaspoon olive oil

1 teaspoon red wine vinegar

1 teaspoon salt

1. Add the couscous and water to the pressure cooker.

2. Lock the lid into place; bring to high pressure and maintain for 2 minutes. Remove from heat and allow pressure to release naturally.

3. Fluff the couscous with a fork. Add all remaining ingredients and stir until combined. Add additional salt, to taste.

4. Refrigerate for 2 hours before serving.

GREEK SALAD TACOS

This fusion of Mediterranean and Central American fare is a wholly North American phenomenon.

Serves 4

8 (6") corn tortillas

8 ounces feta, cut into 8 slices

2 cups shredded romaine or iceberg lettuce

8 thin slices ripe tomato

24 pitted Kalamata olives

¼ cup extra-virgin olive oil

1 teaspoon dried oregano leaves, preferably Mexican

Salt and freshly ground black pepper to taste

1. Soften the tortillas over a stove burner (a few black spots are okay).

2. Place a slice of feta in the center of a tortilla, along with a pinch of lettuce, a slice of tomato, and 3 olives. Repeat with remaining tortillas. In a bowl, whisk together the olive oil, oregano, salt, and pepper. Drizzle the tacos with spoonfuls of dressing, and serve with remaining dressing on the side.

RICOTTA AND GOAT CHEESE CRESPELLE

Crespelle are Italian crepes—paper-thin pancakes filled with anything that inspires you. Here, I use a savory two-cheese filing, but you could just as well roll them with sautéed mushrooms, warm ratatouille, or a dessert filling like fresh peaches, bananas, and chocolate sauce, or berries and crème fraîche . . .

Serves 4

8 ounces ricotta, drained over cheesecloth or a fine strainer

4 ounces (one log) fresh goat cheese, softened at room temperature

¼ cup roughly chopped Italian parsley

1 egg, beaten

Salt and freshly ground black pepper to taste

8 Crepes (see Chapter 12)

Butter

2 cups Quick Tomato Sauce (see Chapter 2) or other tomato sauce

1. Heat oven to 350°F. Whisk together the ricotta, goat cheese, parsley, egg, salt, and pepper. Place 1½ tablespoons filling onto the bottom third of a crepe; roll away from yourself, forming a filled cylinder. Repeat with remaining crepes. Line them up in a buttered 9" × 13" baking dish.

2. Bake for 20 minutes, until tops are slightly crisp. Warm tomato sauce, and make ½-cup pools onto the centers of 4 plates. Place 2 crespelle onto each plate. Garnish with additional chopped parsley or basil leaves, if desired.

CHAPTER 4
HORS D'OEUVRES AND SNACKS

RECIPE LIST

RANCHEROS SALSA **152**
ARTICHOKE DIP **153**
CHEESE FONDUE **154**
CHINESE SOY SAUCE EGGS **155**
VEGAN SPINACH AND ARTICHOKE DIP **156**
POTATO PAKORAS (FRITTERS) **157**
CRUDITÉS WITH THREE DIPS **158**
CURRY DIP **159**
WATERCRESS DIP **160**
BABA GHANOUSH **161**
SLOW COOKER BABA GHANOUSH **162**
STUFFED GRAPE LEAVES **163**
CHICKPEA-PARSLEY-DILL DIP **164**
JALAPEÑO CHEESE DIP **165**
CHILI-CHEESE DIP **166**
BROCCOLI DIP **167**
FRIJOLE DIP **168**
CARAMELIZED ONION DIP **169**
MIXED VEGGIE DIP **170**
SUMMER FRUIT DIP **171**

SUN-DRIED TOMATO PESTO DIP **172**
EGGPLANT CAVIAR **173**
TEXAS CAVIAR **174**
FRIED GREEN TOMATO BRUSCHETTA **175**
GUACAMOLE **176**
HUMMUS **177**
ZESTY LEMON HUMMUS **178**
MANCHEGO-POTATO TACOS WITH PICKLED JALAPEÑOS **179**
MINI LENTIL-SCALLION PANCAKES WITH CUMIN CREAM **180**
MINI GOAT CHEESE PIZZAS **181**
SPICY BUFFALO STRIPS **182**
TERIYAKI "CHICKEN" STRIPS **183**
TOMATILLO SALSA **184**
ROASTED GARLIC SPREAD **185**
STEAMED SPRING ROLLS **186**
DHAL **187**
SWEET AND SOUR "MEATBALLS" **188**
BARBECUE "MEATBALLS" **189**
VEGETABLE GADO-GADO **190**

STUFFED MUSHROOMS **191**

SWEET FENNEL WITH LEMON
AND SHAVED PARMIGIANO **192**

SWEET POTATO AND ROSEMARY PIZZA **193**

TOMATO AND BLACK OLIVE BRUSCHETTA **194**

SPICY WHITE BEAN–CITRUS DIP **195**

BLACK BEAN DIP **196**

WILD MUSHROOM RAGOUT IN
PUFF PASTRY SHELLS **197**

SALSA FRESCA (PICO DE GALLO) **198**

CAJUN PEANUTS **198**

CINNAMON AND SUGAR PEANUTS **199**

BOILED PEANUTS **200**

SPICED PECANS **201**

CHEESE SOUFFLÉ **202**

ARTICHOKE AND CHEESE SQUARES **203**

TWO CHEESE STRATA **204**

FRICOS (CHEESE CRISPS) **205**

RANCHEROS SALSA

This salsa, the best part of Huevos Rancheros (see Chapter 1), freezes exceptionally well. Consider making a double batch and storing half for later.

Yields 4 cups

2 tablespoons olive oil

1 medium white onion, roughly chopped

1 red bell pepper, roughly chopped

1 green bell pepper, roughly chopped

4 plum tomatoes, seeded and roughly chopped

1 tablespoon chopped garlic (about 4 cloves)

1 (14-ounce) can diced tomatoes in tomato purée

1 (7-ounce) can tomatillos, drained

1 (7-ounce) can green chilies, rinsed, drained, and roughly chopped

1 teaspoon chipotle purée (optional)

1 jalapeño pepper, seeded, finely chopped

¼ cup chopped cilantro

1 tablespoon frozen orange juice concentrate

1 teaspoon ground cumin, toasted in a dry pan until fragrant

1 teaspoon dried oregano

¼ teaspoon ground cinnamon

Salt and pepper to taste

In a large, heavy-bottomed pot, heat the oil over medium-high heat until hot but not smoky. Add onion, peppers, and plum tomatoes; cook 5 minutes until onion is translucent. In a food processor, purée garlic, diced tomatoes, and tomatillos; add to onion mixture. Cook 5 minutes more. Add chilies, chipotle, jalapeño, and cilantro; stir in orange juice concentrate, cumin, oregano, cinnamon, salt, and pepper. Cook 5 minutes more.

ARTICHOKE DIP

Serve dip with crackers or bread.

Serves 8

2 (15-ounce) cans quartered artichoke hearts, drained and rinsed

1 red pepper, chopped finely

1 green pepper, chopped finely

3 cloves garlic, minced

2 cups mayonnaise

White pepper

1 pound grated Parmesan cheese

Preheat the oven to 325°F. Mix all ingredients except ¼ of the Parmesan cheese. Spread into a 9" × 9" baking dish or 1½-quart casserole dish, sprinkle remaining Parmesan over the top, and bake 45 minutes until golden brown.

CHEESE FONDUE

Like most families in the early seventies, mine had a fondue pot that would come out of the tippy-top closet once in a blue moon, bringing joy and mess to our dinner table. As a preteen, I'm not sure which I enjoyed more, dipping the veggies and bread cubes in the molten cheese or playing with the Sterno, but now I'm in love.

Serves 6

- 1 garlic clove, halved
- 2 cups dry white wine
- ¾ pound Emmentaler (Swiss) cheese, shredded (3 cups)
- ¾ pound Gruyère cheese, shredded (3 cups)
- 1 tablespoon cornstarch
- 2 tablespoons kirsch
- Assorted steamed vegetables such as carrot sticks, broccoli, cauliflower, and green beans
- Cubes of French bread

1. Rub the inside of a medium saucepot with the cut side of the garlic. Discard the clove, or leave it in. Add the wine and cook over medium heat until it simmers. Whisk in the cheese in small handfuls, making sure that the last addition has completely melted before adding the next. Combine the cornstarch and kirsch into a paste; whisk into cheese mixture. Simmer the fondue gently for 5–7 minutes to allow the cornstarch to thicken.

2. Transfer the cheese mixture to a fondue pot, and set a low flame under it—just enough to keep it at the border of simmering. Assemble a platter with the vegetables and bread cubes, and set the table with either long fondue forks or long wooden skewers.

CHINESE SOY SAUCE EGGS

These strikingly dark, double-cooked spiced eggs are an excellent first course with a salad of baby Asian greens dressed with a few drops of rice vinegar and sesame oil.

Serves 4

8 large eggs

½ cup soy sauce

2 tablespoons sugar

2 tablespoons Chinese 5-spice powder (available in supermarkets)

1 tablespoon chopped garlic

Hard-boil the eggs, about 10 minutes; run them under cold water, and peel them. Bring 4 cups water to a boil in a medium saucepan. Add the soy sauce and sugar. Simmer 5 minutes; add the 5-spice, garlic, and peeled eggs. Cover; simmer slowly for at least an hour, until the soy sauce's color has penetrated well into the eggs, all the way to the yolk. Cool in the cooking liquid, and serve warm or room temperature.

SC VEGAN SPINACH AND ARTICHOKE DIP

Serve with toasted pita points or slices of warm baguette.

Yields 4 cups

- 1 (15-ounce) can artichokes, drained and chopped
- 2 cups water
- 1 teaspoon lemon juice
- 1 tablespoon vegan margarine, such as Earth Balance
- 1 cup thawed frozen spinach, chopped
- 8 ounces vegan cream cheese, such as Tofutti Better Than Cream Cheese
- 16 ounces vegan sour cream, such as Tofutti Sour Supreme
- ⅓ cup vegan Parmesan cheese
- ¼ teaspoon garlic powder
- ¼ teaspoon salt

In a 4-quart slow cooker, add all ingredients. Cover and cook over low heat for 1 hour. Serve warm.

Serving Options

This recipe calls for serving the dip warm, but chilling the dip and serving cool is also delicious. After cooking, let the dip cool to room temperature and store in the refrigerator in an airtight container. Let cool for at least 3 hours before serving.

POTATO PAKORAS (FRITTERS)

Serve these fritters immediately with chutney for dipping.

Serves 8

1¼ cups sifted chickpea flour

2 teaspoons vegetable oil

1½ teaspoons ground cumin

½ teaspoon cayenne or paprika

¼ teaspoon turmeric

2½ teaspoons salt

Approximately ½ cup cold water

1 large or 2 medium baking potatoes (about 8 ounces), peeled, then sliced into ⅛" pieces

Oil for frying

1. In a food processor or blender, pulse flour, oil, cumin, cayenne or paprika, turmeric, and salt 3 or 4 times until fluffy. With blade spinning, gradually add water, processing for 2–3 minutes until smooth. Adjust consistency by adding water until the mixture is slightly thicker than the consistency of heavy cream. Cover and set aside for 10 minutes.

2. Heat fry oil to 350°F. Dip potato slices into batter one by one, and slip them into the fry oil in batches of 6 or 7. Fry 4–5 minutes each side, until golden brown and cooked through.

CRUDITÉS WITH THREE DIPS

Veggies with dip is an essential at virtually any type of party—from the big football game to a family holiday bash to a classy affair.

Serves 8

About 6 cups of assorted vegetables, cut into bite-size pieces, such as carrot sticks, celery sticks, various colored bell peppers, zucchini and yellow squash, radishes, blanched broccoli florets, cauliflower florets, and green beans, fennel, cooked beets, etc.

Assorted black and green olives

Rosemary or thyme sprigs for garnish

Three dressings or dips, such as the ones in this chapter

Arrange vegetables attractively on a serving platter or in a basket, placing different colors beside one another. Garnish with olives and herb sprigs. Serve with dips or drizzled with any dressing.

CURRY DIP

Serve this dip with toasted bread or your favorite cracker!

Yields 2½ cups

1 teaspoon olive oil

½ cup finely chopped onion

½ medium jalapeño pepper, finely chopped (about 1 teaspoon)

2 teaspoons finely chopped red bell pepper

1 teaspoon Madras curry powder

1 teaspoon ground cumin

½ teaspoon ground coriander

½ teaspoon ground turmeric

Pinch of cayenne pepper

¼ teaspoon salt

1 tablespoon very fresh, soft raisins (or any raisins, soaked overnight in ½ cup water, drained)

1½ cups soy mayo

1 tablespoon chopped fresh cilantro

A few drops fresh lemon juice

Salt and pepper to taste

1. Put the oil in a small skillet over medium heat. Add onions, jalapeño, and red pepper; cook stirring occasionally until onion is translucent, about 5 minutes. Add curry powder, cumin, coriander, turmeric, cayenne, and salt. Cook a minute more, until spices are very fragrant. Add raisins and about 1 tablespoon of water. Remove from heat.

2. Transfer to a food processor. Chop on high speed for 30 seconds; scrape down sides of bowl with a rubber spatula. Add soy mayo and cilantro; process 30 seconds more, until smooth and even. Adjust seasonings with lemon, salt, and pepper.

WATERCRESS DIP

This dip is great served with vegetables!

Yields 1½ cups

1 bunch watercress, stems trimmed by 1", roughly chopped

1 cup soy mayo

¼ teaspoon salt

¼ teaspoon black pepper

In a food processor, purée watercress until very fine, about 1 minute. Add soy mayo; pulse to combine. Season with salt and pepper.

BABA GHANOUSH

Serve this Baba Ghanoush with wedges of warm pita bread.

Serves 4

2 cloves garlic, peeled

1 whole eggplant, roasted 1 hour in a 400°F oven, cooled, pulp scooped out

1 tablespoon tahini

1½ teaspoons kosher salt

2–3 teaspoons toasted cumin powder

Juice of 2 lemons

¼ cup extra-virgin olive oil, plus a little extra for garnish

Freshly ground black pepper

Paprika and chopped parsley for garnish (optional)

Pita bread for dipping

1. In a food processor, chop the garlic until it sticks to the walls of the processor bowl. Add eggplant pulp, tahini, salt, cumin, and half of the lemon juice. Process until smooth, gradually drizzling in the olive oil. Season to taste with black pepper, additional salt, and lemon if necessary.

2. Spread onto plates and garnish with a drizzle of extra-virgin olive oil, a few drops of lemon, a dusting of paprika, and some chopped parsley, if using. Serve with wedges of warm pita bread.

SLOW COOKER BABA GHANOUSH

Serve with toasted pita chips or as a vegetable dip.

Yields 1½ cups

1 tablespoon olive oil

1 large eggplant, peeled and diced

4 cloves garlic, peeled and minced

½ cup water

3 tablespoons fresh parsley

½ teaspoon salt

2 tablespoons fresh lemon juice

2 tablespoons tahini

1 tablespoon extra-virgin olive oil

1. In a 4-quart slow cooker, add the olive oil, eggplant, garlic, and water and stir until coated. Cover and cook on high heat for 4 hours.

2. Strain the cooked eggplant and garlic and add to a food processor or blender along with the parsley, salt, lemon juice, and tahini. Pulse to process.

3. Scrape down the side of the food processor or blender container if necessary. Add the extra-virgin olive oil and process until smooth.

PC STUFFED GRAPE LEAVES

A medium (about 5-ounce) lemon will yield about 2 teaspoons of lemon zest and 2–3 tablespoons of juice.

Serves 16

⅓ cup olive oil

4 scallions, minced

⅓ cup fresh mint, minced

⅓ cup fresh parsley, minced

3 cloves garlic, peeled and minced

1 cup long-grain white rice

2 cups vegetable broth

1 teaspoon salt

¼ teaspoon freshly ground black pepper

½ teaspoon lemon zest, grated

1 (16-ounce) jar grape leaves

2 cups water

½ cup fresh lemon juice

1. Bring the oil to temperature in the pressure cooker over medium-high heat. Add the scallions, mint, and parsley; sauté for 2 minutes or until the scallions are soft. Add the garlic and sauté for an additional 30 seconds. Add the rice and stir-fry in the sautéed vegetables and herbs for 1 minute. Add the broth, salt, pepper, and lemon zest; stir to mix. Lock the lid into place. Bring to high pressure; maintain pressure for 8 minutes.

2. Quick-release the pressure. Remove lid and transfer the rice mixture to a bowl.

3. Drain the grape leaves. Rinse them thoroughly in warm water and then arrange them rib-side up on a work surface. Trim away any thick ribs. Spoon about 2 teaspoons of the rice mixture on each grape leaf; fold the sides of each leaf over the filling and then roll it from the bottom to the top. Repeat with each leaf. Pour the water into the pressure cooker. Place a steamer basket in the pressure cooker and arrange the stuffed grape leaves seam-side down in the basket. Pour the lemon juice over the stuffed grape leaves and then press heavy plastic wrap down around them.

4. Lock the lid into place. Bring to high pressure; maintain pressure for 10 minutes.

5. Quick-release the pressure. Remove the lid. Lift the steamer basket out of the pressure cooker and, leaving the plastic in place, let the stuffed grape leaves rest for 5 minutes. Serve hot or cold.

Dolmades

Stuffed grape leaves are often referred to as dolmades. Some versions call for spiced ground lamb or other ground meat to be added to the filling, but you can make them vegetarian with a rice and herb filling.

PC CHICKPEA-PARSLEY-DILL DIP

Try any combination of fresh herbs, such as basil, thyme, or mint, in this versatile dip.

Yields 2 cups

1 cup dried chickpeas

8 cups water

3 tablespoons olive oil

2 garlic cloves, minced

⅛ cup fresh parsley

⅛ cup fresh dill

1 tablespoon fresh lemon juice

2 tablespoons water

¾ teaspoon salt

1. Add the chickpeas and 4 cups water to the pressure cooker. Lock the lid into place; bring to high pressure for 1 minute. Remove from heat and quick-release the pressure.

2. Drain the water, rinse the chickpeas, and add to the pressure cooker again with the remaining 4 cups of water. Let soak for 1 hour.

3. Add 1 tablespoon olive oil. Lock the lid into place; bring to high pressure and maintain for 20 minutes. Remove from heat and allow pressure to release naturally. Drain chickpeas and water.

4. Add the drained, cooked chickpeas, garlic, parsley, dill, lemon juice, and water to a food processor or blender. Blend for about 30 seconds.

5. With the lid still in place, slowly add the remaining oil while still blending, then add the salt.

PC JALAPEÑO CHEESE DIP

To eliminate the spice, just leave the pickled jalapeños out of this recipe.

Serves 12

- 2 tablespoons butter or vegan margarine
- 2 tablespoons flour
- 1 cup milk or vegan soymilk
- 8 ounces shredded Cheddar cheese or vegan Cheddar such as Daiya Cheddar Style Shreds
- 8 ounces shredded Colby cheese or more vegan Cheddar
- ½ cup canned tomatoes
- ½ cup pickled jalapeños
- 2 tablespoons lemon juice
- Salt and pepper, to taste

1. In the pressure cooker, soften butter or margarine over medium-high heat and gradually add flour until you have a paste. Add milk or soymilk and stir until it has thickened and there are no lumps. Bring the mixture to a boil.

2. Add the cheeses and stir until smooth. Add the tomatoes and jalapeños and secure the lid on the pressure cooker. Cook on medium until the pressure indicator rises. Lower heat and cook for 3 minutes. Allow the pressure to release and remove the lid. Add the lemon juice, salt, and pepper.

SC CHILI-CHEESE DIP

The perfect accompaniment for this dip is salty corn tortilla chips.

Serves 12

1 (15-ounce) can vegetarian chili

¼ cup diced onions

½ cup diced tomatoes

1 (8-ounce) package cream cheese or vegan cream cheese

1 cup Cheddar cheese or vegan Cheddar

1 teaspoon garlic powder

1. In a 4-quart slow cooker, place all ingredients.
2. Stir gently; cover, and heat on low for 1 hour.

Vegetarian Chili

Most major grocery stores sell canned vegetarian chili. One of the easiest to find is Hormel Vegetarian Chili with Beans, which contains textured vegetable protein instead of meat.

SC BROCCOLI DIP

Serve this vegetable-rich creamy dip with crisp raw vegetables and pumpernickel pretzels.

Serves 15

4 cups steamed broccoli florets

1 cup fresh baby spinach

1 shallot

1 jalapeño, stem and seeds removed

1 tablespoon vegan Worcestershire sauce

½ tablespoon nonpareil capers

8 ounces cream cheese or vegan cream cheese

8 ounces sour cream or vegan sour cream

¼ teaspoon freshly ground black pepper

2 tablespoons lemon juice

1. In a food processor, place the broccoli, spinach, shallot, jalapeño, Worcestershire sauce, and capers. Pulse until the mixture is mostly smooth.

2. Add the cream cheese, sour cream, pepper, and lemon juice. Pulse until smooth.

3. Pour into a 1½- or 2-quart slow cooker. Cover and cook on low for 1 hour.

How to Steam Vegetables
Bring about 1" of water to boil in a heavy-bottomed pot. Add the vegetables and cook until fork-tender but not soft. Drain and season.

SC FRIJOLE DIP

For best results, serve this dip immediately after cooking or reheat if it cools.

Serves 12

2 (15-ounce) cans pinto beans, drained

1½ cups water

1 tablespoon olive oil

1 small onion, peeled and diced

3 cloves garlic, peeled and minced

1 cup diced tomatoes

1 teaspoon chipotle powder

½ teaspoon cumin

¼ cup fresh cilantro, finely chopped

Salt, to taste

1 cup Monterey jack cheese, grated, or vegan Monterey jack cheese

1. In a 4-quart slow cooker, add the beans, water, olive oil, onion, and garlic. Cover and cook over low heat for 1 hour.

2. Mash the beans until about ½ are smooth and ½ are still chunky.

3. Add all remaining ingredients; stir well, and cook for an additional 30 minutes.

SC CARAMELIZED ONION DIP

Caramelized onions give this dip an amazing depth of flavor.

Yields 1 quart (32 servings)

⅔ cup Slow Cooker Caramelized Onions (Chapter 10)
8 ounces reduced-fat cream cheese
8 ounces reduced-fat sour cream
1 tablespoon vegan Worcestershire sauce
¼ teaspoon white pepper
⅛ teaspoon flour

1. Place all ingredients into a 1½- to 2-quart slow cooker.
2. Heat on low for 2 hours. Whisk before serving.

SC MIXED VEGGIE DIP

Try this vegetable-rich dip with pita chips or baked potato chips.

Serves 20

8 ounces low-fat cream cheese, room temperature
½ cup reduced-fat sour cream
1 teaspoon low-fat mayonnaise
½ teaspoon white pepper
½ teaspoon garlic powder
½ teaspoon onion powder
½ teaspoon vegan Worcestershire sauce
1 carrot, minced
1 stalk celery, minced
3 tablespoons fresh spinach, minced
¼ cup broccoli, minced

1. In a 2-quart slow cooker, thoroughly mix all ingredients.
2. Cook on low for 2 hours. Stir before serving.

SC SUMMER FRUIT DIP

Kiwis, strawberries, star fruit, bananas, and citrus are all excellent dipping choices for this fruity dip, which is also delicious served cold.

Serves 20

½ cup raspberry purée

8 ounces reduced-fat cream cheese or vegan cream cheese, room temperature

1 tablespoon sugar

¾ cup reduced-fat sour cream or vegan sour cream

1 teaspoon vanilla

1. In a small bowl, whisk together all ingredients.

2. Pour into a 2-quart slow cooker; cook on low for 1 hour. Stir before serving.

SC SUN-DRIED TOMATO PESTO DIP

Tart, rich sun-dried tomatoes are the perfect partner for a fresh-tasting pesto in this creamy dip.

Serves 20

2 cloves garlic

1 tablespoon reduced-fat mayonnaise or Vegenaise

¾ ounce fresh basil

1 teaspoon toasted pine nuts

¼ teaspoon white pepper

¼ cup dry (not oil-packed) sun-dried tomatoes, julienne cut

8 ounces reduced-fat cream cheese or vegan cream cheese, room temperature

1. In a food processor, place the garlic, mayonnaise or Vegenaise, basil, pine nuts, and pepper. Pulse until a fairly smooth paste forms.

2. Add the sun-dried tomatoes and pulse 4–5 times.

3. Add the cream cheese and pulse until smooth.

4. Scrape into a 2-quart slow cooker. Cook on low for 1 hour. Stir before serving.

How to Toast Pine Nuts
Preheat the oven to 350°F. Place the pine nuts on a cookie sheet or cake pan. Roast for 5–8 minutes in the oven. Pine nuts will be slightly browned and fragrant when fully toasted. Cool before using.

EGGPLANT CAVIAR

Serve this Eggplant Caviar with crackers or sliced French bread.

Serves 4

1 large eggplant
2 tablespoons olive oil
1 large onion, finely chopped
3 cloves garlic, finely chopped
1 tablespoon tomato paste
Salt and pepper to taste
Crackers or French bread

1. Heat oven to 400°F. Place eggplant in a baking dish and roast on middle rack of the oven until very well done, about 1 hour; cool. Cut the eggplant in half and scoop out the soft pulp with a serving spoon. Place on a cutting board and chop thoroughly, until it has the consistency of oatmeal.

2. Heat the olive oil in a large skillet over medium heat for 1 minute. Add onion; cook until very soft, but not brown, about 10 minutes; add garlic and cook 1 minute more. Stir in tomato paste; cook 1 minute.

3. Add chopped eggplant and cook until mixture is thickened. An indentation should remain when a spoon is depressed into the mixture. Season to taste. Serve with crackers or sliced French bread.

PC TEXAS CAVIAR

Prepare this dip up to 2 days in advance and store in a covered container in the refrigerator.

Yields 5 cups

1 cup dried black-eyed peas
8 cups water
1 pound cooked corn kernels
½ onion, diced
½ bell pepper, diced
1 pickled jalapeño, finely chopped
1 medium tomato, diced
2 tablespoons fresh cilantro
¼ cup red wine vinegar
2 tablespoons olive oil
1 teaspoon salt
½ teaspoon ground black pepper
½ teaspoon ground cumin

1. Rinse and soak the black-eyed peas in 4 cups of water for 1 hour. Drain and rinse.
2. Add the black-eyed peas and remaining 4 cups of water to the pressure cooker. Lock the lid into place; bring to high pressure and maintain for 11 minutes. Remove from heat and allow pressure to release naturally.
3. Pour the drained black-eyed peas into a large mixing bowl; add all remaining ingredients and stir until combined. Refrigerate 1–2 hours before serving.

FRIED GREEN TOMATO BRUSCHETTA

Canapés on grilled bread, called "bruschetta," surprise many visitors to restaurants in Italy, when they appear as complimentary hors d'oeuvres.

Serves 4

4 medium green tomatoes, sliced ½" thick

Flour, eggs, and bread crumbs for dredging

Oil for frying (preferably olive oil)

1 tablespoon balsamic vinegar

¼ cup chopped fresh basil leaves (plus a few whole leaves for garnish)

12 green olives with pimento, halved lengthwise

¼ cup extra-virgin olive oil

1 loaf crusty country bread, sliced 1" thick

1. Dredge tomato slices in flour, egg, and bread crumbs, shaking off excess after each dip, and fry them in oil at low heat (about 325°F) until golden and mostly tender (a little underdone is good). Place the still-hot tomatoes flat on a cutting board and dice them into ½" pieces.

2. In a large mixing bowl, gently toss the diced tomatoes with the vinegar, basil, and olives. Set aside.

3. Brush the bread slices with extra-virgin oil, and grill or oven-toast (400°F) them until lightly browned. This can also be done under the broiler. Top each of 6 slices with tomato mixture, cut each in half, and serve garnished with a small basil sprig.

GUACAMOLE

Serve this dip with tortilla chips, or as an accompaniment to spicy food.

Serves 8

2 cloves garlic, chopped

¼ cup chopped red onion

1 small jalapeño pepper, finely chopped

4 ripe Hass avocados, halved, pitted, and scooped from the skin

2 tablespoons lime juice

½ teaspoon salt

Freshly ground black pepper to taste

¼ cup chopped cilantro

1 plum tomato, seeded and chopped (optional)

With a mortar and pestle, or in a mixing bowl with a fork, mash together the garlic, onion, and jalapeño. Add the avocado and mash until it forms a chunky paste. Add lime juice, salt, pepper, and cilantro, and stir to combine. Garnish with chopped tomato if desired.

HUMMUS

Hummus is delicious when served with wedges of warm pita bread!

Yields 2 cups

1 cup dried garbanzos (chickpeas), soaked overnight if desired, or 1 (16-ounce) can

2 cloves garlic, peeled

3 tablespoons tahini

½ teaspoon kosher salt

2–3 teaspoons toasted cumin powder

Juice of 1 lemon, divided in half

¼ cup extra-virgin olive oil, plus a little extra for garnish

Freshly ground black pepper

Paprika and chopped parsley for garnish (optional)

Pita bread for dipping

1. If using dried chickpeas, cook them in lightly salted water until very, very tender. If using canned chickpeas, drain and rinse them. In a food processor, chop the garlic until it sticks to the sides of the bowl. Add chickpeas, tahini, salt, cumin, and half of the lemon juice. Process until smooth, gradually drizzling in the olive oil. Add up to ¼ cup cold water to achieve a softer hummus if desired. Season to taste with black pepper, and additional salt and lemon to taste.

2. Spread onto plates and garnish with a drizzle of extra-virgin olive oil, a few drops of lemon, a dusting of paprika, and some chopped parsley. Serve with wedges of warm pita bread.

Kosher Salt: The Chefs' Seasoning

Chefs know that judicious use of salt is essential to bring certain flavors to life. Almost all professional chefs, except those creating dishes for people with specific medical conditions, use some amount of salt in their cooking. In finer restaurants, the salt of choice in the kitchen is seldom the fine-powdered table salt most home cooks are familiar with. Instead, they use either complex-tasting crystal sea salt or coarse, flaky white salt known as "kosher" salt. It is so-named because it is the type used for certain processes involved in the Jewish dietary laws, or *kashruth*. It is available at most supermarkets.

SC ZESTY LEMON HUMMUS

Serve this Middle Eastern spread with pita, vegetables, or falafel.

Serves 20

1 pound dried chickpeas

Water, as needed

3 tablespoons tahini

4 tablespoons lemon juice

Zest of 1 lemon

3 cloves garlic

¼ teaspoon salt

1. In a 4-quart slow cooker, place the chickpeas and cover with water. Soak overnight, drain, and rinse. The next day, cook on low for 8 hours. Drain, reserving the liquid.

2. In a food processor, place the chickpeas, tahini, lemon juice, lemon zest, garlic, and salt. Pulse until smooth, adding the reserved liquid as needed to achieve the desired texture.

MANCHEGO-POTATO TACOS WITH PICKLED JALAPEÑOS

Serve these tacos with salsa to boost up the taste!

Serves 8

1 cup leftover mashed potatoes, or instant mashed potatoes, made firm

8 soft corn tortillas

¼ pound Spanish Manchego cheese or sharp Cheddar, cut into 16 small sticks

16 slices pickled jalapeño pepper (available in Mexican sections and ethnic specialty stores)

4 tablespoons unsalted butter

1. Spoon 1 tablespoon of mashed potato into the center of each tortilla. Flatten out the potatoes, leaving a 1" border. Lay 2 pieces of Manchego and 2 pieces pickled jalapeño onto each tortilla, and fold closed into a half-moon shape.

2. In a skillet over medium heat, melt half of the butter. Gently lay 4 of the tacos into the pan, and cook until nicely browned, about 3–4 minutes on each side. Drain on paper towels. Repeat with remaining tacos. Snip tacos in half before serving with salsa.

MINI LENTIL-SCALLION PANCAKES WITH CUMIN CREAM

These delectable crunchy cakes may be easier to make into round shapes with more egg and flour, but they'll be softer—you decide.

Serves 8

1 cup brown lentils, boiled until soft but not broken

3 scallions, chopped fine

1 tablespoon curry powder, toasted in a dry pan until fragrant

Pinch of cayenne

1 teaspoon salt

¼ cup chopped cilantro or parsley

1 egg, beaten

1 tablespoon milk or water

1 tablespoon all-purpose flour

3 tablespoons olive oil for frying

1 cup sour cream

2 teaspoons cumin seeds, toasted in a dry pan, then ground (or 2 teaspoons ground cumin, toasted in a dry pan until fragrant)

1. Gently combine lentils, scallions, curry, cayenne, salt, and cilantro or parsley in a mixing bowl. Mix in the beaten egg and milk or water with your hands, and dust with enough flour to form a cohesive batter.

2. Heat oil in a large nonstick skillet until hot, but not smoky. A bit of the batter should sizzle when placed in the oil. Drop teaspoonfuls of batter into the pan; flatten them out and shape them into round cakes with the back of the spoon. Some lentils may fall away, but the cakes will stick together once they're cooked. Leave at least 1" of space between cakes. Fry 2–3 minutes per side, until lightly browned and crisp. Drain on paper towels.

3. Whisk together the sour cream and cumin. Arrange the lentil cakes on a serving platter, and top each with a dollop of cumin cream.

MINI GOAT CHEESE PIZZAS

To serve, warm again in the oven for 1 minute, until the goat cheese attains a slight shimmer; serve hot.

Serves 8

1 package frozen puff pastry dough (17 ounces—2 sheets), thawed

½ cup marinara sauce

1 (4-ounce) package fresh goat cheese

1 tablespoon chopped fresh thyme or parsley

1. Heat oven to 400°F. Using a 1"-diameter cookie cutter, or the top of a small bottle, cut 24 disks of puff pastry; line onto an ungreased baking sheet. Stack another, matching pan atop the disks, and bake until golden brown, about 15 minutes. The second pan will keep the disks from rising too high.

2. Make a slight indentation on each disk with the tip of a small knife. Spoon in a bit of marinara sauce, crumble on a pinch of goat cheese, and sprinkle with chopped thyme or parsley.

SPICY BUFFALO STRIPS

Most bottled buffalo wing sauces contain butter, so if you're vegan, check the label.

Serves 6

⅓ cup butter or vegan margarine

⅓ cup hot sauce

1 tablespoon vinegar

1 teaspoon garlic powder

2 (7-ounce) packages Gardein Chick'n Strips

1. Place the butter or margarine in a small bowl and microwave for 30 seconds, or until melted.
2. Add the hot sauce, vinegar, and garlic powder and stir well.
3. In a 4-quart slow cooker, add the prepared hot sauce and Chick'n Strips and cook over low heat for 1 hour.

Serving Strips

Faux buffalo chicken strips can be added to sandwiches or salads, but if you'd like to serve them as an appetizer or snack, place in a small basket lined with parchment paper and add sides of celery sticks, carrot sticks, and vegan ranch dressing.

SC TERIYAKI "CHICKEN" STRIPS

Any brand of vegan or vegetarian chicken strips will work in this recipe.

Serves 6

2 (7-ounce) packages Gardein Chick'n Strips

5–6 ounces teriyaki sauce

1 teaspoon hot sauce

In a 4-quart slow cooker, combine all ingredients and cook over low heat for 1 hour.

PC TOMATILLO SALSA

Serve with corn tortilla chips or as an accompaniment to Black Bean Dip (see recipe in this chapter).

Serves 8

1 pound tomatillos, paper removed

Water, as needed

2 jalapeños, stemmed, seeded, and chopped

½ onion, chopped

½ cup cold water

½ cup chopped cilantro

2 teaspoons salt

1. Cut the tomatillos in half and then place in the pressure cooker. Add enough water to cover the tomatillos.
2. Lock the lid into place; bring to high pressure and maintain for 2 minutes. Remove from heat and allow pressure to release naturally.
3. Add the drained, cooked tomatillos, jalapeños, onion, and cold water to a food processor or blender. Blend until well combined. Add the cilantro and salt and pulse until combined. Chill the salsa before serving.

Tomatillo
Tomatillo is the small yellowish or green fruit of a Mexican groundcherry. Surprisingly, it is not a variety of tomato.

PC ROASTED GARLIC SPREAD

Garlic is known for being pungent, but a lesser-known quality is that it may be able to help prevent heart disease and cancer.

Yields ½ cup

2 whole heads garlic

1 cup water

½ cup butter, softened, or vegan margarine such as Earth Balance

2 tablespoons fresh basil

2 tablespoons fresh oregano

½ teaspoon salt

1. Cut the tops off each head of garlic. Pour water into the pressure cooker, then add the steamer basket. Add the garlic. Lock the lid into place; bring to high pressure and maintain for 2 minutes. Remove from heat and allow pressure to quick-release.

2. Once the garlic has cooled, peel away the paper until you are left with only the cloves. In a small bowl, mash the cloves, then add the butter or margarine, basil, oregano, and salt. Refrigerate for 1 hour before serving.

PC STEAMED SPRING ROLLS

Serve with Spicy Peanut Sauce (see Chapter 2) or a sweet and sour dipping sauce.

Serves 12

1 cup cabbage, shredded

1 cup bamboo shoots, sliced

¼ cup cilantro, chopped

2 cloves garlic, minced

5 shiitake mushrooms, sliced

2 carrots, grated

1 teaspoon soy sauce

1 teaspoon rice wine vinegar

12 spring roll wrappers

2 cups water

1. Combine the cabbage, bamboo shoots, cilantro, garlic, mushrooms, carrots, soy sauce, and rice wine vinegar in a medium bowl. Stir until just combined.

2. Place the spring roll wrappers on a flat surface.

3. Top each wrapper with an equal amount of the cabbage mixture, making a row down the center. Roll up the wrappers, tuck in the ends, and place side by side in the pressure cooker steamer basket.

4. Add water to the pressure cooker and lower in the steamer basket.

5. Lock the lid into place. Bring to high pressure; maintain pressure for 3 minutes. Quick-release the pressure, then remove the lid.

Spring Roll Wrappers

Spring roll wrappers are also known as rice paper because they are made from rice flour rolled into thin, translucent sheets. Before using you must briefly soak the papers in water so they become soft and pliable for rolling up the spring roll filling.

PC DHAL

Serve spread on toasted flatbread or as a vegetable dip.

Yields 2 cups

1 tablespoon olive oil

1 teaspoon unsalted butter or vegan margarine

1 small onion, peeled and diced

2 teaspoons fresh ginger, grated

1 serrano chili pepper, seeded and finely diced

1 clove garlic, peeled and minced

½ teaspoon garam masala

¼ teaspoon ground turmeric

½ teaspoon dry mustard

1 cup dried yellow split peas

2 cups water

¼ cup plain yogurt or sour cream or soy sour cream, such as Tofutti Sour Supreme

2 tablespoons fresh cilantro, minced

1. Add the oil and butter or margarine to the pressure cooker and bring to temperature over medium heat. Add the onion, ginger, and chili pepper; sauté for 3 minutes or until soft. Add the garlic, garam masala, turmeric, and dry mustard; sauté for an additional minute. Stir in the split peas. Pour in the water.

2. Lock on the lid. Bring the pressure cooker to high pressure; maintain for 8 minutes. Remove from heat and allow pressure to release naturally. Transfer the cooked split-pea mixture to a bowl; stir until cooled.

3. Add the yogurt or sour cream; whisk until smooth. Stir in the cilantro.

PC SWEET AND SOUR "MEATBALLS"

Worcestershire sauce typically contains anchovies, but some grocery store brands omit this ingredient, making it vegetarian.

Yields 12 "meatballs"

½ cup white sugar

2 tablespoons pineapple juice

⅓ cup white vinegar

⅔ cup water

2 tablespoons soy sauce

2 tablespoons vegetarian Worcestershire sauce

1 tablespoon ketchup

2 tablespoons cornstarch

1 pound vegetarian ground beef, such as Gimme Lean Beef

½ onion, diced

1 clove garlic, minced

½ cup panko bread crumbs

1. In the pressure cooker, bring the sugar, pineapple juice, vinegar, water, soy sauce, Worcestershire sauce, ketchup, and cornstarch to a boil over high heat. Stir continuously until the mixture has thickened, then remove from heat.

2. In a large mixing bowl, combine the vegetarian ground beef, onion, garlic, and bread crumbs, and mix until well combined. (Using your hands is the easiest method.)

3. Roll the "beef" mixture into 12 meatballs; add them to the sauce in the pressure cooker.

4. Lock the lid into place. Bring to high pressure; maintain pressure for 5 minutes. Quick-release the pressure, then remove the lid. Serve warm.

SC BARBECUE "MEATBALLS"

Enjoy these "meatballs" as a two-bite snack or use them as the filling in a hearty sub.

Yields 12 "meatballs"

1 pound vegetarian ground beef, such as Gimme Lean Beef

½ onion, diced

1 clove garlic, minced

½ cup panko bread crumbs

1 (18-ounce) bottle barbecue sauce

1. In a large mixing bowl, combine the vegetarian ground beef, onion, garlic, and bread crumbs, and mix until well combined. (Using your hands is the easiest method.) Roll the "beef" mixture into 12 meatballs.

2. To a 4-quart slow cooker, add the "meatballs."

3. Cover with barbecue sauce. Cover and cook over high heat for 1 hour.

VEGETABLE GADO-GADO

This appetizer of vegetables with a spicy peanut sauce is Indonesian in origin.

Serves 8

16 each: 2-bite carrot sticks, broccoli florets, trimmed green beans, batons of yellow bell pepper and/or yellow summer squash, and assorted other vegetables

½ cup smooth peanut butter

¼ cup honey

¼ teaspoon salt

⅛ teaspoon cayenne pepper

1 tablespoon lime juice

¾ cup (6 ounces) coconut milk

1. Blanch all the vegetables quickly in lightly salted boiling water; plunge immediately into ice-cold water to stop the cooking process. Drain and arrange in an attractive pattern on a serving platter.

2. Combine peanut butter, honey, salt, cayenne, and lemon juice in a food processor or mixing bowl; pulse or whisk together until smooth. Gradually work in coconut milk, until a saucy consistency is reached. Adjust consistency further, if desired, with hot water. Serve as a dipping sauce with blanched vegetables.

STUFFED MUSHROOMS

These mushrooms are best when served hot or warm. If you make them in advance be sure to heat them up before serving.

Serves 6

- 1 pound mushrooms (caps approximately 1½" across)
- 3 tablespoons butter
- ½ cup onion, finely chopped
- ¾ cup bread crumbs
- ½ teaspoon salt
- Freshly ground black pepper to taste
- 1 teaspoon dried thyme
- ¼ cup half-and-half
- ¼ cup grated Parmesan cheese
- 2 tablespoons fresh parsley, chopped

1. Turn on oven broiler. Clean the mushrooms and gently pull the stem from each cap, setting the caps aside. Chop the mushroom stems and set aside. Heat butter in a skillet over medium heat. Add onion and cook for 2 minutes, until translucent. Add mushroom stems, and cook 2–3 minutes more. Stir in bread crumbs, salt, pepper, and thyme; cook 1 minute more. Remove from heat and stir in cream and grated cheese.

2. Using a small spoon, fill each mushroom cap with the mushroom mixture. Place the filled mushrooms on a baking sheet and put under the preheated oven broiler for 5–7 minutes, until the tops are browned and the caps have softened and become juicy. Sprinkle the tops with chopped parsley and serve hot or warm.

SWEET FENNEL WITH LEMON AND SHAVED PARMIGIANO

This simple but delicious snack typifies the essence of Italian cuisine: Use the best ingredients without overcomplicating them.

Serves 4

2 bulbs fresh fennel

½ fresh lemon

1 wedge (at least 4" long) Parmigiano-Reggiano cheese or Asiago cheese

1 tablespoon very high quality extra-virgin olive oil

Pinch of salt

1. Trim the stems and hair-like fronds from the fennel tops. Break the bulbs apart layer by layer, using your hands, to make long, bite-size pieces. Discard the core. Arrange the pieces pyramid-shape onto a small, attractive serving plate.

2. Squeeze the lemon over the fennel. Using a peeler, shave curls of cheese over the fennel, allowing them to fall where they may; make about 10 curls. Drizzle the olive oil over the plate, and sprinkle with salt. Serve at room temperature.

SWEET POTATO AND ROSEMARY PIZZA

Simple 4- or 5-ingredient pizzas like this one perfume every street corner in some parts of Rome. I based this variation on a savory potato and rosemary pie I fell in love with near the Pantheon, one of Rome's ancient architectural wonders.

Serves 6

1 can store-bought pizza crust, or pizza dough of your choice

1½ tablespoons extra-virgin olive oil

1 large sweet potato, peeled

2 sprigs fresh rosemary, or 1 teaspoon dried rosemary leaves

Salt and freshly ground black pepper

1. Preheat oven to 400°F. Spread dough to ¼" thickness on a doubled-up, lightly greased sheet pan. Brush on a light coating of olive oil.

2. Shred the sweet potato into a ¼"-thick layer over the pizza crust using the large-holed side of a box grater. Distribute rosemary leaves evenly on top of potato. Sprinkle remaining olive oil over the pizza, and season it with salt and pepper. Bake 20–25 minutes, until potato is cooked through and begins to brown.

TOMATO AND BLACK OLIVE BRUSCHETTA

This bruschetta will class up any meal!

Serves 8

4 slices Italian country bread, or other crusty rustic bread, about ½" thick

½ cup extra-virgin olive oil

2 cloves garlic, finely chopped

3 ripe tomatoes, roughly chopped

½ teaspoon salt

¼ teaspoon freshly ground black pepper

½ cup black olives (about 24), such as Gaeta, Kalamata, or black oil-cured, pitted

¼ cup roughly chopped Italian parsley

Juice of 1 lemon

1. Heat a stovetop grill, barbecue grill, or broiler. Cut the bread slices in half. Combine the olive oil and garlic; brush the bread liberally with some of this garlic oil, using a pastry brush or your hands. Grill or broil until well toasted on both sides.

2. Toss chopped tomatoes with 1 tablespoon of garlic oil (make sure to get some pieces of garlic in there), salt, pepper, olives, and parsley. Season to taste with lemon juice. Top each piece of grilled bread with a small mound of tomato-olive mixture. Arrange neatly on a serving platter.

SPICY WHITE BEAN–CITRUS DIP

Tangy, spicy, unique, and easy to throw together, this stupendous dip is perfect for tortilla chips, fried plantains, raw vegetables, or as a spread in a burrito.

Serves 12

2 (15-ounce) cans white navy beans, drained and rinsed

¼ cup sour cream

1 tablespoon orange juice concentrate

1 teaspoon chipotle purée or hot pepper sauce

1 teaspoon lime juice

Zest of 1 orange, grated

½ teaspoon salt

½ cup diced white onions

1 tablespoon chopped cilantro

Purée the beans, sour cream, orange juice concentrate, chipotle or hot pepper sauce, lime juice, orange zest, and salt in a food processor until smooth. Add onions and cilantro; mix with a rubber spatula until combined.

PC BLACK BEAN DIP

To give this dip a little kick, you can substitute canned jalapeño peppers for the mild green chilies or add 2 teaspoons of chipotle powder.

Serves 12

1 cup dried black beans

2 cups water

1 tablespoon olive oil

1 small onion, peeled and diced

3 cloves garlic, peeled and minced

1 (14½-ounce) can diced tomatoes

2 (4-ounce) cans mild green chilies, finely chopped

1 teaspoon chili powder

½ teaspoon dried oregano

¼ cup fresh cilantro, finely chopped

Salt, to taste

1 cup Monterey jack cheese, grated, or vegan Monterey jack cheese, such as Follow Your Heart Monterey Jack Vegan Gourmet Cheese Alternative

1. Add the beans and water to a container; cover and let the beans soak 8 hours at room temperature.

2. Add the oil and the onion to the pressure cooker; sauté for 3 minutes or until the onion is soft. Add the garlic and sauté for 30 seconds.

3. Drain the beans and add them to the pressure cooker along with the tomatoes, chilies, chili powder, and oregano. Stir well. Lock the lid into place. Bring to high pressure; maintain pressure for 12 minutes. Remove from heat and allow pressure to release naturally for 10 minutes.

4. Quick-release any remaining pressure. Remove the lid. Transfer the cooked beans mixture to a food processor or blender. Add the cilantro and process until smooth. Taste for seasoning; add salt if desired.

5. Transfer the dip to a bowl. Stir in the cheese. Serve warm.

Other Bean Options

Bean dips are delicious when made with a variety of dried beans. To complement the flavors in this recipe, use black beans, pinto beans, or white beans. If you're pressed for time, use canned beans instead of dried beans, but be sure to drain the liquid first.

WILD MUSHROOM RAGOUT IN PUFF PASTRY SHELLS

Most supermarkets carry small frozen puff pastry hors d'oeuvre shells in the freezer section. They are great for quick homemade bites like these, which have a touch of refinement that store-bought frozen foods can't.

Serves 8

24 pieces frozen puff pastry hors d'oeuvre shells

1 tablespoon unsalted butter

2 cups (about ½ pound) assorted wild mushrooms, such as morels, chanterelles, oysters, shiitakes, and/or domestic and cremini mushrooms

½ teaspoon salt

2 sprigs fresh rosemary, leaves picked and chopped

¼ cup vegetable stock or water

1 teaspoon cornstarch dissolved in 1 tablespoon cold water

Freshly ground black pepper to taste

Squeeze of lemon

1. Bake puff pastry shells according to package directions. In a medium skillet over medium heat, melt the butter. Add the mushrooms and cook without stirring for 5 minutes, until a nice brown coating has developed. Add salt and rosemary; cook 3 minutes more. Add the stock and cornstarch; stir until thickened and bubbling. Remove from heat; adjust seasoning with black pepper, a few drops of lemon, and salt to taste.

2. Spoon ½ teaspoon of mushroom ragout into each shell. Serve piping hot.

Fungus Among Us

The term "wild mushrooms" has come to mean not just foraged fungus, but also a host of "exotic" mushrooms that are cultivated on mushroom farms just like the familiar white button mushrooms. While not as intensely flavorful as their truly wild cousins, they are much cleaner, more uniform, and of higher consistent freshness.

SALSA FRESCA (PICO DE GALLO)

Serve with chips, with a cheese omelet, or as a sauce with other Mexican foods.

Serves 8

4 medium tomatoes, seeded and diced fine (about 1½ cups)

1 small white onion, finely chopped

1 jalapeño pepper, seeded and finely chopped

1 tablespoon puréed chipotle in adobo (optional)

½ teaspoon salt

2 teaspoons lime juice

¼ cup chopped cilantro

In a blender or food processor, purée ⅓ of the tomatoes. Combine with remaining tomatoes, onion, jalapeño, chipotle, salt, lime juice, and cilantro. Best if used within 2 days.

SC CAJUN PEANUTS

Use "green" raw peanuts, not cooked or dried nuts.

Serves 16

2 pounds raw peanuts

12 cups water

⅓ cup salt

1 (3-ounce) package crab boil

1. Rinse the peanuts under cold water, then place in a 6-quart slow cooker.

2. Add the water, salt, and crab boil; cover and cook on high for 7 hours.

SC CINNAMON AND SUGAR PEANUTS

This is a festive treat that can be packaged in cellophane bags and given as party favors or gifts.

Yields 12 ounces

12 ounces unsalted, roasted peanuts

½ tablespoon ground cinnamon

⅓ cup sugar

1 tablespoon melted butter or vegan margarine

1. In a 4-quart slow cooker, place the peanuts.
2. Add the cinnamon and sugar and drizzle with butter or margarine. Stir.
3. Cook on low, uncovered, for 2–3 hours, stirring occasionally.
4. Spread the peanut mixture onto a cookie sheet or parchment paper and cool until dry.

PC BOILED PEANUTS

Use "green" raw peanuts, not cooked or dried nuts.

Serves 16

2 pounds raw peanuts

12 cups water

⅓ cup salt

1. Rinse the peanuts under cold water, then place in the pressure cooker. Add the water and salt.
2. Lock the lid in place; bring to 10 pounds of pressure, or a medium setting, and cook for 45 minutes. Remove from heat and allow pressure to release naturally.
3. Let the peanuts cool in the water, then drain.

Cajun Peanuts

Add a little flavor to plain boiled peanuts by adding Cajun seasoning to the water when boiling. Try a preblended seasoning or make your own by combining red pepper, black pepper, cayenne pepper, garlic powder, and salt.

SPICED PECANS

These pecans are great if you like a little spice in your life.

Yields 3 cups

1 ounce (2 tablespoons) unsalted butter

1 pound whole, shelled pecans

2 tablespoons light soy sauce

1 tablespoon hoisin sauce

A few drops of hot pepper sauce

1. Heat oven to 325°F. Melt butter in a large skillet. Add nuts; cook, tossing occasionally, until nuts are well coated. Add soy sauce, hoisin sauce, and hot pepper sauce; cook 1 minute more. Stir to coat thoroughly.

2. Spread nuts into a single layer on a baking sheet. Bake until all liquid is absorbed and nuts begin to brown. Remove from oven. Cool before serving.

CHEESE SOUFFLÉ

This virtually foolproof soufflé can be prepared in advance and kept in the refrigerator for up to an hour before baking, making it perfect for when guests come over. Serve it with a simple salad such as Mixed Baby Greens with Balsamic Vinaigrette (see Chapter 3).

Serves 6

½ cup unsalted butter

½ cup flour

½ teaspoon table salt

½ teaspoon paprika

Dash of cayenne or pepper sauce

2 cups milk

½ pound sharp Cheddar cheese, diced

8 large eggs, separated

1. Heat oven to 475°F. Butter a 10" soufflé dish and coat the inside with flour. Melt ½ cup butter in a double boiler or a steel bowl set over a pot of simmering water. Add the flour, salt, paprika, and cayenne or pepper sauce; mix well. Gradually stir in the milk with a stiff whisk or wooden spoon. Cook, stirring constantly, until the mixture has become very thick. Stir in the cheese, and continue stirring until all cheese is melted. Remove from heat.

2. Beat the yolks until they are lemon-colored, then gradually stir them into the cheese sauce. In a very clean bowl, whip the egg whites until they are stiff, but not dry. Gently fold them into the cheese sauce, and then pour this batter into the soufflé dish. At this point, the soufflé may be covered and refrigerated for up to 1 hour, or baked right away.

3. Bake at 475°F for 10 minutes. Reduce heat to 400°F, and bake for 25 minutes more. Serve immediately.

ARTICHOKE AND CHEESE SQUARES

These rich vegetable cakes are easy-to-serve, attractive savories that can be made up to 3 days ahead.

Serves 8

1 (12-ounce) jar marinated artichoke hearts, drained, liquid reserved

1 small onion, finely chopped

2 cloves garlic, finely minced

4 whole eggs, beaten

2 tablespoons flour

½ teaspoon salt

¼ teaspoon each of pepper, oregano, and Tabasco sauce

8 ounces shredded Monterey jack cheese

2 tablespoons chopped parsley

1. Chop artichokes and set aside. Heat the marinade liquid in a medium skillet, and sauté the onion and garlic in it until translucent, about 5 minutes.

2. In a mixing bowl, combine eggs, flour, salt, pepper, oregano, and Tabasco. Thoroughly mix in cheese, parsley, artichokes, and onion mixture.

3. Turn into a 7" × 11" baking dish. Bake at 325°F for 30 minutes, until set. Cool to room temperature. Cut into squares and serve room temperature, or reheat at 325°F for 10 minutes.

TWO CHEESE STRATA

This savory bread pudding is the right choice for a dinner party or luncheon, since the assembled casserole has to rest overnight before baking anyway. Just pop it in the oven to bake an hour before the guests arrive.

Serves 6

Unsalted butter

4 large eggs

2 cups milk

1 teaspoon Dijon mustard

1 teaspoon salt

9–10 slices white bread, torn into bite-size pieces

8 ounces Gruyère, Havarti, or Emmentaler (Swiss) cheese, shredded

8 ounces ricotta, drained in a cheesecloth for 1 hour

¼ cup sun-dried tomatoes, roughly chopped

½ cup fresh basil leaves, torn into small pieces

Hot pepper sauce

1. Liberally butter an 8" × 11" baking dish. Whisk together the eggs, milk, mustard, and salt. Make a layer in the baking dish with ⅓ of the bread. Pour on ⅓ of the egg mixture. Distribute ⅓ of the shredded cheese, ½ of the ricotta, ½ of the dried tomatoes, and ½ of the basil into the dish. Season with a few dashes of hot pepper sauce. Repeat for a second layer, finishing with a layer of bread topped with shredded cheese. Cover with plastic wrap, and refrigerate for at least several hours, or overnight.

2. Heat oven to 325°F. Bake the strata for 1 hour, until a toothpick inserted in the center comes out clean and the top is lightly browned. Rest at room temperature for 10 minutes before cutting into portions.

FRICOS (CHEESE CRISPS)

Lacy, cooked wafers of cheese make exquisite garnishes for salads, accompaniments to soups or sandwiches, and handy snack foods. Their Northern Italian origins usually dictate that they be made with Parmigiano-Reggiano, but they're equally good made with Asiago, Cheddar, or provolone.

Serves 4

1 cup finely shredded Parmigiano-Reggiano or other cheese

Heat a nonstick skillet over medium heat. Sprinkle 1 tablespoon of cheese into a small mound on the pan. Cook until the bottom is nicely browned, then transfer to drain on paper towels. They are soft and oozy, and require a little practice to handle them properly, so have a little extra cheese ready in case the first few are "less than perfect."

CHAPTER 5
SOUPS, STEWS, AND CHILIES

RECIPE LIST

VEGETABLE STOCK **208**

PRESSURE COOKER VEGETABLE STOCK **209**

VEGETABLE BROTH **210**

NO-BEEF BROTH **210**

RED BEAN AND PASTA SOUP **211**

WHITE BEAN AND BARLEY SOUP **212**

RED LENTIL SOUP **213**

BLACK BEAN SOUP **214**

CREAM OF ASPARAGUS SOUP **215**

TOMATO SOUP **216**

TOMATO BASIL SOUP **216**

WILD MUSHROOM SOUP WITH THYME **217**

MUSHROOM VEGETABLE STOCK **218**

CARROT PURÉE WITH NUTMEG **219**

SMOKY BLACK-EYED PEA SOUP WITH SWEET POTATOES AND MUSTARD GREENS **220**

PUMPKIN SOUP WITH CARAWAY SEEDS **221**

PUMPKIN-ALE SOUP **222**

CHILLED CURRY POTATO-FENNEL SOUP **223**

SMOOTH CAULIFLOWER SOUP WITH CORIANDER **224**

GAZPACHO **225**

YELLOW SPLIT PEA SOUP WITH CACTUS AND HOMINY **226**

VICHYSSOISE (POTATO AND LEEK SOUP) **227**

MINESTRONE SOUP **228**

MINESTRONE WITH BASIL PESTO **229**

LENTIL SOUP WITH CUMIN **230**

TUSCAN WHITE BEAN SOUP **231**

CUBAN BLACK BEAN SOUP WITH CORIANDER TOFU SOUR CREAM **232**

CORN AND POTATO CHOWDER **233**

MUSHROOM, BARLEY, AND COLLARD GREENS SOUP **234**

PINTO BEAN SOUP WITH SALSA FRESCA **235**

ACORN SQUASH SOUP WITH ANISE AND CARROTS **236**

MISO SOUP **237**

TOFU NOODLE SOUP **238**

HOT AND SOUR SOUP **239**

CAULIFLOWER SOUP **240**

FRENCH ONION SOUP 241

GARDEN VEGETABLE SOUP 242

POTATO-LEEK SOUP 242

BEER-CHEESE SOUP 243

BUTTERNUT SQUASH SOUP 244

CREAMY CHICKPEA SOUP 245

MUSHROOM BARLEY SOUP 246

SUMMER BORSCHT 247

SIMPLE SPLIT PEA SOUP 248

TORTILLA SOUP 249

GREEK-STYLE ORZO AND SPINACH SOUP 250

PHO 251

WILD RICE AND PORTOBELLO SOUP 252

CELERY ROOT SOUP 253

BRUNSWICK STEW 254

JAMAICAN RED BEAN STEW 255

SOUTHWEST CORN CHOWDER 256

OKRA GUMBO 257

MEDITERRANEAN VEGETABLE STEW 258

WHITE BEAN AND TOMATO STEW 259

SEITAN AND MUSHROOM STEW 260

CURRIED SEITAN STEW 261

VEGETABLE DUMPLING STEW 262

ÉTOUFFÉE 263

SEITAN AND CABBAGE STEW 264

POSOLE 265

PUMPKIN STEW 266

CAULIFLOWER CHOWDER 267

WHITE BEAN CASSOULET 268

KOREAN-STYLE HOT POT 269

SEITAN BOURGUIGNONNE 270

SUPER GREENS STEW 271

TEXAS STEW 272

MOCK MEATBALL STEW 273

VEGAN CHILI 274

SOUTHWEST VEGETABLE CHILI 275

CINCINNATI CHILI 276

CHILI CON "CARNE" 277

SHREDDED "CHICKEN" CHILI 278

FIVE PEPPER CHILI 279

SWEET POTATO CHILI 280

THREE BEAN CHILI 281

FAJITA CHILI 282

BLACK BEAN, CORN, AND FRESH TOMATO CHILI 283

RED BEAN CHILI 284

LENTIL CHILI 285

GARDEN VEGETABLE CHILI 286

BLACK BEAN AND "SAUSAGE" CHILI 287

ACORN SQUASH CHILI 288

SUMMER CHILI 289

VEGETABLE STOCK

Other veggies, such as fennel, ginger, parsnips, herbs, and so on, may be substituted for any of the ingredients. This is a very changeable recipe, open to personalization.

Yields about 4 cups

1 onion, sliced

1 leek, white part only, cleaned thoroughly and sliced

1 carrot, peeled and sliced

2 stalks celery, roughly chopped

1 turnip, peeled and sliced

5 cloves garlic, peeled and sliced

6 cups cold water

Small bunch of parsley stems

10 black peppercorns

8 sprigs fresh thyme

1 bay leaf

Salt and pepper (optional)

Combine all ingredients in a large stock pot. Simmer 1 hour; strain. Season with salt and pepper, if desired; cool. Keeps refrigerated for 1 week. Freezes well.

PRESSURE COOKER VEGETABLE STOCK

Save scraps of vegetables to use to make a homemade stock.

Yields 4 cups

2 large onions, peeled and halved

2 medium carrots, cleaned and cut into large pieces

3 stalks celery, cut in half

1 whole bulb garlic

10 peppercorns

1 bay leaf

4½ cups water

1. Add the onions, carrots, and celery to the pressure cooker. Break the bulb of garlic into individual cloves; peel and add to the pressure cooker. Add the peppercorns, bay leaf, and water to completely cover the vegetables. Lock the lid into place and bring to low pressure; maintain pressure for 10 minutes. Remove from heat and allow pressure to release naturally.

2. Strain the stock through a fine-mesh strainer. Store in the refrigerator for 2–3 days, or freeze for up to 3 months.

SC VEGETABLE BROTH

A versatile vegetable broth can be used as the base for almost any soup or stew. Note that it does not contain salt, so you must add that separately when using this broth in recipes.

Yields 4 cups

2 large onions, peeled and halved
2 medium carrots, cleaned and cut into large pieces
3 stalks celery, cut in half
1 whole bulb garlic, crushed
10 peppercorns
1 bay leaf
6 cups water

1. In a 4-quart slow cooker, add all ingredients. Cover and cook on low heat for 8–10 hours.
2. Strain the broth to remove the vegetables. Store broth in the refrigerator.

Storing Broth

Homemade broth can be stored in a covered container in the refrigerator for 2–3 days, or frozen for up to 3 months.

SC NO-BEEF BROTH

Traditional Worcestershire sauce contains anchovies, but several grocery store brands of the sauce are vegan.

Yields 4 cups

4 carrots, washed and cut into large pieces
2 large onions, peeled and quartered
1 celery stalk, chopped
2 cups fresh portobello mushrooms, sliced
1 whole bulb garlic, crushed
1 tablespoon vegan Worcestershire sauce
1 tablespoon brown sugar
6 cups water

1. In a 4-quart slow cooker, add all ingredients. Cover and cook on low heat for 8–10 hours.
2. Strain the broth to remove the vegetables. Store the broth in a covered container in the refrigerator for 2–3 days, or frozen for up to 3 months.

RED BEAN AND PASTA SOUP

This is a hearty winter soup to warm up chilly nights.

Serves 8

1 medium onion, chopped

3 cloves garlic, sliced

3 tablespoons olive oil

1 teaspoon oregano

2 bay leaves

1 (8-ounce) can tomato sauce

2 teaspoons salt

1 tablespoon soy sauce

1 (16-ounce) package red beans, soaked overnight in 1 quart cold water and drained

10 sprigs Italian parsley, including stems

6 cups vegetable stock or water

2 cups cooked pasta (any small shape, such as orzo or ditalini)

1. In a pot large enough to hold all ingredients, cook onions and garlic with olive oil over medium heat for 5 minutes, until onions are translucent. Add oregano, bay leaves, tomato sauce, salt, and soy sauce. Bring to a simmer and add beans, parsley, and stock or water.

2. Bring to a boil, then reduce to a low simmer and cook for 90 minutes, until beans are tender enough to mash between two fingers. In a blender, purée ⅓ of the beans very well; add them back to the soup. Add cooked pasta, and bring back to a boil for 1 minute more before serving garnished with a dollop of sour cream if desired.

SC WHITE BEAN AND BARLEY SOUP

Cool soup to room temperature before refrigerating or freezing in order to save energy.

Serves 8

2 (15-ounce) cans great northern beans, drained and rinsed

½ cup pearl barley

½ onion, diced

2 carrots, peeled and diced

2 cloves garlic, minced

¼ cup fresh parsley, chopped

2 sprigs fresh thyme

6 cups No-Beef Broth (see recipe in this chapter)

1½ teaspoons salt

1. In a 4-quart slow cooker, add all ingredients. Cover, and cook on low for 6–8 hours.
2. Remove the sprig of thyme before serving.

SC RED LENTIL SOUP

Store-bought vegetable broth or stock typically contains much more sodium than the homemade variety, so adjust salt accordingly.

Serves 6

2 cups red lentils

3 tablespoons olive oil

1 small onion, sliced

1½ teaspoons fresh ginger, peeled and minced

2 cloves garlic, minced

6 cups Vegetable Broth (see recipe in this chapter)

Juice of 1 lemon

½ teaspoon paprika

1 teaspoon cayenne pepper

1½ teaspoons salt

1. Rinse the lentils carefully and sort through the bunch to remove any dirt or debris.

2. In a sauté pan, heat the olive oil over medium heat, then sauté the onion, ginger, and garlic for 2–3 minutes.

3. In a 4-quart slow cooker, add the sautéed vegetables and all remaining ingredients. Cover, and cook on low for 6–8 hours. Add more salt, if necessary, to taste.

SC BLACK BEAN SOUP

You can use the leftover green bell pepper, red bell pepper, and red onion from this recipe to make Fajita Chili (see recipe in this Chapter).

Serves 6

2 tablespoons olive oil

½ green bell pepper, diced

½ red bell pepper, diced

½ red onion, sliced

2 cloves garlic, minced

2 (15-ounce) cans black beans, drained and rinsed

2 teaspoons cumin, minced

1 teaspoon chipotle powder

1 teaspoon salt

4 cups Vegetable Broth (see recipe in this chapter)

¼ cup cilantro, chopped

1. In a sauté pan, heat the olive oil over medium heat, then sauté the bell peppers, onion, and garlic for 2–3 minutes.

2. In a 4-quart slow cooker, add the sautéed vegetables, black beans, cumin, chipotle powder, salt, and Vegetable Broth. Cover, and cook on low for 6 hours.

3. Let the soup cool slightly, then pour half into a blender. Process until smooth, then pour back into the pot. Add the chopped cilantro, and stir.

CREAM OF ASPARAGUS SOUP

Asparagus presents a challenge to the frugal chef: what to do with the sizable trimmings from the bottom stalks of this expensive vegetable. Here's the answer:

Serves 6

2 tablespoons olive oil

1 medium onion, chopped

4 cloves garlic, finely chopped

1 bunch of fresh asparagus, or trimmings from several bunches equal to 1 pound, roughly chopped

1 teaspoon salt

¼ cup white wine or sherry (optional)

3 cups vegetable stock or water

1 (10-ounce) package frozen green peas

2 cups cream or half-and-half

Freshly ground black pepper to taste (about ¼ teaspoon)

1 teaspoon dried basil

1. In a large, heavy-bottomed pot over medium heat, heat olive oil for 1 minute. Add onion, garlic, asparagus, and salt; cook 15 minutes, until onion is translucent but not browned. Add wine or sherry; cook 1 minute, until alcohol evaporates; add the stock. Simmer 20 minutes, until asparagus is very tender. Remove from heat; stir in frozen peas.

2. Purée in a blender or food processor until smooth; transfer back to pot, and heat, just to a simmer. Add cream; season with salt, black pepper, and basil. May be served hot or cold.

TOMATO SOUP

This soup is perfect for those long, cold winter nights.

Serves 6

2 tablespoons olive oil

1 medium onion, chopped

2 cloves garlic, finely chopped

4 pounds ripe tomatoes, peeled, seeded, and roughly chopped

1 teaspoon salt

Freshly ground black pepper to taste (about ¼ teaspoon)

In a large soup pot over medium heat, heat olive oil for 1 minute. Add onion and garlic; cook 5–10 minutes, until onions are translucent but not browned. Stir in tomatoes; simmer 25–30 minutes, until tomatoes are submerged in their own juices. Purée in a blender or food processor until smooth. Season with salt and black pepper. May be served hot or cold. Add cream, if desired, for cream of tomato soup.

SC TOMATO BASIL SOUP

Fresh basil adds a different flavor than dried basil to dishes, and the fresh variety is more complementary to this soup.

Serves 5

2 tablespoons butter or vegan margarine

½ onion, diced

2 cloves garlic, minced

1 (28-ounce) can whole peeled tomatoes

½ cup Vegetable Broth (see recipe in this chapter)

1 bay leaf

1 teaspoon salt

1 teaspoon pepper

½ cup unsweetened soymilk

¼ cup chopped fresh basil

1. In a sauté pan over medium heat, melt the butter or margarine, then sauté the onion and garlic for 3–4 minutes.

2. In a 4-quart slow cooker, add the onion and garlic, tomatoes, Vegetable Broth, bay leaf, salt, and pepper. Cover and cook over low heat 4 hours.

3. Allow to cool slightly, then remove the bay leaf. Process the soup in a blender or immersion blender.

4. Return the soup to the slow cooker, then add the soymilk and chopped basil, and heat on low for an additional 30 minutes.

WILD MUSHROOM SOUP WITH THYME

The final purée of this soup should definitely be done in a blender, since it guarantees a smoothness that the food processor can't accomplish.

Serves 8

1 pound white mushrooms

½ pound shiitake mushrooms, stems removed

1 teaspoon olive oil

4 sprigs fresh thyme, or ½ teaspoon dried

4–5 shallots, peeled and chopped very fine

¼ cup dry white wine

2 cups vegetable stock or water

2 teaspoons butter

½ pound assorted wild mushrooms such as chanterelle, shiitake, oyster, cremini, black trumpet, etc., sliced into bite-size pieces or an equal amount of sliced white mushrooms

3 cups cold milk

Salt and freshly ground black pepper

1 tablespoon chives, finely chopped

1. Pulse the white mushrooms in about 4 small batches in a food processor to finely chop them, stopping before they clump. Roughly hand-chop the shiitakes, and pulse them the same way.

2. Heat the oil in a 2½-cup saucepan over medium-high flame, toss in the thyme and allow to sizzle for a moment, then add the shallots and sauté for 3 minutes until translucent. Add the chopped mushrooms. Sprinkle in a pinch of salt and cook 5–7 minutes, until mushrooms are soft.

3. Add white wine and cook 2 minutes, then add the stock. Simmer for 10 minutes.

4. Meanwhile, sauté the sliced wild or white mushrooms in the butter, in small batches over high heat, seasoning them with salt and pepper as they cook. Set aside.

5. Put ⅓ of soup in blender, with 1 cup cold milk, and purée until very smooth. Repeat with remaining soup, then season to taste. Be careful to vent the blender to avoid dangerous splashing. Serve with a spoonful of sautéed mushrooms in each bowl and a sprinkling of chives.

MUSHROOM VEGETABLE STOCK

This stock freezes well so feel free to make some in advance.

Yields about 6 cups

- 1 ounce dried mushrooms, such as porcini or Chinese black mushrooms
- 1 tablespoon olive oil
- 1 onion, sliced
- 1 carrot, peeled and sliced
- 2 stalks celery, roughly chopped
- 1 (8–10-ounce) package white mushrooms, washed and roughly chopped
- 3 cloves garlic, peeled and sliced
- 4 cups cold water
- Small bunch of parsley stems
- 10 black peppercorns
- 8 sprigs fresh thyme
- 1 bay leaf
- 2 teaspoons salt

Soak the mushrooms in 4 cups water for 1 hour. Heat the oil in a stock pot; add onion, carrot, and celery. Cook over medium heat until onions begin to brown, about 15 minutes. Add the dried mushrooms, their soaking liquid, the fresh white mushrooms, garlic, water, parsley stems, peppercorns, thyme, bay leaf, and salt. Bring to a boil, then lower flame. Simmer 45 minutes; strain. Keep refrigerated for 1 week.

CARROT PURÉE WITH NUTMEG

Tasting and feeling like a cream soup, this soup will surprise your guests who won't believe there's no cream in this sweet, delicious soup. For best smoothness, use a blender to purée, not a food processor.

Serves 6

2 tablespoons oil

1 medium onion, chopped

2 tablespoons white wine

4 cups carrots, peeled, halved lengthwise, and sliced thin

2 cups vegetable stock or broth (canned is okay)

1 teaspoon salt

Ground white pepper to taste

Pinch of nutmeg

1¼ cups milk

2 teaspoons freshly chopped chives or parsley

1. Heat oil in large saucepan over medium-high heat. Add onion, sauté for 5 minutes, add wine and carrots. Cook for 1 minute, until wine evaporates.

2. Add stock, salt, pepper, and nutmeg. Bring to a boil, then reduce to simmer for 20 minutes.

3. Ladle into a blender, add 1 cup milk, and blend until very smooth. Adjust consistency with more milk if necessary. Be careful when puréeing the hot liquid, starting the blender on the slowest speed, and/or doing the job in 2 batches. Serve garnished with a sprinkling of chives or parsley.

SMOKY BLACK-EYED PEA SOUP WITH SWEET POTATOES AND MUSTARD GREENS

Use any dark leafy greens you'd like, fresh or frozen, in place of the mustard greens. Julienne kale or collard greens are excellent choices, and are equally antioxidant-rich.

Serves 10–12

- 1 tablespoon olive oil
- 1 medium onion, chopped
- 2 ribs celery, chopped
- 1 carrot, peeled, chopped
- 2 teaspoons salt
- 1 teaspoon dried thyme
- 2 teaspoons dried oregano
- 1 teaspoon ground cumin
- 1 dried chipotle chili, halved
- 2 bay leaves
- 1 pound dried black-eyed peas or navy beans, washed and picked through for stones
- 2 quarts vegetable stock or water
- 1 large sweet potato, peeled, diced into 1" cubes
- 1 (10-ounce) package frozen mustard greens, chopped
- 1 (22-ounce) can diced tomatoes
- Croutons of cornbread or other bread for garnish
- Chopped cilantro for garnish

1. In a large, heavy-bottomed Dutch oven over medium heat, heat the oil for 1 minute. Add onion, celery, carrot, and salt; cook 5 minutes, until onions are translucent. Add thyme, oregano, cumin, chipotle chili, and bay leaves; cook 2 minutes more. Add black-eyed peas or navy beans and vegetable stock. Bring to a boil, then simmer 2 hours until beans are very tender, adding water or stock if necessary.

2. Add the sweet potato and cook 20 minutes more. Stir in chopped mustard greens and diced tomatoes. Cook 10 minutes more, until the potato and greens are tender. Adjust seasoning with salt and pepper, and consistency with additional vegetable stock or water. The soup should be brothy. Serve garnished with cornbread croutons and a sprinkling of chopped cilantro.

PUMPKIN SOUP WITH CARAWAY SEEDS

Butternut squash or even acorn squash substitute very well for pumpkin in this soup. Each imparts its own character, making this three recipes in one. Chipotle and/or Spanish paprika (both in gourmet stores) impart subtle smokiness for an additional dimension.

Serves 8–10

2 tablespoons unsalted butter or olive oil

1 medium onion, chopped

1 large carrot, peeled and sliced thin

2 cups peeled, cubed pumpkin

¼ teaspoon whole caraway seeds

1½ cups vegetable stock or broth (canned is okay)

3 cups cold milk

½ dried chipotle chili or ½ teaspoon smoked Spanish paprika

1. Melt the butter or heat the oil in a heavy-bottomed soup pot over medium heat. Add the onion, carrot, pumpkin, and caraway seeds, and sauté, stirring occasionally, 8–10 minutes, until pumpkin becomes tender and begins to brown (some may stick to pan).

2. Add stock or broth and simmer for 20 minutes. Remove from heat and stir in 2 cups milk.

3. Purée in batches in a blender until smooth, adjusting consistency with remaining milk. Season with salt and pepper to taste. Sprinkle the chipotle chili or Spanish paprika on top.

SC PUMPKIN-ALE SOUP

Use fresh pumpkin in place of the canned pumpkin purée when the ingredient is in season. You'll need 3¾ cups of cooked, puréed fresh pumpkin.

Serves 6

2 (15-ounce) cans pumpkin purée

¼ cup diced onion

2 cloves garlic, minced

2 teaspoons salt

1 teaspoon pepper

¼ teaspoon dried thyme

5 cups Vegetable Broth (see recipe in this chapter)

1 (12-ounce) bottle pale ale beer

1. In a 4-quart slow cooker, add the pumpkin purée, onion, garlic, salt, pepper, thyme, and Vegetable Broth. Stir well. Cover and cook over low heat for 4 hours.

2. Allow the soup to cool slightly, then process in a blender or with an immersion blender until smooth.

3. Pour the soup back into the slow cooker, add the beer, and cook for 1 hour over low heat.

CHILLED CURRY POTATO-FENNEL SOUP

While this soup is delicious hot or cold, I particularly love the way it refreshes in the summer, with enough substance to stand on its own as a main course.

Serves 10–12

1 large Idaho russet potato, peeled

1 large Spanish onion, peeled

1 head sweet fennel, tassel-like fronds removed and set aside

1 red bell pepper

1 tablespoon olive oil

1 (1") piece of fresh ginger, peeled and finely chopped

2 cloves garlic, peeled and finely chopped

2 teaspoons good-quality Madras curry powder

3 cups vegetable stock

1 jalapeño pepper, seeded and finely chopped (optional)

1 quart buttermilk

1 cup half-and-half

Salt and white pepper to taste

1 tablespoon chopped Italian parsley

1. Chop the potato, onion, fennel, and red bell pepper coarsely. In a large soup pot over medium-high heat, heat the oil for 1 minute. Add the chopped vegetables, ginger, and garlic. Cook until onion is translucent, about 5 minutes; stir in curry powder and cook 5 minutes more. Add vegetable stock; raise heat to high and bring to a full boil. Reduce to a simmer; cook until potatoes are falling-apart tender, about 15 minutes.

2. Chill and purée the soup in a blender or food processor. Add the chopped jalapeño, buttermilk, and half-and-half. Season to taste with salt and white pepper. Serve garnished with chopped parsley and/or sprigs from the reserved fennel fronds.

SMOOTH CAULIFLOWER SOUP WITH CORIANDER

Another no-cream "cream soup." This soup is equally delicious hot or chilled.

Serves 4–6

2 tablespoons unsalted butter or olive oil

1 onion

2 tablespoons white wine or dry sherry

1 medium head (about 2 pounds) cauliflower, cut into bite-size pieces

2 cups vegetable stock

1 teaspoon salt

Ground white pepper

1 teaspoon ground coriander

¾ cup cold milk

Chopped chives or parsley

1. In a large saucepan or soup pot, over medium-high heat, melt butter or heat oil. Add onion; cook until it is translucent, but not brown, about 5 minutes. Add wine and cauliflower; cook for 1 minute to steam out the wine. Add the stock, salt, pepper, and coriander; bring up to a rolling boil.

2. Simmer until cauliflower is very tender, about 15 minutes. Transfer to a blender. Add half of the milk and purée until very smooth, scraping down the sides of the blender vase with a rubber spatula. Be very careful during this step, since hot liquids will splash out of blender if it is not started gradually (you may wish to purée in two batches, for safety). Transfer soup back to saucepan, and thin with additional milk if necessary. Season; garnish with chopped herbs just before serving.

GAZPACHO

Nothing could be simpler than buzzing together a refreshing summer soup in minutes in a blender. Serve with a few drops of garlic-infused olive oil drizzled on top and a crust of country bread on the side.

Serves 6

8 tomatoes, seeded

1 large cucumber, peeled

2 green bell peppers, seeded

1 slice bread, torn into postage-stamp-size pieces

1 clove garlic, sliced

2 tablespoons extra-virgin olive oil

1½ teaspoons red wine vinegar

1 teaspoon salt

1 to 2 cups tomato juice

Hot pepper sauce (optional)

Roughly chop the tomatoes, cucumber, and peppers. Combine with bread, garlic, olive oil, vinegar, and salt in a food processor or blender. Purée at high speed until consistency is soupy, but still slightly chunky. Stir in tomato juice to desired consistency, and season with hot pepper sauce to taste.

YELLOW SPLIT PEA SOUP WITH CACTUS AND HOMINY

This Southwestern soup is more like a stew. The Mexican specialty ingredients are increasingly available in ethnic sections of mainstream markets, and certainly in specialty and gourmet shops.

Serves 12

1 tablespoon olive oil

1 medium onion, chopped

2 ribs celery, chopped

1 carrot, peeled and chopped

1 tablespoon dried marjoram or oregano leaves

1 teaspoon ground toasted cumin

½ teaspoon ground coriander

1 bay leaf

1 pound dried yellow split peas

2 quarts vegetable stock or water

2 ancho or guajillo chili pods, oven-toasted for 2 minutes at 350°F, seeded, boiled for 5 minutes in a cup of water, and puréed in a blender

1 (30-ounce) can hominy corn kernels, drained and rinsed

1 small (15-ounce) can cactus (a.k.a. nopalitos), drained and rinsed

Salt and pepper to taste

Chopped cilantro for garnish

Croutons (optional)

1. In a large soup pot over medium heat, heat olive oil for 1 minute. Add onion, celery, and carrot; cook for 5 minutes, until onion turns translucent. Add marjoram or oregano, cumin, coriander, and bay leaf. Cook 1 minute more. Add split peas and stock. Raise heat to high and bring to a full boil; reduce heat to a simmer. Add puréed chili and cook 45 minutes, until peas are very tender and starting to fall apart.

2. Add hominy and cactus; bring back to a boil. Cook 1 minute more; season to taste with salt and pepper, and remove from heat. Serve garnished with chopped cilantro and croutons, if using.

VICHYSSOISE (POTATO AND LEEK SOUP)

Elegant, classic French soups like this make the right first course for a formal occasion. Serve chilled or warm, and make sure to use the prettiest leek pieces, cut very precisely, for the garnish. People will notice.

Serves 12

1 tablespoon olive oil

1 medium onion, chopped

1 pound (about 3 or 4) potatoes, any variety, peeled and cut into 1" chunks

2 bunches leeks, chopped, thoroughly washed twice; 1 cup of the best parts set aside for garnish

1 teaspoon dried sage leaves

1 bay leaf

¼ cup white wine

2 quarts vegetable stock or water

Salt and white pepper to taste

1. In a large soup pot over medium heat, heat olive oil for 1 minute. Add onion, potatoes, and all but 1 cup of the chopped leeks; cook 10 minutes, until onion turns translucent. Add sage, bay leaf, and wine. Cook 1 minute more. Add stock. Bring to a full boil; reduce heat to a simmer and cook for 45 minutes, until potatoes are very tender and starting to fall apart.

2. Carefully purée the soup in a blender in small batches. Season to taste with salt and white pepper. Steam, boil, or sauté the remaining cup of leeks, and serve the soup garnished with a spoonful of leeks in the center.

SC MINESTRONE SOUP

Minestrone is a classic Italian vegetable soup. The zucchini and cabbage are added at the end for a burst of fresh flavor.

Serves 8

- 3 cloves garlic, minced
- 1 (15-ounce) can fire-roasted diced tomatoes
- 1 (28-ounce) can crushed tomatoes
- 2 stalks celery, diced
- 1 medium onion, diced
- 3 medium carrots, diced
- 3 cups Vegetable Broth (see recipe in this chapter)
- 2 (15-ounce) cans kidney beans, drained and rinsed
- 2 tablespoons tomato paste
- 2 tablespoons minced basil
- 2 tablespoons minced oregano
- 2 tablespoons minced Italian parsley
- 1½ cups shredded cabbage
- ¾ cup diced zucchini
- 1 teaspoon salt
- ½ teaspoon pepper
- 8 ounces small cooked pasta

1. In a 4-quart slow cooker, add the garlic, diced and crushed tomatoes, celery, onion, carrots, broth, beans, tomato paste, basil, and spices. Cover and cook on low heat for 6–8 hours.

2. Add shredded cabbage and zucchini and turn to high for the last hour.

3. Stir in the salt, pepper, and pasta before serving.

Suggested Pasta Shapes for Soup

Anchellini, small shells, hoops, alfabeto, or ditalini are all small pasta shapes suitable for soup. For heartier soups, try bow-ties or rotini. Thin rice noodles or vermicelli are better for Asian-style soups.

MINESTRONE WITH BASIL PESTO

Rich and hearty, this Italian vegetable soup has humble origins as a peasant dish, but is elevated to fine dining with a beautiful pesto garnish.

Serves 10–12

2 stalks celery

1 large carrot

1 potato

1 medium zucchini

1 medium yellow "summer" squash

1 large Spanish onion

1 tablespoon olive oil

2 leeks, chopped, thoroughly washed twice

3 cloves garlic, finely chopped

1 teaspoon salt

3 teaspoons chopped fresh oregano or 1 teaspoon dried oregano leaves

3 teaspoons chopped fresh thyme or 1 teaspoon dried thyme leaves

1 bay leaf

2 quarts vegetable stock or water

1 (30-ounce) can diced tomatoes

2 cups cooked pasta (any small shape, such as ditalini)

1 (14-ounce) can red kidney or white cannellini beans

Salt and white pepper to taste

½ recipe Basil Pesto (see Chapter 2), or store-bought pesto

Grated Parmesan cheese (optional)

1. Cut celery, carrot, potato, zucchini, yellow squash, and onion into medium (¼") dice. In a large soup pot or Dutch oven over medium-high heat, heat the olive oil for 1 minute. Add all diced vegetables, leeks, garlic, salt, oregano, thyme, and bay leaf. Cook 10–15 minutes, until onion turns translucent. Add stock and tomatoes. Bring to a full boil; reduce heat to a simmer and cook 45 minutes, until potatoes are cooked through and tender.

2. Add cooked pasta and beans. Bring back to a boil for 1 minute; season to taste with salt and white pepper. Serve in bowls, topped with a teaspoon of Basil Pesto. Serve with grated Parmesan cheese at the table, if desired.

LENTIL SOUP WITH CUMIN

This is the fastest bean soup you can make, ready in about an hour, without any soaking of beans. It gets better as it sits overnight, when the flavors marry, so make enough for two or more meals.

Serves 8

1 large carrot, peeled

1 stalk celery

1 medium onion

1 potato, peeled

2 cloves garlic

1 tablespoon olive oil

½ teaspoon whole cumin seeds, toasted in a dry pan for 1 minute, until fragrant

2 teaspoons salt

1 cup lentils

8 cups vegetable stock

Salt and pepper (optional)

1. Chop carrot, celery, onion, and potato into bite-size pieces; cut garlic into very small slices.

2. Heat the oil over medium flame in a pot large enough to hold everything, and add the cut vegetables, garlic, and cumin, plus 2 teaspoons of salt. Cook for 5 minutes, then add the lentils and vegetable stock. Raise heat to bring to a boil, then reduce flame to medium-low.

3. Simmer 1 hour, season with salt and pepper; serve with a dollop of Tofu Sour Cream (see Chapter 2) if desired.

TUSCAN WHITE BEAN SOUP

One of the trendiest soups of the 1990s, this Northern Italian classic survived that decade with its integrity unscathed. Tuscans place a hunk of rustic bread at the bottom of the bowl before adding the soup. The crust of bread soaks up soup and becomes a velvety "reward" waiting to be found.

Serves 8

1 tablespoon olive oil

1 medium onion, chopped

1 large leek, white part only, finely chopped

3 cloves garlic, finely chopped

3 teaspoons fresh rosemary leaves, or 1 teaspoon dried

1 bay leaf

3 quarts vegetable stock or water

2 cups large white (great northern) beans (soaked overnight if desired)

Salt and white pepper to taste

1 tablespoon extra-virgin olive oil

1. In a large soup pot over medium heat, heat olive oil for 1 minute. Add onion, leek, and garlic; cook 10 minutes, until onion turns translucent, stirring frequently. Add rosemary and bay leaf; cook 5 minutes more. Add stock and beans. Bring to a full boil; reduce heat to a simmer, and cook 90 minutes, until beans are very tender and starting to fall apart (cooking time will vary depending on age of beans and whether or not they were soaked—assume 30 minutes less for soaked beans).

2. Carefully purée ⅔ of the soup in a blender; add back to rest of soup. Season to taste with salt and white pepper. Serve with a few drops of fine extra-virgin olive oil sprinkled on top.

CUBAN BLACK BEAN SOUP WITH CORIANDER TOFU SOUR CREAM

Cubans flavor this soup with a smoked pork bone. The same smoky effect comes from chipotle, a smoked jalapeño chili, or smoked Spanish paprika, available in specialty stores, or via the Internet.

Serves 10–12

- 1 tablespoon olive oil
- 1 medium onion, chopped
- 1 large leek, white part only, finely chopped
- 4 cloves garlic, finely chopped
- 1 teaspoon cumin seeds, toasted lightly then ground, or 1½ teaspoons ground cumin, heated in a dry pan until fragrant
- 1 bay leaf
- 1 teaspoon smoked Spanish paprika or half of a seeded chipotle chili (optional)
- 2 cups black beans (soaked overnight, if desired)
- 3 quarts vegetable stock or water
- ½ bunch fresh cilantro (optional)
- Salt and pepper to taste
- 1 recipe Tofu Sour Cream (see Chapter 2) or store-bought equivalent
- 2 teaspoons ground coriander
- 1 tablespoon chopped cilantro, for garnish

1. In a large soup pot over medium heat, heat olive oil for 1 minute. Add onion, chopped leek, and garlic; cook 5 minutes, until onion turns translucent, stirring frequently. Add cumin, bay leaf, and paprika or chipotle if using. Cook 5 minutes more. Add beans and stock. Bring to a full boil; reduce heat to a simmer, and cook 90 minutes, adding cilantro halfway through, until beans are very tender and starting to fall apart (cooking time will vary depending on age of beans and whether or not they were soaked—assume 30 minutes less for soaked beans). Carefully purée ⅔ of the soup in a blender; add back to rest of soup. Season to taste with salt and white pepper.

2. Whisk together the Tofu Sour Cream and coriander until well combined. Serve the soup topped with a teaspoon of the sour cream and a sprinkling of chopped cilantro.

CORN AND POTATO CHOWDER

Corn and dairy form a complete protein, making this a very nourishing dish for vegetarians.

Serves 12

8 ears sweet corn, shucked

1 tablespoon olive oil

2 large onions, chopped

2 stalks celery, chopped

1 pound red potatoes, cut into 1" chunks

3 sprigs fresh thyme or 1 teaspoon dried thyme leaves

1 bay leaf

3 teaspoons salt

1 smoked chili (optional)

4 ounces (1 stick) unsalted butter

3 quarts vegetable stock or water

4 teaspoons cornstarch, dissolved in ¼ cup water

1 quart cream or milk

White pepper and additional salt to taste

2 tablespoons chopped fresh chives

1. Cut corn kernels from the cob using a slicing motion with a kitchen knife. Reserve the cobs, and set kernels aside. In a large soup pot over medium-high heat, heat olive oil for 1 minute. Add the corn cobs, onions, celery, potatoes, thyme, bay leaf, salt, and chili if using. Cook until onions are translucent, about 5 minutes. Add the butter and cook gently, allowing the vegetables to stew in the butter, for about 5 more minutes.

2. Add the vegetable stock or water. Raise flame to high and bring to a full boil. Lower to a simmer and cook 10 minutes more. Remove the corn cobs; add cornstarch mixture and simmer 5 minutes more. Stir in the cream or milk, and adjust seasoning with white pepper and salt to taste. Serve sprinkled with chives.

MUSHROOM, BARLEY, AND COLLARD GREENS SOUP

This should be called "Health Soup" for its concentration of cancer-fighting antioxidants, folate-rich greens, nourishing whole grains, and complete protein-forming combinations. Who knew medicine for the body and soul could taste so good?

Serves 12

2 tablespoons olive oil

2 pounds mushrooms (any variety)

1 large onion, chopped

1 carrot, peeled and chopped

2 stalks celery, chopped

4 cloves garlic, roughly chopped

2 bay leaves

2 tablespoons fresh or 2 teaspoons dried marjoram or oregano leaves

1½ teaspoons fresh or ½ teaspoon dried rosemary leaves

2 teaspoons salt

½ teaspoon fresh ground black pepper

2 cups pearl barley, rinsed

3 quarts vegetable stock or water

1 bunch fresh collard greens, cooked until tender in boiling water and chopped, or 2 (10-ounce) packages frozen chopped collards

1. Heat the oil in a large soup pot over medium-high heat for 1 minute. Add mushrooms, onion, carrot, celery, garlic, bay leaves, marjoram or oregano, rosemary, salt, and pepper. Cook until vegetables have softened significantly and are stewing in their natural broth, about 15 minutes. Stir in barley and stock or water. Bring the soup up to a full boil, then reduce to a medium simmer and cook until barley is tender, about 40 minutes.

2. Add the collards; cook about 10 minutes more. Season to taste.

PINTO BEAN SOUP WITH SALSA FRESCA

A restaurant secret to elevating simple soups to finer cuisine is to place an attractive garnish right in the middle of the portion just before serving. In this case, we use a refreshing Salsa Fresca to brighten this Mexican soup.

Serves 6

1½ cups dried pinto beans

7 cups water

¼ cup olive oil

2 medium yellow onions, diced

1 teaspoon salt

½ teaspoon freshly ground black pepper

4 cloves garlic, crushed

¼ teaspoon dried thyme

6 cups vegetable stock or water

1 cup Salsa Fresca (see Chapter 4)

Tofu Sour Cream (see Chapter 2), optional

1. Rinse the beans well and place in a saucepan with the water, bring to a boil, lower to a simmer, and cook until very tender, about 1½ hours.

2. In a large soup pot, heat the oil over a medium flame. Add the onions, salt, and pepper; cook until the onions brown slightly, about 10 minutes. Add the garlic and thyme; cook 2 minutes more. Add the beans, along with their cooking liquid and the stock or water. Bring to a boil; reduce heat and simmer uncovered, stirring occasionally, until the beans start to break apart, about 30 minutes.

3. Purée the beans in a blender until smooth (work carefully in small batches, so as not to splash hot liquid—a blender works best for this). Adjust seasoning. Ladle the soup into warmed shallow soup plates, topping each with a spoonful of Salsa Fresca and, if desired, a dollop of Tofu Sour Cream.

ACORN SQUASH SOUP WITH ANISE AND CARROTS

When the weather turns chilly, fall and winter squashes like acorn squash start showing up in the markets—just in time to make this smooth, soothing, velvety soup. Remove the seeds from the squash. Salt and toast them for twenty minutes in a medium-temperature oven for a crunchy soup garnish.

Serves 6

1 tablespoon olive oil

2 medium onions, chopped

1 teaspoon salt

1 medium acorn squash (about 2 pounds), peeled, cut into 1" chunks

2 carrots, peeled and cut into 1" chunks

1 teaspoon anise seeds, toasted in a dry pan for 2 minutes, until fragrant

¼ cup Cognac or brandy

1 pint vegetable stock

1–2 cups skim milk

Fresh parsley, chopped

1. Heat the olive oil in a heavy medium saucepot over a medium flame. Add the onions and salt; cook until translucent and slightly browned, about 10 minutes. Lower the flame. Add the squash, carrots, and anise seeds; cook slowly, stirring the browned bits from the bottom of the pan frequently with a wooden spoon. These browned natural sugars will give the soup its caramelized complexity.

2. When the squash is soft and nicely browned, add the Cognac; cook for 2 minutes to steam off the alcohol. Add the stock; simmer 15 minutes.

3. In a blender, purée the soup with as much skim milk as necessary for a thick but soupy consistency. Season to taste. Serve garnished with toasted squash seeds and a sprinkling of chopped parsley.

MISO SOUP

The delicious cloudy broth you've been served in Japanese restaurants, with diced tofu and seaweed, is made with a fermented soybean and grain paste called miso.

Serves 4

5 cups vegetable or mushroom stock

1 piece kombu (kelp, a dried seaweed), about 5" square

1 teaspoon soy sauce

3 tablespoons light (yellow) miso, such as shiro mugi miso

2 scallions, chopped

2 ounces firm tofu, diced into small cubes

4 teaspoons wakame seaweed (instant)

1. Bring stock and kombu to a boil in a soup pot. Cover; remove from heat and let stand 5 minutes. Strain; stir in soy sauce.

2. In a mixing bowl, mix about ¼ cup of the warm stock into the miso paste with a wire whisk until the miso is dissolved. Pour this mixture back into the remaining stock. Place scallions, diced tofu, and wakame into 4 bowls. Gently ladle soup into the bowls.

[SC] TOFU NOODLE SOUP

For added texture, freeze the tofu and bake before adding to the soup.

Serves 4

2 tablespoons olive oil

1 medium onion, diced

3 cloves garlic, minced

2 ribs celery, sliced in ½" pieces

7 ounces extra-firm tofu, cubed

5 cups Vegetable Broth (see recipe in this chapter)

1 bay leaf

1 teaspoon salt

Juice of 1 lemon

2 teaspoons fresh parsley, chopped

2 teaspoons fresh thyme, chopped

8 ounces cooked egg noodles or linguine

1. In a large sauté pan heat the olive oil over medium heat. Add the onion, garlic, and celery and sauté for 3 minutes.
2. Add the tofu and cook 5 additional minutes.
3. In a 4-quart slow cooker, pour the sautéed vegetables, tofu, Vegetable Broth, bay leaf, and salt. Cover, and cook on low for 8 hours.
4. Add the lemon juice, parsley, thyme, and pasta. Cover and cook for an additional 20 minutes.

SC HOT AND SOUR SOUP

Adjust the spiciness of this soup by adding more or less chili paste, to taste.

Serves 6

4 cups Vegetable Broth (see recipe in this chapter)

2 tablespoons soy sauce

2 tablespoons rice vinegar

1 teaspoon sesame oil

2 ounces dried Chinese mushrooms

½ cup canned bamboo shoots, sliced

4 ounces extra-firm tofu, cubed

1 tablespoon red chili paste

1 teaspoon white pepper

2 tablespoons cornstarch mixed with ¼ cup water

1. In a 4-quart slow cooker, add all ingredients except for the cornstarch mixture; cook on low for 6 hours.
2. Pour in the cornstarch mixture; stir, and cook on high heat for 20 additional minutes.

SC CAULIFLOWER SOUP

Cauliflower's peak season is the fall, so try this soup on a crisp autumn night.

Serves 6

1 small head cauliflower, chopped

½ onion, diced

1 teaspoon salt

1 teaspoon pepper

2 tablespoons butter or vegan margarine

4 cups Vegetable Broth (see recipe in this chapter)

Zest of ½ lemon

1. In a 4-quart slow cooker, add all ingredients except zest. Cover, and cook on low for 6 hours.

2. Turn off slow cooker and let soup cool about 10 minutes. Using a blender or immersion blender, process until very smooth.

3. Return soup to the slow cooker; add lemon zest, and heat until warm.

Zest Versus Juice

Lemon zest is obtained by grating the outer peel of the lemon. It contains a more intense lemon flavor than the juice of the citrus fruit, although many recipes call for both lemon zest and lemon juice.

SC FRENCH ONION SOUP

Vidalia onions are a sweet variety of onion that work particularly well in French Onion Soup.

Serves 4

¼ cup olive oil

4 Vidalia onions, sliced

4 cloves garlic, minced

1 tablespoon dried thyme

1 cup red wine

4 cups Vegetable Broth (see recipe in this chapter)

1 teaspoon salt

1 teaspoon pepper

4 slices French bread

4 ounces Swiss cheese or vegan cheese such as Daiya Mozzarella Style Shreds

1. In a sauté pan, heat the olive oil over medium-high heat and cook the onions until golden brown, about 3 minutes. Add the garlic and sauté for 1 minute.

2. In a 4-quart slow cooker, pour the sautéed vegetables, thyme, red wine, Vegetable Broth, salt, and pepper. Cover and cook on low heat for 4 hours.

3. While the soup is cooking, preheat the oven to the broiler setting. Lightly toast the slices of French bread.

4. To serve, ladle the soup into a broiler-safe bowl, place a slice of the toasted French bread on top of the soup, put a slice of the Swiss cheese on top of the bread, and place the soup under the broiler until the cheese has melted.

SC GARDEN VEGETABLE SOUP

Leave the skin on the potatoes in this recipe, and others, for a more rustic, richer potato flavor.

Serves 6

- ½ red onion, diced
- 1 small squash, diced
- 4 red potatoes, quartered
- 1 cup okra, sliced
- 1 cup fresh corn
- 1 cup green beans, cut into ½" pieces
- 6 cups Vegetable Broth (see recipe in this chapter)
- 6 ounces diced tomatoes
- 1½ teaspoons salt
- 1 teaspoon pepper

In a 4-quart slow cooker, add all ingredients. Cover and cook over low heat for 6–8 hours.

Choosing the Right Broth

In most soup recipes, you can use Vegetable Broth (see recipe in this chapter) or No-Beef Broth (see recipe in this chapter), depending on how rich you would like the flavor to be. For a full-flavored taste, choose No-Beef Broth, but remember to adjust the salt because No-Beef Broth already has sodium from the vegan Worcestershire sauce.

SC POTATO-LEEK SOUP

If you'd like to omit the alcohol from this recipe, just add another ½ cup of Vegetable Broth.

Serves 6

- 2 tablespoons butter or vegan margarine
- 2 small leeks, chopped (white and light green parts only)
- 3 large russet potatoes, peeled and diced
- 4 cups Vegetable Broth (see recipe in this chapter)
- ½ cup white wine
- ½ cup water
- 1 teaspoon salt
- 1 teaspoon pepper
- ¼ teaspoon dried thyme

1. In a sauté pan over medium heat, melt the butter or vegan margarine, then add the leeks. Cook until softened, about 5 minutes.

2. In a 4-quart slow cooker, add the sautéed leeks, potatoes, broth, wine, water, salt, pepper, and thyme. Cover and cook over low heat 6–8 hours.

3. Allow soup to cool slightly, then use an immersion blender or traditional blender to process until smooth.

SC BEER-CHEESE SOUP

For the best results, use a pale ale beer in this recipe.

Serves 12

½ cup butter or vegan margarine

½ white onion, diced

2 medium carrots, peeled and diced

2 ribs celery, diced

½ cup flour

3 cups Vegetable Broth (see recipe in this chapter)

1 (12-ounce) beer

3 cups milk or unsweetened soymilk

3 cups Cheddar cheese or vegan Daiya Cheddar Style Shreds

1 teaspoon salt

1 teaspoon pepper

½ teaspoon dry ground mustard

1. In a sauté pan over medium heat, melt the butter or vegan margarine, then sauté the onion, carrots, and celery until just softened, about 5–7 minutes. Add the flour and stir to form a roux. Let cook for 2–3 minutes.

2. In a 4-quart slow cooker, add the cooked vegetables and roux, then slowly pour in the Vegetable Broth and beer while whisking.

3. Add the milk or soymilk, cheese, salt, pepper, and mustard. Cover and cook on low for 4 hours.

4. Let the soup cool slightly, then blend until smooth, or you can skip this step and serve it chunky.

Unsweetened Soymilk

Plain or original soymilk typically contains sugar and has a distinct flavor that will stand out in savory dishes. For these recipes, use plain unsweetened soymilk instead.

SC BUTTERNUT SQUASH SOUP

You can substitute an extra cup of Vegetable Broth for the white wine in this soup.

Serves 6

1 medium butternut squash, peeled and diced

1 russet potato, peeled and diced

1 large carrot, chopped

1 rib celery, sliced

1 onion, diced

4 cups Vegetable Broth (see recipe in this chapter)

1 cup white wine

1 bay leaf

¼ teaspoon dried thyme

1½ teaspoons salt

Pinch of nutmeg

1. In a 4-quart slow cooker, add all of the ingredients. Cover and cook over low heat for 6 hours.

2. Cool the soup slightly and remove the bay leaf. Process in a blender or using an immersion blender.

SC CREAMY CHICKPEA SOUP

Beans can be puréed to make a creamy soup without the cream.

Serves 6

1 small onion, diced

2 cloves garlic, minced

2 (15-ounce) cans chickpeas, drained and rinsed

5 cups Vegetable Broth (see recipe in this chapter)

1 teaspoon salt

½ teaspoon cumin

Juice of ½ lemon

1 tablespoon olive oil

¼ fresh parsley, chopped

1. In a 4-quart slow cooker, add all ingredients except for the lemon juice, olive oil, and parsley. Cover, and cook over low heat for 4 hours.

2. Allow to cool slightly, then process the soup in a blender or using an immersion blender.

3. Return the soup to the slow cooker, then add the lemon juice, olive oil, and parsley, and heat on low for an additional 30 minutes.

MUSHROOM BARLEY SOUP

Using three types of mushrooms in this soup adds a more robust flavor.

Serves 8

1 ounce dried porcini mushrooms

1 cup boiling water

1½ teaspoons butter or vegan margarine

5 ounces fresh shiitake mushrooms, sliced

4 ounces fresh button mushrooms, sliced

1 large onion, diced

1 clove garlic, minced

⅔ cup medium pearl barley

¼ teaspoon ground black pepper

½ teaspoon salt

6 cups No-Beef Broth (see recipe in this chapter)

1. In a heat-safe bowl, place the dried porcini mushrooms; pour the boiling water over the mushrooms. Soak for 15 minutes.

2. Meanwhile, in a medium sauté pan, melt the butter or vegan margarine. Sauté the fresh mushrooms, onion, and garlic until the onion is soft, about 3 minutes.

3. Drain the porcini mushrooms and discard the water.

4. In a 4-quart slow cooker, add all of the mushrooms, onion, garlic, barley, pepper, salt, and the broth. Stir, cover, and cook 6–8 hours on low.

SC SUMMER BORSCHT

Serve this cooling soup with a dollop of sour cream or vegan sour cream. Try Tofutti Sour Supreme.

Serves 6

3½ cups cooked beets, shredded

¼ cup onion, diced

½ teaspoon salt

1 teaspoon sugar

¼ cup lemon juice

½ tablespoon celery seed

2 cups Vegetable Broth (see recipe in this chapter)

2 cups water

1. In a 4-quart slow cooker, place all of the ingredients. Cover and cook on low for 6–8 hours, or on high for 4 hours.

2. Refrigerate the soup for 4 hours or overnight. Serve cold.

Can't Beat Beets

Beets, also known as beetroot, can be peeled, steamed, cooked, pickled, and shredded; they are good hot or cold. They are high in folate, vitamin C, potassium, and fiber. Although they have the highest sugar content of all vegetables, beets are very low in calories; one beet is only 75 calories.

SC SIMPLE SPLIT PEA SOUP

Immersion blenders are handheld blenders that can be used in the pot where food is cooked, which eliminates the need to transfer soup to a blender.

Serves 6

2 cups dried green split peas

Water, as needed

6 cups Vegetable Broth (see recipe in this chapter)

2 medium potatoes, peeled and diced

2 large carrots, chopped

3 stalks celery, chopped

2 cloves garlic, minced

1 teaspoon cumin

1 teaspoon thyme

1 bay leaf

1 teaspoon salt

1. Rinse the green split peas; soak overnight in enough water to cover them by more than 1". Drain.

2. In a 4-quart slow cooker, add all ingredients; cook over low heat for 6–8 hours.

3. Let the soup cool slightly, then remove the bay leaf. Process in a blender, or use an immersion blender, until smooth.

SC TORTILLA SOUP

Turn this soup into a complete meal by adding pieces of cooked vegetarian chicken, such as Morningstar Farms Meal Starters Chik'n Strips or Gardein Seasoned Bites.

Serves 8

2 tablespoons olive oil

1 large onion, chopped

2 cloves garlic, minced

2 tablespoons soy sauce

7 cups Vegetable Broth (see recipe in this chapter)

12 ounces firm silken tofu, crumbled

2 cups tomato, diced

1 cup corn kernels

1 teaspoon chipotle powder

1 teaspoon cayenne pepper

2 teaspoons ground cumin

2 teaspoons salt

1 teaspoon dried oregano

10 small corn tortillas, sliced

8 ounces shredded Monterey Jack cheese or vegan cheese, such as Daiya Mozzarella Style Shreds

1. In a sauté pan over medium heat, add the olive oil; sauté the onion until just soft, about 3 minutes. Add the garlic and sauté for an additional 30 seconds.

2. In a 4-quart slow cooker, add all ingredients except tortillas and cheese. Stir, cover, and cook over low heat for 4 hours.

3. While the soup is cooking, preheat oven to 450°F. Slice the corn tortillas into thin strips and place them on an ungreased baking sheet. Bake for about 10 minutes, or until they turn golden brown. Remove from heat and set aside.

4. After the soup has cooled slightly, use an immersion blender or regular blender to purée the soup.

5. Serve with cooked tortilla strips and 1 ounce of shredded cheese in each bowl of soup.

Chipotle Powder

Chipotle powder is made from ground chipotle peppers, a type of dried jalapeño. They bring a smoky spiciness to dishes, but can be replaced with cayenne pepper or chili powder.

GREEK-STYLE ORZO AND SPINACH SOUP

Lemon zest adds a bright, robust flavor to this simple soup.

Serves 6

2 cloves garlic, minced

3 tablespoons lemon juice

1 teaspoon lemon zest

5 cups Vegetable Broth (see recipe in this chapter)

1½ teaspoons salt

1 small onion, thinly sliced

1 package extra-firm tofu, cubed

⅓ cup dried orzo

4 cups fresh baby spinach

1. In a 4-quart slow cooker, add the garlic, lemon juice, zest, broth, salt, and onion. Cover and cook on low for 6–8 hours.

2. Stir in the tofu and cook for 30 minutes on high.

3. Add the orzo and spinach. Stir and continue to cook on high for an additional 15 minutes. Stir before serving.

SC PHO

This Vietnamese noodle soup is easy to make in the slow cooker. Try it instead of vegetable soup on a cold night.

Serves 6

1 tablespoon coriander seeds

1 tablespoon whole cloves

6 star anises

1 cinnamon stick

1 tablespoon fennel seed

1 tablespoon whole cardamom

4 knobs fresh ginger, sliced

1 onion, sliced

1 quart No-Beef Broth (see recipe in this chapter)

1 teaspoon soy sauce

8 ounces Vietnamese rice noodles

1 cup shredded seitan

½ cup chopped cilantro

½ cup chopped Thai basil

2 cups mung bean sprouts

¼ cup sliced scallions

1. In a dry nonstick skillet, quickly heat the spices, ginger, and onion until the seeds start to pop, about 5 minutes. The onion and ginger should look slightly caramelized. Place them in a cheesecloth packet and tie it securely.

2. In a 4-quart slow cooker, place the cheesecloth packet. Add the broth, soy sauce, noodles, and seitan. Cover and cook on low for 4 hours.

3. Remove the cheesecloth packet after cooking. Serve each bowl topped with cilantro, basil, sprouts, and scallions.

SC WILD RICE AND PORTOBELLO SOUP

Any variety of rice will work in this soup. It's fine to substitute white rice or brown rice if that's what you have on hand.

Serves 4

½ yellow onion, diced
2 small carrots, peeled and diced
2 ribs celery, sliced
1 cup chopped portobello mushroom
½ cup uncooked wild rice
4 cups Vegetable Broth (see recipe in this chapter)
1 bay leaf
1 sprig rosemary
1 teaspoon salt
½ teaspoon pepper

1. In a 4-quart slow cooker, add all ingredients. Cover and cook over low heat for 6 hours.
2. Remove the bay leaf and rosemary sprig before serving.

SC CELERY ROOT SOUP

Serve a bowl of this soup topped with green apple crisps.

Serves 6

2 tablespoons butter or vegan margarine

1 small leek (white and light green parts only), chopped

2 cloves garlic, minced

1 large celery root, peeled and cubed

2 medium russet potatoes, peeled and cubed

6 cups Vegetable Broth (see recipe in this chapter)

1½ teaspoons salt

1 teaspoon pepper

1. In a large sauté pan over medium heat, melt the butter or margarine, then add the leek and sauté about 4 minutes. Add the garlic and sauté an additional 30 seconds.

2. In a 4-quart slow cooker, add the sautéed leek and garlic, celery root, potatoes, broth, salt, and pepper. Cover and cook over low heat for 6–8 hours.

3. Let the soup cool slightly, then process in a blender or with an immersion blender until smooth.

Celery Root

Celery root, also known as celeriac, is not the root of the celery you know. It is similar in texture to a potato, and is cultivated for its root, not its leaves or stalk. It is grown in cool weather and is best in the fall, right after it has been pulled. The roots and crevices have to be trimmed away, so a 1-pound root will only yield about 2 cups after it is peeled and sliced or grated, something to keep in mind when buying for a recipe.

SC BRUNSWICK STEW

Try adding barbecue sauce to this stew to spice things up.

Serves 4

4 cups Vegetable Broth (see recipe in this chapter)
1 (15-ounce) can diced tomatoes
1 (6-ounce) can tomato paste
1 cup okra, sliced
1 cup corn
1 cup frozen lima beans
2 cups seitan, diced
¼ teaspoon dried rosemary
¼ teaspoon dried oregano
2 teaspoons vegan Worcestershire sauce
Salt and pepper, to taste

In a 4-quart slow cooker, add all ingredients. Cover and cook on low heat for 5–6 hours.

SC JAMAICAN RED BEAN STEW

Make your own jerk seasoning by combining thyme, allspice, black pepper, cinnamon, cayenne, onion powder, and nutmeg.

Serves 4

2 tablespoons olive oil

½ onion, diced

2 garlic cloves, minced

1 (15-ounce) can diced tomatoes

3 cups sweet potatoes, peeled and diced

2 (15-ounce) cans red kidney beans, drained

1 cup coconut milk

3 cups Vegetable Broth (see recipe in this chapter)

2 teaspoons jerk seasoning

2 teaspoons curry powder

Salt and pepper, to taste

1. In a sauté pan over medium heat, add the olive oil, then sauté the onion and garlic for about 3 minutes.

2. In a 4-quart slow cooker, add all ingredients. Cover and cook on low heat for 6 hours.

SC SOUTHWEST CORN CHOWDER

The russet potatoes in this recipe will slowly break up during the cooking process and add to the creaminess of the chowder.

Serves 4

¼ cup butter or vegan margarine

1 onion, diced

1 jalapeño, minced

1 cup diced tomato

2 medium russet potatoes, peeled and diced

2 (15-ounce) cans creamed corn

2 cups water

2 cups unsweetened soymilk

1 teaspoon chili powder

1 teaspoon cumin

¼ teaspoon cayenne pepper

Salt and pepper, to taste

1. In a sauté pan over medium heat, melt the butter or vegan margarine; add the onion and jalapeño, and sauté for about 3 minutes.

2. In a 4-quart slow cooker, add all ingredients. Cover and cook on low heat for 6 hours.

SC OKRA GUMBO

The roux—a combination of oil or butter and flour—is the base for many classic New Orleans dishes.

Serves 6

½ cup vegetable oil

½ cup flour

1 white onion, diced

1 bell pepper, diced

4 cloves garlic, minced

4 cups water

2 cups Vegetable Broth (see recipe in this chapter)

1 tablespoon vegan Worcestershire sauce

1 (16-ounce) package frozen chopped okra

1 tablespoon Cajun seasoning

1 bay leaf

2 teaspoons salt

2 teaspoons pepper

1 (7-ounce) package Gardein Chick'n Strips, chopped

½ cup flat-leaf parsley, chopped

½ cup scallions, sliced

½ teaspoon file powder

6 cups cooked white rice

1. In a sauté pan, bring the oil and flour to medium heat, stirring continuously until the roux achieves a rich brown color, at least 10 minutes.
2. In a 4-quart slow cooker, add the roux and all remaining ingredients except the rice. Cover and cook on low heat for 6 hours.
3. Once done, remove the bay leaf. Pour each serving over 1 cup of cooked rice.

Filé Powder

Filé (pronounced FEE-lay) powder is made from ground sassafras leaves. It is an essential ingredient for authentic Cajun or Creole gumbo. Used to both thicken and flavor, filé powder is thought to have been first used by the Choctaw Indians from the Louisiana bayou region. It can be found in most well-stocked grocery stores.

MEDITERRANEAN VEGETABLE STEW

Try serving this stew with large pieces of pita bread and a scoop of hummus.

Serves 6

2 tablespoons extra-virgin olive oil

4 garlic cloves, chopped

1 red onion, chopped

1 red bell pepper, seeded and chopped

1 eggplant, chopped

1 (15-ounce) can artichokes, drained and chopped

⅓ cup Kalamata olives, pitted and chopped

2 (15-ounce) cans diced tomatoes

4 cups Vegetable Broth (see recipe in this chapter)

1 teaspoon red pepper flakes

½ teaspoon dried oregano

½ teaspoon dried parsley

1 teaspoon salt

½ teaspoon pepper

In a 4-quart slow cooker, add all ingredients. Cover and cook on low heat for 4–6 hours.

Preparing Eggplant
Some people salt eggplant prior to cooking in order to remove bitterness, but this step is not required for making delicious recipes using eggplant. The skins can be removed, but this also is not necessary. Eggplants, called aubergine in almost all other parts of the world, can be boiled, steamed, sautéed, stir-fried, deep-fried, braised, baked, grilled, broiled, and microwaved.

SC WHITE BEAN AND TOMATO STEW

Enjoy this hearty stew over rice or with a piece of crusty white bread.

Serves 4

1 (15-ounce) can cannellini beans, drained
4 cups Vegetable Broth (see recipe in this chapter)
1 tablespoon vegetable oil
1 teaspoon salt
2 cloves garlic, minced
½ teaspoon dried sage
¼ teaspoon dried thyme
½ teaspoon black pepper
1 cup tomato, diced

1. In a 4-quart slow cooker, add all ingredients except for tomato. Cover and cook on low heat for 5–6 hours.
2. Add the tomato; stir, and cook for an additional 30 minutes.

SC SEITAN AND MUSHROOM STEW

Homemade or store-bought seitan will work well in this recipe, but if you use store-bought seitan, be sure to drain the liquid first.

Serves 4

2 tablespoons extra-virgin olive oil

1 yellow onion, sliced

4 garlic cloves, minced

1 cup carrots, chopped

2 cups mushrooms, sliced

2 cups seitan, cubed

3 cups Vegetable Broth (see recipe in this chapter)

2 tablespoons soy sauce

1 cup potatoes, peeled and cubed

1 cup frozen peas

½ teaspoon sage

½ teaspoon salt

¼ teaspoon pepper

1. In a sauté pan over medium heat, add the extra-virgin olive oil. Add the onion and garlic and sauté for 3 minutes.
2. In a 4-quart slow cooker, add the sautéed vegetables and all remaining ingredients. Cover and cook on low heat for 4–5 hours.

SC CURRIED SEITAN STEW

Adding a small amount of soy sauce to a curry dish gives it a richness that is normally achieved with fish sauce in recipes that aren't vegetarian.

Serves 4

2 tablespoons olive oil

½ onion, chopped

2 cloves garlic, minced

1 teaspoon fresh ginger, minced

2 tablespoons panang curry paste

1 teaspoon paprika

1 teaspoon sugar

½ teaspoon cayenne pepper

1 teaspoon soy sauce

1 (14-ounce) can coconut milk

3 cups Vegetable Broth (see recipe in this chapter)

2 cups seitan, cubed

½ teaspoon salt

¼ teaspoon pepper

¼ cup cilantro, chopped

1. In a 4-quart slow cooker, add all ingredients except for the cilantro. Cover and cook on low heat for 4 hours.
2. Garnish with cilantro before serving.

SC VEGETABLE DUMPLING STEW

Surprisingly, some popular brands of uncooked biscuits in a tube are actually vegan.

Serves 6

2 tablespoons olive oil

½ large onion, diced

2 cloves garlic, minced

2 carrots, chopped

2 stalks celery, chopped

½ cup corn kernels

½ cup okra, chopped

2 (14½-ounce) cans diced tomatoes

4 cups Vegetable Broth (see recipe in this chapter)

¼ teaspoon dried rosemary

1 teaspoon dried parsley

¼ teaspoon dried oregano

½ teaspoon salt

¼ teaspoon black pepper

1 (6-ounce) package vegan refrigerated biscuits

1. In a sauté pan over medium heat, add the olive oil, onion, and garlic and sauté for 3 minutes.

2. In a 4-quart slow cooker, add all ingredients except for the biscuits. Cover and cook on low heat for 4–5 hours.

3. While the stew is cooking, flatten the biscuits with a rolling pin on a floured surface, then cut each into fourths.

4. Drop the biscuit pieces into the stew and cook for 30 more minutes.

ÉTOUFFÉE

Vegan shrimp can be purchased online at VegeUSA.com.

Serves 6

½ cup butter or vegan margarine
1 onion, diced
3 celery ribs, chopped
1 carrot, diced
3 cloves garlic, minced
1 green bell pepper, chopped
¼ cup flour
1 cup water
2 teaspoons Cajun seasoning
1 (10½-ounce) package vegan shrimp
Juice of 1 lemon
½ teaspoon salt
¼ teaspoon black pepper
4 cups cooked white rice
½ cup chopped parsley

1. In a sauté pan over medium heat, add the butter or vegan margarine. Sauté the onion, celery, carrot, garlic, and green bell pepper until soft, about 5–7 minutes. Stir in the flour to make a roux.

2. Add the roux to a 4-quart slow cooker. Whisk in the water, Cajun seasoning, vegan shrimp, lemon juice, salt, and pepper. Cover and cook on low heat for 4–5 hours.

3. Serve over the white rice and garnish with parsley.

SC SEITAN AND CABBAGE STEW

This dish is reminiscent of beef and cabbage stew, minus the meat.

Serves 4

- 1 onion, chopped
- 1 carrot, chopped
- 2 celery ribs, chopped
- 4 cups cabbage, shredded
- 2 potatoes, chopped
- 3 cups seitan, cubed
- 4 cups Vegetable Broth (see recipe in this chapter)
- 2 tablespoons vegan Worcestershire sauce
- ½ teaspoon salt
- ¼ teaspoon black pepper

In a 4-quart slow cooker, add all ingredients. Cover and cook on low heat for 5–6 hours.

SC POSOLE

This rich-tasting stew just needs a sprinkling of shredded red cabbage to finish it to perfection.

Serves 6

8 large dried New Mexican red chilies

1½ quarts Vegetable Broth (see recipe in this chapter)

3 cloves garlic, minced

2 tablespoons lime juice

1 tablespoon ground cumin

1 tablespoon oregano

1 (7-ounce) package Gardein Chick'n Strips

¾ cup flour

1 teaspoon canola oil

1 large onion, sliced

40 ounces canned hominy

1. Seed the chilies, reserving the seeds.
2. In a dry, hot frying pan, heat the chilies until warmed through and fragrant, about 2–3 minutes. Do not burn or brown them.
3. In a medium pot, place the chilies and seeds, 1 quart broth, garlic, lime juice, cumin, and oregano. Bring to a boil and continue to boil for 20 minutes.
4. Meanwhile, in a plastic bag, toss the Chick'n Strips with the flour to coat. Heat the oil in a large nonstick skillet and brown the vegan meat on all sides, about 3 minutes.
5. Add the onion and cook about 5 minutes, or until the onion is soft.
6. In a 4-quart slow cooker, pour the unused broth, hominy, onion, and Chick'n mixture.
7. Strain the chili-stock mixture through a mesh sieve into the slow cooker insert, mashing down with a wooden spoon to press out the pulp and juice. Discard the seeds and remaining solids.
8. Cook on low for 8 hours.

Citrus Leftovers

If you have a small amount of juice left, pour it into an ice cube tray in your freezer, one well at a time, and freeze. Leftover zest can also be saved. Place the zest in a freezer bag and refrigerate up to 1 week or frozen in a freezer-safe container up to 1 month.

SC PUMPKIN STEW

In chunky stews, fresh pumpkin works best, but if you are going to purée it into a creamy soup, then canned pumpkin is the better choice.

Serves 8

6 cups Vegetable Broth (see recipe in this chapter)
2 cups pumpkin, cubed and peeled
2 cups potatoes, cubed and peeled
1 cup corn kernels
1 onion, diced
2 cloves garlic, minced
2 bay leaves
2 tablespoons tomato paste
1½ teaspoons salt
½ teaspoon dried thyme
½ teaspoon dried parsley

In a 4-quart slow cooker, add all ingredients. Cover and cook over low heat for 8 hours.

SC CAULIFLOWER CHOWDER

In this rich chowder, puréed cauliflower takes the place of heavy cream or soymilk.

Serves 6

2 pounds cauliflower florets

2 quarts Vegetable Broth (see recipe in this chapter)

1 onion, chopped

3 cloves garlic, minced

1 teaspoon white pepper

1½ teaspoons salt

1½ cups broccoli florets

2 carrots, cut into coins

1 stalk celery, diced

1. In a 4-quart slow cooker, place the cauliflower, broth, onion, garlic, pepper, and salt; stir. Cook on low for 6 hours, or until the cauliflower is fork-tender.

2. Use an immersion blender to purée the cauliflower in the slow cooker until very smooth.

3. Add the broccoli, carrots, and celery. Cook for 30 minutes, or until the vegetables are fork-tender.

SC WHITE BEAN CASSOULET

The longer you cook this cassoulet, the creamier it gets.

Serves 8

1 pound dried cannellini beans
2 cups boiling water
1 ounce dried porcini mushrooms
2 leeks, sliced
1 teaspoon canola oil
2 parsnips, diced
2 carrots, diced
2 stalks celery, diced
½ teaspoon ground fennel
1 teaspoon crushed rosemary
1 teaspoon dried chervil
⅛ teaspoon cloves
¼ teaspoon salt
¼ teaspoon freshly ground black pepper
2 cups Vegetable Broth (see recipe in this chapter)

1. The night before making the soup, place the beans in a 4-quart slow cooker. Fill with water to 1" below the top of the insert. Soak overnight.
2. Drain the beans and return them to the slow cooker.
3. In a heatproof bowl, pour the boiling water over the dried mushrooms and soak for 15 minutes.
4. Slice only the white and light green parts of the leeks into ¼ rounds. Cut the rounds in half.
5. In a nonstick skillet, heat the oil; add the parsnip, carrots, celery, and leeks. Sauté for 1 minute, just until the color of the vegetables brightens.
6. Add to the slow cooker along with the spices. Add the mushrooms, their soaking liquid, and the broth; stir.
7. Cook on low for 8–10 hours.

Using Dried Beans
Dried beans must be soaked overnight and boiled for at least 10 minutes before being added to a slow cooker, if you'd prefer to use them over canned beans.

SC KOREAN-STYLE HOT POT

Serve this hot and spicy main dish with sides of steamed rice and kimchi.

Serves 8

3 bunches baby bok choy

8 cups water

8 ounces sliced cremini mushrooms

12 ounces extra-firm tofu, cubed

3 cloves garlic, thinly sliced

¼ teaspoon sesame oil

1 tablespoon crushed red pepper flakes

7 ounces enoki mushrooms

1. Remove the leaves of the baby bok choy. Wash thoroughly.
2. Place the leaves whole in a 4-quart slow cooker. Add the water, cremini mushrooms, tofu, garlic, sesame oil, and crushed red pepper. Stir.
3. Cook on low for 8 hours.
4. Add the enoki mushrooms and stir. Cook an additional 30 minutes.

SEITAN BOURGUIGNONNE

Better Than Bouillon No Beef Base is a good vegetarian alternative to beef stock.

Serves 6

2 tablespoons olive oil

1 pound cooked seitan, cut into 2" cubes

2 carrots, sliced

1 onion, sliced

1 teaspoon salt

2 tablespoons flour

2 cups red wine

2 cups No-Beef Broth (see recipe in this chapter)

1 tablespoon tomato paste

2 cloves garlic, minced

½ teaspoon dried thyme

1 bay leaf

¼ teaspoon pepper

1 tablespoon butter or vegan margarine

18 whole pearl onions, peeled

2 cups sliced button mushrooms

1. Heat the olive oil in a sauté pan over medium heat. Sauté the seitan, carrots, and onion until soft, about 7 minutes. Stir in the salt and flour.

2. In a 4-quart slow cooker, add the vegetables and roux. Whisk in the red wine and No-Beef Broth, then add all remaining ingredients.

3. Cover and cook over low heat for 6–8 hours.

SC SUPER GREENS STEW

Kale and Swiss chard can hold up during long cooking times, but a more delicate green, such as spinach, would break down more.

Serves 6

2 cups chopped kale

2 cups chopped Swiss chard

1 (15-ounce) can chickpeas, drained

¼ onion, diced

1 carrot, peeled and sliced

2 cloves garlic, minced

6 cups Vegetable Broth (see recipe in this chapter)

1½ teaspoons salt

½ teaspoon pepper

1 sprig rosemary

½ teaspoon dried marjoram

In a 4-quart slow cooker, add all ingredients. Cover, and cook on low heat for 6 hours.

SC TEXAS STEW

Simple yet hearty is the goal for this cowboy-style stew.

Serves 6

2 tablespoons olive oil

1 (12-ounce) package frozen veggie crumbles

1 (15-ounce) can pinto beans, drained

1 (14-ounce) can diced tomatoes

1 (12-ounce) package frozen corn

½ onion, diced

½ green bell pepper, diced

4 cups Vegetable Broth (see recipe in this chapter)

1 teaspoon salt

1. In a sauté pan over medium, heat the olive oil and cook the frozen veggie crumbles until browned, about 10 minutes.

2. In a 4-quart slow cooker, add the cooked veggie crumbles and all other ingredients. Cover, and cook on low heat for 4–6 hours.

SC MOCK MEATBALL STEW

Unlike a traditional pasta dish, this stew has more sauce and just a little bit of pasta.

Serves 4

1 tablespoon olive oil
¼ onion, diced
3 cloves garlic, minced
1 teaspoon dried oregano
1 teaspoon dried basil
½ teaspoon crushed red pepper
1 teaspoon salt
2 cups Vegetable Broth (see recipe in this chapter)
2 (15-ounce) cans diced tomatoes
12 small vegan meatballs
2 cups cooked pasta shells

1. In a sauté pan over medium heat, heat the olive oil. Add the onion and sauté for 2–3 minutes.
2. Add the garlic and sauté for an additional 30 seconds.
3. In a 4-quart slow cooker, add the sautéed onion and garlic and all other ingredients except for the pasta. Cover and cook on low for 4–6 hours.
4. Add the pasta and cook 1 additional hour.

VEGAN CHILI

This hearty warm-up goes especially well with Spicy Southwestern Cornbread (see Chapter 12) and a tall glass of lemonade.

Serves 8

¼ cup olive oil

2 cups chopped onions

1 cup chopped carrots

2 cups chopped assorted bell peppers

2 teaspoons salt

1 tablespoon chopped garlic

2 chopped, seeded jalapeño peppers

1 tablespoon ground ancho chili pepper or ½ teaspoon crushed red pepper flakes

1 chipotle in adobo, chopped

1 tablespoon toasted cumin seeds, ground or 4 teaspoons ground cumin, toasted briefly in a dry pan

1 (28-ounce) can plum tomatoes, roughly chopped, juice included

3 (16-ounce) cans beans: 1 each red kidney, cannellini, and black beans, rinsed and drained, or an equal amount of home-cooked beans (start with about 1½ cups dried beans)

1 cup of tomato juice

Finely chopped red onions

Chopped fresh cilantro

1. Heat the oil in a heavy-bottomed Dutch oven or soup pot. Add the onions, carrots, bell peppers, and salt; cook 15 minutes over medium heat, until the onions are soft. Add the garlic, jalapeños, ancho, chipotle, and cumin; cook 5 minutes more.

2. Stir in tomatoes, beans, and tomato juice. Simmer about 45 minutes. Serve garnished with red onions and cilantro.

SOUTHWEST VEGETABLE CHILI

Southwest cuisine is similar to Mexican food and includes a wide variety of peppers, such as the jalapeños, bell peppers, chipotle, and chili powder found in this recipe.

Serves 4

1 (28-ounce) can diced tomatoes

1 (15-ounce) can red kidney beans

1 onion, chopped

1 green bell pepper, chopped

1 red bell pepper, chopped

1 zucchini, chopped

1 squash, chopped

¼ cup chopped, pickled jalapeños

⅛ cup chili powder

2 tablespoons garlic powder

2 tablespoons cumin

1 teaspoon chipotle powder

⅛ teaspoon dried thyme

1 teaspoon salt

¼ teaspoon black pepper

In a 4-quart slow cooker, add all ingredients. Cover and cook on low heat for 5 hours.

SC CINCINNATI CHILI

Cincinnati Chili is native to the state of Ohio and is typically eaten over spaghetti or on hot dogs.

Serves 4

1 onion, chopped

1 (12-ounce) package frozen veggie burger crumbles

3 cloves garlic, minced

1 cup tomato sauce

1 cup water

2 tablespoons red wine vinegar

2 tablespoons chili powder

½ teaspoon cumin

½ teaspoon ground cinnamon

½ teaspoon paprika

½ teaspoon ground allspice

1 tablespoon light brown sugar

1 tablespoon unsweetened cocoa powder

1 teaspoon hot pepper sauce

16 ounces cooked spaghetti

1. In a 4-quart slow cooker, add all ingredients except for the spaghetti. Cover and cook on low heat for 5 hours.

2. Serve the chili over the spaghetti and top with cheese, onions, and/or pinto beans.

Ways to Serve

Cincinnati Chili is known for being served up to five ways: Two-way means chili and spaghetti; three-way means chili, spaghetti, and Cheddar cheese; four-way means chili, spaghetti, cheese, and onions or pinto beans; and five-way means all of the above!

SC CHILI CON "CARNE"

Try Boca Ground Crumbles in this fast recipe as a vegan alternative to ground beef.

Serves 4

½ cup onion, diced

½ cup bell pepper, diced

1 (12-ounce) package frozen veggie burger crumbles

2 cloves garlic, minced

1 (15-ounce) can kidney beans, rinsed and drained

2 cups Vegetable Broth (see recipe in this chapter)

1 tablespoon chili powder

½ tablespoon chipotle powder

½ tablespoon cumin

1 teaspoon thyme

1 tablespoon oregano

2 cups fresh diced tomatoes

1 tablespoon tomato paste

1 tablespoon cider vinegar

2 teaspoons salt

In a 4-quart slow cooker, add all ingredients. Cover and cook on low heat for 5 hours.

SC SHREDDED "CHICKEN" CHILI

There are many vegan and vegetarian chicken substitutes on the market, but you can also use shredded seitan to replace the meat.

Serves 4

½ cup diced onion

½ cup diced bell pepper

1 (8-ounce) package Morningstar Farms Meal Starters Chik'n Strips, shredded by hand

2 cloves garlic, minced

1 (15-ounce) can kidney beans, rinsed and drained

2 cups Vegetable Broth (see recipe in this chapter)

1 tablespoon chili powder

½ tablespoon chipotle powder

½ tablespoon cumin

1 teaspoon thyme

1 tablespoon oregano

1 (15-ounce) can diced tomatoes, drained

1 tablespoon tomato paste

1 tablespoon cider vinegar

2 teaspoons salt

In a 4-quart slow cooker, add all ingredients. Cover and cook on low heat for 5 hours.

SC FIVE PEPPER CHILI

Sound the alarm! This chili will set mouths aflame.

Serves 8

1 onion, diced
1 jalapeño, seeded and minced
1 habanero pepper, seeded and minced
1 bell pepper, diced
1 poblano pepper, seeded and diced
2 cloves garlic, minced
2 (15-ounce) cans crushed tomatoes
2 cups fresh tomatoes, diced
2 tablespoons chili powder
1 tablespoon cumin
½ tablespoon cayenne pepper
⅛ cup vegan Worcestershire sauce
2 (15-ounce) cans pinto beans
1 teaspoon salt
¼ teaspoon black pepper

In a 4-quart slow cooker, add all ingredients. Cover and cook on low heat for 5 hours.

SWEET POTATO CHILI

Sweet potatoes are great sources of fiber and beta-carotene, making this chili healthy and delicious.

Serves 4

1 red onion, diced

1 jalapeño, seeded and minced

3 cloves garlic, minced

1 (15-ounce) can black beans, drained

1 sweet potato, peeled and diced

3 tablespoons chili powder

1 tablespoon paprika

1 teaspoon dried oregano

1 teaspoon ground cumin

½ teaspoon chipotle powder

1 (28-ounce) can diced tomatoes, drained

2 cups Vegetable Broth (see recipe in this chapter)

1 teaspoon salt

¼ teaspoon black pepper

1 lime, juiced

¼ cup cilantro, chopped

1. In a 4-quart slow cooker, add all ingredients except the lime and cilantro. Cover and cook on low heat for 8 hours.

2. When the chili is done cooking, mix in the lime juice and garnish with the cilantro.

SC THREE BEAN CHILI

Using dried beans will save you a little money on this recipe, but be sure to soak the beans overnight and boil for 10 minutes on the stovetop before using.

Serves 8

1 (15-ounce) can pinto beans, drained

1 (15-ounce) can black beans, drained

1 (15-ounce) can great northern white beans, drained

1 onion, diced

3 cloves garlic, minced

3 cups Vegetable Broth (see recipe in this chapter)

1 tablespoon chili powder

½ tablespoon chipotle powder

½ tablespoon cumin

½ tablespoon paprika

1 (15-ounce) can diced tomatoes

1 teaspoon salt

¼ teaspoon black pepper

In a 4-quart slow cooker, add all ingredients. Cover and cook on low heat for 5 hours.

SC FAJITA CHILI

Recreate the flavor of sizzling restaurant fajitas in your own home!

Serves 6

1 red onion, diced

1 jalapeño, seeded and minced

3 cloves garlic, minced

1 (15-ounce) can black beans, drained

1 (15-ounce) can diced tomatoes, drained

1 (8-ounce) package Morningstar Farms Meal Starters Chik'n Strips, cut into bite-size pieces

2 cups Vegetable Broth (see recipe in this chapter)

2 teaspoons chili powder

1 teaspoon sugar

1 teaspoon paprika

¼ teaspoon garlic powder

¼ teaspoon cayenne pepper

¼ teaspoon cumin

1 teaspoon salt

¼ teaspoon black pepper

In a 4-quart slow cooker, add all ingredients. Cover and cook on low heat for 5 hours.

BLACK BEAN, CORN, AND FRESH TOMATO CHILI

Tofutti makes a delicious nondairy sour cream called Sour Supreme, and it can be found in some national grocery store chains.

Serves 4

1 red onion, diced

1 jalapeño, seeded and minced

3 cloves garlic, minced

1 (15-ounce) can black beans, drained

1 (15-ounce) can corn, drained

3 tablespoons chili powder

1 tablespoon paprika

1 teaspoon dried oregano

1 teaspoon ground cumin

½ teaspoon chipotle powder

2 cups Vegetable Broth (see recipe in this chapter)

1 teaspoon salt

¼ teaspoon black pepper

2 cups tomato, diced

¼ cup cilantro, chopped

4 tablespoons sour cream or vegan sour cream

1. In a 4-quart slow cooker, add all ingredients except tomato, cilantro, and sour cream. Cover and cook on low heat for 5 hours.

2. When the chili is done cooking, mix in the tomato and garnish with the cilantro. Top with sour cream or vegan sour cream.

SC RED BEAN CHILI

In the United States, "red beans" most commonly refers to kidney beans.

Serves 4

2 (15-ounce) cans red kidney beans, drained
½ cup onion, diced
2 cloves garlic, minced
2 cups Vegetable Broth (see recipe in this chapter)
1 tablespoon chili powder
½ tablespoon chipotle powder
½ tablespoon cumin
½ tablespoon paprika
1 (15-ounce) can tomatoes, diced
1 teaspoon salt
¼ teaspoon black pepper

In a 4-quart slow cooker, add all ingredients. Cover and cook on low heat for 5 hours.

SC LENTIL CHILI

Before using dried lentils, rinse them well and pick through to remove any debris or undesirable pieces.

Serves 6

1 cup lentils, uncooked

1 onion, diced

3 cloves garlic, minced

4 cups Vegetable Broth (see recipe in this chapter)

¼ cup tomato paste

1 cup carrots, chopped

1 cup celery, chopped

1 (15-ounce) can diced tomatoes, drained

2 tablespoons chili powder

½ tablespoon paprika

1 teaspoon dried oregano

1 teaspoon cumin

1 teaspoon salt

¼ teaspoon black pepper

In a 4-quart slow cooker, add all ingredients. Cover and cook on low heat for 8 hours.

GARDEN VEGETABLE CHILI

A true garden vegetable recipe requires some flexibility, since all ingredients aren't available year-round, and you should use what's actually growing in your garden.

Serves 8

1 large onion, diced

3 cloves garlic, minced

1 large green bell pepper, chopped

2 cups zucchini, chopped

1½ cups corn kernels

1 (28-ounce) can diced tomatoes

2 cups Vegetable Broth (see recipe in this chapter)

1 (15-ounce) can kidney beans, drained

1 (15-ounce) can pinto beans, drained

1 (15-ounce) can cannellini beans, drained

2 tablespoons chili powder

1 teaspoon cumin

1 teaspoon dried oregano

1 teaspoon salt

¼ teaspoon black pepper

In a 4-quart slow cooker, add all ingredients. Cover and cook on low heat for 6 hours.

SC BLACK BEAN AND "SAUSAGE" CHILI

Gimme Lean is a brand of vegan sausage that is sold in major grocery store chains and is usually found in the produce section.

Serves 6

1 red onion, diced

1 jalapeño, seeded and minced

2 carrots, peeled and chopped

3 cloves garlic, minced

1 (15-ounce) can black beans, drained

1 (14-ounce) package Gimme Lean Sausage, crumbled

3 tablespoons chili powder

1 tablespoon paprika

1 teaspoon dried thyme

1 teaspoon ground cumin

½ teaspoon chipotle powder

1 (28-ounce) can diced tomatoes, drained

2 cups Vegetable Broth (see recipe in this chapter)

1 teaspoon salt

¼ teaspoon black pepper

In a 4-quart slow cooker, add all ingredients. Cover and cook on low heat for 5 hours.

ACORN SQUASH CHILI

Acorn squash keeps its shape in this chili, giving it a chunky texture.

Serves 8

2 cups acorn squash, cubed

2 (15-ounce) cans petite diced tomatoes

2 stalks celery, diced

1 medium onion, diced

3 cloves garlic, minced

2 carrots, diced

1 teaspoon mesquite liquid smoke

2 teaspoons hot sauce

1 teaspoon chili powder

1 teaspoon paprika

1 teaspoon oregano

1 teaspoon smoked paprika

1 (15-ounce) can kidney beans, drained and rinsed

1 (15-ounce) can cannellini beans, drained and rinsed

1 cup fresh corn kernels

1. In a 4-quart slow cooker, add all ingredients except the corn. Cover and cook for 8 hours on low.

2. Add the corn and stir. Cover and continue to cook on low for 30 minutes. Stir before serving.

SC SUMMER CHILI

This chili is full of summer vegetables, and you can add vegetarian chicken for a heartier dish.

Serves 8

1 bulb fennel, diced

4 radishes, diced

2 stalks celery including leaves, diced

2 carrots, cut into coin-size pieces

1 medium onion, diced

1 shallot, diced

4 cloves garlic, sliced

1 habanero pepper, diced

1 (15-ounce) can cannellini beans, drained and rinsed

1 (12-ounce) can tomato paste

½ teaspoon dried oregano

½ teaspoon black pepper

½ teaspoon crushed rosemary

½ teaspoon cayenne

½ teaspoon ground chipotle

1 teaspoon chili powder

1 teaspoon tarragon

¼ teaspoon cumin

¼ teaspoon celery seed

2 zucchini, cubed

10 campari tomatoes, quartered

1 cup corn kernels

1. In a 4-quart slow cooker, add the fennel, radishes, celery, carrots, onion, shallot, garlic, habanero, beans, tomato paste, and all spices; stir. Cook on low for 6–7 hours.

2. Stir in the zucchini, tomatoes, and corn. Cook for an additional 30 minutes on high. Stir before serving.

Campari Tomatoes

Campari is a type of tomato that is grown on the vine and has a sweet, juicy taste. It is round and on the small side, but not as small as a cherry tomato.

CHAPTER 6

ROOT VEGETABLES

RECIPE LIST

WHITE POTATO PIE **292**

BASIC PIE DOUGH **293**

ROASTED YUKON GOLD POTATOES **294**

TURNIP AND POTATO GRATIN **295**

PARSNIP PURÉE **296**

SLOW COOKER PARSNIP PURÉE **297**

YUCA CON MOJO (YUCA WITH GARLIC AND LIME) **298**

ROASTED BEETS **299**

CITRUSY BEETS **300**

FRENCH FRIES **301**

CARROT TIMBALES **302**

HONEY-ORANGE BEETS **303**

BUTTERED BEETS **304**

RUTABAGA OVEN FRIES **305**

HERB-MIXED TURNIPS **306**

CURRIED PARSNIPS **307**

"STEAMED" ARTICHOKES **308**

CELERY ROOT, ARTICHOKE, AND POTATO GRATIN **309**

CELERY ROOT MASH **310**

GINGERED MASHED SWEET POTATOES **311**

PARSNIP AND CARROT BAKE **312**

CARROT AND MUSHROOM TERRINE **313**

CARROTS AND GINGER **314**

CREAMED CARROTS **315**

MASHED TURNIPS **316**

BRAISED BEET GREENS **317**

TURNIP AND CARROT PURÉE **318**

SAVORY TURNIP GREENS **319**

PARSNIP PURÉE **320**

CRISP POTATO PANCAKES **321**

ROSEMARY NEW POTATOES **322**

ROASTED GARLIC MASHED POTATOES **323**

MOROCCAN ROOT VEGETABLES **324**

GARLIC PARSLEY MASHED POTATOES **325**

ROSEMARY MASHED POTATOES **326**

TWICE-BAKED POTATOES **327**

POTATO MESSAROUND **328**

SWEET POTATO CASSEROLE **329**

POTATOES PAPRIKASH **330**

ROSEMARY-GARLIC MASHED POTATOES **331**

SOUTHWESTERN CASSEROLE **332**

CHEESY PEASY POTATOES **333**

POTATO RISOTTO **334**

SCALLOPED POTATOES **335**

POTATOES AU GRATIN **336**

ROSEMARY FINGERLING POTATOES **337**

BRAISED FINGERLING POTATOES **338**

DILL RED POTATOES **339**

CHIPOTLE AND THYME SWEET POTATOES **340**

MAPLE-GLAZED SWEET POTATOES **341**

HERBED POTATOES **342**

POTATO PICCATA **343**

CHIPOTLE AND THYME MASHED SWEET POTATOES **344**

MASHED SWEET POTATOES **345**

PRESSURE COOKER MAPLE-GLAZED SWEET POTATOES **346**

MEXICAN SPICE POTATOES **347**

GARLIC-PARMESAN MASHED POTATOES **348**

POTATO-BROCCOLI CASSEROLE **349**

GARLIC-PARSLEY POTATOES **350**

OLD-FASHIONED GLAZED CARROTS **351**

WHITE POTATO PIE

This pie is great as an appetizer or side dish or as a meal if you add some other sides!

Serves 8 as side dish, or as lunch with a green salad and cold cuts

7 cups diced thin-skinned white potatoes

1 stick butter or margarine, chopped

1 medium onion, chopped

½ cup chopped parsley

2 teaspoons salt

1 package frozen pie dough (not sweet) or 1 recipe Basic Pie Dough (see recipe in this chapter)

1 egg, beaten, mixed with 1 tablespoon cold water (egg wash)

1 cup cream

1. Heat oven to 350°F. Combine potatoes, butter, onion, parsley, and salt. Roll half of the pie dough ¼" thin, and settle it into a 10" pie pan. Brush the rim of the crust with egg wash. Arrange the potato mixture in the crust so that it mounds slightly. Roll the top crust ¼" thin, and place it onto the pie. Trim edges and crimp the pie firmly shut, using either fingers or the tines of a fork. Cut a circular vent in the center of the pie.

2. Bake 90 minutes. Bring cream to a boil, and add it through the vent (it may not all fit—that's okay). Bake 30 minutes more.

3. Make sure potatoes are very soft. Allow to cool about 15 minutes.

BASIC PIE DOUGH

This recipe is perfect for any pie you want to make. Enjoy!

Yields enough dough for 1 pie

2 cups flour (pastry flour is best, but you can use all-purpose)

½ teaspoon salt

6 ounces (1½ sticks) unsalted butter, cold, cut into pea-size pieces

½ cup very cold water

1. Sift flour and salt together over a bowl containing the diced butter. Using your hands, break up the butter into the flour until the flour assumes the color of the butter. There should still be some nuggets of unmixed butter.

2. Sprinkle in most of the water, and work quickly with your hands until dough clumps together. Add extra water if the dough feels too dry to roll. Do not overmix. Separate dough into 2 balls, wrap separately, and refrigerate for at least 30 minutes.

ROASTED YUKON GOLD POTATOES

Here's a mess-free way of making Roasted Yukon Gold Potatoes, which works as well on the barbecue grill as in the oven. It calls for wrapping the seasoned, cut potatoes in a foil pouch before cooking.

Serves 4

1 medium onion, roughly chopped

2 tablespoons olive oil

¼ cup chopped parsley

3 or 4 cloves garlic, minced

1½ pounds Yukon Gold potatoes, washed, sliced ½" thick

1 teaspoon salt

Pepper

1. Heat oven to 425°F. Put onion, olive oil, parsley, and garlic in blender or food processor, and purée until smooth. Toss with potatoes and salt, then wrap in a ready-made foil oven bag, or a sheet of foil crimped to seal. Potatoes should be no more than 2 layers deep.

2. Bake on a sheet pan in center rack for 45 minutes, until potatoes are tender when poked with a fork. Season with pepper.

TURNIP AND POTATO GRATIN

This dish is perfect for a home-style meal with your family!

Serves 8

2 garlic cloves, finely chopped

2 tablespoons unsalted butter

2½ pounds all-purpose potatoes, peeled and cut into ½" cubes

2 pounds turnips or rutabagas, peeled and cut into ½" cubes

4 cups heavy cream

Salt and freshly ground black pepper

1. Preheat the oven to 350°F. Grease the bottom and sides of a 9" square baking dish with the butter and spoon the garlic all over.

2. Mix the potatoes and turnips and arrange them in the pan. Bring the cream to a boil on the stove and season with salt and pepper (about 2 teaspoons salt and 1 teaspoon pepper), then pour it over the vegetables, and cover the pan with foil.

3. Bake 30 minutes, then uncover and cook another 20–25 minutes. The potatoes and turnips should be very tender and the sauce should be bubbling and browned on top when done.

PARSNIP PURÉE

In New England, farmers leave some parsnips in the ground at the end of the fall harvest season. Through the winter, starches turn to sugars in these parsnips deep below the frozen earth. When the ground thaws in the spring, the farmers dig these super-sweet roots and send them to market, bringing a rare treat to lucky cooks-in-the-know.

Serves 6

2 pounds parsnips

½ cup milk

8 tablespoons unsalted butter

Salt

1. Peel the parsnips and boil in salted water. Cook until very tender, about 10 to 15 minutes. Drain in a colander. While the parsnips are draining, heat the milk in a small pot.

2. Combine the parsnips and milk in a food processor or blender. With the motor going, gradually add the butter, making sure it is well mixed and the purée very smooth. Season lightly with salt.

SLOW COOKER PARSNIP PURÉE

Parsnips are long white root vegetables related to carrots. Due to the starchiness of their texture, they can frequently be used in place of potatoes.

Serves 6

5 medium parsnips, peeled and chopped

½ cup Vegetable Broth (see Chapter 5)

½ cup 2% milk or unsweetened soymilk

1 teaspoon salt

1 tablespoon butter or vegan margarine

1. Add the parsnips, Vegetable Broth, milk, and salt to a 4-quart slow cooker. Cover, and cook over low heat for 4 hours.

2. Allow the parsnips to cool slightly, then use an immersion blender to process, or use a blender or food processor and blend in batches.

3. Return to the slow cooker, add the butter or margarine, and heat until melted.

YUCA CON MOJO (YUCA WITH GARLIC AND LIME)

Earthy-tasting yuca (a.k.a. cassava) has a potato-like texture, but a nutty, somewhat mushroom-like fragrance and taste. A woody spine in the center can be removed after cooking. To peel the waxy brown skin, cut the root into cross sections and pare using a cook's knife. Frozen yuca is also available, and is fine for this dish.

Serves 8

1½ pounds peeled yuca, cut into 1½" chunks

½ teaspoon salt

2½ tablespoons fresh-squeezed lime juice

¼ cup extra-virgin olive oil

3 large cloves garlic, finely chopped

1 tablespoon chopped fresh herb, such as cilantro or parsley (optional)

1. Simmer the yuca about 25 minutes in enough water to cover it, along with the salt and ½ teaspoon of the lime juice, in a covered pot. It should be fork-tender, but not mushy. Drain; remove woody center core. Transfer to a plate, and cover to keep warm.

2. In a small skillet, heat the oil. Remove pan from heat, and add the garlic. Stir in remaining lime juice and herbs. Pour this sauce over the yuca, and serve immediately.

ROASTED BEETS

Roasting brings natural juices to the surface of these magenta roots and caramelizes them into a sweet, intensely flavored crust.

Serves 8

2 pounds beets (about 8, tangerine-size), peeled, cut into 1" wedges

1 tablespoon olive oil

¼ teaspoon ground cinnamon

¼ teaspoon salt

Chopped Italian parsley (optional)

Heat oven to 350°F. Toss beets with olive oil, cinnamon, and salt. Spread into a single layer on a baking sheet (preferably nonstick). Roast on the middle rack of the oven until tender, about 1 hour, turning once, after 30 minutes. If desired, serve sprinkled with chopped parsley.

SC CITRUSY BEETS

Beets can be served as a warm side dish or a chilled salad over a bed of greens.

Serves 4

12 baby beets, halved, ends trimmed

1 cup orange juice

Juice of ½ lime

¼ red onion, sliced

½ teaspoon pepper

Add all ingredients to a 2-quart or 4-quart slow cooker and cook on low for 4 hours.

FRENCH FRIES

The key to crispy, golden french fries is cooking the rinsed, high-starch potatoes twice—once at a moderate temperature to cook them through, then a second time at a higher temperature to crisp them.

Serves 8

2 pounds (about 5) high-starch potatoes, such as Burbank Russets (a.k.a. Idaho baking potatoes) or Yukon Golds, peeled

Peanut oil for frying

Salt

1. Cut potatoes into 2½"-long strips, ½" wide and thick; soak in enough cold water to cover them for 30 minutes. Drain and dry with absorbent towels.

2. Heat oil to 350°F. Fry potatoes in small batches until they are soft and tender enough to mash between your fingers, about 2 minutes (make sure to allow time between each batch for the oil to come back up to temperature—a fry thermometer is essential); drain on paper towels. The potatoes may be fried again once cooled (about 5 minutes), or set aside to be refried later.

3. Heat the oil to 365°F. Fry again in small batches, stirring lightly with a tool, so they don't stick together. When golden brown (about 2–3 minutes), remove from oil, shake off any excess, and drain on paper towels. Sprinkle immediately with salt, and serve in a napkin-lined basket.

CARROT TIMBALES

The wine in this dish is optional, but it sure is delicious!

Serves 4

1 tablespoon unsalted butter

2 cups peeled, sliced carrots, cooked soft, chopped in a food processor

¼ cup chopped shallots

2 tablespoons port wine (optional)

½ teaspoon salt

Pinch of freshly grated nutmeg

Black pepper to taste

1 cup cream or half-and-half

3 large eggs

¼ cup grated Parmesan cheese to garnish

Chopped tarragon or parsley to garnish

1. Heat oven to 375°F. Butter 4 (6-ounce) ramekins or custard cups. In a small skillet over medium heat, melt 1 tablespoon of butter; add the carrots and cook until soft, about 3 minutes. Add the shallots to the carrots, along with the port wine, salt, nutmeg, and pepper. Heat the cream until steaming but not boiling. Whisk the eggs into the vegetable mixture, then gradually whisk in the cream.

2. Divide the mixture into prepared cups, and line them up in a shallow casserole or roasting pan. Add enough hot tap water to come ⅔ up the sides of the custard cups. Cover pan with foil, and bake in center of oven until almost set, 25–30 minutes. Open oven door, loosen but do not remove foil, and bake for 10 minutes more. Allow to rest at room temperature for 10 minutes before loosening with a knife, inverting, and unmolding. Garnish with Parmesan and chopped tarragon or parsley.

HONEY-ORANGE BEETS

If you are able to find fresh beets with the greens still attached, wash the greens thoroughly, dress them with lemon and olive oil, and use them as a bed for this dish, creating a warm-salad main course.

Serves 4

6 medium-size fresh beets

1 teaspoon grated orange zest

2 tablespoons orange juice

2 teaspoons butter

1 teaspoon honey

¼ teaspoon ground ginger

Salt and freshly ground pepper to taste

Boil beets in enough water to cover for 40 minutes, or until tender. Drain beets and let cool slightly. Slip off skins and slice. In a saucepan, heat the orange zest, orange juice, butter, honey, and ginger over low heat until the butter melts. Add the beets and toss to coat. Season with salt and pepper to taste.

PC BUTTERED BEETS

This down-on-the-farm comfort food side dish goes well with just about any entrée.

Serves 8

4 large golden or red beets

1 cup water

Butter or vegan margarine, such as Earth Balance, to taste

Salt and black pepper, to taste

1. Scrub the beets and trim both ends. Place the beets on the rack in the pressure cooker. Pour in the water.

2. Lock the lid into place and bring to high pressure; maintain pressure for 25 minutes.

3. Remove the pressure cooker from the heat, quick-release the pressure, and remove the lid. Transfer the beets to a cutting board. Test for doneness. If beets aren't cooked, simmer on the stovetop, or cook, covered, in the microwave for a few extra minutes.

4. When the beets are cool enough to handle, use a paring knife to remove the peel. Slice the beets. Reheat the beets and melt butter or margarine to taste over the heated beets. Season with salt and pepper to taste.

Beet Peak Season

During the spring months, beets are in bloom. Look for this root vegetable in your grocery store or farmers' market in April.

RUTABAGA OVEN FRIES

Though not really fried, these golden batons look and feel like french fries, and are great for dipping in ketchup or aioli (garlic mayonnaise).

Serves 4

- 1 large rutabaga ("wax turnip"), thickly peeled
- 1 tablespoon olive or vegetable oil
- Kosher salt
- 1 tablespoon finely chopped thyme, rosemary, or parsley
- Freshly ground black pepper

Heat oven to 400°F. Slice rutabaga into 2½" × ½" sticks (batons); soak in cold water for 30 minutes. Dry thoroughly with towels. Toss gently with oil and a light sprinkling of salt. Spread fries into a single layer on a sheet pan and bake, turning occasionally, until lightly browned and tender, about 30 to 40 minutes. Remove from oven and toss with thyme, salt, and fresh ground pepper.

HERB-MIXED TURNIPS

Rutabagas and turnips have a naturally buttery flavor, especially when young and fresh in the autumn. This makes the pairing with herbs and crisp bread crumbs natural.

Serves 4

1½ pounds turnips and rutabagas, peeled

2 tablespoons butter

1 tablespoon chopped parsley

2 teaspoons chopped chervil or tarragon

2 tablespoons chopped chives

1 clove garlic, finely chopped

Kosher salt and black pepper

½ cup fresh bread crumbs browned in 1 tablespoon olive oil or butter

Cook the turnips and rutabagas separately in salted water until they're al dente (tender, but firm—approximately 10 minutes for turnips, 20 minutes for rutabagas); drain. In a large skillet over medium heat, melt the butter. Add the turnips and rutabagas, and cook over medium-high flame until golden brown. Add herbs, garlic, salt, and pepper, and toss to coat. Serve topped with bread crumbs.

CURRIED PARSNIPS

The herby sweetness of parsnips lends itself well to curries. Try this one over brown rice with a little lentil dal for a delicious dinner that's a complete protein dish to boot!

Serves 4

- 1½ pounds parsnips, peeled, cut into bite-size pieces
- 2 tablespoons butter or oil
- 1 red onion, thinly sliced
- 2 Bosc pears or Golden Delicious apples, cored, thinly sliced
- 1 teaspoon Madras curry powder, toasted in a dry pan until fragrant
- ½ teaspoon ground coriander, toasted in a dry pan until fragrant
- Kosher salt and black pepper
- ¼ cup yogurt
- ¼ cup mango chutney (such as Major Grey's)
- 2 tablespoons chopped cilantro

Boil the parsnips until halfway done, about 5 minutes; drain. Melt the butter or heat the oil in a large, heavy-bottomed skillet. Add the onion, pears, curry, and coriander and cook over medium flame, stirring regularly until onion is soft, about 10 minutes. Add the parsnips, season well, and cook 5 minutes more, until the parsnips brown lightly. Remove from heat before stirring in the yogurt, chutney, and cilantro.

SC "STEAMED" ARTICHOKES

Choose artichokes that are all the same size so they will finish cooking at the same time.

Serves 4

4 large artichokes

1 cup water

1 lemon, cut into 8 wedges

2 tablespoons lemon juice

1 teaspoon dried oregano

1. Place the artichokes stem-side down in an oval 4-quart slow cooker. Pour the water into the bottom of the slow cooker. Add the lemons, lemon juice, and oregano.

2. Cook on low for 6 hours, or until the leaves are tender.

CELERY ROOT, ARTICHOKE, AND POTATO GRATIN

Rich and savory, this is the perfect cold weather supper, with a watercress-endive salad and a glass of Zinfandel.

Serves 8

4 tablespoons butter or olive oil

3 cloves garlic, chopped

4 large artichokes, trimmed, choke removed, cut into 8 pieces

1 large celery root (about 1 pound) trimmed and cut into 1" cubes

8 ounces potatoes, peeled and cut into 1" cubes

1½ teaspoons kosher salt

Freshly ground black pepper

4 cups heavy cream

½ cup parsley

1. Heat oven to 400°F. Butter or oil an 11" × 13" casserole or gratin dish and sprinkle the chopped garlic evenly around, rubbing some onto the sides of the pan. Blanch the artichoke for about 10 minutes in rapidly boiling salted water, adding the celery root for the last 3 minutes. Drain well, combine with potatoes, and add to casserole. Season thoroughly with salt and pepper; add cream and parsley.

2. Place the casserole onto a sheet pan to catch any overflow. Cover with aluminum foil and bake for 1 hour, until cream is bubbling and potatoes are tender. Uncover and cook 15–20 minutes more, until sauce is thick and starting to brown on top. Allow the casserole to rest at room temperature for at least 10 minutes before serving.

CELERY ROOT MASH

Serve this recipe in place of mashed potatoes if you're looking for something light!

Serves 6

2 pounds celery root (sometimes called "celeriac" or "apio")

1 pound white potatoes

½ cup milk

8 tablespoons unsalted butter

1 tablespoon snipped chives (optional)

Salt

1. Peel and dice the celery root and potatoes roughly into 1" pieces. Boil in lightly salted boiling water until very tender, about 20 minutes. Drain in a colander, then return to the pot and heat for 30 seconds to steam out any residual water. Heat the milk and butter in a small pot.

2. Using a stiff wire whisk or potato masher, crush the vegetables until they are a soft mash. Gradually mash in the milk-butter mixture, making sure it is well mixed before adding more; fold in the chives if desired. Season lightly with salt.

GINGERED MASHED SWEET POTATOES

This may become a staple on your Thanksgiving table.

Serves 5 or 6

4 medium sweet potatoes or yams (about 1½ pounds)

¼ cup milk

2 tablespoons butter

1 tablespoon mashed candied ginger or 1 tablespoon brown sugar plus ½ teaspoon ground ginger

Peel and quarter the sweet potatoes, and cook in boiling salted water until tender, about 20 minutes. Drain and return to the pan. In a small saucepan or in the microwave, heat the milk and butter; add to the potatoes, along with the candied ginger; mash by hand or with an electric mixer. Texture will be thicker than mashed white potatoes.

PARSNIP AND CARROT BAKE

This dish is great as a side or an appetizer.

Serves 4

- 1 pound carrots, peeled, cut roughly into 2½" × ½" batons
- 8 ounces parsnips, peeled, cut roughly into 2½" × ½" batons
- ¾ cup vegetable stock
- 2 tablespoons butter, chopped
- ½ teaspoon salt
- Chopped fresh chervil or tarragon
- Freshly ground black pepper

Heat oven to 375°F. Place carrots, parsnips, stock, butter, and salt into a shallow baking dish. Cover with aluminum foil and bake until the vegetables are soft, about 45 minutes. Uncover and bake until vegetables brown lightly, 10–15 minutes more. Sprinkle with chervil and black pepper before serving.

CARROT AND MUSHROOM TERRINE

This dish is best when served warm, so if you make it ahead, heat it up before serving.

Serves 8

¼ cup butter, plus 1 tablespoon

1 pound mushrooms, chopped

2 cloves garlic, chopped

1 cup roughly chopped shallots

4½ cups grated carrots

5 eggs

1 cup bread crumbs

1 cup grated Pecorino Romano or Parmesan cheese

Salt and pepper to taste

½ teaspoon oregano

½ teaspoon rosemary

1. Heat oven to 350°F. Butter a 2-quart terrine or loaf pan. Melt ¼ cup of butter in a heavy-bottomed skillet. Add the mushrooms, garlic, and shallots; cook until shallots soften, about 10 minutes.

2. In a mixing bowl, combine the shallot mixture with the carrots, eggs, half of the bread crumbs, the cheese, salt and pepper to taste, oregano, and rosemary. Pour mixture into terrine and sprinkle with remaining bread crumbs and dot with remaining butter; cover with foil. Bake 30 minutes, then uncover and bake 5 minutes more, until browned. Let stand 10 minutes before serving.

CARROTS AND GINGER

Boost the flavor in this dish by adding a dash of cinnamon or allspice after cooking.

Serves 4

1 pound carrots, peeled and sliced diagonally

¼ cup butter or vegan margarine, such as Earth Balance

1 teaspoon fresh ginger, minced

1 cup water

Salt and black pepper, to taste

1. Add the carrots, butter or margarine, ginger, and water to the pressure cooker. Stir to mix. Lock the lid into place and bring to high pressure; maintain pressure for 1 minute.

2. Remove from heat and quick-release the pressure. Remove the lid and stir the contents of the pressure cooker. Add salt and pepper, to taste.

Fresh Versus Ground Ginger

Ground ginger is more pungent than fresh and has a slightly different taste, so it is recommended that you don't substitute one for the other in all recipes. In this recipe, however, either will work well. If using ground ginger, use ⅛ teaspoon or less.

CREAMED CARROTS

With their appealing color and gentle bite, these carrots supply a nice array of colors, textures, and flavors to your meal. Also, since the vitamin A in carrots is lipid-soluble, this ingredient combination aids in the release of this important nutrient.

Serves 4

1 pound carrots, peeled, quartered lengthwise, cut into 2" sticks

½ cup water

2 tablespoons unsalted butter

1½ teaspoons sugar

½ teaspoon salt

½ cup light cream

Pinch of grated nutmeg

White pepper (optional)

Combine the carrots, water, butter, sugar, and salt in a large skillet. Simmer over medium heat until most of the water has evaporated and the carrots are tender. Add the cream; simmer until it lightly coats the carrots and has a saucy consistency. Season carrots with nutmeg, and white pepper if desired.

PC MASHED TURNIPS

Serve this low-carb dish in place of mashed potatoes.

Serves 4

4 medium turnips, peeled and diced

1 small onion, diced

½ cup Pressure Cooker Vegetable Stock (see Chapter 5)

¼ cup sour cream, or vegan sour cream, such as Tofutti Sour Supreme

Salt and pepper, to taste

1. Add the turnips, onion, and stock to the pressure cooker. Lock the lid into place and bring to high pressure; maintain for 5 minutes. Remove from heat and allow pressure to release naturally for 10 minutes.

2. Use a slotted spoon to transfer turnips to a serving bowl, reserving the broth in the pressure cooker. Use a hand-held mixer or immersion blender to purée the turnips, adding some of the broth from the pressure cooker if necessary. Stir in the sour cream. Taste for seasoning, and add salt and pepper to taste if necessary.

Flavor Variations

Some of the ingredients one would typically use in mashed potatoes also work well in mashed turnips. A couple of unique ingredients to try are nutmeg or horseradish, but not both in the same dish.

PC BRAISED BEET GREENS

Young, fresh greens will cook quicker than older, tougher ones. Adjust the cooking time accordingly.

Serves 4

1 tablespoon olive oil

1 large shallot or small red onion, minced

1 pound beet greens

Salt and pepper, to taste

¼ cup Pressure Cooker Vegetable Stock (see Chapter 5)

1 tablespoon white wine

1. Bring the oil to temperature in the pressure cooker over medium heat. Add the shallot or onion; sauté for 3 minutes. Add the beet greens. Sprinkle with salt and pepper. Stir the greens to coat them in the oil. Once they're slightly wilted, add the stock, making sure not to exceed the fill line in your pressure cooker.

2. Lock the lid into place and bring to low pressure; maintain pressure for 1–3 minutes. Quick-release the pressure and remove the lid. Simmer and stir for 1 minute or until the remaining moisture in the pan evaporates.

3. Taste for seasoning, and add more salt and pepper if needed. Add white wine, stir, and serve warm.

PC TURNIP AND CARROT PURÉE

The nutmeg in this recipe makes it a great side dish on a crisp fall evening or for Thanksgiving dinner.

Serves 6

2 cups turnips, peeled and quartered

2 cups carrots, peeled and cut into 2" pieces

2 cups water

1 teaspoon salt, plus extra, to taste

2 tablespoons extra-virgin olive oil

½ teaspoon nutmeg, freshly grated

2 tablespoons sour cream, or vegan sour cream, such as Tofutti Sour Supreme

1. Put the turnips, carrots, water, and 1 teaspoon salt in the pressure cooker. Lock the lid into place and bring to high pressure; maintain pressure for 8 minutes. Remove the pressure cooker from the heat, quick-release the pressure, and remove the lid.

2. Drain the vegetables. Return them to the pressure cooker and put it over low heat for 1–2 minutes to evaporate any residual moisture. Mash the vegetables together with the oil, nutmeg, and sour cream. Taste for seasoning, and add salt if needed.

SAVORY TURNIP GREENS

Use fresh or frozen turnip greens for best flavor and optimal nutrition.

Serves 4

1 pound turnip greens

1 tablespoon olive oil

½ onion, diced

1 garlic clove, minced

1 teaspoon dried red pepper flakes

2 cups Pressure Cooker Vegetable Stock (see Chapter 5)

1 teaspoon Dijon mustard

Salt and pepper, to taste

1. To prepare the greens, cut away the tough stalks and stems. Wash greens, chop into large pieces, and set aside.

2. Bring the pressure cooker to medium heat. Add the olive oil, onion, garlic, and red pepper flakes. Cook until the onions begin to soften, about 5 minutes. Add the stock, mustard, and chopped greens; stir well.

3. Lock the lid into place and bring to high pressure; maintain for 5 minutes. Remove from heat and release pressure naturally. Add salt and pepper, to taste.

PC PARSNIP PURÉE

The techniques in this recipe are inspired by Julia Child's famous preparation of this dish.

Serves 4

1 pound parsnips, peeled and diced

Water, as needed

3 tablespoons butter or vegan margarine, such as Earth Balance

½ teaspoon salt

½ teaspoon pepper

1. Place the parsnips in the pressure cooker and add enough water to just cover.

2. Lock on the lid. Bring to high pressure; maintain pressure for 3 minutes. Remove the pan from the heat, quick-release the pressure, and remove the lid. Remove the parsnips but reserve the cooking water.

3. Add the drained parsnips and ¼ cup cooking water to a food processor. Blend until smooth, adding more water if necessary.

4. Return the purée to the cleaned pressure cooker or a saucepan. Add the butter or margarine, salt, and pepper, and cook over low heat for 10 minutes, stirring often, before serving.

Parsnips

Parsnips are mildly flavored root vegetables that look like off-white carrots. Because of the mild flavor, they can be used in a variety of ways, such as baking with other herbed root vegetables or whipping into a purée to serve like mashed potatoes. Look for parsnips during the peak seasons of fall and winter.

CRISP POTATO PANCAKES

These scrumptious, simple "latkes" make wonderful snacking, and can be made as miniature hors d'oeuvres. It's traditional to serve them with either sour cream or applesauce.

Serves 4

1 large egg

3 large baking potatoes (such as Burbank Russets or other high-starch variety), peeled

1 medium onion

1 teaspoon salt

1 tablespoon flour

Clarified butter (ghee) or olive oil for frying

1. Beat the egg in a large bowl. Using the large-hole side of a box grater, shred the potatoes in long motions, forming the lengthiest shreds possible. Quickly grate in the onion. Add the salt and sprinkle in the flour; toss with your hands to combine well.

2. Heat the clarified butter until it shimmers but does not smoke (a piece of potato should sizzle upon entry). Form 8 pancakes from the batter, and pan-fry them in batches of 3 or 4, squeezing out excess water before gently sliding them into the pan. Cook slowly, without moving them for the first 5 minutes; then loosen with a spatula. Turn after about 8 minutes, when the top appears $\frac{1}{3}$ cooked. Finish cooking on other side, about 4 minutes more. Drain on paper towels.

ROSEMARY NEW POTATOES

Fresh rosemary perfumes the cooking oil in this Italian classic, imparting its robust herbal flavor to the browning potatoes. "New" connotes young, small potatoes.

Serves 4

1 pound golf-ball-size red new potatoes

2 tablespoons extra-virgin olive oil

3 sprigs fresh rosemary

Kosher salt and freshly ground black pepper

1. Heat oven to 375°F. Slice the potatoes into ½"-thick rounds, and boil them in lightly salted water until crisp-tender, about 7 minutes. Drain well, and dry very well with a towel.

2. Heat the olive oil in a large, heavy, oven-safe skillet until it shimmers, but does not smoke. Add the rosemary sprigs (they should sizzle), and then slip in the potatoes. Cook without disturbing for 5 minutes. Once potatoes have browned lightly on the first side, turn them over, and put the pan in the oven. Cook 10 minutes. Transfer potatoes to a serving platter, season with salt and pepper, and garnish with additional rosemary sprigs.

ROASTED GARLIC MASHED POTATOES

The amount of garlic in this recipe may seem huge, but the garlic mellows and sweetens as it roasts. All your guests will taste is heavenly, heady, light potatoes "to die for."

Serves 6

3 heads garlic

2 pounds potatoes (preferably thin-skinned creamers, red bliss, or round white Eastern potatoes), peeled

8 tablespoons butter

½ cup milk or cream

1½ teaspoons salt

White pepper (optional)

1. Heat oven to 350°F. Wrap all 3 garlic heads into a pouch fashioned from aluminum foil, and place in the center of the oven. Roast until garlic is very soft and yields to gentle finger pressure, about 1 hour and 15 minutes. Roughly cut potatoes into large chunks, and boil in enough lightly salted water to cover until very tender, about 25–30 minutes depending on type and size of potato pieces. Cut the garlic bulbs in half laterally. Using your hands, squeeze out the roasted garlic, and push it through a sieve. Heat the butter and milk or cream together in a small pan until the butter melts. Drain the potatoes well, then return them to the pot, put them on the stove, and cook over moderate heat for 30 seconds to 1 minute to steam off any excess moisture.

2. For the smoothest mashed potatoes, force the potatoes through a ricer (see "For Supersmooth Spuds" in this chapter). Otherwise, mash them with a potato masher or stiff wire whisk. Add the roasted garlic purée, salt, pepper, and the cream mixture to the potatoes, and mix just enough to incorporate. Serve immediately, or keep warm for later service in a double boiler.

SC MOROCCAN ROOT VEGETABLES

These vegetables are good served with couscous and a yogurt or vegan side salad.

Serves 8

1 pound parsnips, peeled and diced
1 pound turnips, peeled and diced
2 medium onions, chopped
1 pound carrots, peeled and diced
6 dried apricots, chopped
4 pitted prunes, chopped
1 teaspoon ground turmeric
1 teaspoon ground cumin
½ teaspoon ground ginger
½ teaspoon ground cinnamon
¼ teaspoon ground cayenne pepper
1 tablespoon dried parsley
1 tablespoon dried cilantro
2 cups Vegetable Broth (see Chapter 5)
1 teaspoon salt

1. Add the parsnips, turnips, onions, carrots, apricots, prunes, turmeric, cumin, ginger, cinnamon, cayenne pepper, parsley, and cilantro to a 4-quart slow cooker.
2. Pour in the Vegetable Broth and salt.
3. Cover and cook on low for 9 hours, or until the vegetables are cooked through.

PC GARLIC PARSLEY MASHED POTATOES

Russet potatoes are also commonly called Idaho potatoes.

Serves 6–8

1 cup water

8 cups russet potatoes, quartered

8 tablespoons butter or vegan margarine, such as Earth Balance

½ onion, diced

4 cloves garlic, minced

½ cup milk or unsweetened soymilk

½ cup parsley

2 teaspoons salt

½ teaspoon black pepper

1. Pour the water into the pressure cooker and add the potatoes. Lock the lid into place and bring to high pressure. Once the pressure is achieved, turn the heat to low and cook for 5 minutes. Remove from heat and allow pressure to release naturally.

2. Drain the potatoes into a colander. Add the butter to the pressure cooker and sauté the onion and garlic for 3 minutes. Add the milk or soymilk and potatoes, and remove from heat. Mash the potatoes using a potato masher. Mix in the parsley, salt, and pepper.

ROSEMARY MASHED POTATOES

These basic flavors can be used in other potato dishes if you're not in the mood for mashed potatoes. Instead, try roasting quartered red potatoes or whole fingerlings with rosemary.

Serves 6–8

1 cup water

8 cups russet potatoes, quartered

¼ cup extra-virgin olive oil

4 cloves garlic, minced

1 tablespoon rosemary

½ cup milk or unsweetened soymilk

2 teaspoons salt

½ teaspoon black pepper

1. Pour the water into the pressure cooker and add the potatoes. Lock the lid into place and bring to high pressure. Once the pressure is achieved, turn the heat to low and cook for 5 minutes. Remove from heat and allow pressure to release naturally.

2. Drain the potatoes into a colander. Add the olive oil to the pressure cooker and sauté the garlic and rosemary until golden brown. Add the milk and potatoes and remove from heat. Mash the potatoes using a potato masher. Season with salt and pepper.

Growing Rosemary

Rosemary is one of the easiest herbs to grow—in many areas it can grow year-round, and does not need constant sunlight.

TWICE-BAKED POTATOES

This is an elegant way to serve flavored potatoes. Prepare them up to two days ahead, and then bake them whenever you wish, easy as pie.

Serves 4–6

4 large potatoes

2 tablespoons unsalted butter

2 tablespoons chopped onion or shallot

⅓ cup sour cream

Salt and pepper to taste

½ cup shredded Gruyère or Swiss cheese

1 egg, beaten, divided

About ¼ cup milk

1. Bake the potatoes and allow to cool until they can be handled. Meanwhile, melt the butter in a small skillet and cook the onion until softened, about 3 minutes. Halve the potatoes lengthwise and scoop out the flesh, being careful to leave a ¼"–½" shell.

2. In a large bowl, combine the potatoes, sour cream, onion and butter, salt and pepper, and half of the beaten egg. Mash them together thoroughly, then beat by hand or with an electric mixer, adding as much milk as necessary for a smooth consistency, slightly firmer than mashed potatoes. Stir in the cheese.

3. Heat oven to 350°F. Mound the mixture in the potato shells (for extra beauty, pipe the mixture in through a pastry bag with a wide star tip). Whisk the remaining egg with a teaspoon of water, and brush the tops of the stuffed potatoes with this mixture. Bake them for 30 minutes, until nicely browned on top and hot all the way through.

For Supersmooth Spuds

Pro chefs often force cooked potatoes through a device known as a "ricer" to break up any lumps and avoid over-mashing, which could result in gluey or gummy mashed potatoes. The ricer looks much like an oversized garlic press, with a plunger and a grate with small holes.

SC POTATO MESSAROUND

"Messaround" means a little bit of everything, which is what this recipe has! Try playing with it by adding different cheeses and peppers or swap out the broth and soup, to your taste.

Serves 4

8 cups red potatoes, cubed

1 red onion, diced

1 poblano pepper, diced

1 red pepper, diced

1 jalapeño pepper, minced

3 cups vegetarian "chicken" broth

1 (14½-ounce) can cream of mushroom soup or vegan cream of mushroom soup

1 teaspoon salt

¼ teaspoon black pepper

1 cup shredded Cheddar cheese or vegan Cheddar

2 tablespoons chives to garnish

1. Add all of the ingredients to a 4-quart slow cooker except for the chives.

2. Cover and cook on medium-high heat for 4–5 hours. Garnish with the chives.

SC SWEET POTATO CASSEROLE

If you'd like to use fresh sweet potatoes in this casserole, steam or roast them before using in the dish.

Serves 4

2 (18-ounce) cans sweet potatoes, drained and slightly mashed

1 cup unsweetened soymilk

½ cup butter or vegan margarine, melted

½ cup white sugar

1 teaspoon cinnamon

½ teaspoon nutmeg

½ cup pecans, chopped

½ cup brown sugar

2 tablespoons flour

1. Add the mashed sweet potatoes, soymilk, ¼ cup of butter or vegan margarine, sugar, cinnamon, and nutmeg to a 4-quart slow cooker.

2. In a bowl, mix the pecans, brown sugar, flour, and remaining ¼ cup of butter or margarine.

3. Pour the mixture over the top of the casserole. Cover and cook on medium-high heat for 4–5 hours.

SC POTATOES PAPRIKASH

This Hungarian classic is the perfect spicy side dish to serve with a seitan roast.

Serves 8

1½ teaspoons olive oil

1 medium onion, halved and sliced

1 shallot, minced

4 cloves garlic, minced

½ teaspoon salt

½ teaspoon caraway seeds

¼ teaspoon freshly ground black pepper

1 teaspoon cayenne

3 tablespoons paprika

2 pounds red potatoes, thinly sliced

2 cups Vegetable Broth (see Chapter 5)

2 tablespoons tomato paste

½ cup reduced-fat sour cream or vegan sour cream

1. In a nonstick pan, heat the oil. Add the onion, shallot, and garlic and sauté for 1–2 minutes, or until they begin to soften. Add the salt, caraway seeds, pepper, cayenne, and paprika, and stir. Immediately remove from heat.

2. Add the onion mixture, potatoes, broth, and tomato paste to a 4-quart slow cooker. Stir to coat the potatoes evenly.

3. Cover and cook on high for 2½ hours, or until the potatoes are tender.

4. Turn off the heat and stir in the sour cream.

SC ROSEMARY-GARLIC MASHED POTATOES

Slow-cooked mashed potatoes are the perfect side for busy holiday cooks. Not only does this dish leave a burner free for other cooking, there is no need to boil the potatoes before mashing them.

Serves 10

3 pounds red potatoes, quartered

4 cloves garlic, minced

¾ cup Vegetable Broth (see Chapter 5)

1 tablespoon minced, fresh rosemary

2 teaspoons salt

¼ cup 1% milk or unsweetened soymilk

1 tablespoon butter or vegan margarine

⅓ cup reduced-fat sour cream or vegan sour cream

1. Place the potatoes in a 4-quart slow cooker. Add garlic, broth, rosemary, and salt. Stir.

2. Cover and cook on high until potatoes are tender, about 3–4 hours.

3. Pour in milk, butter, and sour cream or the vegan alternatives. Mash with a potato masher.

SC SOUTHWESTERN CASSEROLE

Unless you're vegan, serve this delicious dish with a poached egg on top.

Serves 6

4 large red potatoes, diced

1 (15-ounce) can black beans, drained

1 large onion, diced

1 jalapeño, seeded and diced

1 tablespoon butter or vegan margarine

1 (15-ounce) can diced tomatoes

4 ounces button mushrooms, sliced

¼ teaspoon salt

¼ teaspoon pepper

¼ cup shredded Mexican-blend cheese or vegan Cheddar

1. In a 4-quart slow cooker, stir all ingredients together except the cheese.

2. Cover and cook on low for 8–9 hours.

3. Stir in the cheese shortly before serving.

CHEESY PEASY POTATOES

Cheese, potatoes, and peas are a classic dinner combo! Use whatever variety of potato you like most, and if you don't like mushrooms, feel free to use cream of celery soup instead.

Serves 4

8 cups potatoes, cubed

1 (14½-ounce) can cream of mushroom soup or vegan cream of mushroom soup

3 cups vegetarian "chicken" broth

2 cups frozen peas

1 cup chopped vegetarian "bacon"

1 cup shredded Cheddar cheese or vegan Cheddar

1 teaspoon salt

¼ teaspoon black pepper

Add all ingredients to a 4-quart slow cooker, cover, and cook on medium-high heat for 4–5 hours.

SC POTATO RISOTTO

Finely diced potato replaces arborio rice in this spin on a classic. You can replace the spinach with peas if you like.

Serves 4

2 leeks (white part only)

¼ cup olive oil

3 sprigs fresh thyme, chopped

3 pounds russet potatoes, peeled and finely diced

2 cups dry white wine

5 cups Vegetable Broth (see Chapter 5)

1 teaspoon salt

¼ teaspoon black pepper

4 cups fresh spinach

1. Thinly slice the leeks crosswise into semicircles and rinse.
2. Add the olive oil to a 4-quart slow cooker and sauté the leeks on high heat until translucent, about 5–7 minutes.
3. Add the rest of the ingredients except for the spinach. Cover and cook on medium-high heat for 4 hours.
4. Mix the spinach into the risotto and continue cooking for 1 more hour.

SCALLOPED POTATOES

These easy scalloped potatoes go well with a piece of mock meatloaf and a heaping scoop of green beans.

Serves 8

½ white onion, julienned

2 cloves garlic, minced

3 cups Alfredo sauce

1 teaspoon salt

¼ teaspoon black pepper

½ cup water

4 potatoes, thinly sliced

1 teaspoon salt

¼ teaspoon black pepper

Add all ingredients to a 4-quart slow cooker. Cover and cook on medium-high heat for 4 hours.

Choosing Onions
Choosing the right type of onion is important for the outcome of your dish because each has a distinct flavor. Yellow onions are a little sweeter, especially Vidalia onions. White onions should be used in dishes like this, where you don't want the flavor to stand out.

SC POTATOES AU GRATIN

For rich dishes high in fat, serve a smaller portion and balance it with a healthy veggie on the side.

Serves 8

½ cup water

8 cups potatoes, peeled and diced

2 cups Alfredo sauce

1 cup shredded Cheddar cheese or vegan Cheddar

1 teaspoon salt

¼ teaspoon black pepper

Add all ingredients to a 4-quart slow cooker. Cover and cook on medium-high heat for 4 hours.

SC ROSEMARY FINGERLING POTATOES

Fingerling potatoes are small, long potatoes that look a little like fingers.

Serves 6

2 tablespoons extra-virgin olive oil

1½ pounds fingerling potatoes

1 teaspoon salt

¼ teaspoon black pepper

2 tablespoons fresh rosemary, chopped

1 tablespoon fresh lemon juice

1. Add the olive oil, potatoes, salt, and pepper to a 4-quart slow cooker. Cover and cook on low heat for 3–4 hours.

2. Remove the cover and mix in the rosemary and lemon juice.

PC BRAISED FINGERLING POTATOES

Braising is a technique that involves browning food first and then slowly cooking in liquid until softened.

Serves 3–4

2 tablespoons extra-virgin olive oil

1 pound fingerling potatoes, halved (root to stem)

1 cup Pressure Cooker Vegetable Stock (see Chapter 5)

4 whole garlic cloves

1 tablespoon rosemary, chopped

1 tablespoon thyme, chopped

Salt and pepper, to taste

1. Add olive oil to the pressure cooker and cook the potatoes over medium-high heat, 3 minutes on each side. Add the Vegetable Stock and whole garlic cloves to the pressure cooker.

2. Lock the lid into place and bring to high pressure. Once the pressure is achieved, turn the heat to low and cook for 5 minutes. Remove from heat and allow pressure to release naturally.

3. Drain the potatoes and garlic in a colander. Put the potatoes in a mixing bowl and mince the cooked garlic.

4. Add the garlic, rosemary, and thyme to the potatoes, then season with salt and pepper to taste.

SC DILL RED POTATOES

Fresh dill is the perfect herb to season a summer dish.

Serves 6

2 tablespoons extra-virgin olive oil
1½ pounds red potatoes
1 teaspoon salt
¼ teaspoon black pepper
2 tablespoons fresh dill, chopped
½ teaspoon lemon pepper

1. Add the olive oil, potatoes, salt, and pepper to a 4-quart slow cooker. Cover, and cook on low heat for 3–4 hours.
2. Remove the cover and mix in the dill and lemon pepper.

SC CHIPOTLE AND THYME SWEET POTATOES

To substitute fresh thyme for dried thyme, use ½ tablespoon of the fresh herb.

Serves 6

6 cups sweet potatoes, cubed

4 tablespoons butter or vegan margarine

3 cloves garlic, minced

1 teaspoon dried chipotle pepper

½ teaspoon dried thyme

1 teaspoon salt

¼ teaspoon black pepper

Add all ingredients to a 4-quart slow cooker. Cover and cook on medium heat for 4 hours.

SC MAPLE-GLAZED SWEET POTATOES

You can reduce the amount of sugar in this recipe by choosing a no-sugar-added syrup.

Serves 4

4 cups sweet potatoes, cubed

2 tablespoons butter or vegan margarine

¼ cup maple syrup

⅓ cup chopped pecans

Add all ingredients to a 4-quart slow cooker. Cover and cook on medium heat for 4 hours.

Recipe Substitutions

It's okay to use inexpensive pancake syrup instead of pure maple syrup in this recipe. It won't be as flavorful as pure maple syrup, but it will do the job.

SC | HERBED POTATOES

Any combination of herbs will work in this potato dish. Rosemary, thyme, dill, and coriander are great alternatives.

Serves 4

2 tablespoons olive oil

1 onion, diced

8 cups red potatoes, quartered

1 teaspoon dried oregano

1 teaspoon dried basil

1 teaspoon salt

¼ teaspoon black pepper

1. Add the olive oil to a 4-quart slow cooker and sauté the onion on high heat until translucent, about 3–5 minutes.
2. Add the remaining ingredients to the slow cooker. Cover, and cook on medium heat for 4 hours.

SC POTATO PICCATA

Piccata typically means a dish that contains butter, lemon, and herbs. Italian parsley, capers, garlic, and shallots are also commonly used.

Serves 4

2 tablespoons butter or vegan margarine
1 onion, julienned
1 red pepper, sliced
4 russet potatoes, sliced
¼ cup Vegetable Broth (see Chapter 5)
2 tablespoons fresh lemon juice
1 teaspoon salt
¼ teaspoon black pepper
¼ cup parsley, chopped

1. Add the butter or margarine to a 2-quart slow cooker and sauté the onions and peppers on high heat until they are golden brown, about 5–7 minutes.

2. Add the rest of the ingredients except for the parsley. Cover and cook on medium heat for 4 hours. Mix in the parsley.

⏹PC CHIPOTLE AND THYME MASHED SWEET POTATOES

To substitute fresh thyme for dried thyme, use ½ tablespoon of the fresh herb.

Serves 4–6

2 cups water

6 cups sweet potatoes, cubed

4 tablespoons butter or vegan margarine, such as Earth Balance

3 cloves garlic, minced

½ teaspoon dried chipotle pepper

½ teaspoon dried thyme

Salt and pepper, to taste

1. Pour water into the pressure cooker and add potatoes. Lock the lid into place and bring to high pressure. Once achieved, turn the heat to low and cook for 5 minutes. Remove from heat and release pressure naturally.

2. Drain the potatoes into a colander. Add the butter to the pressure cooker and sauté the garlic for about 2 minutes. Remove the pressure cooker from the heat. Add the sweet potatoes, chipotle pepper, and thyme. Mash the potatoes using a potato masher or electric mixer. Season with salt and pepper, to taste.

PC MASHED SWEET POTATOES

Turn this into a sweet potato casserole by covering with vegetarian marshmallows, such as Sweet & Sara brand, and baking in an uncovered dish. Traditional marshmallows contain gelatin, which is made from animal skin and bones.

Serves 3–5

1 cup water

5 cups sweet potatoes, cubed

4 tablespoons butter or vegan margarine, such as Earth Balance

¼ cup Pressure Cooker Vegetable Stock (see Chapter 5)

⅛ cup orange juice

2 tablespoons maple syrup

Salt and pepper, to taste

1. Add water and potatoes to the pressure cooker. Lock the lid into place and bring to high pressure. Once achieved, turn heat to low and cook 5 minutes. Remove from heat and allow pressure to release naturally for 20 minutes.

2. Drain the sweet potatoes in a colander. Add the butter or margarine, stock, orange juice, and maple syrup to the pressure cooker, and heat until the butter or margarine has melted. Remove from heat and add the sweet potatoes. Mash with a potato masher. Season with salt and pepper, to taste.

PRESSURE COOKER MAPLE-GLAZED SWEET POTATOES

You can remove the sugar from this recipe by replacing it with a sweetener, such as Splenda or Stevia.

Serves 2–4

1 cup water

4 cups sweet potatoes, diced

1 tablespoon butter or vegan margarine, such as Earth Balance

¼ cup maple syrup

1 tablespoon brown sugar

⅓ cup chopped pecans

1. Add water and potatoes to the pressure cooker. Lock the lid and bring to high pressure. Once achieved, turn the heat to low and cook for 5 minutes. Remove from heat and allow pressure to release naturally.

2. Drain potatoes in a colander. Preheat the oven to 375°F. Place the butter or margarine, syrup, and sugar in a small bowl and microwave for 30 seconds, or until the butter or margarine is melted. In a bowl, toss potatoes, butter or margarine mixture, and pecans, then pour into the casserole dish. Bake for 10 minutes.

MEXICAN SPICE POTATOES

If you like things spicy, really kick it up by adding an extra teaspoon of cayenne to these potatoes!

Serves 4

6 cups red potatoes, cubed
1 teaspoon chili powder
½ teaspoon sugar
½ teaspoon paprika
⅛ teaspoon cayenne pepper
⅛ teaspoon garlic powder
¼ teaspoon cumin
½ teaspoon salt
⅛ teaspoon black pepper
½ cup water

Add all ingredients to a 4-quart slow cooker. Cover and cook on medium heat for 4 hours.

SC GARLIC-PARMESAN MASHED POTATOES

Red potatoes break down easily, but become creamy, not crumbly, when mashed.

Serves 8

½ cup butter or vegan margarine
6 cloves garlic, minced
1½ pounds red potatoes, quartered
2 cups unsweetened soymilk
1 cup Parmesan cheese or vegan Parmesan
1 teaspoon salt
¼ teaspoon black pepper
¼ cup fresh parsley, chopped

1. Add the butter or vegan margarine to the slow cooker and sauté the garlic on high heat until it is golden brown, about 1 minute.
2. Add the rest of the ingredients except for the parsley. Cover and cook on medium heat for 4 hours.
3. Mix in the parsley and mash the potatoes to the desired consistency.

SC POTATO-BROCCOLI CASSEROLE

For a lighter and thinner sauce, use milk or unsweetened soymilk instead of Alfredo sauce.

Serves 8

1½ pounds red potatoes

2 cups broccoli florets

3 cups Alfredo sauce

1 teaspoon lemon pepper

½ teaspoon red pepper flakes

½ teaspoon garlic powder

1 teaspoon salt

¼ teaspoon black pepper

Add all ingredients to a 4-quart slow cooker. Cover and cook on medium heat for 4 hours.

GARLIC-PARSLEY POTATOES

The ingredients in this dish are similar to mashed potatoes, but you enjoy a stronger potato flavor by leaving them in bigger pieces.

Serves 8

½ cup butter or vegan margarine
6 cloves garlic, minced
1 onion, diced
1½ pounds red potatoes, quartered
½ cup unsweetened soymilk
1 teaspoon salt
¼ teaspoon black pepper
¼ cup parsley
1 tablespoon fresh lemon juice

1. Add the butter or vegan margarine to a 4-quart slow cooker and sauté the garlic and onion on high heat until they are golden brown, about 2–3 minutes.

2. Add the rest of the ingredients except for the parsley and lemon juice. Cover and cook on medium heat for 4 hours.

3. Mix in the parsley and lemon juice and cook for an additional 30 minutes.

OLD-FASHIONED GLAZED CARROTS

For added finesse to this lovely, classic dish, cut the carrots on a 45-degree bias, rotating them a quarter-turn after each cut, to make an angular shape chefs refer to as "oblique."

Serves 8

1 pound carrots, peeled, cut into 1" chunks

2 tablespoons unsalted butter

½ cup water

1½ teaspoons sugar

¼ teaspoon salt

Combine all ingredients in a heavy-bottomed skillet or pan large enough to accommodate a crowded single layer. Over medium-high heat, simmer about 5 minutes, then toss or flip the carrots. Continue cooking until the liquid is mostly evaporated, and what remains is a glaze adhering to the carrots. Be careful not to go too far, or the glaze will break and become oily.

CHAPTER 7
GRAINS, BEANS, AND LEGUMES

RECIPE LIST

BROWN RICE 354

WHITE RICE 354

WILD RICE 355

QUINOA 355

COUSCOUS 356

RED BEANS AND YELLOW RICE 357

RED BEANS AND RICE PIE WITH OREGANO AND TOMATOES 358

NEW ORLEANS RED BEANS AND RICE 359

RED BEANS AND RICE 360

PUERTO RICAN GANDULES (PIGEON PEAS) 361

QUINOA SALAD WITH TOMATOES AND CILANTRO 362

MINTED SWEET PEAS 362

SUSHI RICE 363

AVOCADO KAPPA MAKI SUSHI ROLLS 364

CHICKPEAS IN POTATO-ONION CURRY 365

INDIAN CHAPATI PAN BREAD 366

AVOCADO-BEET WRAPS WITH SUCCOTASH 367

KASHA VARNISHKES 368

WHEAT AND CORN WRAPS WITH TOFU 369

FRIED RICE WITH GREEN PEAS AND EGG 370

TUSCAN WHITE BEAN RAGOUT 371

RAJ'S CHICKPEAS IN TOMATO SAUCE 372

WILD RICE VEGETABLE PANCAKES 373

WILD RICE WITH APPLES AND ALMONDS 374

WILD RICE WITH MIXED VEGETABLES 374

EGYPTIAN LENTILS AND RICE 375

MEXICAN RICE 375

CUBAN BLACK BEANS AND RICE (MOROS Y CRISTIANOS) 376

BLACK BEAN BURRITOS 377

BARLEY RISOTTO 378

PEPPERY BROWN RICE RISOTTO 379

PUMPKIN RISOTTO 380

EASY SAFFRON VEGETABLE RISOTTO 381

WILD MUSHROOM RISOTTO 382

WILD MUSHROOM RISOTTO WITH TRUFFLES 383

BEET RISOTTO CAKES 384

POLENTA WITH BUTTER AND CHEESE 385

PAN-FRIED POLENTA WITH MARINARA 386

CREAMY THYME POLENTA 387

CHINESE BLACK RICE 387

CREOLE JAMBALAYA 388

MEXICAN FRIJOLES REFRITOS (REFRIED BEANS) 389

- HUMMUS BI TAHINI WITH SPROUTS AND CHERRY TOMATOES IN A PITA POCKET 390
- COUSCOUS-STUFFED RED PEPPERS 391
- BULGUR STUFFING 392
- THREE GRAIN PILAF 393
- RICE PILAF 394
- VEGETABLE RICE PILAF 395
- CRANBERRY-PECAN PILAF 396
- GREEN RICE PILAF 396
- TOMATILLO RICE 397
- STUFFED PEPPERS 398
- VEGETABLE FRIED RICE 399
- PAELLA 400
- PRESSURE COOKER PAELLA 401
- VEGAN CHORIZO PAELLA 402
- EGGPLANT "LASAGNA" 403
- PORTOBELLO BARLEY 404
- SAFFRON RICE 405
- BULGUR WITH BROCCOLI AND CARROT 405
- MOCK CHICKEN AND RICE 406
- SPANISH RICE 407
- BROWN RICE AND VEGETABLES 408
- CURRIED RICE 408
- CHIPOTLE BLACK BEAN SALAD 409
- MEDITERRANEAN CHICKPEAS 410
- OPEN-FACED BEAN BURRITO 411
- SLOW COOKER REFRIED BEANS 412
- CUBAN BLACK BEANS 413
- PRESSURE COOKER CUBAN BLACK BEANS AND RICE 414
- CURRIED LENTILS 415
- HOPPIN' JOHN 416
- CHIPOTLE-THYME BLACK BEANS 417
- BEER-LIME BLACK BEANS 418
- BLACK BEAN–CILANTRO FRITTERS 419
- BOSTON-STYLE BAKED BEANS 420
- BOURBON BAKED BEANS 421
- PINTO BEANS 422
- ADZUKI BEANS 422
- LIMA BEANS 423
- LIMA BEANS AND DUMPLINGS 424
- BLACK BEANS 425
- WHITE BEANS 426
- BLACK-EYED PEAS 427
- LENTILS 428
- MEXICAN BEER BLACK BEANS 429
- WHITE BEANS WITH ROSEMARY AND FRESH TOMATO 430
- WASABI-BARBECUE CHICKPEAS 431
- LENTILS WITH SAUTÉED SPINACH, WHITE WINE, AND GARLIC 432
- CHANA MASALA 433
- EASY EDAMAME 434
- SUMMER VEGETABLE BEAN SALAD 435
- BLACK BEAN SALSA 436
- SPICY BLACK-EYED PEAS AND KALE 437
- RED BEANS WITH PLANTAINS 438
- RED BEAN FRITTERS 439
- WHITE BEANS WITH GARLIC AND FRESH TOMATO 440
- WHITE BEANS AND RICE 441
- WHITE BEAN–LEEK PURÉE 442
- PRESSURE COOKER WASABI-BARBECUE CHICKPEAS 443
- CHICKPEA "TUNA" SALAD SANDWICH 444
- PRESSURE COOKER HOPPIN' JOHN 445
- LENTIL-SPINACH CURRY 446
- LENTIL PÂTÉ 447
- RED LENTIL CURRY 448
- PRESSURE COOKER CHANA MASALA 449
- SEA SALT EDAMAME 450
- DINNER LOAF 451

PC BROWN RICE

For short- or medium-grain brown rice, you will need to allow for additional cooking time.

Serves 4

1 cup long-grain brown rice

2 cups water

1. Add the rice and water to the pressure cooker.
2. Lock the lid into place; bring to high pressure and maintain for 15 minutes. Remove from heat and allow pressure to release naturally.
3. Fluff with a fork before serving or using in a recipe.

Nutritional Benefits

Brown rice is partially milled rice and has only the outer husk removed. Removing only the inedible outer part of the rice helps retain key nutrients, such as fiber and iron.

PC WHITE RICE

As with brown rice, the shorter the grain, the longer the cooking time.

Serves 4

1 cup long-grain white rice

1½ cups water

1. Add the rice and water to the pressure cooker.
2. Lock the lid into place; bring to high pressure and maintain for 5 minutes. Remove from heat and allow pressure to release naturally.
3. Fluff with a fork before serving or using in a recipe.

PC WILD RICE

Try a blend of cooked wild rice and cooked white or brown rice for a more subtle flavor.

Serves 4

1 cup wild rice

4 cups water

1. Add the wild rice and water to the pressure cooker.
2. Lock the lid into place; bring to high pressure and maintain for 22 minutes. Remove from heat and allow pressure to release naturally.
3. Fluff with a fork before serving or using in a recipe.

Wild Rice

Wild rice is actually a type of grass, not rice, that grows in marshlands. Most wild rice has a nutty flavor, but it varies slightly depending on the type.

PC QUINOA

Quinoa is an excellent source of protein for vegans and vegetarians.

Serves 4

1 cup quinoa

2 cups water

1. Add the quinoa and water to the pressure cooker.
2. Lock the lid into place; bring to high pressure and maintain for 6 minutes. Remove from heat and allow pressure to release naturally.
3. Fluff with a fork before serving or using in a recipe.

[PC] COUSCOUS

Couscous is really a type of pasta cut into tiny balls, but it is often served as a grain, with vegetables as a topping or on the side.

Serves 4

1 cup couscous

2 cups water

1. Add the couscous and water to the pressure cooker. Lock the lid into place; bring to high pressure and maintain for 2 minutes. Remove from heat and allow pressure to release naturally.

2. Fluff with a fork before serving or using in a recipe.

RED BEANS AND YELLOW RICE

This combination of red beans and yellow rice is both colorful and delicious!

Serves 8

DOMINICAN RED BEANS:

1 medium onion, chopped

3 cloves garlic, sliced

3 tablespoons olive oil

1 teaspoon oregano

2 bay leaves

1 (8-ounce) can Goya brand Spanish-style tomato sauce

2 teaspoons adobo con pimienta (seasoned salt with white pepper)

1 packet Goya brand sazón (optional)

1 (16-ounce) package red beans soaked overnight in 1 quart cold water, drained

½ small bunch fresh cilantro, including stems, roughly chopped (optional)

YELLOW RICE:

2 tablespoons achiote (annatto seeds)

3 tablespoons oil

1 medium onion, chopped

1 tablespoon adobo con pimienta

4 cups long-grain rice, such as Canilla or Goya brand

1. For Dominican Red Beans: Sauté onions and garlic with olive oil over medium heat for 5 minutes in a pot large enough to hold all ingredients. Add oregano, bay leaves, tomato sauce, adobo, and sazón. Bring to a simmer and add beans and cilantro, adding enough water to cover them (about 3 cups).

2. Bring to a boil, then reduce to a low simmer, and cook 90 minutes, until beans are tender enough to mash between 2 fingers.

3. For Yellow Rice: Heat achiote in oil, in a large pot with a tight-fitting lid, over a medium-high flame until seeds sizzle and give up their color. Oil should be a dark orange hue. Remove from heat and carefully remove seeds with a slotted spoon or skimmer.

4. Add onion and adobo to achiote oil and sauté over medium heat for 5 minutes, until translucent. Add rice and stir until it is well coated with oil. Add 6 cups water, and raise flame to high.

5. Bring to boil, and then reduce to simmer, cover tightly, and cook 20 minutes, until all water is absorbed. Remove from heat and let stand, covered, 5 minutes. Fluff with a fork.

RED BEANS AND RICE PIE WITH OREGANO AND TOMATOES

Rice and beans have long been recognized by nutritionists as providing the building blocks for proteins required for good health.

Serves 6

1 cup pastry or all-purpose flour

¼ teaspoon salt

6 tablespoons unsalted butter, cold, cut into small pieces

About 3 tablespoons water, ice-cold

1 bag dried beans (any kind) for prebaking the crust

1 medium onion, chopped

1 tablespoon olive oil

½ bunch fresh oregano, roughly chopped, or 1 tablespoon dried

1 (15½-ounce) can red kidney beans, drained and rinse

Salt and pepper to taste

1 egg, beaten

1 cup brown rice, cooked

1 (16-ounce) can stewed tomatoes, drained

1. Make the pie dough in advance: Mix together the flour, salt, and butter with your hands until butter is mostly, but not completely, incorporated. Add the water, a little at a time, mixing until the dough comes together. Knead briefly, just to smooth out. Some small nuggets of butter may still be seen in the dough, which will make the crust flaky. Wrap the dough in plastic and refrigerate for no less than 30 minutes.

2. Roll the dough thin (¼"), on a floured surface, mold into a buttered 9" pie pan, and trim the edges. Cover with wax paper, then fill with dried, uncooked beans, and bake 25–30 minutes in a 350°F oven until golden. This precooking is called "blind baking" the pie shell. Allow to cool before removing the baking beans. Throw these beans away, or use for another pie crust.

3. Meanwhile, sauté onion in olive oil until translucent, add the oregano, and cook for 1 minute longer. Toss in the red beans, season with salt and pepper, and remove from heat. Separately, stir beaten egg into cooked brown rice.

4. Spread half of rice-egg mixture into bottom of pie shell. Distribute beans evenly over the rice, and layer on 1 can of stewed tomatoes. Cover with remaining rice. Bake for 30 minutes at 350°F.

SC NEW ORLEANS RED BEANS AND RICE

Red beans and rice is a New Orleans staple that is traditionally served on Mondays.

Serves 8

¼ cup butter or vegan margarine

1 cup onion, diced

1 cup green bell pepper, diced

1 cup celery, diced

5 cloves garlic, minced

2 (15-ounce) cans red kidney beans, drained

1½ cups water

4 teaspoons salt

2 teaspoons liquid smoke

1 teaspoon vegan Worcestershire sauce

2 teaspoons hot sauce

1 teaspoon dried thyme

2 teaspoons cayenne pepper

4 bay leaves

8 cups cooked long-grain white rice

1. Add the butter or vegan margarine to a 4-quart slow cooker and sauté the onion, green bell pepper, celery, and garlic for 3–5 minutes over high heat.

2. Add the red kidney beans, water, salt, liquid smoke, Worcestershire sauce, hot sauce, dried thyme, cayenne pepper, and bay leaves. Cover and cook on low heat for about 6 hours.

3. Remove the bay leaves and serve over the cooked white rice.

Make It "Meaty"
Sausage and ham hocks are the most common meats used in red beans and rice. To make a vegetarian "meaty" version, add cooked, sliced vegetarian sausage and chunks of cooked vegetarian bacon right before serving.

SC RED BEANS AND RICE

Red beans and rice is a classic Big Easy dish that can be cooked with the rice and beans mixed together.

Serves 4

3 cups water

3½ cups vegetarian chicken stock

2 tablespoons butter or vegan margarine

1 (15-ounce) can kidney beans, drained

2 cups white rice, uncooked

1 onion, chopped

1 green bell pepper, chopped

1 cup celery, chopped

1 teaspoon thyme

1 teaspoon paprika

1 teaspoon Cajun seasoning

½ teaspoon red pepper flakes

1 teaspoon salt

¼ teaspoons black pepper

1. Add all ingredients to a 4-quart slow cooker. Cover and cook on low heat for 6 hours.
2. Check the rice to see if it is tender and if not, cook for an additional hour.

PUERTO RICAN GANDULES (PIGEON PEAS)

Pigeon peas are the beloved bean of Puerto Rico, where they are served over oily, long-grain white rice.

Serves 6

1½ cups pigeon peas, soaked overnight, rinsed and drained

1 tablespoon olive oil

1 small Spanish onion, chopped

⅓ green pepper, chopped

2 cloves garlic, minced

2 bay leaves

1½ teaspoons salt

¼ teaspoon fresh ground black pepper

¼ cup chopped fresh thyme or 1 tablespoon dried

1 medium tomato, seeded, chopped

1. Simmer peas in 4 cups water for 1 hour, until tender. Meanwhile, heat the olive oil in a 10" skillet, then add onion, green pepper, garlic, bay leaves, salt, pepper, and thyme, and sauté until onion is translucent (about 5 minutes). Add chopped tomato and cook 2 minutes more.

2. Add the vegetables to the peas and cook 45 minutes more, until peas are very soft. Serve with white or yellow rice.

QUINOA SALAD WITH TOMATOES AND CILANTRO

Quinoa, an ancient grain that has made a comeback in the last few years due to much attention from high-profile chefs, has a very attractive light golden hue and a springy, crunchy texture, and the kernels have an appealing, ringlet-like shape. It cooks quickly.

Serves 6

1 cup quinoa, boiled for 15 minutes, drained

1 cup Red and Yellow Plum Tomato Chutney (see Chapter 9)

¼ teaspoon kosher salt

1 tablespoon extra-virgin olive oil

Combine the cooked quinoa and tomato chutney. Season to taste. Dress with olive oil, and serve with extra olive oil at the table. (Herb-infused olive oil is great here. Try rosemary-flavored.)

MINTED SWEET PEAS

This recipe is great to serve as a side dish!

Serves 4

2 cups shelled fresh peas (about 2 pounds unshelled)

½ teaspoon sugar

2 tablespoons butter or vegan margarine

Salt and pepper to taste

3 tablespoons chopped fresh mint leaves

Simmer the peas and sugar until bright green and tender, about 5 minutes; drain. Toss peas with butter or margarine, salt, pepper, and mint.

SUSHI RICE

Contrary to popular belief, the term "sushi" does not connote raw fish. Instead, it refers to the vinegar-seasoned, short-grain rice central to the Japanese diet. Sushi forms the base for delicious appetizers and dinners, which need not involve any fish at all.

Yields 4½ cups

2 cups Japanese-style short-grain rice

1 (1"-square) kelp (optional)

3 tablespoons sake (optional)

¼ cup rice vinegar

1 tablespoon sugar

½ teaspoon salt

1. In a bowl or pot, under cold running water, rinse the rice very well, agitating it with your hands until all the starch has been washed off and the wash water runs clear; drain. Place the drained rice in a pot with a tight-fitting lid, along with the kelp and 2¼ cups water. Cover pot, and bring to a boil; lower to a simmer. Cook until all water is absorbed, about 8 minutes. Remove from heat, and let stand, covered, for at least 10 minutes.

2. Combine the sake, vinegar, sugar, and salt. Transfer the rice to a large bowl; sprinkle with vinegar mixture and gently fold to combine. Spread rice onto a large sheet pan or platter to cool and dry, fanning and gently turning it occasionally. Keep covered and slightly warm for use in making sushi preparations.

AVOCADO KAPPA MAKI SUSHI ROLLS

These crunchy, simple rolls feature protein-rich tofu. They're equally delicious made with brown sushi rice, a heart-healthy option.

Yields 6 rolls

7 sheets of nori

1 recipe Sushi Rice (see recipe in this chapter), 4½ cups total

2 teaspoons wasabi

1 cup fine julienne of cucumber (use a mandoline to make these strips extra fine)

1 ripe Hass avocado, cut into thin strips, sprinkled with lemon juice and salt

½ recipe marinated tofu from Tofu Salad (see Chapter 3), store-bought marinated tofu, or flavored tempeh, cut into small strips

Pickled ginger

Place 1 sheet of nori on a sushi-rolling mat, long edge toward you. Spread about ¾ cup rice onto the nori, leaving a 1" strip free at the far end. Use your hands, moistened with water, to smooth the rice into an even layer. At the part closest to you, spread a thin line of wasabi. Arrange ⅙ of the cucumber, ⅙ of the avocado, and ⅙ of the tofu into a strip near the wasabi-laced edge. Using the mat as a helper, roll the assembly jelly-roll style away from yourself. Keep pressure even and firm, and keep the mat clear of the roll. Repeat the procedure with remaining nori and fillings. Allow to stand for 5 minutes before slicing each roll into 6 pieces. Serve with wasabi and pickled ginger.

CHICKPEAS IN POTATO-ONION CURRY

Thirty-minute main dishes like this are a lifesaver when you come home hungry and nothing's ready. Put on a pot of basmati rice before you start this dish, and you'll be dining before you know it.

Serves 4

- 2 cups onions, cut into 1" pieces
- 3 tablespoons oil, divided
- 1½ cups cubed (1") potatoes
- 1 (14-ounce) can coconut milk
- 1 (15-ounce) can chickpeas (garbanzos), drained and rinsed
- 5–6 cloves garlic, peeled
- 1 teaspoon kosher salt
- 1½ teaspoons ground coriander
- ½ teaspoon ground turmeric
- 1 teaspoon chili powder
- 1 teaspoon ground cumin
- Juice of ½ a lemon

1. In a skillet over high heat, cook the onions in 1 tablespoon oil until lightly browned, about 5 minutes. Add the potatoes and coconut milk; cover and cook until potatoes are tender, about 20 minutes; add the chickpeas. In a food processor, combine the garlic, salt, coriander, turmeric, chili powder, and cumin; process until it becomes a paste, scraping down sides as needed.

2. Heat remaining oil in a small skillet, and fry the garlic mixture for 1 minute, allowing it to become fragrant and slightly browned. Add the garlic mixture to the chickpea pot. Simmer for 2 to 3 minutes; season to taste with lemon and additional salt. Serve with basmati rice and/or Indian breads.

INDIAN CHAPATI PAN BREAD

This recipe takes under an hour for 16 breads. It's the traditional partner to Indian curries, which are eaten by scooping up morsels into the bread, to be eaten from the hand. If you work with a partner, one of you can be cooking the chapatis while the other one rolls, saving up to a quarter of the preparation time.

Yields 16 chapati

1 cup chapati flour (Indian whole-wheat flour)

⅓ cup warm water (generous)

1 teaspoon oil

1. In a mixing bowl, make a well in the center of the flour. Pour the warm water and oil into this depression; fold ingredients together with a fork until a dough forms. Knead the dough in the bowl for 10 minutes. It should be smooth and elastic.

2. Divide the dough into 4 pieces. Roll 1 of the pieces against the table with your hands to form a cylinder; cut the cylinder into 4 nuggets. Cover remaining dough with a damp cloth while you work. Form each nugget into a ball the size of a marble, and roll it on a floured surface with a rolling pin into thin disks (1/16"—a little thicker than a CD). Repeat with remaining dough. They can be stacked.

3. Heat an iron skillet over a medium flame for 5 minutes, until hot enough for a drop of water to sizzle on it. Dust off the excess flour from a chapati and place it flat into the dry pan. Leave it until bubbles and air pockets are visible on the top; flip it to cook the other side. Some brown spots are fine. Repeat with remaining dough. Stack the cooked chapatis on a plate, and cover with a dry towel to keep warm.

AVOCADO-BEET WRAPS WITH SUCCOTASH

Have these wraps as your lunch or as an appetizer!

Serves 4

4 flour tortillas (10" diameter or larger)

2 tablespoons vegan mayonnaise or vegan sour cream

2 cups Succotash Salad (see Chapter 3)

1 large or 2 small beets (about 8 ounces), boiled until tender, peeled

1 ripe Florida avocado, peeled and cut into 1" wedges

1. Soften and lightly brown the tortillas by placing them directly over the burner of a gas stove, and flipping them until the surface blisters slightly (alternately, steam, broil, or toast them for a minute until soft). Spread ½ tablespoon of mayonnaise or sour cream into a line across the center of each tortilla. Spoon ½ cup of succotash onto each tortilla. Halve the beets, and cut the halves into ½" slices. Divide the beets and avocado slices evenly onto the tortillas, placing them on the side of the succotash line closest to you.

2. Place 1 of the tortillas on a work surface directly in front of yourself. Fold the near edge of the tortilla over the fillings, and roll it, jelly-roll fashion, away from yourself, keeping even pressure to ensure a tight roll. Place seam-side down on a plate; repeat with remaining tortillas.

KASHA VARNISHKES

This is a classic Jewish dish. While Jewish cooking is pretty meat-centric, there are a few really good vegetarian dishes like this one.

Serves 8

2 cups coarse or medium granulation kasha (toasted buckwheat)

2 eggs (or 3 egg whites)

4 cups stock or water, hot

3 tablespoons butter or margarine

1 tablespoon olive oil

1 medium onion, roughly chopped

1 (10-ounce) package mushrooms, sliced

1 pound bow-tie–shaped pasta (farfalle) or egg noodles, cooked medium-soft

1 (10½-ounce) can condensed cream of mushroom soup

Salt and pepper to taste

1. Heat a large skillet over high heat. Combine kasha and eggs, and mix with a wooden spoon until well coated. Pour the kasha mixture into the hot pan and cook, stirring and breaking up lumps, until the egg has dried onto the kasha, and grains are separate. Add the hot stock or water and the butter or margarine carefully (it may spatter). Lower flame to low heat, cover tightly, and cook 7–10 minutes, until all liquid is absorbed.

2. In a separate pan, heat the olive oil. Sauté the onion and mushrooms together until soft, about 5 minutes. In a mixing bowl, combine the cooked kasha, onion, mushrooms, cooked pasta, and cream of mushroom soup; mix well. Salt and pepper to taste. Transfer to a casserole and bake 20 minutes at 350°F until hot and slightly crusty on top.

WHEAT AND CORN WRAPS WITH TOFU

Neater to eat and easier to carry than sandwiches, wraps like these are catching on all over. Substitute almost any grain you like for the wheat berries used here.

Serves 4

½ cup wheat berries, spelt, faro, or other whole grain, boiled until tender, usually about 30 minutes

2 ears corn, kernels sheared from the cob and boiled 1 minute, or 1 (10-ounce) package frozen sweet corn, thawed.

Juice of 1 lemon

1 tablespoon extra-virgin olive oil

½ teaspoon ground cumin

Salt and pepper to taste

2 tablespoons salad dressing

4 medium flour tortillas (10"–12")

½ recipe marinated tofu from Tofu Salad (see Chapter 3), or 1 cup store-bought flavored tofu

1. In a bowl, toss the cooked grain, corn, lemon juice, olive oil, cumin, salt, and pepper until combined.

2. Spread the dressing in a line across the equator of each tortilla. Spoon in the grain salad; arrange the tofu alongside the grain.

3. Roll, jelly-roll style, away from yourself. Tuck in ends.

FRIED RICE WITH GREEN PEAS AND EGG

An all-purpose fried rice that can be adapted to your taste—try it with sliced mushrooms, snow peas, water chestnuts, or your own favorite garnishes.

Serves 4

3 eggs, beaten

2 tablespoons peanut or other oil

2 tablespoons chopped fresh ginger

2 tablespoons chopped garlic

½ cup chopped scallions, plus extra for garnish (optional)

4 cups cooked white rice

1 (10-ounce) package frozen green peas

1 small carrot, peeled, diced, and blanched (optional)

1 tablespoon soy sauce (optional)

Sesame seeds, for garnish (optional)

1. Heat a 10" nonstick skillet with a few drops of oil over medium heat; add the eggs. Cook without stirring until completely cooked through, about 3 minutes. Slide the cooked egg sheet onto a cutting board; let it cool for 5 minutes. Roll the egg into a cylinder, and crosscut to form long julienne.

2. Heat the oil in a large skillet or wok. Add the ginger, garlic, and scallions, and cook for 1 minute; they should sizzle. Add the rice. Over high heat, chop and stir the rice to break up any lumps; cook until very hot and some rice forms crunchy bits, about 5 minutes. Add the peas, and the carrot if using. Cook until peas are hot, then stir in the egg julienne, and soy sauce if desired. Serve garnished with additional chopped scallions and/or sesame seeds if desired.

TUSCAN WHITE BEAN RAGOUT

Eaten on its own, or as a base for a larger item, this hearty stew packs flavor and nutrition.

Serves 8

1 pound great northern (large white) beans, cooked very soft; retain cooking liquid, or 1 (28-ounce) can of large white beans

2 tablespoons olive oil

2 tablespoons chopped garlic (about 5 cloves)

2 medium onions, diced

2 teaspoons chopped fresh rosemary, or 1 teaspoon dried rosemary leaves

1 dried New Mexico chili, or ¼ teaspoon crushed red pepper flakes

1 head escarole (about 6 cups washed leaves), or an equal amount of spinach, torn into large pieces

6 ripe plum tomatoes, seeded and diced (about 1½ cups)

2 ounces unsalted butter

¼ cup roughly chopped Italian parsley

½ cup grated Parmigiano-Reggiano cheese (optional)

Kosher salt and freshly ground black pepper

A few drops top-quality extra-virgin olive oil

1. Strain the cooking liquid from the beans and reserve (you should have about 2 cups of liquid—add water if necessary to reach this amount). Heat the olive oil in a large skillet or Dutch oven over medium heat; add the garlic and cook until it turns white and fragrant, only about 30 seconds. Stir in the onions, rosemary, and chili. Cook gently until the onions are very soft, about 10 minutes, stirring occasionally. Add the beans, and enough bean-cooking liquid to make the mixture brothy; simmer 5 minutes.

2. Stir in the escarole; simmer until it is all wilted. Add the tomatoes, butter, parsley, and cheese if using. Remove from heat, and stir until the butter is melted in, adding additional bean liquid as necessary to keep it brothy. Season well with salt and pepper. Serve warm, drizzled with extra-virgin olive oil.

Note: This stew can be prepared through Step 1, and refrigerated for up to 3 days. The flavors will mingle, and the dish will be even better.

RAJ'S CHICKPEAS IN TOMATO SAUCE

This quick, delicious, healthful dish can be thrown together in minutes using ingredients from the pantry.

Serves 6

2 tablespoons peanut or safflower oil

1 tablespoon cumin seeds

1 tablespoon chopped fresh ginger

¼ teaspoon crushed red pepper flakes

1 large onion, halved and sliced into half-moons

1 medium (15–20-ounce) can tomatoes, either crushed or diced

Salt and black pepper

2 (15-ounce) cans chickpeas (garbanzos), drained and rinsed

Chopped cilantro (optional)

1. Heat the oil in a large saucepan over medium heat. Add the cumin seeds and cook until they are fragrant, about 1 minute. Stir in the ginger, crushed red pepper, and onion; cook until the onion is soft, about 5 minutes. Add the tomatoes and cook 5 minutes more, until they become saucy.

2. Season the sauce with salt and pepper and add the chickpeas; cook 5 minutes more. Sprinkle with chopped cilantro, if desired. Serve with basmati rice and Indian breads.

WILD RICE VEGETABLE PANCAKES

Crunchy, earthy-tasting wild rice cakes satisfy a comfort-food-loving part of the soul. They're easy to make and can be kept at room temperature for hours before serving. Try them with Braised Red Cabbage (see Chapter 8), or as an appetizer, with a light Asian soy-vinegar dipping sauce.

Serves 6–8

4 ounces wild rice

1 cup julienne carrots

1 cup julienne celery

1 cup julienne white onion

3 scallions, chopped

2 eggs

½ cup flour

Kosher salt and freshly ground black pepper

Olive oil for frying

1. Boil the wild rice in 2 quarts of lightly salted water until very tender and most grains have burst open, about 40 minutes. Drain, reserving liquid, and cool the rice by spreading it on a platter or pan. Toss the rice with the carrots, celery, onion, scallions, egg, and flour. Season with salt and pepper. Moisten with a few drips of rice cooking liquid to help the mixture adhere to itself.

2. Heat 2 tablespoons olive oil in a nonstick skillet over medium heat until a piece of onion sizzles when added, about 2 minutes. Place ¼-cup mounds of rice mixture into the pan; shape them into rough-hewn pancakes. Cook without moving them until they brown on the first side and are visibly cooked around the edges, about 5 minutes. Flip the pancakes with a spatula, and cook until lightly browned. Drain. Serve.

WILD RICE WITH APPLES AND ALMONDS

For extra texture with an Indian curry dinner, such as Aloo Gobi (see Chapter 8) or Curried Parsnips (see Chapter 6), serve them in a ring of this chewy, crunchy mixture of nuts and fruits.

Serves 8

½ cup wild rice

½ cup shelled almonds, whole or in slivers

1 tablespoon oil

1 large onion, roughly chopped

1 Rome or Golden Delicious apple, peeled, cored, and diced

¼ cup raisins

Salt and freshly ground black pepper to taste

1 tablespoon olive oil or butter, optional

¼ cup chopped cilantro or parsley

1. Boil the rice in 2½ quarts salted water until tender, about 40 minutes; drain, saving cooking liquid. Crisp the almonds by toasting them dry until fragrant and visibly shiny (see "Toasting Nuts," Chapter 2). Heat the oil in a large skillet or Dutch oven over medium heat for 1 minute. Add onion; cook until softened, about 5 minutes. Add the apple, raisins, and a splash of the rice cooking liquid. Cook 5 minutes more, until the apple is translucent.

2. Combine the cooked rice, apple mixture, nuts, salt, and pepper. Stir in olive oil or butter, if desired, and serve garnished with cilantro or parsley.

SC WILD RICE WITH MIXED VEGETABLES

Wild rice cooks up perfectly in the slow cooker. Try it as a high-fiber alternative to white rice or potatoes.

Serves 8

2½ cups water

1 cup wild rice

3 cloves garlic, minced

1 medium onion, diced

1 carrot, diced

1 stalk celery, diced

1. Place all ingredients into a 4-quart slow cooker and stir. Cover and cook on low for 4 hours.

2. After 4 hours, check to see if the kernels are open and tender. If not, put the lid back on and continue to cook for an additional 15–30 minutes.

3. Stir before serving.

EGYPTIAN LENTILS AND RICE

Amino acids in the lentils and rice combine to form complete proteins, making this warming, comforting dish nutritionally powerful.

Serves 8

1 tablespoon olive oil

¼ teaspoon cumin seeds

1 medium onion, roughly chopped

1 cup rice

½ cup brown or green lentils

2 teaspoons juice plus ½ teaspoon zest from a lemon

1 teaspoon salt

3 cups vegetable stock or water

Heat the oil and cumin seeds in a medium saucepan over medium heat until the seeds are fragrant, about 30 seconds. Add the onion; cook until translucent, about 5 minutes. Stir in the rice and lentils, mixing with a wooden spoon until well coated. Add the lemon juice, zest, salt, and stock. Cover tightly and simmer until all water is absorbed, about 20 minutes. Remove from heat and allow to stand for 5 minutes before fluffing with a fork and serving. Goes great with a dab of Tunisian chili sauce ("harissa") or other chili paste.

MEXICAN RICE

This rice combines nicely with Mexican Frijoles Refritos (see recipe in this chapter) for an excellent lunchtime meal.

Serves 6

1½ cups long-grain white rice

1 large tomato, peeled, seeded, and chopped

⅓ medium white onion, roughly chopped

1 clove garlic, peeled and roughly chopped

⅓ cup peanut or safflower oil

3½ cups vegetable stock

2 teaspoons salt

½ carrot, peeled and finely chopped

⅓ cup green peas (frozen are okay)

1. Soak rice in hot water for 15 minutes, then rinse and drain. Purée the tomato, onion, and garlic in a blender.

2. Fry the rice in the oil, in a large saucepot, until it turns light gold in color, about 10 minutes. Pour off excess oil. Stir in the tomato purée and cook until almost dry, about 3 minutes.

3. Add stock, salt, carrot, and peas, cover, and simmer over low heat for 18 minutes; liquid should be absorbed and rice tender. Remove from heat and let stand 5 minutes, then fluff with a fork.

CUBAN BLACK BEANS AND RICE (MOROS Y CRISTIANOS)

Use the black beans in this recipe for many other uses, including Black Bean Burritos (see recipe in this chapter).

Serves 8

1½ cups black beans, soaked overnight, drained

6 cups water

2 tablespoons vegetable oil

2 cloves garlic, minced

½ Spanish onion, finely chopped

¼ teaspoon ground cumin

¼ teaspoon oregano

1 bay leaf

1 teaspoon salt

¼ teaspoon fresh ground black pepper

½ cup chopped fresh cilantro leaves and stems

1 clove garlic, peeled and crushed with the side of a knife

4 teaspoons vegetable oil

1½ cups long-grain white rice, rinsed and drained

2 cups water

1½ teaspoons salt

Prepare the Beans:

1. Simmer beans in water until very tender (about 90 minutes).

2. Meanwhile, heat the oil. Add the garlic, onion, cumin, oregano, bay leaf, salt, and pepper and sauté until onion is soft. Add this mixture to the beans and simmer 20 minutes more. Stir in cilantro.

Prepare the Rice:

1. Sauté garlic gently in 3 teaspoons oil until it begins to brown. Add rice and stir to coat.

2. Add water and salt; bring to a boil, and cover. Lower heat and simmer 20 minutes.

3. Remove from heat; pour in remaining oil, and fluff to separate grains. Serve topped with a ladle of Cuban black beans.

BLACK BEAN BURRITOS

It's probably no accident that these burritos (which can be made vegan by substituting soy cheese for the Cheddar and Monterey jack) are a source of complete protein, since their origins are hot Mexican lands, where many local residents considered animal protein a luxury.

Serves 4

1 tablespoon oil

1 cup chopped onions

4 large (12") flour or whole-wheat tortillas

1 cup shredded cheese, such as a combination of Cheddar and Monterey jack or soy cheese

2 cups cooked brown or white rice, hot

1½ cups cooked black beans in sauce, hot, or 1 (15-ounce) can of black beans, heated with some cumin and garlic

½ cup Salsa Fresca (see Chapter 4) or chopped tomatoes and onions

1 ripe Hass avocado, peeled and sliced

½ cup fresh cilantro sprigs

Tofu Sour Cream (optional, see Chapter 2)

1. Brown the onions in the oil until soft. Soften a tortilla over a gas burner or in a hot oven; place on a clean work surface. Spoon a quarter of the hot onions into a line, ⅓ of the way up on the tortilla; sprinkle on ¼ of the shredded cheese. Immediately spoon on ½ cup hot rice; this should be hot enough to melt the cheese. Ladle on ¼ of the beans, including some of the sauce; top with the salsa, avocado slices, cilantro, and Tofu Sour Cream, if desired.

2. Fold edge nearest to you up to cover the fillings. Fold side flaps in to seal ingredients into a pocket. Roll the burrito away from yourself, keeping even tension, and tucking with your fingers as you roll. Repeat with remaining tortillas.

PC BARLEY RISOTTO

If you're not a fan of Parmigiano-Reggiano cheese, you can substitute crumbled blue cheese or grated Cheddar cheese to taste.

Serves 4

- 1 tablespoon butter or vegan margarine, such as Earth Balance
- 1 tablespoon olive oil
- 1 large onion, diced
- 1 clove garlic, minced
- 1 stalk celery, finely minced
- 1½ cups pearl barley, well rinsed
- ⅓ cup dried mushrooms
- 4 cups Pressure Cooker Vegetable Stock (see Chapter 5)
- 2¼ cups water
- 1 cup Parmigiano-Reggiano cheese, grated, or vegan cheese, such as Daiya Mozzarella Style Shreds
- 2 tablespoons fresh parsley, minced
- Salt, to taste

1. Bring the butter or margarine and oil to temperature in the pressure cooker over medium heat. Add the onion; sauté for 3 minutes or until the onion is soft. Add the garlic; sauté for 30 seconds. Stir in the celery and barley until the barley is coated with the fat. Add the mushrooms, stock, and water. Lock the lid into place and bring to high pressure; maintain pressure for 18 minutes. Quick-release the pressure and remove the lid.

2. Drain off any excess liquid not absorbed by the barley, leaving just enough to leave the risotto slightly soupy. Reduce heat to low and stir in the cheese and parsley. Taste for seasoning, and add salt if needed.

Flavor Variations

To further enhance the earthy flavor of the mushrooms and barley, add ½ teaspoon of dried thyme and ½ teaspoon of dried sage instead of fresh parsley.

PC PEPPERY BROWN RICE RISOTTO

If you avoid alcohol, replace the wine in this recipe with ¼ cup Pressure Cooker Vegetable Stock (see Chapter 5).

Serves 8

2 medium leeks

1 small fennel bulb

3 tablespoons butter or vegan margarine, such as Earth Balance

2 cups short-grain brown rice, rinsed and drained

½ teaspoon salt

2½ cups water

¼ cup white wine

¾ cup fontina cheese, grated, or vegan cheese, such as Daiya Mozzarella Style Shreds

1½ teaspoons freshly ground or cracked black pepper

1. Cut the leeks into quarters lengthwise, and then slice into ½" slices; wash thoroughly, drain, and dry.

2. Clean the fennel. Trim the fronds from the fennel, chop, and set aside. Dice the bulb.

3. Melt the butter or margarine in the pressure cooker over medium heat. Add the leeks and fennel bulb; sauté for 1 minute or until the leeks begin to wilt.

4. Add the rice and stir-fry into the leeks until the rice begins to turn golden brown. Stir in the salt, water, and white wine.

5. Lock the lid into place and bring to high pressure; maintain pressure for 20 minutes. Remove from heat and allow pressure to release naturally for 10 minutes. Quick-release any remaining pressure. Remove the lid.

6. Fluff the rice with a fork. Stir in the cheese, fennel fronds, and pepper. Taste for seasoning and add additional salt if needed.

Italian Cheese

Fontina is an Italian cheese with a mild flavor that is creamy and melts easily. Mozzarella is a more common alternative to fontina in this recipe.

PC PUMPKIN RISOTTO

This seasonal risotto will make for a unique entrée on any Thanksgiving table.

Serves 6–8

1 tablespoon olive oil

1 cup diced sweet yellow onion

2 cups arborio rice

1 cup white wine

2 cups Pressure Cooker Vegetable Stock (see Chapter 5)

2 cups water

1 cup canned pumpkin purée

1 teaspoon grated fresh ginger

1 teaspoon grated nutmeg

Salt and pepper, to taste

1. Bring the oil to medium heat in the pressure cooker. Sauté the onion until translucent. Add the rice and sauté until opaque, about 4 minutes. Add the wine and stir until the liquid is absorbed. Add stock and 1 cup water.

2. Lock the lid into place; bring to high pressure and maintain for 6 minutes. Quick-release the pressure and remove the lid.

3. Add the remaining cup of water, pumpkin purée, ginger, and nutmeg. Simmer over medium heat until the liquid is absorbed. Season with salt and pepper, to taste.

EASY SAFFRON VEGETABLE RISOTTO

This is about the fastest risotto you can make, and still achieve the creamy, saucy, flavorful dish of Northern Italy. The key is the gradual addition of hot liquid while stirring, which extracts natural starches in the short-grain rice, thickening the sauce. The dish is even better if you use freshly sautéed veggies, but frozen are a suitable convenience.

Serves 6

3 pinches saffron

10 cups vegetable stock (or 5 cups canned vegetable broth combined with an equal amount of water)

2 tablespoons olive oil

1 onion, roughly chopped

1 pound short-grain Italian rice for risotto, such as arborio, carnaroli, or roma

½ cup dry white wine

1½ cups grated Parmesan cheese

1 pound frozen mixed vegetables, or an equal amount of sautéed fresh vegetables

Salt and freshly ground black pepper to taste

1 tablespoon unsalted butter

Lemon wedges (optional)

1. Combine the saffron with 1 cup of the stock and let steep for 10 minutes; heat the remaining stock separately until hot but not boiling. Heat the oil in a heavy-bottomed saucepan over medium heat; add the onion and cook until translucent, about 5 minutes. Stir in the rice and mix with a wooden spoon until rice is well coated and begins to change color, about 5 minutes.

2. Add the white wine; cook until all wine is absorbed. Add the saffron mixture; cook, stirring, until the liquid is absorbed. Begin adding the hot stock in 1-cup increments, stirring each time until all the liquid is absorbed before adding the next cup, until rice is soft and creamy, and you have only 1 cup of liquid left. Fold in the cheese, vegetables, salt, pepper, and butter. Stir until well combined; remove from heat. Adjust consistency with remaining stock. Rice should have a saucy consistency and be soft, but still have a little bite. Serve with lemon wedges, if desired.

SC WILD MUSHROOM RISOTTO

This makes a great side dish, but you can also try it as a main course, paired with a green salad.

Serves 6

1 teaspoon olive oil

1 shallot, minced

2 cloves garlic, minced

8 ounces sliced assorted wild mushrooms

2 cups Vegetable Broth (see Chapter 5)

2 cups arborio rice

3 cups water

½ teaspoon salt

1. Heat the oil in a nonstick pan. Sauté the shallot, garlic, and mushrooms until soft, about 4–5 minutes.

2. Add ½ cup broth and the rice and cook until the liquid is fully absorbed, about 5 minutes.

3. Scrape the rice mixture into a 4-quart slow cooker. Add the water, salt, and remaining broth.

4. Cover and cook on low for 1 hour. Stir before serving.

WILD MUSHROOM RISOTTO WITH TRUFFLES

The earthy taste of wild mushrooms and the musky perfume of truffles marry incredibly well with the natural richness of risotto. This recipe works as well using dried wild mushrooms, which are easier to find out of season. Practice with cultivated "exotics" like shiitake, cremini, and oyster mushrooms before delving into the $28-per-pound chanterelles.

Serves 8

4 tablespoons unsalted butter, divided

6 shallots or 1 large onion, roughly chopped (about 1½ cups)

1 pound assorted wild and exotic mushrooms

1 pound short-grain Italian rice for risotto, such as arborio, carnaroli, or roma

½ cup dry white wine

10 cups Mushroom Vegetable Stock (see Chapter 5), hot

1½ cups grated Parmesan cheese

Salt and freshly ground black pepper to taste

Fresh or canned truffle for shaving (optional)

Lemon wedges (optional)

1. Melt 3 tablespoons butter in a heavy-bottomed saucepan over medium heat; add the shallots or onion and cook until translucent, about 2 minutes. Add the mushrooms; cook 5 minutes more until they have wilted and given up some juices. Stir in the rice and mix with a wooden spoon until rice is well coated and begins to look chalky white, about 5 minutes.

2. Add the white wine; cook until all wine is absorbed. Start adding the hot stock in 1-cup increments, stirring each time until all the liquid is absorbed before adding the next cup, until rice is soft and creamy and you have only 1 cup of liquid left. Fold in the cheese, salt, pepper, and remaining 1 tablespoon of butter. Stir until well combined; remove from heat. Adjust consistency with remaining stock. Rice should have a saucy consistency and be soft, but still have a little bite. If using, shave white or black truffles over the finished plates at the table. Serve with lemon wedges, if desired.

BEET RISOTTO CAKES

This dish is great for a side or even as a dinner! Enjoy!

Serves 10

- 2–3 medium-size beets (about 1 pound), peeled and diced (¼") or 2 (14½-ounce) cans beets, diced, liquid reserved
- 1 tablespoon red wine vinegar (if using fresh beets)
- 3 tablespoons butter, divided
- 1 large onion, chopped
- 1 pound Italian arborio short-grain rice for risotto
- ½ cup red wine (optional)
- Vegetable stock or water
- Kosher salt and freshly ground black pepper
- 1 cup grated Parmesan cheese
- 2 tablespoons olive oil or butter for frying
- Cornmeal

1. If starting with fresh, cook the diced beets in enough water to cover them, along with the vinegar and a pinch of salt. Drain, reserving the cooking liquid. Combine the cooking or canning liquid with enough water to total 8 cups. Melt 2 tablespoons of butter in a large, heavy-bottomed saucepan; add the onion and cook until soft, about 5 minutes. Stir in the rice and cook over medium heat until it attains a chalky, cooked color, about 5 minutes.

2. Add the wine to the cooking rice; stir constantly with a wooden spoon until all liquid is absorbed. Gradually start to add the stock mixture in ½-cup increments, stirring constantly, waiting until all liquid is absorbed before adding the next cup. Continue until rice is saucy, but still slightly "al dente." Season with salt and pepper; stir in the Parmesan, cooked beets, and remaining 1 tablespoon of butter. The risotto is now ready to be served as a soft entrée, garnished with Parmesan shavings. If using for Beet Risotto Cakes, transfer mixture into a buttered 9" × 13" glass baking dish; set aside to cool. Refrigerate at least 4 hours or overnight, until risotto is firm to the touch.

3. Using a 3" cookie cutter or other shaping device (a 15-ounce can with both ends removed works quite well), cut out as many round cakes as you can (ball up and reflatten all the remaining bits). Heat a large nonstick skillet over medium heat; add 2 tablespoons olive oil or butter. Dip the flat surfaces of the risotto cakes in cornmeal, and fry them until a crisp crust forms and they are golden brown on the outside and hot on the inside, about 4 minutes per side. Serve hot or warm.

POLENTA WITH BUTTER AND CHEESE

Delicious as a base for stews and ragouts, such as chunky tomato sauce, sautéed wild mushroom ragout, or a vegetable stew, polenta is also excellent when allowed to chill, then grilled or fried.

Serves 4

1 teaspoon salt

4 cups water or stock, boiling

1 cup coarse yellow cornmeal (polenta)

½ cup grated Parmesan cheese

1 tablespoon butter

1. Add salt to the boiling water. Whisking constantly with a stiff wire whisk, gradually pour cornmeal into water in a steady stream, whisking out any lumps. Continue whisking constantly until mixture thickens noticeably.

2. Lower heat to a very low simmer. You should see only the occasional bubble plopping up through the polenta, but beware: The polenta is molten lava at this point, and spattering can be hazardous. Stir regularly with a wooden spoon until full thickening is achieved, about 25 minutes. Stir in cheese and butter; remove from heat. Serve immediately, or allow to cool for grilling or frying.

PAN-FRIED POLENTA WITH MARINARA

Similar to grits, polenta is made from boiled cornmeal, and can be enjoyed firm or creamy.

Serves 4–5

2 tablespoons butter or vegan margarine, such as Earth Balance

½ onion, diced

2 cloves garlic, minced

4 cups Pressure Cooker Vegetable Stock (see Chapter 5), or water

1 teaspoon salt

½ teaspoon thyme

½ cup cornmeal

½ cup coarse polenta

1 cup corn kernels, canned or fresh

¼ cup olive oil

2 cups Basic Marinara Sauce (see Chapter 2)

1. Add the butter to the pressure cooker and sauté the onion until it begins to turn golden brown. Add the garlic and sauté for 1 minute more. Add the stock or water, salt, and thyme, and bring to a boil. Slowly add the cornmeal, coarse polenta, and corn, stirring so they will not clump.

2. Lock the lid into place and bring to high pressure; maintain pressure for 10 minutes. Remove from heat and quick-release the pressure. Allow the polenta to cool and firm for at least 30 minutes.

3. When the polenta is firm, cut into 2½" squares, and remove from the pressure cooker. Add the olive oil to a sauté pan and fry the polenta squares until brown on both sides. Serve with Basic Marinara Sauce.

Flavor Variations

Jazz up this dish by adding cooked vegetables to the polenta before you allow it to cool. Chopped and sautéed leeks are a nice addition, as well as fresh sautéed bell pepper.

PC CREAMY THYME POLENTA

To substitute fresh herbs in this recipe, increase the amount of thyme to 1 tablespoon.

Serves 4–5

3½ cups water

½ cup coarse polenta

½ cup fine cornmeal

1 cup corn kernels

1 teaspoon dried thyme

1 teaspoon salt

1. Add all of the ingredients to the pressure cooker and stir.
2. Lock the lid into place and bring to high pressure; maintain pressure for 10 minutes. Remove from heat and quick-release the pressure. Season with additional salt, if necessary.

PC CHINESE BLACK RICE

Chinese black rice can be used in savory or sweet dishes. For a sweet approach, try adding coconut milk and sugar.

Serves 4

1 cup Chinese black rice

2 cups Pressure Cooker Vegetable Stock (see Chapter 5)

1 teaspoon rice wine vinegar

1 teaspoon Chinese 5-spice powder

½ teaspoon salt

1. Add the rice and stock to the pressure cooker.
2. Lock the lid into place; bring to high pressure and maintain for 15 minutes. Remove from heat and allow pressure to release naturally.
3. Once the pressure has released, open the lid and stir in the rice wine vinegar, Chinese 5-spice powder, and salt.

PC CREOLE JAMBALAYA

Try Morningstar Farms Meal Starters Chik'n Strips and Tofurky sausage as an alternative to real meat in this recipe.

Serves 8

½ cup butter or vegan margarine, such as Earth Balance

1 cup onion, chopped

1 medium bell pepper, chopped

2 stalks celery, chopped

3 cloves garlic, minced

3 cups Pressure Cooker Vegetable Stock (see Chapter 5)

1 cup water

8 ounces tomato sauce

2 cups white rice

2 bay leaves

2 teaspoons thyme

2 teaspoons cayenne

2 teaspoons Cajun seasoning

2 cups cooked vegetarian chicken and sausage, optional

Salt, to taste

1. Melt the butter or margarine in the pressure cooker over medium-low heat, then add the onion, bell pepper, celery, and garlic. Cook for about 15 minutes, until soft.

2. Add the stock, water, tomato sauce, rice, bay leaves, thyme, cayenne, and Cajun seasoning, then stir.

3. Lock the lid into place; bring to high pressure and maintain for 6 minutes. Remove from heat and allow pressure to release naturally.

4. Stir in prepared chopped vegetarian chicken and sausage, if using, and let stand for 5 minutes. Season with salt, to taste.

Creole Cuisine

Creole cuisine is similar to, but more refined than, Cajun cooking, and both use the Holy Trinity of onion, bell pepper, and celery as the base of many dishes. It hails from southern Louisiana, but is influenced by Spanish, French, and African cuisines.

MEXICAN FRIJOLES REFRITOS (REFRIED BEANS)

The sweet-corny taste of pinto beans is favored by Mexicans for this rich preparation, which is usually made with bacon fat, but sometimes with vegetable oil instead for economical reasons.

Serves 6

PREPARE THE BEANS:

½ pound pinto beans, washed

¼ white onion, roughly chopped

1 tablespoon oil

1 teaspoon salt

½ cup chopped white onion

6 tablespoons olive oil

The cooked beans (about 4 cups with broth)

Prepare the Beans:

Bring beans to a boil with onions, oil, salt, and 5 cups water in a 2½-quart pot. Lower flame and simmer 2½–3 hours, until very tender, skimming occasionally and adding water if necessary to keep it brothy.

Fry the Beans:

1. Cook the onion in the oil until translucent in a 10" skillet (iron is best), then add the beans (broth included) 1 cup at a time, mashing with a wooden spoon over high heat.

2. Constantly mash and stir until beans dry out and sizzle around the edges. They should start coming away from the surface of the pan. Rock the pan back and forth to make sure they loosen, and turn them out, omelet style, onto a warm serving platter.

3. Garnish with radishes, lettuce, shredded queso blanco (a fresh Mexican cheese sold in most Hispanic food sections), or feta cheese.

HUMMUS BI TAHINI WITH SPROUTS AND CHERRY TOMATOES IN A PITA POCKET

These beautiful, healthful sandwiches are colorful and attractive to serve when afternoon guests arrive. They're quick to make.

Serves 4

- 1 (15½-ounce) can chickpeas (garbanzos), drained and rinsed
- 2 tablespoons tahini (sesame paste)
- 1 tablespoon ground cumin
- Juice of 1 lemon (about 2 ounces)
- ⅓ cup, plus 1 tablespoon, olive oil
- Coarse salt and freshly ground black pepper
- 4 (7") loaves pita bread
- 1 cello box alfalfa sprouts
- 12 ripe cherry tomatoes, washed and halved

1. To make the hummus, purée together the chickpeas, tahini, cumin, and half of the lemon juice at high speed in a food processor. While machine is running, gradually add ⅓ cup olive oil. Adjust flavor to taste with salt, pepper, and remaining lemon juice.

2. Make an opening at the top of each pita, and slather each generously with hummus. Into each pocket, stuff a tuft of alfalfa sprouts the size of a golf ball, and 6 cherry tomato halves. Drizzle remaining olive oil over contents of all sandwiches.

PC COUSCOUS-STUFFED RED PEPPERS

Pine nuts are also known as pignoli or pignolia, and are most commonly known for being a key ingredient in pesto.

Serves 4

1 cup couscous

2 cups water

2 tablespoons pine nuts

4 ounces crumbled feta cheese, or vegan feta, such as Vegcuisine Soy Feta Cheese

1 teaspoon dried oregano

1 teaspoon salt

4 large red bell peppers, stemmed and seeded

1. Preheat the oven to 350°F. Add the couscous and water to the pressure cooker.

2. Lock the lid into place; bring to high pressure and maintain for 2 minutes. Remove from heat and allow pressure to release naturally.

3. While the couscous is cooking, toast the pine nuts in a small sauté pan over low heat, stirring often to avoid burning. Once they begin to turn golden brown, remove from heat.

4. When the couscous is done, remove the lid of the pressure cooker. Fluff the couscous, and add the cooked pine nuts, feta, oregano, and salt. Stir well to combine.

5. Stuff ¼ of the couscous mixture into each of the red bell peppers and place in an ungreased baking dish. Bake for 15 minutes, or until the pepper begins to soften.

PC BULGUR STUFFING

Bulgur is a healthier alternative to white bread in stuffing.

Serves 4–5

1 cup bulgur

3 cups Pressure Cooker Vegetable Stock (see Chapter 5)

2 tablespoons butter or vegan margarine, such as Earth Balance

½ onion, diced

½ cup celery rib, diced

½ cup chopped mushrooms

½ teaspoon dried thyme

½ teaspoon dried sage

½ teaspoon salt

¾ teaspoon black pepper

1. Add the bulgur and Pressure Cooker Vegetable Stock to the pressure cooker.
2. Lock the lid into place; bring to high pressure and maintain for 9 minutes. Remove from heat and allow pressure to release naturally.
3. In a large sauté pan over medium heat, melt the butter or margarine and sauté the onion and celery until soft, about 7 minutes. Add the mushrooms, thyme, sage, salt, and pepper, and sauté for an additional 2 minutes.
4. Pour the vegetable mixture into the cooked bulgur and stir until well combined.

PC THREE GRAIN PILAF

Millet is a good source of protein and B vitamins.

Serves 4

2 tablespoons extra-virgin olive oil

½ cup scallions, sliced

1 cup jasmine rice

½ cup millet

½ cup quinoa

2½ cups Pressure Cooker Vegetable Stock (see Chapter 5) or water

Salt and pepper, to taste

1. Add the olive oil to the pressure cooker and sauté the scallions for 2–3 minutes. Add the grains and sauté for 2–3 minutes. Add the stock and bring to a boil.

2. Lock the lid into place and bring to high pressure; maintain for 4 minutes. Remove from heat and release pressure naturally for 5 minutes.

3. Quick-release any remaining pressure and remove the lid. Fluff the pilaf with a fork. Taste for seasoning and add salt and pepper to taste, if necessary.

PC RICE PILAF

A pilaf is a rice dish seasoned with spices, vegetables, and/or meat.

Serves 6–8

1½ tablespoons unsalted butter or vegan margarine, such as Earth Balance
1 medium carrot, peeled and grated
1 stalk celery, finely diced
1 medium onion, diced
2 cups long-grain white rice
¼ teaspoon salt
½ teaspoon black pepper
3 cups Pressure Cooker Vegetable Stock (see Chapter 5)

1. Melt the butter or margarine in the pressure cooker over medium heat. Add the carrot and celery; sauté for 3 minutes.

2. Add the onion; sauté for 3 minutes or until the onion is tender. Add the rice and stir into the vegetables. Add the salt, pepper, and stock; stir.

3. Lock the lid into place and bring to high pressure; maintain pressure for 3 minutes. Remove from heat and allow pressure to release naturally for 5 minutes.

4. Quick-release any remaining pressure and remove the lid. Fluff the rice with a fork. Serve.

White Rice

Rice is a culinary staple around the world and has been used as food for thousands of years. It provides some nutritional benefits, as it is a source of protein, iron, and vitamins, but white rice is less healthy than brown rice.

VEGETABLE RICE PILAF

Instant pilaf that comes in cardboard boxes at the supermarket is no match for this dish.

Serves 4

1 tablespoon butter or vegan margarine, such as Earth Balance
1 tablespoon vegetable oil
½ small yellow onion, thinly sliced
2 cloves garlic, minced
1½" piece fresh ginger, peeled and grated
1 serrano pepper, seeded and minced
1½ cups cauliflower florets, quartered
1 cup green beans, cleaned, and cut into 1" pieces
½ cup carrot, peeled and sliced diagonally
1 teaspoon ground cumin
½ teaspoon ground turmeric
¼ teaspoon cardamom seeds
1 teaspoon chili powder
⅛ teaspoon ground cloves
⅛ teaspoon hot paprika
½ teaspoon salt
1 cup long-grain white rice
1½ cups water
¼ cup slivered almonds, toasted

1. Melt the butter or margarine in the pressure cooker over medium heat. Add the oil and bring to temperature.

2. Add the onion, garlic, ginger, and serrano pepper; sauté for 2 minutes. Stir in the cauliflower, green beans, carrot, cumin, turmeric, cardamom seeds, chili powder, ground cloves, paprika, salt, rice, and water.

3. Lock the lid into place and bring to high pressure; maintain pressure for 6 minutes. Remove from heat and allow pressure to release naturally for 15 minutes. Quick-release any remaining pressure and remove the lid.

4. Fluff rice with a fork. Transfer to a serving bowl. Top with toasted almonds.

PC CRANBERRY-PECAN PILAF

To make this a complete meal, add vegan beef, such as Gardein Beefless Tips.

Serves 4

1 cup long-grain white rice

2 cups Pressure Cooker Vegetable Stock (see Chapter 5)

⅓ cup dried cranberries

1 teaspoon dried thyme

1 bay leaf

1 cup pecan pieces

2 tablespoons butter or vegan margarine, such as Earth Balance

Salt and pepper, to taste

1. Add the rice, Vegetable Stock, cranberries, thyme, and bay leaf to the pressure cooker.
2. Lock the lid into place and bring to high pressure; maintain pressure for 5 minutes. Remove from heat and allow pressure to release naturally.
3. Stir in the pecans and butter, then season with salt and pepper.

GREEN RICE PILAF

Green with fresh herbs, this rice is a great stuffing for vegetables, base for curries, or accompaniment to a hearty vegetable stew.

Serves 4

3 tablespoons butter

2 cups chopped onion

2 cups long-grain rice

½ cup (packed) mixed chopped herbs, such as chives, chervil, tarragon, parsley, and dill

4 cups vegetable stock

Salt and pepper, to taste

1 bay leaf

1. In a medium saucepan, melt the butter over a medium flame. Add the onion; cook until translucent, about 5 minutes. Add the rice; cook, stirring often, until the rice is well coated and becomes golden.
2. In a blender, combine the herbs, stock, salt, and pepper; blend until herbs are finely chopped. Add to the rice; bring to a boil, add the bay leaf, and then lower to a very slow simmer. Cover tightly; cook until rice has absorbed all liquid, about 25 minutes. Fluff with a fork, then cover and let stand for 5 minutes before serving.

SC TOMATILLO RICE

This recipe is similar to jambalaya, in that you cook the rice in a tomato-based sauce so the flavors are completely absorbed.

Serves 4

2 tablespoons olive oil
½ red onion, diced
½ red bell pepper, diced
2 cloves garlic, minced
Juice of 1 lime
1 cup tomatillo salsa
1 cup water
1 teaspoon salt
1 cup long-grain white rice
½ cup cilantro, chopped

1. Heat the olive oil in a sauté pan over medium heat. Add the onion, bell pepper, and garlic and sauté about 5 minutes.
2. Transfer to a 4-quart slow cooker. Add all the remaining ingredients except for the cilantro.
3. Cover and cook over low heat for 6–8 hours. Check the rice periodically to make sure the liquid hasn't been absorbed too quickly and the rice is not burning.
4. Stir in the cilantro before serving.

SC STUFFED PEPPERS

Try a mixture of green, red, orange, and yellow peppers for this dish.

Serves 4

4 large bell peppers
½ teaspoon ground chipotle pepper
¼ teaspoon hot Mexican chili powder
¼ teaspoon freshly ground black pepper
⅛ teaspoon salt
1 (15-ounce) can fire-roasted diced tomatoes with garlic
1 cup cooked long-grain rice
1½ cups broccoli florets
¼ cup diced onion
½ cup water

1. Cut the tops off of each pepper to form a cap. Remove the seeds from the cap. Remove the seeds and most of the ribs from inside the pepper.

2. Place the peppers open-side up in a 4- or 6-quart slow cooker.

3. In a medium bowl, mix the spices, tomatoes, rice, broccoli, and onion. Spoon the mixture into each pepper until they are filled to the top. Replace the cap.

4. Pour the water into the bottom of the slow cooker insert. Cook on low for 6 hours.

SC VEGETABLE FRIED RICE

Sriracha is a popular type of hot sauce that features a rooster on the bottle and is sometimes called "rooster sauce."

Serves 4

1 tablespoon butter or vegan margarine

2 cups white rice, uncooked

3 garlic cloves, minced

2 cups water

2 cups Vegetable Broth (see Chapter 5)

2½ teaspoons soy sauce

1 teaspoon brown sugar

½ teaspoons sriracha sauce

1 teaspoon lime juice

1 cup carrots, diced

1 cup broccoli, chopped

1. Rub the butter or margarine around the inside of a 4-quart slow cooker to ensure that the rice will not stick to the edges.
2. Add the rest of the ingredients. Cover and cook on low heat for 4–5 hours.

SC PAELLA

The spice saffron can be very expensive, but you can use the more affordable turmeric in its place.

Serves 6

1 tablespoon olive oil

½ onion, diced

1 cup diced tomato

½ teaspoon saffron or turmeric

1 teaspoon salt

2 tablespoons fresh parsley

1 cup long-grain white rice

1 cup frozen peas

2 cups water

1 (12-ounce) package vegan chorizo, crumbled

1. Heat the olive oil in a sauté pan over medium heat. Add the onion and sauté for 3 minutes.
2. Add the tomato, saffron or turmeric, salt, and parsley and stir.
3. Pour the sautéed mixture into a 4-quart slow cooker. Add the white rice, then frozen peas and water.
4. Cover, and cook on low heat for 4 hours.
5. Pour the crumbled chorizo on top of the rice. Cover and cook for an additional 30 minutes. Stir before serving.

PC PRESSURE COOKER PAELLA

Turmeric is a budget-friendly alternative to saffron in any recipe.

Serves 4–6

3 tablespoons olive oil

1 medium onion, chopped

1 cup grated carrot

1 red bell pepper, seeded and chopped

1 cup green peas, fresh or frozen

1 clove garlic, minced

1 cup basmati rice

1½ teaspoons turmeric

2 cups Pressure Cooker Vegetable Stock (see Chapter 5)

¼ cup chopped parsley

Salt and pepper, to taste

1. Add the olive oil to the pressure cooker over medium heat and sauté the onion, carrot, bell pepper, and peas until they begin to soften, about 5 minutes. Add the garlic, rice, and turmeric, and stir until well coated.

2. Add the Vegetable Stock and parsley. Lock the lid into place; bring to high pressure and maintain for 7 minutes. Remove from heat and allow pressure to release naturally.

3. Season with salt and pepper, to taste, before serving.

Paella Staples

There aren't many right or wrong ingredients for paella because it comes in many varieties. The two ingredients that are consistently used are rice and saffron (or turmeric).

VEGAN CHORIZO PAELLA

Trader Joe's grocery store chain carries a delicious kind of vegan chorizo sausage.

Serves 4

¼ cup olive oil

14 ounces vegan chorizo, cut into 1" slices

1 cup onion, diced

4 garlic cloves, minced

½ cup fresh parsley, chopped

1 (14-ounce) can diced tomatoes, drained

1 cup grated carrot

1 red bell pepper, seeded and chopped

1 cup green peas, fresh or frozen

1½ teaspoons turmeric

1 cup basmati rice

2 cups Pressure Cooker Vegetable Stock (see Chapter 5)

Salt and pepper, to taste

1. Add the oil to the pressure cooker and sauté the sausage until it is browned. Remove the sausage and add the onion, garlic, half the parsley, tomatoes, carrot, red bell pepper, peas, and turmeric. Sauté for 3–5 minutes. Add the rice and stock and return the sausage to the pressure cooker. Bring to a boil.

2. Lock the lid; bring to high pressure and maintain for 7 minutes. Remove from heat and allow pressure to release naturally. Garnish with the rest of the parsley. Season with salt and pepper, to taste, before serving.

SC EGGPLANT "LASAGNA"

This no-noodle dish makes for a hearty vegetarian meal. Serve it with a side salad.

Serves 8

2 (1-pound) eggplants

1 tablespoon kosher salt

30 ounces skim-milk ricotta or tofu ricotta (see sidebar)

2 teaspoons olive oil, divided use

1 medium onion, diced

3 cloves garlic, minced

1 tablespoon fresh, minced Italian parsley

1 tablespoon fresh, minced basil

1 (28-ounce) can crushed tomatoes

1 shallot, diced

4 ounces fresh spinach

1 tablespoon dried mixed Italian seasoning

¼ teaspoon salt

½ teaspoon freshly ground black pepper

1. Slice the eggplant lengthwise into ¼"-thick slices. Place in a bowl or colander and sprinkle with the salt. Allow it to sit for 15 minutes. Drain off the liquid. Rinse off the salt. Pat dry. Set aside. Line a colander with cheesecloth or paper towels. Pour the ricotta into the colander and drain for 15 minutes. (If you are using tofu ricotta, skip the draining step.)

2. Heat 1 teaspoon olive oil in a nonstick pan. Sauté the onion and garlic until just softened, about 1–2 minutes. Add the parsley, basil, and crushed tomatoes. Sauté until the sauce thickens and the liquid has evaporated, about 20 minutes.

3. In a second nonstick pan, heat the remaining oil. Sauté the shallot and spinach until the spinach has wilted, about 30 seconds–1 minute. Drain off any extra liquid.

4. Stir the shallot-spinach mixture, Italian seasoning, salt, and pepper into the ricotta mixture. Set aside.

5. Preheat the oven to 375°F. Place the eggplant slices on baking sheets. Bake for 10 minutes. Cool slightly.

6. Pour ⅓ of the sauce onto the bottom of a 4-quart slow cooker. Top with a single layer of eggplant. Top with ⅓ of the cheese mixture. Add ⅓ of the sauce. Top with the rest of the cheese mixture.

7. Layer the remaining eggplant on top, then top with remaining sauce. Cover, and cook for 4 hours on low, then uncovered 30 minutes on high.

Tofu Ricotta

You can make your own tofu ricotta by crumbling 1 package of drained tofu, then adding 1 tablespoon lemon juice, 1 teaspoon salt, 1 teaspoon dried parsley, and ½ teaspoon pepper.

SC PORTOBELLO BARLEY

This method of cooking barley makes it as creamy as risotto, but with the bonus of being high in fiber.

Serves 8

1 teaspoon olive oil
2 shallots, minced
2 cloves garlic, minced
3 portobello mushroom caps, sliced
1 cup pearl barley
3¼ cups water
¼ teaspoon salt
½ teaspoon freshly ground black pepper
1 teaspoon crushed rosemary
1 teaspoon dried chervil
¼ cup grated Parmesan or vegan Parmesan

1. Heat the oil in a nonstick skillet. Sauté the shallots, garlic, and mushrooms until softened, about 3–4 minutes.

2. Place the mushroom mixture into a 4-quart slow cooker. Add the barley, water, salt, pepper, rosemary, and chervil. Stir.

3. Cover, and cook on low for 8–9 hours or on high for 4 hours.

4. Turn off the slow cooker and stir in the Parmesan. Serve immediately.

SC SAFFRON RICE

Better Than Bouillon makes a delicious No Chicken base that can be used to make stock.

Serves 4

2 cups white rice, uncooked
2 tablespoons margarine
2 cups water
2 cups vegetarian chicken stock
¾ teaspoons saffron threads
1 teaspoon salt

1. Add all ingredients to a 4-quart slow cooker. Cover and cook on low heat for 4–5 hours.
2. Check the rice to see if it is tender. If not, cook for another 30–45 minutes.

SC BULGUR WITH BROCCOLI AND CARROT

This filling and delicious dish makes a comforting meal on a cold day.

Serves 4

2 cups bulgur, uncooked
2 tablespoons butter or vegan margarine
1 cup carrots, diced
1 cup broccoli, chopped
2 cups Vegetable Broth (see Chapter 5)
1 teaspoon salt

1. Add all ingredients to a 4-quart slow cooker. Cover and cook on low heat for 6 hours.
2. Check the rice to see if it is tender and if not, cook for 1 more hour.

MOCK CHICKEN AND RICE

Brown rice, white rice, or wild rice will all work in this recipe.

Serves 8

2 tablespoons olive oil

1 cup mushrooms, sliced

½ cup onions, sliced

2 cups white rice, uncooked

2 tablespoons butter or vegan margarine

2 cups water

2 cups vegetarian chicken broth

2 (7-ounce) packages Gardein Chick'n Strips

½ teaspoon salt

⅛ teaspoon black pepper

1. Add the olive oil to a 4-quart slow cooker and sauté the mushrooms and onions on high heat until browned, about 3–5 minutes.

2. Add the rest of the ingredients to the slow cooker. Cover and cook on low heat for 6 hours.

SC SPANISH RICE

Cooking rice in tomatoes, chili powder, and bell pepper is the key to Spanish rice.

Serves 8

2 cups white rice, uncooked
2 tablespoons butter or vegan margarine
2 cups water
2 cups Vegetable Broth (see Chapter 5)
1 onion, diced
1 green bell pepper, diced
1 cup canned tomatoes, diced
⅛ cup pickled jalapeños, diced
1 teaspoon chili powder
½ teaspoon garlic powder
1 teaspoon salt
¼ teaspoon black pepper

Add all ingredients to a 4-quart slow cooker. Cover and cook on low heat for 4–5 hours.

SC BROWN RICE AND VEGETABLES

This recipe is simple, easy, and healthy. Yum!

Serves 8

2 cups brown rice, uncooked
2 tablespoons butter or vegan margarine
3 cups Vegetable Broth (see Chapter 5)
2 cups water
½ cup yellow squash, chopped
½ cup zucchini, chopped
½ onion, chopped
½ cup button mushrooms, sliced
½ cup red bell pepper, chopped
1 teaspoon salt
¼ teaspoon black pepper

Add all ingredients to a 4-quart slow cooker. Cover and cook on low heat for 4–5 hours.

SC CURRIED RICE

Curried Rice is a great side dish.

Serves 4

2 cups white rice, uncooked
2 tablespoons olive oil
2 cups water
2 cups No-Beef Broth (see Chapter 5)
2 tablespoons curry powder
1 teaspoon salt
¼ teaspoon black pepper
1 tablespoon lime juice
¼ cup cilantro, chopped

1. Add all the ingredients to a 4-quart slow cooker except the lime juice and cilantro.
2. Cover and cook on low heat for 4–5 hours.
3. Stir in the lime juice and cilantro and cook for 30 more minutes before serving.

SC CHIPOTLE BLACK BEAN SALAD

There are actually 5 different varieties of black beans, but when you purchase black beans, they are often just labeled as black beans.

Serves 8

1 (16-ounce) bag dried black beans

Enough water to cover beans by 1"

2 teaspoons salt

1 tablespoon chipotle powder

2 teaspoons thyme

2 fresh tomatoes, diced

1 red onion, diced

¼ cup cilantro, chopped

1. Add black beans, water, and salt to a 4-quart slow cooker. Cover and cook on medium heat for about 5–6 hours. Check the beans at about 5 hours and continue cooking if necessary.

2. Once the beans are done, drain in a colander and allow to cool to room temperature.

3. Mix in the remaining ingredients and serve.

Prepping Dried Beans
Before cooking with dried beans, you must first rinse the beans, soak them overnight in a pot full of water, and then boil them for 10 minutes. They are then ready for Step 1 of the recipe.

SC MEDITERRANEAN CHICKPEAS

Chickpeas, also known as garbanzo beans, are the main ingredient in this delicious dish that can be served hot or cold.

Serves 8

2 (15-ounce) cans chickpeas, drained

1 cup water

4 teaspoons salt

¼ cup extra-virgin olive oil

1 teaspoon black pepper

1 cup fresh basil, chopped

5 cloves garlic, minced

2 tomatoes, diced

½ cup Kalamata olives, sliced

Add all ingredients to a 4-quart slow cooker. Cover and cook on low heat for 4 hours.

SC OPEN-FACED BEAN BURRITO

Salsas come in many different flavors depending on which ingredients are used but any type of salsa (except fruit-based salsa) will work in this recipe.

Serves 8

1 (16-ounce) bag dried black beans

Water, enough to cover beans by 1"

4 teaspoons salt

1 tablespoon chili powder

2 teaspoons cumin

2 teaspoons garlic powder

1 teaspoon black pepper

1 (15-ounce) can corn, drained

2 fresh tomatoes, diced

8 large flour tortillas

4 cups cooked brown rice

2 cups shredded Cheddar cheese or vegan Cheddar cheese (optional)

2 cups salsa (optional)

¼ cup cilantro, chopped (optional)

1. Rinse the black beans, then soak overnight. Drain the water, rinse again, then add to a large pot and cover with water. Boil on high heat for 10 minutes, then drain.

2. Add black beans, water, and 2 teaspoons of salt to a 4-quart slow cooker. Cover and cook on medium heat for about 5–6 hours. Check the beans at about 5 hours to see if they are fork-tender and continue cooking if necessary.

3. Once the beans are done, drain in a colander and allow to cool to room temperature. Then, in a large bowl, mix in the remaining salt, chili powder, cumin, garlic powder, black pepper, corn, and tomatoes.

4. Place a tortilla on a plate, add a scoop of the brown rice and then a scoop of the black bean mixture. Top with the cheese, salsa, and cilantro, if desired.

SC SLOW COOKER REFRIED BEANS

Refried beans can be made with black beans or the more commonly used pinto beans. Serve them as a side dish at your next Mexican meal.

Serves 8

1 (16-ounce) bag dried pinto beans

Enough water to cover beans by 1"

4 teaspoons salt

¼ cup olive oil

6 cloves garlic, minced

1 teaspoon black pepper

1. Rinse the pinto beans, then soak overnight. Drain the water, rinse again.

2. In a large pot, add the beans and cover with water. Boil on high heat for 10 minutes, then drain.

3. Add pinto beans, water, salt, olive oil, and garlic to a 4-quart slow cooker. Cover and cook on medium heat for about 5–6 hours. Check the beans at about 5 hours and continue cooking if necessary.

4. Once the beans are done, drain in a colander. Add the black pepper and mash the beans with a potato masher or the back side of a wooden spoon. Add water, if necessary, to create the desired consistency.

SC CUBAN BLACK BEANS

Traditionally served with rice, Cuban-style black beans are also great served with tortillas and fresh avocado slices.

Serves 4

½ teaspoon apple cider vinegar

¼ cup diced onion

1 (15-ounce) canned black beans, drained

2 cloves garlic, minced

1 jalapeño, minced

½ teaspoon oregano

¼ teaspoon cumin

1. Place all ingredients into a 2-quart slow cooker. Stir to distribute all the ingredients evenly.
2. Cover and cook on low for 6–8 hours. Stir before serving.

PRESSURE COOKER CUBAN BLACK BEANS AND RICE

Cuban food is the combination of African, Caribbean, and Spanish cuisines.

Serves 6

1 cup dried black beans

4 cups water

3 tablespoons olive or vegetable oil

1 medium green bell pepper, seeded and diced

½ stalk celery, finely diced

½ cup carrots, peeled and grated

1 medium onion, diced

2 cloves garlic, minced

¾ cup medium- or long-grain white rice

2 cups Pressure Cooker Vegetable Stock (see Chapter 5)

2 teaspoons paprika

½ teaspoon cumin

¼ teaspoon chili powder

1 bay leaf

Salt and freshly ground black pepper, to taste

1. Rinse the beans and add them to a covered container. Pour in the water, cover, and let the beans soak overnight. Drain.

2. Bring the oil to temperature in the pressure cooker over medium-high heat. Add the green bell pepper, celery, and carrots; sauté for 2 minutes. Add the onion; sauté for 3 minutes or until the onion is soft. Stir in the garlic and sauté for 30 seconds.

3. Stir in the rice and stir-fry until the rice begins to brown. Add the drained beans, stock, paprika, cumin, chili powder, and bay leaf.

4. Lock the lid into place and bring to low pressure; maintain pressure for 18 minutes. Remove from heat and allow pressure to release naturally. Stir, taste for seasoning, and add salt and pepper to taste. Remove bay leaf and serve.

SC CURRIED LENTILS

Serve this Indian-style dish with hot rice or naan, an Indian flatbread. It can also be served with plain yogurt or vegan yogurt as garnish or on the side.

Serves 6

2 teaspoons butter or canola oil
1 large onion, thinly sliced
2 cloves garlic, minced
2 jalapeños, diced
½ teaspoon red pepper flakes
½ teaspoon ground cumin
1 pound yellow lentils
6 cups water
½ teaspoon salt
½ teaspoon ground turmeric
4 cups chopped fresh spinach

1. Heat the butter or oil in a nonstick pan. Sauté the onion slices until they start to brown, about 8–10 minutes.

2. Add the garlic, jalapeños, red pepper flakes, and cumin. Sauté for 2–3 minutes.

3. Add the onion mixture to a 4-quart slow cooker.

4. Sort through the lentils and discard any rocks or foreign matter. Add the lentils to the slow cooker. Stir in the water, salt, and turmeric.

5. Cover and cook on high for 2½ hours.

6. Add the spinach and stir. Cook on high for an additional 15 minutes.

SC HOPPIN' JOHN

Hoppin' John is traditionally eaten on New Year's Day. Eating it as the first meal of the day is supposed to ensure health and prosperity for the coming year.

Serves 8

1 cup dried black-eyed peas, rehydrated
¾ cup water
1 teaspoon liquid smoke
1 teaspoon red pepper flakes
3 cups diced mustard or collard greens
1 (14-ounce) can tomatoes
½ teaspoon freshly ground black pepper
¼ teaspoon salt
1 teaspoon dried oregano

1. Place all ingredients into a 4-quart slow cooker. Stir.
2. Cover and cook on high for 5 hours.

Quick Prep for Black-Eyed Peas

Here's a method to quickly and easily prepare black-eyed peas. Place the peas in a large stockpot. Cover completely with water, and bring to a boil. Boil 2 minutes, reduce heat, and simmer for 1 hour.

PC CHIPOTLE-THYME BLACK BEANS

According to recent research, black beans provide special digestive tract support.

Serves 8

2 cups dried black beans

16 cups water

1 tablespoon vegetable oil

1 teaspoon chipotle powder

2 teaspoons fresh thyme, minced

1 teaspoon salt

1. Add the beans and 8 cups water to the pressure cooker. Lock the lid into place; bring to high pressure for 1 minute. Remove from heat and quick-release the pressure.

2. Drain the water, rinse the beans, and add to the pressure cooker again with the remaining 8 cups water. Let soak for 1 hour.

3. Add the vegetable oil, chipotle, thyme, and salt. Lock the lid into place; bring to high pressure and maintain for 12 minutes. Remove from heat and allow pressure to release naturally.

PC BEER-LIME BLACK BEANS

Try a Mexican beer, such as Negra Modelo, Tecate, or Corona, to complement the beans in this recipe.

Serves 8

2 cups dried black beans

14 cups water

1 tablespoon vegetable oil

½ red onion, diced

1 clove garlic, minced

2 teaspoons salt

2 (12-ounce) bottles light-colored beer, such as an ale

¼ cup cilantro, chopped

1 tablespoon lime juice

1. Add the beans and 8 cups water to the pressure cooker. Lock the lid into place; bring to high pressure for 1 minute. Remove from heat and quick-release the pressure.

2. Drain the water, rinse the beans, and add to the pressure cooker again with the remaining 6 cups water. Soak for 1 hour.

3. Lock the lid into place; bring to high pressure and maintain for 10 minutes. Remove from heat and quick-release the pressure.

4. Remove the lid and add the oil, onion, garlic, salt, and beer to the pressure cooker, then stir. Lock the lid into place; bring to high pressure and maintain for 2 minutes. Remove from heat and allow pressure to release naturally.

5. Stir in the chopped cilantro and lime juice before serving.

PC BLACK BEAN–CILANTRO FRITTERS

For an extra-crunchy exterior, try rolling the fritters in panko bread crumbs before frying.

Serves 8–10

1 cup black beans

8 cups water

1 tablespoon vegetable oil

1 teaspoon salt

1 red bell pepper, diced

1 jalapeño, minced

½ cup onion, diced

¼ cup cilantro

1 cup flour

1 cup cornmeal

1 tablespoon baking powder

½ cup heavy cream or unsweetened soymilk

2 eggs, beaten, or 2 teaspoons cornstarch mixed with 2 tablespoons water

2 quarts canola oil, for frying

Salt and pepper, to taste

1. Add the beans and 4 cups water to the pressure cooker. Lock the lid into place; bring to high pressure for 1 minute. Remove from heat and quick-release the pressure.

2. Drain the water, rinse the beans, and add to the pressure cooker again with the remaining 4 cups water. Soak for 1 hour.

3. Add the vegetable oil and salt. Lock the lid into place; bring to high pressure and maintain for 12 minutes. Remove from heat and allow pressure to release naturally. Drain and set aside.

4. In a bowl, combine the red bell pepper, jalapeño, onion, cilantro, and black beans.

5. In another bowl combine the flour, cornmeal, baking powder, heavy cream or soymilk, and 2 eggs or cornstarch mixture. Add the vegetable and bean mixture to the flour mixture and stir until well combined. Form the batter into 1" fritters.

6. In a large pot, heat the oil to 350°F and fry the fritters until golden brown, about 3–4 minutes. Season with salt and pepper, to taste.

Egg Replacements

Other options for replacing eggs in fritters are using mixes such as Ener-G Egg Replacer or tofu. If using tofu, use half a cup of soft tofu to replace two eggs.

BOSTON-STYLE BAKED BEANS

If you're missing the bacon in these baked beans, add pieces of Lightlife Fakin' Bacon.

Serves 8

2 cups dried navy beans
16 cups water
2 tablespoons vegetable oil
1 teaspoon salt
1 teaspoon liquid smoke
¼ cup onion, diced
1 tablespoon yellow mustard
1 tablespoon brown sugar
1 teaspoon molasses

1. Add the beans and 8 cups water to the pressure cooker. Lock the lid into place; bring to high pressure for 1 minute. Remove from heat and quick-release the pressure.

2. Drain the water, rinse the beans, and add to the pressure cooker again with the remaining 8 cups water. Soak for 1 hour.

3. Add 1 tablespoon vegetable oil, salt, and liquid smoke. Lock the lid into place; bring to high pressure and maintain for 10 minutes. Quick-release the pressure.

4. Add all remaining ingredients; stir and lock the lid into place. Bring to high pressure and maintain for 5 minutes. Remove from heat and allow pressure to release naturally.

SC BOURBON BAKED BEANS

Serve these at your next cookout or as a side dish for barbecue tempeh or tofu.

Serves 8

1 large sweet onion, peeled and diced

3 (15-ounce) cans cannellini, great northern, or navy beans

1 (15-ounce) can diced tomatoes

¼ cup maple syrup

3 tablespoons apple cider vinegar

1 teaspoon liquid smoke

4 cloves garlic, peeled and minced

2 tablespoons dry mustard

1½ teaspoons freshly ground black pepper

½ teaspoon ground ginger

¼ teaspoon dried red pepper flakes

2 tablespoons bourbon

Salt, to taste

1. Add all ingredients to a 4-quart slow cooker. Stir until combined.
2. Cover and cook on low heat for 6 hours. Taste for seasoning and add additional salt, if needed.

SC PINTO BEANS

Try mashing pinto beans with a little vegetable broth to make vegetarian refried beans.

Serves 8

1 (16-ounce) bag dried pinto beans
Enough water to cover beans by 1"
2 teaspoons salt

1. Rinse the pinto beans, then soak overnight. Drain the water and rinse the beans again.
2. In a large pot, add beans and cover them with water. Boil on high heat for 10 minutes, then drain.
3. Add pinto beans, water, and salt to a 4-quart slow cooker. Cover and cook on medium heat for about 5–6 hours. Check the beans at about 5 hours and continue cooking if necessary.
4. Once the beans are done, drain in a colander.

SC ADZUKI BEANS

Adzuki beans are an Asian bean typically enjoyed sweetened, but they are good served savory, too.

Serves 8

1 (16-ounce) bag dried adzuki beans
Enough water to cover beans by 1"
2 teaspoons salt

1. Rinse the adzuki beans, then soak overnight. Drain the water and rinse the beans again.
2. In a large pot, add beans and cover with water. Boil on high heat for 10 minutes, then drain.
3. Add adzuki beans, water, and salt to a 4-quart slow cooker. Cover and cook on medium heat for about 5–6 hours. Check the beans at about 5 hours and continue cooking if necessary.
4. Once the beans are done, drain in a colander.

PC LIMA BEANS

All beans should be finished using the natural-release method.

Serves 4

1 cup dried lima beans

4 cups water

4 cups Pressure Cooker Vegetable Stock (see Chapter 5)

1 tablespoon vegetable oil

1. Add the beans and water to the pressure cooker. Lock the lid into place; bring to high pressure for 1 minute. Remove from heat and quick-release the pressure. Drain the water, rinse the beans, and add to the pressure cooker again with the stock. Let soak for 1 hour.

2. Add the vegetable oil and salt. Lock the lid into place; bring to high pressure and maintain for 6 minutes. Remove from heat and allow pressure to release naturally.

SC LIMA BEANS AND DUMPLINGS

Dumplings can be added to just about any dish that has a fair amount of liquid in it to create a home-style flavor.

Serves 8

1 (16-ounce) bag dried lima beans

Enough water to cover beans by 1"

2 teaspoons salt

1 (10-ounce) package vegan refrigerated biscuit dough

1. Rinse the lima beans, then soak overnight. Drain the water and then rinse the beans again.
2. In a large pot, add the beans and cover with water. Boil on high heat for 10 minutes, then drain.
3. Add lima beans, water, and salt to a 4-quart slow cooker. Cover and cook on medium heat for about 5–6 hours. Check the beans at about 5 hours and continue cooking if necessary.
4. While the beans cook, roll out the biscuit dough, then tear each biscuit into fourths.
5. Once the beans are nearly done, drop in the biscuit pieces, cover, and cook for an additional 30 minutes.

SC BLACK BEANS

Black beans are a versatile ingredient, and you can kick up the flavor by adding dried chili powder to them while cooking.

Serves 8

1 (16-ounce) bag dried black beans

Enough water to cover beans by 1"

2 teaspoons salt

1. Rinse the black beans, then soak overnight. Drain the water and rinse the beans again.

2. In a large pot, add the beans and cover with water. Boil on high heat for 10 minutes, then drain.

3. Add black beans, water, and salt to a 4-quart slow cooker. Cover and cook on medium heat for about 5–6 hours. Check the beans at about 5 hours to see if they are fork-tender and continue cooking if necessary.

4. Once the beans are done, drain in a colander.

SC WHITE BEANS

Adding a little salt while cooking will help bring out the flavor of the beans, but this ingredient is optional.

Serves 8

1 (16-ounce) bag dried white beans

Enough water to cover beans by 1"

2 teaspoons salt

2 bay leaves

1. Rinse the white beans, then soak overnight. Drain the water and rinse the beans again.

2. In a large pot, add the beans and cover with water. Boil on high heat for 10 minutes, then drain.

3. Add white beans, water, salt, and bay leaves to a 4-quart slow cooker. Cover and cook on medium heat for about 5–6 hours. Check the beans at about 5 hours and continue cooking if necessary.

4. Once the beans are done, drain in a colander and remove the bay leaves.

SC BLACK-EYED PEAS

Beans can be stored in the freezer for several months as long as they are sealed in an airtight bag.

Serves 8

1 (16-ounce) bag dried black-eyed peas

Enough water to cover black-eyed peas by 1"

2 teaspoons salt

1 teaspoon liquid smoke

1. Rinse the black-eyed peas, then soak overnight. Drain the water and then rinse the peas again.

2. Add the peas to a large pot and cover with water. Boil on high heat for 10 minutes, then drain.

3. Add black-eyed peas, water, salt, and liquid smoke to a 4-quart slow cooker. Cover and cook on medium heat for about 5–6 hours. Check the black-eyed peas at about 5 hours and continue cooking if necessary.

4. Once the black-eyed peas are done, drain in a colander.

SC LENTILS

Lentils are commonly used in Indian cuisine and are delicious with curry paste mixed in.

Serves 8

1 (16-ounce) bag dried lentils

Enough water to cover lentils by 1"

2 teaspoons salt

1. Add lentils, water, and salt to a 4-quart slow cooker. Cover and cook on medium heat for about 3–4 hours. Check the lentils at about 5 hours and continue cooking if necessary.

2. Once the lentils are done, drain in a colander.

SC MEXICAN BEER BLACK BEANS

Try a Mexican beer, such as Negra Modelo, Tecate, or Corona, to complement the beans in this recipe.

Serves 8

1 (16-ounce) bag dried black beans

Enough water to cover beans by ½"

2 (12-ounce) bottles light-colored beer

4 teaspoons salt

1 red onion, diced

4 cloves garlic, minced

2 fresh tomatoes, diced

½ cup cilantro, chopped

1 lime, juiced

1. Rinse the black beans, then soak overnight. Drain the water and then rinse the beans again.
2. Add the beans to a large pot and cover with water. Boil on high heat for 10 minutes, then drain.
3. Add black beans, water, beer, and 2 teaspoons salt to a 4-quart slow cooker. Cover and cook on medium heat for about 5–6 hours. Check the beans at about 5 hours and continue cooking if necessary.
4. Once the beans are done, drain in a colander.
5. In a large bowl, combine the beans, remaining salt, red onion, garlic, tomatoes, cilantro, and lime.

WHITE BEANS WITH ROSEMARY AND FRESH TOMATO

Rosemary is a cheap and easy herb to maintain in your garden.

Serves 8

2 (15-ounce) cans white beans, drained

1 cup water

4 teaspoons salt

3 tablespoons extra-virgin olive oil

4 cloves garlic, minced

2 cups tomatoes, diced

2–3 tablespoons fresh rosemary, chopped

¼ teaspoon black pepper

Add all ingredients to a 4-quart slow cooker. Cover and cook on low heat for about 5–6 hours.

SC WASABI-BARBECUE CHICKPEAS

Use a store-bought barbecue sauce if you're short on time, but if you do have time to spare, the Barbecue Sauce recipe in this book (see Chapter 2) will be well worth it.

Serves 8

1 (16-ounce) bag dried chickpeas

Enough water to cover beans by 1"

2 teaspoons salt

1 onion, diced

2½ tablespoons wasabi powder

3 cups barbecue sauce

1. Rinse the chickpeas, then soak overnight. Drain the water and then rinse the chickpeas again.
2. Add the chickpeas to a large pot and cover with water. Boil on high heat for 10 minutes, then drain.
3. Add chickpeas, water, and salt to a 4-quart slow cooker. Cover and cook on medium heat for about 5–6 hours. Check the beans at about 5 hours and continue cooking if necessary.
4. Once the chickpeas are done, drain in a colander and allow to cool to room temperature.
5. In a large bowl, combine the chickpeas with the rest of the ingredients.

Wasabi

Wasabi is a condiment also known as Japanese horseradish or mountain hollyhock, due to the fact that it grows naturally in cool, wet, mountain river valleys. It has a spicy and pungent flavor that is known to clear nasal passages if enough is consumed.

SC LENTILS WITH SAUTÉED SPINACH, WHITE WINE, AND GARLIC

Keep a close eye on this one, as spinach takes only a few seconds to sauté perfectly.

Serves 8

1 (16-ounce) bag dried lentils

Enough water to cover lentils by 1"

4 teaspoons salt

2 tablespoons olive oil

8 cups packed fresh spinach

5 cloves garlic, minced

⅛ cup white wine

1 teaspoon black pepper

1. Add lentils, water, and salt to a 4-quart slow cooker. Cover and cook on medium heat for about 3–4 hours. Check the lentils at about 5 hours and continue cooking if necessary.

2. Once the lentils are done, drain in a colander and allow them to cool to room temperature.

3. While the lentils are cooling, add the olive oil to a large pan and sauté the spinach with the garlic and white wine.

4. In a large bowl, combine the lentils with the sautéed spinach, the remaining salt, and pepper.

SC CHANA MASALA

The main ingredient in the popular Indian dish chana masala is chickpeas.

Serves 8

2 (15-ounce) cans chickpeas, drained
1 cup water
4 teaspoons salt
¼ cup butter or vegan margarine
1 onion, diced
5 cloves garlic, minced
1 tablespoon cumin
½ teaspoon cayenne pepper
1 teaspoon ground turmeric
2 teaspoons paprika
1 teaspoon garam masala
1 cup tomatoes, diced
1 lemon, juiced
2 teaspoons grated fresh ginger

Add all ingredients to a 4-quart slow cooker. Cover and cook on low heat for 6 hours.

SC EASY EDAMAME

Edamame are baby soybeans, and they're often enjoyed as an appetizer or in salads.

Serves 8

1 (16-ounce) package frozen edamame, shelled

Enough water to cover edamame by 1"

1 teaspoon coarse sea salt

¼ cup soy sauce

1. Add edamame and water to a 4-quart slow cooker. Cover and cook on high heat for about 1–2 hours. Check the edamame after an hour and continue cooking if necessary.
2. Once the edamame is done, drain in a colander.
3. Sprinkle with coarse sea salt and serve with soy sauce on the side for dipping.

SC SUMMER VEGETABLE BEAN SALAD

Serve this salad warm, straight out of the slow cooker, or chilled and over a bed of lettuce.

Serves 8

1 (15-ounce) can black beans
1 (15-ounce) can red kidney beans
1 (15-ounce) can white beans
1 cup water
4 teaspoons salt
1 red onion, diced
1 green bell pepper, diced
1 red bell pepper, diced
¼ cup cilantro, chopped
½ cup red wine vinegar
½ cup extra-virgin olive oil
1 teaspoon black pepper

Add all ingredients to a 4-quart slow cooker. Cover and cook on low heat for 4 hours.

White Beans

Great northern beans, navy beans, and cannellini beans are all referred to as white beans. Each has its own unique qualities; cannellini beans work best if you want the bean to hold its shape and texture after a long cooking time.

SC BLACK BEAN SALSA

This recipe makes a lot of salsa, so it's great for parties or large gatherings.

Serves 8

1 (16-ounce) bag dried black beans
Enough water to cover beans by 1"
4 teaspoons salt
2 (15-ounce) cans tomatoes, drained
1 cup corn
1 onion, diced
1 jalapeño, minced
3 cloves garlic, minced
3 teaspoons apple cider vinegar
2 teaspoons sugar
¼ teaspoon black pepper
¼ cup cilantro, chopped

1. Rinse the black beans, then soak overnight. Drain the water and rinse the beans again.
2. In a large pot, add the beans and cover with water. Boil on high heat for 10 minutes, then drain.
3. Add the black beans, water, and 2 teaspoons salt to a 4-quart slow cooker. Cover and cook on medium heat for about 5–6 hours. Check the beans at about 5 hours and continue cooking if necessary.
4. Once the beans are done, drain in a colander and allow to cool to room temperature.
5. In a large bowl, combine the beans with the rest of the ingredients.

SC SPICY BLACK-EYED PEAS AND KALE

Black-eyed peas are a good source of fiber, protein, and iron.

Serves 8

1 (16-ounce) bag dried black-eyed peas

Enough water to cover black-eyed peas by 1"

4 teaspoons salt

2 tablespoons olive oil

1 onion, diced

5 cloves garlic, minced

1 pound kale, chopped

½ teaspoon cayenne pepper

2 teaspoons cumin

1 teaspoon black pepper

1. Rinse the black-eyed peas, then soak overnight. Drain the water and rinse the peas again.
2. In a large pot, add the peas and cover with water. Boil on high heat for 10 minutes, then drain.
3. Add black-eyed peas, water, and 2 teaspoons salt to a 4-quart slow cooker. Cover and cook on medium heat for about 5–6 hours. Check the black-eyed peas at about 5 hours and continue cooking if necessary.
4. Once the black-eyed peas are done, drain in a colander.
5. Add the olive oil to the slow cooker and sauté the onion, garlic, and kale for about 5 minutes.
6. Add the rest of the ingredients, including the black-eyed peas, to the slow cooker. Cover and allow to cook for 15–20 minutes more.

RED BEANS WITH PLANTAINS

Beans served with plantains is a common dish in the West African country of Ghana.

Serves 8

2 cups red beans

16 cups water

4 tablespoons olive oil

2 teaspoons salt, plus more to taste

1 cup onion, diced

4 cloves garlic, minced

1 teaspoon fresh ginger, peeled and minced

½ teaspoon cayenne pepper

1 cup tomatoes, diced

3 ripened plantains, peeled and sliced diagonally

1 cup canola oil

Pepper, to taste

1. Add the beans and 8 cups water to the pressure cooker. Lock the lid into place; bring to high pressure for 1 minute. Remove from heat and quick-release the pressure.

2. Drain the water, rinse the beans, and add to the pressure cooker again with the remaining 8 cups water. Soak for 1 hour.

3. Add 2 tablespoons olive oil and 2 teaspoons salt. Lock the lid into place; bring to high pressure and maintain for 11 minutes. Remove from heat and allow pressure to release naturally.

4. While cooking the beans, add the remaining olive oil in a pan and sauté the onion until caramelized. Add the garlic, ginger, and cayenne and sauté 1 minute more. Add the tomatoes and bring to a simmer for 3–5 minutes. Add the mixture to the beans.

5. For the plantains, simply fry in the canola oil. Season with salt and pepper and serve with the red beans.

PC RED BEAN FRITTERS

Serve these fritters with a side of sour cream or vegan sour cream, for dipping.

Serves 6–8

1 cup red beans

8 cups water

1 tablespoon olive oil

1 teaspoon salt

1 jalapeño, minced

½ onion, diced

4 cloves garlic, minced

¼ cup cilantro

1 cup flour

1 cup cornmeal

1 tablespoon baking powder

½ cup heavy cream or unsweetened soymilk

2 eggs, beaten, or 2 teaspoons cornstarch mixed with 2 tablespoons water

2 quarts canola oil, for frying

Salt and pepper, to taste

1. Add the beans and 4 cups water to the pressure cooker. Lock the lid into place; bring to high pressure for 1 minute. Remove from heat and quick-release the pressure.

2. Drain the water, rinse the beans, and add to the pressure cooker again with the remaining 4 cups water. Soak for 1 hour.

3. Add the olive oil and salt. Lock the lid into place; bring to high pressure and maintain for 11 minutes. Remove from heat and allow pressure to release naturally. Drain and set aside.

4. In a bowl, combine the jalapeño, onion, garlic, cilantro, and red beans.

5. In another bowl combine the flour, cornmeal, baking powder, heavy cream or soymilk, and 2 eggs or cornstarch mixture. Add the bean mixture to the flour mixture and stir until well combined. Form the batter into 1" fritters.

6. In a large pot, heat the canola oil to 350°F and fry the fritters until golden brown, about 3–4 minutes. Season with salt and pepper, to taste.

Alternate Methods of Preparation

To reduce the amount of oil used in this recipe, pan-fry the fritters instead of deep frying. After the fritters are formed, heat 1 tablespoon of oil in a sauté pan over medium heat and cook the fritters for 3 minutes on each side.

PC WHITE BEANS WITH GARLIC AND FRESH TOMATO

Cherry or Roma tomatoes work best for this recipe, but in a pinch, any variety will do.

Serves 4–6

1 cup dried cannellini beans

4 cups water

4 cups Pressure Cooker Vegetable Stock (see Chapter 5)

1 tablespoon vegetable oil

1 teaspoon salt

2 cloves garlic, minced

½ cup tomato, diced

½ teaspoon dried sage

½ teaspoon black pepper

1. Add the beans and water to the pressure cooker. Lock the lid into place; bring to high pressure for 1 minute. Remove from heat and quick-release the pressure.
2. Drain the water, rinse the beans, and add to the pressure cooker again with the stock. Soak for 1 hour.
3. Add the vegetable oil and salt. Lock the lid into place; bring to high pressure and maintain for 10 minutes. Quick-release the pressure.
4. Add all remaining ingredients to the pressure cooker and lock the lid. Bring to high pressure and maintain for 4 minutes. Remove from heat and allow the pressure to release naturally.

[PC] WHITE BEANS AND RICE

It may sound like an odd condiment, but a touch of yellow mustard finishes off this dish surprisingly well.

Serves 8

2 cups dried white beans

16 cups water

3 tablespoons canola oil

1 cup onion, diced

1 green bell pepper, chopped

1 stalk celery, chopped

3 cloves garlic, minced

2 bay leaves

¼ teaspoon cayenne pepper

Salt and pepper, to taste

4 cups cooked white rice

1. Add the beans and 8 cups water to the pressure cooker. Lock the lid into place; bring to high pressure for 1 minute. Remove from heat and quick-release the pressure. Drain the water, rinse the beans, and add to the pressure cooker again with the remaining 8 cups water. Soak for 1 hour. Lock the lid into place; bring to high pressure and maintain for 12 minutes. Remove from heat and allow pressure to release naturally.

2. Add the oil to a pan and sauté the onion, green pepper, celery, and garlic until they are fragrant and browned. Add the mixture to the pressure cooker along with the bay leaves and cayenne pepper.

3. Lock the lid into place; bring to high pressure and maintain for 10–15 minutes. Remove from heat and allow pressure to release naturally.

4. Season with salt and pepper and serve over the white rice.

WHITE BEAN–LEEK PURÉE

Tarragon is a pungent herb that isn't enjoyed by all. If you don't care for tarragon, replace it with sage in this recipe.

Serves 4

1 cup dried cannellini beans

4 cups water

4 cups Pressure Cooker Vegetable Stock (see Chapter 5)

1 tablespoon vegetable oil

½ teaspoon salt

1 cup thinly sliced leeks

1 teaspoon lemon juice

2 cloves garlic, minced

¼ teaspoon dried tarragon

1. Add the beans and water to the pressure cooker. Lock the lid into place; bring to high pressure for 1 minute. Remove from heat and quick-release the pressure.

2. Drain the water, rinse the beans, and add to the pressure cooker again with the stock. Soak for 1 hour.

3. Add the vegetable oil and salt. Lock the lid into place; bring to high pressure and maintain for 10 minutes. Quick-release the pressure.

4. Add all remaining ingredients to the pressure cooker and lock the lid. Bring to high pressure and maintain for 4 minutes. Remove from heat and allow the pressure to release naturally.

5. Pour the beans and remaining liquid into a large food processor or blender and blend until creamy. Season with additional salt, if desired.

PRESSURE COOKER WASABI-BARBECUE CHICKPEAS

Most bottled barbecue sauces in your local grocery store are vegetarian, but to be sure, read the label before purchasing.

Serves 4

1 cup dried chickpeas
8 cups water, plus 1 tablespoon
2 tablespoons vegetable oil
½ cup onion, diced
1 tablespoon wasabi powder
1 cup barbecue sauce

1. Add the chickpeas and 4 cups water to the pressure cooker. Lock the lid into place; bring to high pressure for 1 minute. Remove from heat and quick-release the pressure.

2. Drain the water, rinse the chickpeas, and add to the pressure cooker again with the remaining 4 cups water. Soak for 1 hour.

3. Add 1 tablespoon vegetable oil. Lock the lid into place; bring to high pressure and maintain for 20 minutes. Remove from heat and allow pressure to release naturally. Drain chickpeas and water. Set chickpeas aside.

4. Add the remaining tablespoon of oil to the pressure cooker over medium heat. Sauté the onion until just soft, about 5 minutes.

5. Reconstitute the wasabi powder by combining with 1 tablespoon water, then add to the sautéed onion. Stir in the barbecue sauce and cooked chickpeas.

6. Lock the lid into place; bring to high pressure and maintain for 3 minutes. Remove from heat and allow pressure to release naturally.

PC CHICKPEA "TUNA" SALAD SANDWICH

Chickpeas are also commonly known as garbanzo beans.

Serves 4

1 cup dried chickpeas
8 cups water
6" piece dried kombu
1 tablespoon vegetable oil
2 tablespoons sweet relish
½ celery stalk, minced
¼ red onion, minced
4 tablespoons mayonnaise or vegan mayonnaise, such as Vegenaise
1 teaspoon lemon juice
½ teaspoon dried dill
1 teaspoon salt
4 sandwich buns
4 lettuce leaves and 4 slices tomato, optional

1. Add the chickpeas and 4 cups water to the pressure cooker. Lock the lid into place; bring to high pressure for 1 minute. Remove from heat and quick-release the pressure.

2. Drain the water, rinse the chickpeas, and add to the pressure cooker again with the remaining 4 cups water. Soak for 1 hour.

3. Add the kombu and vegetable oil. Lock the lid into place; bring to high pressure and maintain for 20 minutes. Remove from heat and allow pressure to release naturally.

4. Once the pressure is released, remove the lid, remove the kombu, and drain the chickpeas.

5. Transfer the drained chickpeas to a large bowl and mash.

6. Add the relish, celery, red onion, mayonnaise, lemon juice, dill, and salt, and stir until well combined. Scoop into a small dish, cover, and refrigerate for 1–2 hours.

7. Divide the mixture evenly over the 4 sandwich buns, top with lettuce and tomato, if desired, and serve.

Kombu

Kombu is a type of edible seaweed that is often sold in sheets. It is often used to flavor soups and other savory dishes because it adds the umami flavor.

PRESSURE COOKER HOPPIN' JOHN

Hoppin' John is a New Year's Day tradition in the southern United States.

Serves 4

1 tablespoon olive oil

½ cup onion, diced

1 clove garlic, minced

1 cup dried black-eyed peas

4¾ cups Pressure Cooker Vegetable Stock (see Chapter 5)

1 bay leaf

1 teaspoon chipotle powder

1 teaspoon salt

½ cup dried white rice

1. Pour the olive oil into the pressure cooker and bring to medium heat. Add the onion and sauté for 5 minutes. Add the garlic and sauté 30 seconds.

2. Add the black-eyed peas, stock, bay leaf, chipotle powder, and salt to the pressure cooker. Lock the lid into place; bring to high pressure and maintain for 5 minutes. Quick-release the pressure. Open the lid and pour in the rice. Lock the lid into place; bring to high pressure and maintain for 6 minutes. Allow the pressure to release naturally. Remove the bay leaf before serving.

[PC] LENTIL-SPINACH CURRY

Once-exotic curry powder can now be found in almost any grocery store. There are several varieties, and any will work in this recipe.

Serves 4

1 cup yellow lentils

4 cups water

1 tablespoon olive oil

½ cup onion, diced

1 clove garlic, minced

½ teaspoon coriander

½ teaspoon turmeric

½ teaspoon curry powder

½ cup tomato, diced

2 cups fresh spinach

1. Add the lentils and water to the pressure cooker. Lock the lid into place; bring to high pressure and maintain for 6 minutes. Quick-release the pressure, then drain the beans. Clean the pressure cooker.

2. Add the oil to the pressure cooker over medium heat. Sauté the onion for 3 minutes; add the garlic, coriander, turmeric, and curry powder and sauté for an additional 30 seconds. Stir in the tomato, fresh spinach, and cooked lentils. Simmer for 10 minutes before serving.

PC LENTIL PÂTÉ

Pâté is typically made from ground meat, but for a vegetarian version try ground beans or mushrooms.

Serves 8–10

2 cups dried lentils

8 cups water

2 tablespoons olive oil

1 teaspoon salt, plus more to taste

3 tablespoons butter or vegan margarine, such as Earth Balance

1 cup onion, diced

3 cloves garlic, minced

1 teaspoon red wine vinegar

Pepper, to taste

1. Add the beans, water, 1 tablespoon olive oil, and 1 teaspoon salt to the pressure cooker.

2. Lock the lid into place; bring to high pressure and maintain for 7 minutes. Remove from heat and allow pressure to release naturally.

3. Add the butter or margarine to a pan and sauté the onion until it begins to turn golden brown. Add the garlic and vinegar, and sauté 1 minute more. Add the mixture to the lentils. Pour the mixture into a food processor and blend until smooth. Taste and season with salt and pepper, if desired.

Serving Suggestions

For an eye-pleasing presentation, pour the pâté into a lightly oiled ramekin and pack tightly. Flip the ramekin over onto a serving dish and gently remove the ramekin. Serve with a variety of crackers and baguette slices.

PC RED LENTIL CURRY

You can simplify the seasoning in this dish by omitting the turmeric and ginger.

Serves 8

2 cups dried red lentils
8 cups water
3 tablespoons olive oil
1 teaspoon salt, plus more to taste
1 cup onion, diced
1 teaspoon garlic, minced
1 teaspoon fresh ginger, peeled and minced
3 tablespoons curry powder
1 teaspoon turmeric
1 teaspoon cumin
1 teaspoon chili powder
1 teaspoon sugar
1 (6-ounce) can tomato paste
Pepper, to taste

1. Add the beans, water, 1 tablespoon oil, and 1 teaspoon salt to the pressure cooker.
2. Lock the lid into place; bring to high pressure and maintain for 7 minutes. Remove from heat and allow pressure to release naturally.
3. In a pan, add the remaining oil and sauté the onion until it is caramelized. Add the garlic and ginger and sauté for 1 minute more. Add the curry powder, turmeric, cumin, chili powder, sugar, and tomato paste, and bring the mixture to a simmer for 2–3 minutes, stirring constantly.
4. Drain the lentils and add to the curry mixture. Taste for seasoning and add salt and pepper if desired.

PC PRESSURE COOKER CHANA MASALA

Serve this delicious dish warm!

Serves 4–6

1 cup dried chickpeas
8 cups water
1 tablespoon vegetable oil
1 tablespoon butter or vegan margarine, such as Earth Balance
½ onion, diced
1 garlic clove, minced
1 teaspoon ground cumin
¼ teaspoon ground cayenne pepper
½ teaspoon ground turmeric
¼ cup tomatoes, diced
½ cup water
1 teaspoon paprika
½ teaspoon garam masala
1 teaspoon salt
1 tablespoon lemon juice
1 teaspoon fresh ginger, grated

1. Add the chickpeas and 4 cups water to the pressure cooker. Lock the lid into place; bring to high pressure for 1 minute. Remove from heat and quick-release the pressure.

2. Drain the water, rinse the beans, and add to the pressure cooker again with the remaining 4 cups water. Soak for 1 hour.

3. Add the vegetable oil. Lock the lid into place; bring to high pressure and maintain for 20 minutes. Remove from heat and allow pressure to release naturally. Drain and set chickpeas aside.

4. Add the butter or margarine to the pressure cooker over medium heat and sauté the onion and garlic. Add all remaining ingredients, including the cooked chickpeas, and let simmer until the sauce has reduced, about 15–20 minutes.

PC SEA SALT EDAMAME

Edamame, a preparation of immature soybeans in the pod, is a staple in Japanese, Chinese, and Hawaiian cuisine.

Serves 4

1 cup edamame, shelled

8 cups water

1 tablespoon vegetable oil

1 teaspoon coarse sea salt

1 tablespoon soy sauce

1. Add the edamame and 4 cups water to the pressure cooker. Lock the lid into place; bring to high pressure for 1 minute. Remove from heat and quick-release the pressure.

2. Drain the water, rinse the edamame, and add to the pressure cooker again with the remaining 4 cups water. Soak for 1 hour.

3. Add the vegetable oil. Lock the lid into place; bring to high pressure and maintain for 11 minutes. Remove from heat and allow pressure to release naturally.

4. Once the pressure has released, drain the edamame and transfer to a serving bowl. Sprinkle with coarse sea salt and serve with soy sauce on the side, for dipping.

PC DINNER LOAF

You won't be missing the meatloaf on your dinner table if you try this dinner loaf instead!

Serves 6–8

1 cup dried pinto beans
8 cups water
1 tablespoon vegetable oil
1 teaspoon salt
1 cup onion, diced
1 cup chopped walnuts
½ cup plain dried oats
1 egg, beaten, or 1 teaspoon cornstarch combined with 1 tablespoon water
¾ cup ketchup
1 teaspoon garlic powder
1 teaspoon dried basil
1 teaspoon dried parsley
Salt and pepper, to taste

1. Add the beans and 4 cups water to the pressure cooker. Lock the lid into place; bring to high pressure for 1 minute. Remove from heat and quick-release the pressure.

2. Drain the water, rinse the beans, and add to the pressure cooker again with the remaining 4 cups water. Soak for 1 hour.

3. Add the vegetable oil and salt. Lock the lid into place; bring to high pressure and maintain for 11 minutes. Remove from heat and allow pressure to release naturally. Drain the beans and pour into a large mixing bowl.

4. Combine the rest of the ingredients with the beans. Spread the mixture into a loaf pan and bake at 350°F for 30–35 minutes.

Mock Meatloaf

There are many ingredients you can use to make mock meatloaf. For the easiest option, use vegetarian ground beef, such as Gimme Lean Ground Beef, instead of real meat in your favorite recipe.

CHAPTER 8
LEAFY GREENS AND CRUCIFEROUS VEGETABLES

RECIPE LIST

ARTICHOKES IN COURT BOUILLON WITH LEMON BUTTER 454

SPINACH AND TOMATO SAUTÉ 455

ALOO GOBI (CAULIFLOWER AND POTATO CURRY) 456

PRESSURE COOKER ALOO GOBI 457

CURRIED CAULIFLOWER 458

STIR-FRIED ASIAN GREENS 459

SHANGHAI BOK CHOY WITH GARLIC AND BLACK BEAN SAUCE 460

BRAISED SWISS CHARD 461

CABBAGE STEWED IN TOMATO SAUCE 462

SPINACH WITH PINE NUTS (PIGNOLI) AND GARLIC 462

VEGAN CREAMED SPINACH 463

BASIC BUTTERED BRUSSELS SPROUTS 464

PAN-SEARED BRUSSELS SPROUTS 465

CRANBERRY-WALNUT BRUSSELS SPROUTS 466

SMOKY SPICED COLLARD GREENS WITH TURNIP 466

BRAISED RED CABBAGE (CHOU ROUGE À LA FLAMANDE) 467

SCENTED ESCAROLE WITH FENNEL 468

BROCCOLI FLORETS WITH LEMON BUTTER SAUCE 469

SAUTÉED BROCCOLI RAAB 470

BROCCOLI IN LEMON BUTTER SAUCE 471

CREAMED SPINACH 472

STUFFED CABBAGE 473

KIMCHI-STYLE CABBAGE 474

GAI LAN (CHINESE BROCCOLI) WITH TOASTED GARLIC 475

SWISS CHARD ROLLS WITH ROOT VEGETABLES 476

SPINACH PANCAKES WITH CARDAMOM 477

SPINACH-STUFFED VEGETABLES 478

SPINACH AND FETA PIE 479

GRILLED RADICCHIO 480

KALE WITH GARLIC AND THYME 481

KALE WITH RED PEPPER FLAKES AND CUMIN 482

SZECHUAN STIR-FRIED CABBAGE WITH HOT PEPPERS 483

GARLICKY BROCCOLI RAAB 484

COLLARD GREENS WITH TOMATOES AND CHEDDAR **485**

SOUTHERN-STYLE COLLARDS **486**

SOY-GLAZED BOK CHOY **487**

BABY BOK CHOY **488**

HOMEMADE SAUERKRAUT **489**

ARTICHOKES IN COURT BOUILLON WITH LEMON BUTTER

The elegant artichoke stands on its own as a self-contained snack or appetizer. Each part has its own character, from the earthy bits of meat on the outer leaves, to the sweet, wholly edible, purple-tinged inner leaves, to the vegetal bottom. This court bouillon is a standard cooking medium for artichokes.

Serves 4

4 whole artichokes (preferably pointed-leaf, not "globe," artichokes)

4 lemons

2 tablespoons whole coriander seeds

2 tablespoons salt

8 ounces salted whole butter

1. Trim the stems of the artichokes to about 2". Bring 5 quarts water to a rapid boil. Halve 3 of the lemons, squeeze them into the boiling water, and toss the squeezed lemon fruits into the water, along with the coriander seeds and salt. Boil 5 minutes.

2. Place the artichokes in the cooking liquid and cover with a heavy plate or other object to keep them from floating. Boil until a paring knife, inserted where the stem meets the bottom, comes out very easily, about 15 minutes. Meanwhile, melt the butter in a microwave for 30 seconds on high, then mix with the juice of the remaining lemon.

3. Serve each person a whole artichoke, accompanied by a ramekin of butter sauce and a large bowl for discarded leaves. Eat the artichoke leaf by leaf, starting by dipping them in the butter and nibbling at the tender bits at the bottoms of the outer leaves, gradually reaching fully edible inner leaves. When you reach the hair-like "choke," scoop it out with a spoon, discard it, and carve the prized "heart" at bottom into pieces for easy consumption.

SPINACH AND TOMATO SAUTÉ

The subtle addition of coriander brings this dish an understated elegance, perfect for a dinner main course. Always wash spinach twice, submerging it in fresh water each time and agitating it well by hand. Growing low to the ground, spinach usually hides plenty of soil in its crevices.

Serves 4

3 teaspoons butter

6 plum tomatoes, roughly chopped

1 teaspoon coriander

2 bunches flat-leaf spinach, washed very thoroughly

½ teaspoon salt

Freshly ground black pepper

In a large skillet or heavy-bottomed Dutch oven, melt 2 teaspoons of the butter over medium-high heat. Add the tomatoes and coriander; cook until softened, about 5 minutes. Add the spinach in handfuls, allowing each handful to wilt before adding the next. Season it well with salt and pepper. Finish by swirling in the remaining butter.

ALOO GOBI (CAULIFLOWER AND POTATO CURRY)

This classic North Indian curry is a hearty main course. It's also an excellent filling for wraps known as roti.

Serves 8

1 large head cauliflower

2 pounds potatoes

3 tablespoons oil

2 large onions, finely chopped (about 5 cups)

4 jalapeño or other chili peppers, finely chopped

1 (1") piece fresh ginger, finely chopped

3 tomatoes, finely chopped

1¼ teaspoons chili powder

1 teaspoon turmeric

1 teaspoon coriander

2 teaspoons kosher salt

1 teaspoon garam masala (spice mixture available at specialty stores—or make your own by combining 1 teaspoon each of ground cardamom, cumin seed, cloves, black pepper, and cinnamon)

Cilantro or parsley, chopped, for garnish

1. Cut the cauliflower and potatoes into large chunks. Heat the oil in a heavy skillet over medium-high heat, and cook the onions, chilies, and ginger until brown, about 10 minutes. Add the tomatoes, chili powder, turmeric, coriander, and salt; cook 5 minutes more, until spices are fragrant and evenly dispersed. Mix in the potatoes and cauliflower, plus enough water to come halfway up the vegetables.

2. Cover the pan and cook for 20 minutes, stirring occasionally, until the potatoes and cauliflower are very tender. Add the garam masala powder; cook 5 minutes more. Serve garnished with cilantro.

PRESSURE COOKER ALOO GOBI

Aloo Gobi is a vegetarian Indian dish made from potatoes and cauliflower.

Serves 4–6

2 cups potatoes, peeled and cubed

Water, as needed, plus 2 tablespoons

2 cups cauliflower, chopped

2 tablespoons vegetable oil

1 teaspoon cumin seeds

1 clove garlic, minced

1 teaspoon fresh ginger, minced

1 teaspoon turmeric

1 teaspoon garam masala

1 teaspoon salt

1. Add the potatoes to the pressure cooker and enough water to cover. Lock on the lid. Bring to high pressure; maintain pressure for 4 minutes. Remove the pan from the heat, quick-release the pressure, and remove the lid.

2. Add the cauliflower and reattach the lid. Bring to high pressure; maintain pressure for 2 minutes. Remove the pan from the heat, quick-release the pressure, and remove the lid. Drain all ingredients.

3. Place the vegetable oil in the cleaned pressure cooker over low heat. Add the cumin seeds, garlic, and ginger; cook for 1 minute. Add the turmeric, garam masala, and salt; cook for an additional minute.

4. Stir in 2 tablespoons water, then add the cooked potatoes and cauliflower. Simmer over low heat, stirring occasionally, for 10 minutes.

SC CURRIED CAULIFLOWER

Heating herbs and spices before adding them to water intensifies the flavor.

Serves 6

1 tablespoon olive oil
¼ cup finely diced onion
1½ teaspoons curry powder
½ teaspoon cumin
½ teaspoon coriander
1 teaspoon chili powder
1 teaspoon salt
1 cup diced tomatoes
1 cup water
1 head cauliflower, chopped

1. Heat the olive oil in the bottom of a 4-quart slow cooker set to medium heat. Add the onion and cook for 5 minutes.

2. Add the curry powder, cumin, coriander, chili powder, salt, and tomatoes and stir until well combined.

3. Add the water and cauliflower to the spice mixture in the slow cooker and stir until the cauliflower is coated. Cover and cook over medium heat for about 3 hours.

STIR-FRIED ASIAN GREENS

Heaping ceramic bowls of jasmine rice with portions of this stir-fry constitute Asian "comfort food" at its best. This may require two large pans, or need to be cooked in two batches.

Serves 8

1 bunch (about 1 pound) collard greens, thinly sliced

1 small head (about 1 pound) Chinese cabbage (barrel-shaped Napa cabbage), thinly sliced

1 bunch watercress, stem ends trimmed

2 tablespoons peanut oil

1 (10-ounce) package white or cremini mushrooms

1 large "horse" carrot or 2 cello carrots, peeled, sliced thinly on the bias (diagonal)

¼ pound snow peas, halved diagonally

1 medium red onion, halved and sliced with the grain

2" piece fresh ginger, julienne

3 cloves garlic, finely chopped

Salt and white pepper to taste

2 tablespoons soy sauce

1 tablespoon Chinese cooking wine or dry sherry (optional)

1 teaspoon Asian sesame oil

Black sesame seeds or toasted white sesame seeds for garnish (optional)

Mix together the collards, cabbage, and watercress; wash thoroughly and dry. Heat the peanut oil in a large skillet (13") over high heat until it is shimmery, but not smoky. Add the mushrooms, carrots, snow peas, onion, ginger, and garlic; sauté 2 minutes, stirring frequently, allowing some parts to brown. Season it well with salt and white pepper. Add the greens, soy sauce, wine, if using, and sesame oil. Toss or stir; cook only 1 minute, until the greens begin to wilt. Serve immediately, with jasmine rice and a sprinkling of sesame seeds, if desired.

SHANGHAI BOK CHOY WITH GARLIC AND BLACK BEAN SAUCE

Miniature jade green heads of Shanghai bok choy, often labeled "baby bok choy," are increasingly available in groceries where Asian greens are sold. If you can't find these attractive miniature heads, regular bok choy is

Serves 4

8 heads Shanghai ("baby") bok choy

2 cups Mushroom Vegetable Stock (see Chapter 5) or other strong vegetable stock

1 teaspoon sugar

1 tablespoon Chinese fermented black bean sauce, or 1 teaspoon Chinese fermented black beans

2 teaspoons hoisin sauce (available in the Asian section of most supermarkets)

2 teaspoons cornstarch, dissolved in ¼ cup cold water

2 teaspoons peanut or other oil

2 teaspoons (about 3 cloves) chopped garlic

Salt to taste

Dash of Asian hot chili paste (optional)

1. Halve the bok choy heads lengthwise, and blanch in rapidly boiling salted water for 3–4 minutes, until crisp tender. Drain and plunge immediately into ice water to stop the cooking. In a saucepan, bring the stock to a boil. Whisk in sugar, bean sauce or beans, and hoisin sauce. Simmer 10 minutes, then whisk in cornstarch slurry to thicken; cook 5 minutes more, covered. It should have the consistency of honey. Taste for seasoning.

2. Heat the oil in a skillet, over medium heat. Add garlic, and allow it to sizzle until it begins to turn golden brown. Immediately add the blanched bok choy, season lightly with salt, and cook until vegetable is warmed through. Add chili paste if desired. Transfer to a serving platter, and spoon on the black bean sauce, reserving any extra to be served on the side at the table.

BRAISED SWISS CHARD

Handsome, broad-leafed, and cool, Swiss chard has come back into vogue in recent years, thanks in great part to the devotion of gourmet chefs and nutritionists who have rediscovered its striking beauty (especially of the red-veined varieties) and unearthed its cancer-fighting possibilities. The juicy stems and tender leaves are cooked separately.

Serves 4

- 1 large bunch red or green Swiss chard (about 1½ pounds)
- 1 cup strong vegetable stock, mushroom stock, or liquid from cooking beans
- Salt and freshly ground black pepper to taste
- 1 tablespoon olive oil
- 2 medium shallots, finely chopped (about ¼ cup)
- 1 tablespoon unsalted butter
- Lemon wedges

1. Wash the chard thoroughly under running water, and shake dry. Using your hands, tear the leafy parts away from the stems; set aside. Cut the stems into bite-size pieces. In a nonreactive skillet, bring the stock to a boil; add the stem pieces. Season with salt and pepper; cook until tender. Transfer them to a bowl or plate, reserving their cooking liquid. Wipe out the skillet.

2. Return the skillet to the heat and add the olive oil and shallots. Cook 1 minute until they sizzle and soften slightly. Add the chard leaves, and cook only until they wilt. Add back the stems, plus 2 tablespoons of their cooking liquid. Bring to a simmer, and swirl in the butter. Taste for seasoning. Serve with lemon wedges.

CABBAGE STEWED IN TOMATO SAUCE

Hearty winter food like stewed cabbage goes beautifully with seasoned brown rice.

Serves 8

2 tablespoons olive oil

1 medium onion, roughly chopped

1 small head green or red cabbage (about 2 pounds, chopped)

1 teaspoon caraway seeds

Salt and freshly ground black pepper

2 cups tomato sauce

2 teaspoons brown sugar

Heat the oil in a large Dutch oven. Add the onion and cook until translucent, about 5 minutes. Add the cabbage, caraway seeds, and a little salt and pepper; cook over medium heat until soft and saucy, about 5 minutes more. Stir in tomato sauce and brown sugar. Lower flame to a simmer, and cook covered, stirring occasionally, for 1 hour, until the cabbage is very tender and has taken on color from the sauce.

SPINACH WITH PINE NUTS (PIGNOLI) AND GARLIC

Based on a Roman dish, this antioxidant-rich spinach dish picks up nuttiness not just from the pignoli, but also from the toasted garlic.

Serves 4

¼ cup pine nuts (pignoli)

3 tablespoons extra-virgin olive oil

2 cloves garlic, finely chopped

2 pounds washed spinach leaves, stems removed

Salt and freshly ground black pepper

Lemon wedges

1. Gently toast the nuts in a dry sauté pan until they start to brown. Set aside. In a very large pan, heat the olive oil and garlic over medium heat until the garlic sizzles and starts to brown.

2. Add ⅓ of the spinach and the pine nuts, and sauté until the spinach is wilted, and lets off some liquid. Add the rest of the spinach in batches, seasoning with salt and pepper as it cooks. Serve with lemon wedges.

VEGAN CREAMED SPINACH

Fresh spinach reduces greatly when cooked, so to get a bigger bang for your buck, use frozen spinach when possible.

Serves 6

- 1 tablespoon vegan margarine
- 1 clove garlic, minced
- 1 tablespoon flour
- 1 cup unsweetened soymilk
- ½ teaspoon salt
- ½ crushed teaspoon red pepper
- ¼ teaspoon dried sage
- 1 (12-ounce) package frozen spinach, thawed

1. Melt the margarine in a 2-quart slow cooker over medium heat. Add the garlic, and cook for 2 minutes before stirring in the flour.
2. Slowly pour in the soymilk and whisk until all lumps are removed.
3. Add all remaining ingredients. Stir, and cook over low heat for 1–2 hours.

Variations
You can simplify this recipe by going with a simple butter or margarine sauce that is flavored with salt, pepper, and sage, or make this savory dish even richer by adding a sprinkling of vegan cheese such as Daiya Mozzarella Style Shreds.

BASIC BUTTERED BRUSSELS SPROUTS

Brussels sprouts are an excellent fall and winter vegetable that holds very well for a long time, making them perfect for busy working people who can keep them on hand in the refrigerator for whenever they're needed.

Serves 4

1 pint Brussels sprouts

2 ounces (½ stick) unsalted butter

Salt and white pepper

Pinch nutmeg (optional)

1. Remove outer leaves from sprouts, and trim the stems so that they're flush with the sprout bottoms. Halve the sprouts by cutting through the stem end.

2. Boil in small batches, in 4 quarts of well-salted, rapidly boiling water. Drain.

3. In a medium (10") sauté pan, over medium heat, melt the butter, and add the cooked sprouts, tossing with the seasonings to coat. Serve with lemon wedges.

PC PAN-SEARED BRUSSELS SPROUTS

Pan-searing Brussels sprouts brings out a buttery sweetness that is otherwise missing from the vegetable.

Serves 4

1 pound Brussels sprouts

2 tablespoons olive oil, divided

¼ cup water

Salt and pepper, to taste

1. Trim the stems of the Brussels sprouts and remove the discolored outer leaves. Cut in half, from the stem to the top, and place into a medium bowl. Add 1 tablespoon of the oil and gently toss until coated.
2. Add the remaining tablespoon of oil to the pressure cooker and bring to medium-high heat. Place the Brussels sprouts in the pressure cooker and cook for about 5 minutes, stirring often, or until the sides begin to brown. Add the water.
3. Lock on the lid. Bring to high pressure; maintain pressure for 1 minute. Remove the pan from the heat, quick-release the pressure, and remove the lid. Season with salt and pepper, to taste.

SC CRANBERRY-WALNUT BRUSSELS SPROUTS

The combination of cranberries and walnuts makes this a perfect Thanksgiving side dish.

Serves 6

- 1 pound Brussels sprouts, trimmed and quartered
- 2 tablespoons olive oil
- 2 tablespoons water
- ½ teaspoon salt
- ¼ teaspoon pepper
- ¼ cup dried cranberries
- ¼ cup walnuts, chopped

1. Place all ingredients in a 2-quart slow cooker and stir until the olive oil coats the other ingredients.
2. Cover and cook on high heat for 2½ hours.

SMOKY SPICED COLLARD GREENS WITH TURNIP

The smokiness in this dish comes from the chipotle chili (a smoked jalapeño pepper) available dried or canned in most supermarkets in the Mexican foods section, or at Latino specialty markets. For milder greens, remove the seeds and veins from the chili before use. Collards are high in usable calcium, essential in the vegetarian diet.

Serves 4

- 1 bunch collards or turnip greens
- 1 medium white turnip, peeled and diced into ¼" pieces
- 1 medium onion, chopped
- 1 chipotle chili, dried or canned, cut in half
- 1 tablespoon olive oil
- 1 teaspoon salt
- 1 cup vegetable stock or water

1. Wash greens and remove the stems. Cut leaves into long thin strips (julienne).
2. In a heavy-bottomed pot, sauté the turnip, onion, and chili in olive oil until the onion is translucent. Add the greens and salt, and sauté a few minutes more, until greens are wilted.
3. Add stock or water, bring to a boil, and reduce heat to simmer for 20 minutes, or until greens are very tender and turnips are soft.

BRAISED RED CABBAGE (CHOU ROUGE À LA FLAMANDE)

Cruciferous vegetables, such as cabbage, broccoli, radishes, and collard greens, contain phytochemicals that may help to protect against some of the most deadly cancers.

Serves 8

1 small head red cabbage (about 2 pounds)

1 teaspoon salt

Pinch of grated nutmeg

1 tablespoon oil

1 tablespoon red wine vinegar

4 Granny Smith or pippin apples, peeled and cut into ¼" slices

1 tablespoon brown sugar

Wash cabbage and discard tough outer leaves; quarter, core, and thinly slice it (julienne). Sprinkle shredded cabbage with salt and nutmeg. Heat oil in a large Dutch oven or ovenproof casserole dish with a tight-fitting lid; add cabbage and red wine vinegar. Cover and cook over a low heat for at least 1 hour, either on the stovetop or in a low (325°F) oven. Add the apples and sugar; cook for another 30 minutes, until cabbage is very tender and apples are mostly dissolved.

SCENTED ESCAROLE WITH FENNEL

Serve this dish garnished with grated cheese.

Serves 6 as an appetizer, 3 as a main dish

2 tablespoons extra-virgin olive oil

2 cloves garlic, finely chopped

1 small onion, finely chopped

12 cups coarsely chopped escarole

1½ teaspoons fennel seeds, lightly toasted in a dry pan

Salt and freshly ground black pepper

1 tablespoon grated Parmesan cheese (Parmigiano-Reggiano)

1. Heat the oil over a medium heat. Add the garlic, and cook about 1 minute, until it starts to brown. Add onion, and cook until translucent, about 5 minutes.

2. Add the escarole and fennel seeds, season with salt and pepper, and cover. Cook until escarole is wilted, and simmer in its own juices. Remove cover, raise heat to medium-high, and cook to evaporate most of the liquid, about 5 minutes. Serve garnished with grated cheese.

BROCCOLI FLORETS WITH LEMON BUTTER SAUCE

White butter sauce, or beurre blanc, is a simple, smooth base, which can be tailored to whatever it is served with—whole-grain mustard, herbs, and/or various citrus flavors.

Serves 4

2 small shallots, finely chopped

¼ cup white cooking wine

Juice of 1 lemon

8 ounces cold, unsalted butter, cut into small pieces

Salt and white pepper

1 large head broccoli, broken into florets

1. Place the shallots, wine, and half of the lemon juice in a small saucepan, over a medium heat. Simmer until almost dry. Reduce heat to very low, and stir in a few small pieces of butter, swirling it in with a wire whisk until it is mostly melted. Gradually add the remaining butter, whisking constantly, until all is used, and sauce is smooth. Never boil. Season the sauce with salt, white pepper, and remaining lemon juice to taste. Keep in a warm place, but not over a flame.

2. Wash the broccoli and boil in 4 quarts of rapidly boiling, salted water. Drain, and serve with lemon butter sauce.

PC SAUTÉED BROCCOLI RAAB

Broccoli raab, also known as rapini, can be prepared in the same way as broccoli.

Serves 6

1 pound broccoli raab, trimmed

1 teaspoon salt

1 cup water

2 tablespoons olive oil

2 cloves garlic, sliced

2 shallots, sliced

Pepper, to taste

1. Put the broccoli, salt, and water in the pressure cooker. Lock the lid and bring to low pressure; maintain pressure for 2 minutes. Remove from heat, quick-release the pressure, and remove the lid. Drain and transfer to a bowl.

2. In the cleaned pressure cooker or in a sauté pan, bring the olive oil to medium heat. Add the garlic and shallots; sauté for 1 minute, stirring often. Add the broccoli raab and sauté for an additional minute, until heated through and coated with the olive oil mixture. Season with pepper, to taste.

PC BROCCOLI IN LEMON BUTTER SAUCE

Serve as a side dish or toss with pasta for a complete meal.

Serves 6

4 cups broccoli florets

¼ teaspoon salt

1 cup water

4 tablespoons butter, melted, or vegan margarine, such as Earth Balance

1 tablespoon fresh lemon juice

¼ teaspoon Dijon mustard

1. Put the broccoli, salt, and water in the pressure cooker. Lock the lid into place and bring to low pressure; maintain pressure for 2 minutes.

2. Remove the pressure cooker from the heat, quick-release the pressure, and remove the lid. Drain and transfer the broccoli to a serving bowl.

3. While the broccoli cooks, whisk together the butter, lemon juice, and mustard. Pour over the cooked broccoli and toss to coat.

CREAMED SPINACH

To add richness and silky texture to a meal, add a spoonful of this savory classic vegetable dish to the plate. It works especially well as a counterpoint to crunchy foods.

Serves 4

2 pounds spinach, stemmed and washed

½ cup heavy cream

½ teaspoon salt

Grated nutmeg

Freshly ground black pepper

1. Heat a large nonreactive skillet or Dutch oven over medium heat, and cook the spinach with a few drops of water until just wilted. Drain, rinse, and squeeze dry in a colander. Chop the spinach finely.

2. In a skillet, bring the cream to a boil; add the salt, nutmeg, and pepper. Stir in the spinach; cook until most of the water has cooked out, and the spinach is thick. If desired, purée in a food processor.

STUFFED CABBAGE

Comfort foods like these neat little packets of rice feel like Thanksgiving all over again. This recipe is time-consuming, so plan on making it a day ahead, or on a leisurely day in the kitchen. They freeze well.

Serves 6

1 head green cabbage (about 1½ pounds), stem core cut out

2 tablespoons olive oil

1 large onion, roughly chopped

1 bunch of scallions, chopped

1 bunch of basil, leaves picked, washed well, and cut into julienne

½ cup chopped Italian parsley

1 teaspoon oregano

½ teaspoon thyme

Kosher salt and freshly ground black pepper

1 cup of cooked barley, spelt, brown rice, or other whole grain

¼ cup puréed silken tofu

¼ cup vegetable stock

2 cups tomato sauce

1. Bring a large stockpot of water to a boil; submerge the cabbage in it for about 5 minutes. Peel off the first few softened leaves, then put the cabbage back in to soften some more. Repeat this process until you have 12 softened leaves; cut the thick vein from their stem ends. Finely shred the remaining cabbage.

2. Heat the olive oil in a large skillet over high heat for 1 minute; add the chopped cabbage, onion, scallions, basil, parsley, oregano, and thyme. Season thoroughly with salt and pepper. Cover and cook until vegetables are tender, about 15 minutes, stirring occasionally; drain. Combine with cooked barley and puréed tofu. Taste for seasoning, adding more salt if necessary—it should be highly seasoned.

3. Place the softened cabbage leaves on a work surface, with the stem end closest to you. Distribute the filling onto the leaves, placing it closest to the stem end. Fold the sides in to envelop the filling, then roll away from yourself, providing even tension to keep the rolls plump. Place the rolls in a baking dish; add the vegetable stock. Bake 30 minutes at 350°F. Make small pools of tomato sauce on 6 plates, and serve 2 rolls atop the sauce for each portion.

KIMCHI-STYLE CABBAGE

If you can't find Korean chili powder, substitute plain chili powder, which is also made from crushed red peppers.

Yields 1 quart

1 clove garlic, minced

1 teaspoon fresh ginger, minced

1 bunch scallions, sliced

½ cup water

¼ cup soy sauce

1 tablespoon Korean chili powder

4 cups Napa cabbage, cut into 2" pieces

1 cup carrots, julienned

Add the garlic, ginger, scallions, water, soy sauce, and chili powder to the pressure cooker and stir well. Add the cabbage and carrots. Lock on the lid. Bring to high pressure; maintain pressure for 2 minutes. Remove the pan from the heat, quick-release the pressure, and remove the lid.

Kimchi

Kimchi is a popular Korean condiment that is often used as the base for other recipes. Traditional recipes call for fermenting the mixture until pickled, but you can make "kimchi-style" cabbage by pressure-cooking the ingredients instead of fermenting.

GAI LAN (CHINESE BROCCOLI) WITH TOASTED GARLIC

Darker, leafier, and more slender-stemmed than Western broccoli, gai lan is nonetheless a cousin in the Brassica genus, which also includes most cabbages, cauliflower, mustard greens, and bok choy. It's worth seeking out in Asian grocery markets, but if you can't find it, this recipe will work just as well with regular broccoli or broccoli raab.

Serves 4

1 pound gai lan (Chinese broccoli) or other type of broccoli

2 tablespoons peanut oil

5 cloves garlic, finely chopped

Pinch of crushed red pepper flakes (optional)

Kosher salt and freshly ground black pepper

Lemon wedges

1. Prepare a deep bowl full of salted ice water; set aside. Bring a large pot of salted water (it should be as salty as tears) to a rapid, rolling boil. Trim any frayed ends from the stems of the gai lan. Cook it by handfuls, only until crisp-tender; plunge immediately into the ice bath. Drain.

2. In a large skillet or wok, heat the oil over a medium heat until it is hot. Add the garlic and red pepper (if using), and cook without stirring, until the garlic begins to turn golden brown. Immediately add the blanched vegetable, and toss gently to stop the garlic from browning further. Cook until the vegetable is thoroughly hot. Season well with salt and pepper. Serve with lemon wedges.

SWISS CHARD ROLLS WITH ROOT VEGETABLES

This dish is particularly attractive with red Swiss chard, though green is fine.

Serves 4

- 8 large leaves Swiss chard, thoroughly washed
- 3 tablespoons olive oil, divided
- 2 cups roughly chopped red onion
- 2 carrots, roughly chopped
- 2 sweet potatoes (about ½ pound), peeled and finely diced
- 8 cups chopped root vegetables (such as celery root, parsnips, turnips, and white potatoes—try Latino roots, such as yuca or taro)
- ¼ cup roughly chopped Italian parsley
- Juice of 2 limes (about 4 tablespoons)
- 2 teaspoons chopped cilantro (optional)
- Kosher salt and freshly ground black pepper
- 1 cup stock or water

1. Remove the stems from the chard; chop them finely. Heat 2 tablespoons of the olive oil over a medium flame in a heavy-bottomed Dutch oven or large skillet. Add the chard stems, red onion, carrots, sweet potatoes, root vegetables, parsley, lime juice, and cilantro; season well with salt and pepper.

2. Bring a large pot of salted water to a boil. Blanch the chard leaves for 3–4 minutes, then drain and cool. Spoon ¼ cup of filling onto the stem end of a chard leaf. Fold in the sides to envelop the filling; roll away from yourself, keeping even tension so the rolls remain plump. Line the rolls up in a greased skillet; add 1 cup of water or stock, season lightly with salt. Cook 10 minutes; serve garnished with remaining filling.

SPINACH PANCAKES WITH CARDAMOM

Serve with a glass of Sprite or white Riesling wine on a hot August midday.

Serves 4

1 tablespoon olive oil

2 teaspoons finely chopped garlic

2 pounds fresh spinach, washed and stemmed

4 pods cardamom, cracked open, or ½ teaspoon ground

1 teaspoon salt

Freshly ground black pepper

2 ounces egg substitute

1 cup plus 2 tablespoons bread crumbs

Oil for frying

Lemon wedges

1. Heat the olive oil in a large skillet or Dutch oven over high heat; add the garlic. Cook for 30 seconds, until garlic becomes clear and fragrant; add the spinach, cardamom pods, salt, and pepper to taste. Cook just until spinach is wilted; transfer to a colander to cool.

2. Squeeze all excess water from spinach. Combine with egg substitute and 2 tablespoons of bread crumbs; mix well. Form into 4 pancakes; dredge in remaining bread crumbs. Heat fry oil in a heavy-bottomed skillet, and fry cakes until browned on both sides, and hot in the center. Serve with lemon wedges.

SPINACH-STUFFED VEGETABLES

The little child in all of us loves stuffed things. Maybe it's the sense of something hidden, mysterious. Or maybe it's just the sneaky feeling that we're getting two things instead of just one. But the best reason to treasure this colorful cornucopia is that it's easy.

Serves 4

1 tablespoon olive oil

1 tablespoon whole coriander seeds

3 medium shallots, roughly chopped

¼ teaspoon crushed red pepper flakes (optional)

2 pounds spinach, washed and stemmed

½ teaspoon salt

¼ cup crumbled feta cheese (optional; not vegan)

4 plum tomatoes, tops cut off, insides scooped out

1 medium zucchini, cut into 4 (2") cylinders

1 medium yellow squash, cut into 4 (2") cylinders

White pepper

4 large stuffing mushrooms, stems removed

Lemon wedges

1. Heat the olive oil and coriander seeds in a small pan until very hot but not smoking—the coriander seeds should become fragrant, but not brown. Strain the oil into a large skillet or Dutch oven; discard the seeds. Over a medium heat, cook the shallots and crushed pepper, if using, for 1 minute—they should sizzle but not brown. Add the spinach all at once; season with salt and cook, stirring, just until spinach is wilted. Transfer to a colander to cool.

2. Chop the spinach roughly on a cutting board. Add the feta cheese, if using. Trim the bottoms of the tomatoes just enough to help them stand straight. Using a small spoon or melon-baller, scoop enough of the seeded center from the zucchini and yellow squash to form a teaspoon-size pocket. Season all the vegetables liberally with salt and white pepper, including the mushrooms. Spoon the spinach mixture into them, mounding slightly on top. Any extra spinach may be used to line the plates when serving.

3. Arrange the vegetables in a steamer basket. Steam over rapidly boiling water just until the zucchini becomes tender, about 6 minutes. Serve hot or at room temperature, along with remaining spinach filling and lemon wedges.

SPINACH AND FETA PIE

Every June on Manhattan's Ninth Avenue, there's an international food festival. The owners of a Greek bakery near 46th Street set up a favorite booth, which features spinach and feta pie to die for.

Serves 8

1 bunch fresh spinach (about 4 cups)
3 tablespoons olive oil
1 yellow onion, chopped
1 cup grated Swiss cheese
2 eggs
1¼ cups light cream
½ teaspoon salt
¼ teaspoon freshly ground black pepper
Pinch of nutmeg
¼ cup grated Parmesan cheese
1 (10") deep-dish pie crust, prebaked 5 minutes at 375°F
6 ounces feta cheese, crumbled
2 medium tomatoes, sliced (optional)

1. Heat oven to 350°F. Wash and stem the spinach; steam until wilted. Squeeze out excess water and chop. Heat the olive oil in a small skillet and cook the onion until golden, about 7 minutes; toss with the spinach. Stir in the Swiss cheese.

2. Combine the eggs, cream, salt, pepper, nutmeg, and Parmesan cheese in a blender. Blend 1 minute. Spread the spinach mixture into the crust. Top with feta cheese and decorate with tomatoes if desired. Pour on the egg mixture, pressing through with your fingers to make sure it soaks through to the crust. Bake 45 minutes, until a knife inserted in the pie comes out clean. Serve hot or room temperature.

GRILLED RADICCHIO

Though it's usually thought of as a salad leaf, radicchio, a bittersweet, purplish-red head lettuce, mellows and becomes juicy when it's lightly dressed and cooked on a grill or in a grill pan. Select tight round heads that are heavy for their size, without wilted leaves or blemishes.

Serves 4

4 heads radicchio

1 tablespoon extra-virgin olive oil

1 lemon, halved

Salt and pepper to taste

Lemon wedges to garnish

1. Quarter the radicchio heads through the root end. In a mixing bowl, drizzle the olive oil over the pieces, squeeze on the lemon juice, and season with salt and pepper to taste; toss to coat.

2. Heat a grill or stovetop grill pan to medium heat. Lay the radicchio, cut-side down, across the grill ribs. Cook until wilting is visible from the sides, only about 2 minutes. Turn to the other cut side and cook for 1 or 2 minutes more, pulling it from the grill before it goes completely limp. Serve with extra lemon wedges on the side.

KALE WITH GARLIC AND THYME

Antioxidant-rich dark leafy greens like kale are nutritional powerhouses loaded with calcium, beta-carotene, and vitamin C. They're also high in fiber and phytochemicals. One could say they're the liver of the vegetable world!

Serves 4

2 pounds kale, stems and ribs removed

1 tablespoon olive oil

1 medium red onion, chopped

1 tablespoon chopped garlic

Pinch of crushed red pepper

2 teaspoons chopped fresh thyme leaves or ½ teaspoon dried

¼ cup dry sherry or white wine

Salt and fresh ground black pepper

Grated Parmesan cheese (optional; not vegan)

1. Bring a large pot of well-salted water to a rolling boil. Add the kale and cook for 10 minutes, until it has lost its waxy coating and the leaves are tender. Transfer to a colander to drain, reserving about ½ cup of the cooking liquid. Roughly chop the kale.

2. Heat the oil in a large skillet or Dutch oven. Add the onion, garlic, red pepper, and thyme. Cook over medium heat until the onion is soft and starting to brown around the edges. Splash in the sherry; cook for 5 minutes until all alcohol has evaporated. Add back the kale; cook 10 minutes more. Season with salt and pepper. Serve sprinkled with grated Parmesan cheese if desired.

PC KALE WITH RED PEPPER FLAKES AND CUMIN

Kale can be enjoyed while still tough and chewy, or completely softened. Adjust cooking times to reach the consistency you enjoy.

Serves 4

2 cups water

½ teaspoon salt, plus more to taste

8 cups kale, washed, drained, and chopped

1 tablespoon olive oil

1 clove garlic, minced

1 teaspoon dried red pepper flakes

½ cup Pressure Cooker Vegetable Stock (see Chapter 5)

½ teaspoon cumin

1. Bring water to a boil in the pressure cooker. Stir in ½ teaspoon salt. Blanch kale for 1 minute, drain, and set aside.

2. Add the olive oil to the pressure cooker over medium heat. Add the garlic and red pepper flakes; cook for 30 seconds. Add the stock, cumin, and kale, then stir.

3. Lock the lid into place and bring to high pressure; maintain pressure for 6 minutes. Remove from heat and allow pressure to release naturally. Serve.

SZECHUAN STIR-FRIED CABBAGE WITH HOT PEPPERS

Chinese cabbage dishes are so delectable that they can make you forget about other things.

Serves 4–6

- ¼ cup plus 2 tablespoons peanut or other neutral oil
- 8 dried red chili peppers, quartered and seeded
- 1 (1") piece fresh ginger, peeled and finely chopped
- 1 medium head cabbage (preferably Chinese cabbage, but any variety is okay), washed and chopped into 2" pieces
- ½ teaspoon cornstarch
- 1 tablespoon soy sauce
- 1 teaspoon dry sherry or Chinese cooking wine
- 1 teaspoon sugar
- 1 teaspoon rice wine vinegar
- 1 teaspoon Asian sesame oil

1. Heat ¼ cup of the oil in a wok or skillet over high heat. Stir in the peppers and fry, stirring, for 1 minute, until the peppers darken in color. Transfer the peppers and oil to a bowl and set aside.

2. Pour remaining 2 tablespoons of oil into the wok; add the ginger and cook for a few seconds until fragrant. Add the cabbage all at once. Fry, stirring, for 1 minute. Combine the cornstarch, soy sauce, and sherry or cooking wine together in a small bowl. Add to the wok. Stir until the cornstarch cooks and forms a thick sauce; add the sugar and vinegar. Sprinkle in the sesame oil and pour in the red peppers and their oil. Stir to combine well. Transfer to a serving bowl.

GARLICKY BROCCOLI RAAB

The key to the toasty flavor of this dish is to brown the garlic to a golden color before adding the blanched raabs. Their moisture stops the garlic from cooking, preserving its browned, but not burned, flavor.

Serves 4

- 1 pound broccoli raab florets, bottoms trimmed
- 2 tablespoons good quality olive oil
- 2 tablespoons finely chopped garlic
- Pinch of crushed red pepper flakes (optional)
- Salt and freshly ground black pepper
- Lemon wedges

Blanch the florets in rapidly boiling salted water; shock in ice water and drain. Heat the olive oil in a large, heavy-bottomed skillet over medium heat for 1 minute. Add the garlic and red pepper flakes, if using, and cook stirring with a wooden spoon until garlic is golden. Add all of the raab at once; toss to coat. Season well with salt and pepper (make sure to taste as you season, remembering that the raab florets should have been blanched and shocked in salted water!). When the vegetable is hot, serve with lemon wedges on the side.

COLLARD GREENS WITH TOMATOES AND CHEDDAR

The assertive vegetal taste of collards benefits from marriage with equally gutsy tomatoes and Cheddar cheese. White Cheddar from Vermont is my favorite. Try this with a grain pilaf, such as soaked bulgur wheat, for a chewy textural contrast.

Serves 4

- 2 pounds collard greens, stems and ribs removed
- 2 tablespoons olive oil
- 1 tablespoon finely chopped garlic (about 2 cloves)
- 4 ripe red or yellow tomatoes (or a combination)
- 1 teaspoon salt
- 1 teaspoon oregano
- 4 ounces Cheddar cheese, shredded

Bring a large pot of salted water to a rolling boil. Cook the greens until tender, about 10 minutes; drain and roughly chop. Heat the oil in a large, heavy-bottomed skillet over medium-high heat. Add the garlic; allow it to sizzle for 30 seconds before adding the collards, tomatoes, salt, and oregano. Cook for 4 minutes, just until the tomatoes are hot. Serve topped with the shredded cheese.

PC SOUTHERN-STYLE COLLARDS

Collard greens are a southern staple typically flavored with animal fat, but a tasty vegetarian version can be made by adding liquid smoke and soy sauce to the broth.

Serves 4–6

1 pound collard greens

1 tablespoon olive oil

½ onion, diced

1 garlic clove, minced

1 chipotle chili pepper

4 cups Pressure Cooker Vegetable Stock (see Chapter 5)

1 teaspoon liquid smoke

1 tablespoon soy sauce

1 teaspoon white vinegar

Salt and pepper, to taste

1. To prepare the greens, cut away the tough stalks and stems and discard any leaves that are bruised or yellow. Wash the collards 2–3 times thoroughly to remove the grit, chop into large pieces, and set aside.

2. Bring the pressure cooker to medium heat. Add the olive oil, onion, garlic, and chipotle pepper. Cook until the onion begins to soften, about 5 minutes. Add all remaining ingredients, except salt and pepper, and the chopped collards; stir well.

3. Lock the lid into place and bring to high pressure; maintain pressure for 10 minutes. Remove from heat and allow pressure to release naturally.

4. Remove the chipotle before serving. Season with salt and pepper, to taste.

PC SOY-GLAZED BOK CHOY

Any type of bok choy—such as Chinese cabbage or baby bok choy—works well in this recipe.

Serves 4

1 pound bok choy

½ cup water, plus 2 teaspoons warm water

¼ cup soy sauce

1 teaspoon rice wine vinegar

1 teaspoon peanut oil

1 teaspoon fresh ginger, minced

1 teaspoon cornstarch

1. Trim the ends off the bok choy and slice in half lengthwise. Add to the steamer basket, then pour in ½ cup water.

2. Lock on the lid. Bring to high pressure; maintain pressure for 1 minute. Remove the pan from the heat, quick-release the pressure, and remove the lid. Remove the steamer basket and drain water.

3. Add the soy sauce, rice wine vinegar, peanut oil, and ginger to the pressure cooker and bring to medium heat. Combine the cornstarch with remaining 2 teaspoons of water, then slowly add to the pressure cooker, stirring constantly. Add the bok choy and stir until it's completely coated.

4. Lock on the lid. Bring to high pressure; maintain pressure for 1 minute. Remove the pan from the heat, quick-release the pressure, and remove the lid.

SC BABY BOK CHOY

Bok choy is also known as Chinese cabbage. Baby bok choy is simply a smaller, more tender version of mature bok choy.

Serves 6

2 tablespoons soy sauce
2 tablespoons apple cider vinegar
2 tablespoons sesame oil
½ teaspoon garlic powder
1 teaspoon crushed red pepper flakes
3 heads baby bok choy, halved lengthwise

1. In a small bowl, whisk together all ingredients except for the bok choy.
2. Place the bok choy in a 4-quart slow cooker; pour the soy sauce mixture over the bok choy. Cover and cook on low heat for 3 hours.

SC HOMEMADE SAUERKRAUT

This isn't your traditional sauerkraut recipe, which requires fermentation, but is a delicious spin on the classic.

Serves 12

1 head cabbage, finely shredded

1 tablespoon kosher salt

Water, as needed

1 teaspoon sugar

1 sprig dill

1. Place the shredded cabbage in a 4- or 6-quart slow cooker and toss with the salt until juice from the cabbage begins to appear. Pack the cabbage down into the liquid, then fill with enough water to just cover the cabbage.

2. Add the sugar and dill and cook over low heat for 8–10 hours. Remove the dill before serving.

Veggie Dogs
There are many brands of vegetarian and vegan hot dogs for sale in grocery stores around the country, and you can even find them at Walmart. Use homemade sauerkraut as a topping for your dog.

CHAPTER 9
TOMATOES AND OTHER VEGETABLES

RECIPE LIST

TOMATO AND CHEESE TART **492**

CUMIN-ROASTED BUTTERNUT SQUASH **493**

MUSHROOM-STUFFED TOMATOES **494**

HERB-STUFFED TOMATOES **495**

STEWED TOMATOES **495**

HERBED RED AND YELLOW TOMATOES ON HONEY-NUT BREAD **496**

FRIED GREEN TOMATOES WITH RÉMOULADE SAUCE **497**

TOMATO CONFIT WITH FINE HERBS **498**

RED AND YELLOW PLUM TOMATO CHUTNEY **499**

CHILAQUILES (TORTILLA STEW) **500**

AVOCADO SASHIMI WITH MISO DRESSING **501**

RATATOUILLE **502**

QUICK TOMATO AND OREGANO SAUTÉ **503**

ZUCCHINI "LASAGNA" **504**

EGGPLANT ROLATINE **505**

SIMPLE SALSA **506**

STIR-FRIED SNOW PEAS WITH CILANTRO **506**

EGGPLANT PARMIGIANO **507**

PRESSURE COOKER RATATOUILLE **508**

EGGPLANT CAPONATA **509**

MASHED EGGPLANT AND TOMATO SALAD **510**

STEAMED ASPARAGUS WITH HOLLANDAISE SAUCE **511**

PRESSURE COOKER ASPARAGUS WITH VEGAN HOLLANDAISE SAUCE **512**

EGGPLANT AND TOMATO SAUTÉ **513**

MEATLESS MOUSSAKA **514**

SPICED "BAKED" EGGPLANT **515**

STUFFED EGGPLANT **516**

ZUCCHINI RAGOUT **517**

ASPARAGUS-SHALLOT SAUTÉ **518**

ROASTED VEGETABLES **519**

CHINESE WRINKLED STRING BEANS **520**

GREEN BEANS AND PINE NUT SAUTÉ **521**

FRESH GREEN BEANS WITH TOASTED SESAME **522**

ROSEMARY-THYME GREEN BEANS **522**

FENNEL COOKED IN WHITE WINE **523**

BUTTERNUT SQUASH **524**

STEWED SQUASH **525**

SPAGHETTI SQUASH **525**

WINTER VEGETABLE MEDLEY **526**

CORN ON THE COB **527**

CILANTRO-LIME CORN ON THE COB **528**

CREAMED CORN **529**

CORN AND PEPPER PUDDING **530**

PRESSURE COOKER CREAMED CORN **531**

OKRA WITH CORN AND TOMATO **532**

SUCCOTASH **533**

CORN MAQUE CHOUX **534**

CHEESY POBLANO PEPPERS **535**

ROASTED RED BELL PEPPER PURÉE **536**

BRIE TIMBALES WITH ROASTED RED PEPPER SAUCE **537**

TOMATO AND CHEESE TART

Store-bought puff pastry makes this an easy, attractive brunch item. Always look for puff made with real butter rather than shortening—guests can tell.

Serves 4–6

8 ounces store-bought (or homemade) puff pastry, thawed

1 tablespoon olive oil

4 leeks, sliced and thoroughly washed

3 sprigs fresh thyme leaves, picked (about 2 teaspoons), or a scant teaspoon dried

Kosher salt and freshly ground black pepper

6 ounces raclette or other semisoft cheese, such as Havarti or Gouda, sliced

2–3 tomatoes, thinly sliced

Pinch of sugar

1. Heat oven to 375°F. Roll the pastry out to fit a 14" × 4" oblong rectangular tart pan (you can also use a 10" circular tart pan—adjust dough dimensions accordingly); prick the rolled dough with the tines of a fork in several places. Arrange the dough in the pan and refrigerate until ready to use.

2. Heat the olive oil in a medium skillet over moderate heat; sauté the leeks and thyme until the leeks are soft and translucent, about 5 minutes; season with salt and pepper, remove from heat and cool to room temperature. Spoon the leeks into the tart shell; cover with the cheese. Arrange the tomatoes in rows or concentric circles (depending on what type of pan you're using), and sprinkle them with a little sugar. Bake 40–45 minutes, until cheese begins to brown and the crust is golden.

CUMIN-ROASTED BUTTERNUT SQUASH

Choose butternuts with a large cylindrical barrel and small bulbous bottom, so you yield the most squash and fewest seeds. Since the squash is peeled for this dish, the longer barrel means easier preparation.

Serves 8

1 medium butternut squash (2–3 pounds)

2 tablespoons ground cumin

2 tablespoons olive oil

Salt and coarsely ground black pepper

1 tablespoon roughly chopped Italian (flat-leaf) parsley

1. Cut the butternut in two, crosswise, just above the bulbous bottom. Place the cut side of the cylindrical barrel down on a cutting board, and peel it with a knife or potato peeler, removing all rind. Repeat with the bottom part, then cut bottom in half and remove seeds.

2. Dice squash into 1" chunks. In a large mixing bowl, toss squash with cumin, oil, salt, and pepper.

3. Spread into a single layer on a doubled baking sheet, and roast in a 375-degree oven for 40 minutes, turning after 25 minutes, until browned and tender. Serve sprinkled with chopped parsley.

MUSHROOM-STUFFED TOMATOES

Use any ripe tomato you prefer for this dish. Late in the season, Roma plum tomatoes are usually the best choice, since they keep a long time even when ripe. If using a processor to chop the mushrooms, "pulse" them in small batches, stopping before they clump.

Serves 6 as an appetizer or side dish, or up to 12 as a tasty garnish

- 4 shallots, chopped fine
- 2 tablespoons olive oil, divided
- 1 pound white mushrooms, washed and chopped fine
- 1 teaspoon salt plus 2 pinches
- Splash of white wine (about ¼ cup)
- ¼ cup finely chopped parsley
- Freshly ground black pepper
- 6 large ripe plum tomatoes, halved crosswise, bottoms trimmed flat
- 3 tablespoons bread crumbs

1. Sauté chopped shallots with 1 tablespoon olive oil in a large skillet over medium heat. Add chopped mushrooms (if some don't fit, you can add them later, when the rest have wilted down) and 1 teaspoon salt, and raise heat to high. Cook, stirring occasionally, until mushrooms have given up their water, and most of it has evaporated.

2. Add the white wine and cook until it has mostly evaporated. Stir in chopped parsley, remove from heat, and season with freshly ground black pepper.

3. Scoop the innards from the tomatoes, and season the tomato cups with 2 pinches salt. Fill each tomato with mushroom filling so that it mounds slightly, topping each with a sprinkle of bread crumbs. Line into a baking dish and drizzle with remaining olive oil. Bake 25 minutes, until soft, at 350°F.

SC HERB-STUFFED TOMATOES

Serve these Italian-influenced stuffed tomatoes with a simple salad for an easy, light meal.

Serves 4

4 large tomatoes

1 cup cooked quinoa

1 stalk celery, minced

1 tablespoon fresh garlic, minced

2 tablespoons fresh oregano, minced

2 tablespoons fresh Italian parsley, minced

1 teaspoon dried chervil

1 teaspoon fennel seeds

¾ cup water

1. Cut out the core of each tomato and discard. Scoop out the seeds, leaving the walls of the tomato intact.
2. In a small bowl, stir together the quinoa, celery, garlic, and spices. Divide evenly among the 4 tomatoes.
3. Place the filled tomatoes in a single layer in an oval 4-quart slow cooker. Pour the water into the bottom of the slow cooker. Cook on low for 4 hours.

SC STEWED TOMATOES

For an Italian variation, add basil and Italian parsley.

Serves 6

1 (28-ounce) can whole tomatoes in purée, diced

1 tablespoon minced onion

1 stalk celery, diced

½ teaspoon oregano

½ teaspoon thyme

Place all ingredients into a 2-quart slow cooker. Stir. Cook on low up to 8 hours.

HERBED RED AND YELLOW TOMATOES ON HONEY-NUT BREAD

Golden or yellow tomatoes have a sweet, mellow flavor that, at its best, is grassy like fresh garden tomatoes, but without excessive tartness. The combination of two colors of tomatoes makes this a very festive summer sandwich.

Serves 4

¼ cup extra-virgin olive oil

¼ cup balsamic vinegar

1 tablespoon Dijon mustard

½ bunch fresh oregano or marjoram, roughly chopped

½ bunch Italian parsley, roughly chopped

1 small bunch chives, chopped

2 ripe beefsteak or other sweet variety red tomatoes, sliced ½" thick

2 yellow acid-free tomatoes, sliced ½" thick

8 slices Branola or other type sweet-dough bread containing whole grains, ½" thick

Coarse salt and black pepper to taste

1. Whisk together oil, vinegar, and mustard in a small steel bowl. Fold in chopped herbs.

2. Lay tomato slices in a single layer into a glass (nonreactive) dish and pour most of the dressing over them, reserving about 2 tablespoons. Allow to marinate at room temperature for about 10 minutes.

3. Toast the whole grain bread and drizzle with remaining dressing. Shingle tomatoes in alternating colors. Season with coarse salt and freshly ground black pepper.

FRIED GREEN TOMATOES WITH RÉMOULADE SAUCE

These classic, tart, flavorful American favorites go particularly well with light summer salads.

Serves 4 as an appetizer or side dish

1 cup mayonnaise (preferably homemade)

1 hard-boiled egg, finely chopped

1 tablespoon capers, chopped

1 tablespoon chopped cornichons or dill pickle

1 teaspoon chopped parsley

Dash of hot pepper sauce, or cayenne

3 large green tomatoes, sliced ½" thick (should total 12–14 slices)

Flour for dredging

6 beaten eggs, diluted with ½ cup milk

4 cups plain or seasoned bread crumbs, preferably homemade

3 cups light oil, such as canola or peanut, for frying

Salt, to taste

1. Make the rémoulade sauce: Combine mayonnaise with chopped egg, capers, pickle, parsley, and hot sauce or cayenne. Taste for seasoning and refrigerate.

2. Dredge each tomato slice in flour, then eggs, then bread crumbs, pressing the bread crumbs to ensure adherence. Fry in small batches over low-medium heat (325°F oil temperature), until they feel tender when tested with a fork. Season with salt to taste and serve immediately with rémoulade sauce.

TOMATO CONFIT WITH FINE HERBS

The term "confit" refers to items cooked in their own liquid, which these tomatoes do inside their skins. Oven roasting intensifies the sweetness of tomatoes by cooking out some of their water. These slow-cooked summer jewels benefit from the essence released by herbs steaming in the tomatoes' juices. They keep, refrigerated, for four days.

Serves 5 as a side dish, or up to 10 as a tasty garnish

5 large ripe but firm beefsteak tomatoes, cored, halved crosswise, seeded

12 big sprigs assorted fresh herbs like thyme, oregano, rosemary, parsley, etc.

3 tablespoons olive oil

1 teaspoon salt

1. Preheat oven to 275°F. Toss the tomatoes gently with the herbs, olive oil, and salt, then arrange cut-side down in a baking dish, so that the herbs are under and touching them.

2. Bake 2 hours, until flesh is very soft to the touch, and skin looks wrinkled.

3. Cool until you can touch them, and carefully remove the skins. Serve warm.

RED AND YELLOW PLUM TOMATO CHUTNEY

This summer salsa accompanies fried tofu very well, and is also a great base for grain salads.

Yields about 3 cups

⅓ cup sugar

Juice of 1 lemon

6 ripe red plum tomatoes, seeded and roughly chopped

6 ripe yellow plum tomatoes, seeded and roughly chopped

¼ cup finely diced red onion

¼ cup fresh cilantro, roughly chopped (optional)

Mix sugar with ½ cup water in a medium saucepan. Cook over high heat until water is evaporated and molten sugar begins to turn golden brown. Pour in lemon juice to stop the sugar from cooking and bring it up from the bottom of the pan. Add the chopped tomatoes and red onion. Simmer for no more than 5 minutes (this is to warm the tomatoes, not cook them). Remove from heat. Allow to cool in a colander, letting the excess water released from the warmed tomatoes drain out. Stir in chopped cilantro.

CHILAQUILES (TORTILLA STEW)

Pronounced "chill-uh-KILL-ehs," these softened tortilla chips are a favorite hearty breakfast item in Mexico. They're perfect for brunch because they only take a few minutes to throw together once the ingredients are assembled.

Serves 2

4 cups tortilla chips (any color)

2 cups vegetable stock

1 cup New Mexico Chili Sauce (see Chapter 2) or spicy tomato sauce

4 large eggs (optional)

2 tablespoons sour cream or Tofu Sour Cream (see Chapter 2)

Chopped cilantro

Place the chips in a large skillet over a high flame. Add 1 cup of vegetable stock and the New Mexico Chili Sauce. Bring to a boil, then lower to a simmer, adding more stock as needed to keep the mixture soupy. Cook until the tortillas are well softened, but not mushy. If desired, fry the eggs in a little butter. Serve the chilaquiles on 2 plates, topped with fried eggs, a dollop of sour cream, and a sprinkling of chopped cilantro.

AVOCADO SASHIMI WITH MISO DRESSING

The wasabi and pickled ginger give this recipe a bit of a kick!

Serves 2

1 ripe Hass avocado, halved, seeded, and peeled
1 lemon
1 teaspoon white or yellow miso
1 teaspoon grated fresh ginger
1 teaspoon light soy sauce
1 teaspoon sugar
1 teaspoon sesame oil
Wasabi paste for garnish
Pickled ginger for garnish

1. Place the avocado halves cut-side down on a board; score them at ⅛" intervals, leaving the stem end connected to hold them together. Squeeze the lemon over the scored avocados to prevent browning. Fan the avocados onto 2 small plates.

2. Whisk together the miso, ginger, soy sauce, sugar, and sesame oil until the sugar is dissolved. Spoon some of the dressing over the avocadoes. Serve garnished with wasabi and pickled ginger.

RATATOUILLE

A classic Provençal dish, this is a perfect way to make the most of summer's harvest.

Serves 6

2 tablespoons olive oil

1 large onion, diced

2 medium zucchini, diced

2 medium yellow squash, diced

1 small eggplant, diced

1 bell pepper, diced

1 tablespoon flour

3 tomatoes, seeded, and cut into 6 pieces

2 teaspoons dried Herbes de Provence (or a combination of oregano, thyme, rosemary, marjoram, savory and/or lavender)

1 teaspoon salt

Freshly ground black pepper

Fresh basil leaves, chopped (optional)

1. Heat the olive oil in a heavy-bottomed Dutch oven until hot, but not smoky. Add onion; cook until translucent, about 5 minutes. Combine the zucchini, yellow squash, eggplant, and bell pepper in a large paper bag; dust with flour, fold bag closed, and shake to coat. Add floured vegetables to the pot, along with the tomatoes, herbs, salt, and pepper.

2. Reduce heat to a simmer, cover, and cook gently for 1 hour, until all vegetables are tender. Serve hot or at room temperature. Garnish with freshly chopped basil, if desired.

QUICK TOMATO AND OREGANO SAUTÉ

This versatile pan stew accompanies steamed, baked, or sautéed mushrooms as easily as it does grilled tempeh or fried tofu. It also works beautifully as a simple pasta sauce.

Serves 4

1 tablespoon olive oil

2 cloves garlic, finely minced

2 cups chopped tomatoes (any variety)

Scant ½ teaspoon salt

Ground black pepper

2 tablespoons chopped fresh oregano, or ½ teaspoon dried

1. Heat olive oil in 10" skillet over medium flame. Sprinkle in chopped garlic, and stir with a wooden spoon for only a moment, until the garlic whitens, and releases its aroma. Do not allow it to brown.

2. Add chopped tomato, salt, and, if you are using dried oregano, add that now. Simmer 10 minutes, until most water has evaporated, stirring occasionally.

3. Season with fresh ground black pepper, and if you are using fresh oregano, stir it in and simmer 1 minute more.

ZUCCHINI "LASAGNA"

Layered and baked like the beloved Italian-American pasta dish, this wheat-free casserole is best made a day in advance and cut while cold, then warmed before serving. If you don't have a mandoline or slicing machine, the deli counter person is usually glad to slice your zucchini at the store.

Serves 8

- 3 cups tomato sauce
- 4 large zucchini, sliced very thin on a mandoline or slicing machine, about ⅛" thick
- Kosher salt and freshly ground black pepper
- 1 pound ricotta cheese
- 1 pound provolone, fontina, mozzarella, or cheese of your choice, shredded
- 2 cups sautéed onions and mushrooms, or 2 cups frozen mixed vegetables, thawed

1. Heat oven to 350°F. Spread 1 cup sauce onto the bottom of a 9" × 13" baking dish. Arrange a layer of zucchini slices into the pan, overlapping the pieces by a third. Season with salt and black pepper.

2. Dot the zucchini layer with half of the ricotta, distributing teaspoonfuls evenly around the casserole. Layer on ⅓ of the shredded cheese, and half of the vegetables.

3. Arrange another layer of zucchini, and repeat fillings, using remaining ricotta, vegetables, and another third of the shredded cheese. Add a final layer of zucchini on top, and spread on 2 more cups of tomato sauce.

4. Sprinkle top with remaining cheese; bake 1 hour until casserole is bubbly and cheese is lightly browned. Cool to room temperature, and then refrigerate until cold. Cut into portions, and reheat in the oven or microwave until hot.

EGGPLANT ROLATINE

These spinach-and-ricotta-filled roulades make a very beautiful dinner presentation served atop a heap of tomato-sauced linguine, garnished with a sprig of fresh basil. The finished rolatine keep well for several days, and are delicious at room temperature or as sandwich fillings.

Serves 8

1 large eggplant, sliced lengthwise into even ⅛" slices (as thick as the cover of a hardcover book)

Flour for dredging

Egg wash of about 6 beaten eggs, mixed with ½ cup water

4 cups bread crumbs

Oil for frying

1 pound ricotta cheese

8 ounces shredded mozzarella cheese

½ cup grated Parmesan (good quality, like Parmigiano-Reggiano or Grana Padano)

Salt and pepper

1½ pounds fresh spinach, washed and cooked, or 1 pound frozen spinach, thawed

4 cups tomato sauce

Fresh basil

1. Bread and fry the eggplant: Dip a slice of eggplant in the flour to coat both sides; shake off excess flour, submerge in egg wash, shake off excess, and coat in bread crumbs, pressing to make sure they adhere well. Place on a holding tray and repeat with remaining slices. Heat oil to about 350°F (a piece of vegetable should sizzle visibly when dropped into the oil). Fry the breaded eggplant slices, dripping any excess oil off before stacking them between layers of paper towels.

2. Fill and roll: Heat oven to 350°F. Combine the 3 cheeses in a mixing bowl and season lightly with salt and pepper. Place 1 teaspoon of cooked spinach and a generous teaspoon of cheese mixture at the wide end of a fried eggplant slice. Roll away from yourself, jelly-roll style, and place into a baking dish, with the seam on the bottom. Repeat with remaining eggplant and fillings, lining the finished roulades close together in the baking dish. Bake until cheeses are visibly hot, and the edges begin to brown lightly. Serve on a pool of tomato sauce, garnished with basil leaves. One piece per appetizer portion, 2 per main course.

SIMPLE SALSA

This simple condiment pairs magnificently with burritos, tacos, empanadas, tortilla chips, and all kinds of other Mexican savories.

Yields 1 cup

2 large tomatoes

1 small onion, finely diced

1 or 2 jalapeño peppers, finely chopped

½ teaspoon fresh-squeezed lime juice

Salt and freshly ground black pepper

½ teaspoon chipotle purée (optional)

Quarter the tomatoes. Cut out the inside viscera; reserve. Cut the remaining petals into a fine dice. Purée the insides in a food processor until smooth. Toss together with the tomato dice, the diced onion, jalapeños, lime juice, salt, pepper, and chipotle if desired. Keeps in the refrigerator for 2 days, but is best used the day it's made.

STIR-FRIED SNOW PEAS WITH CILANTRO

This is a quick and easy dish that's perfect to serve your family on a weeknight.

Serves 4

2 tablespoons peanut or other light oil

1 cup thinly sliced scallions

1 cup snow peas

½ cup strong vegetable stock

2 teaspoons cornstarch

½ cup finely chopped cilantro leaves (a.k.a. "Chinese parsley" or "coriander leaf")

Dash of soy sauce

Pinch of sugar

1. Heat oil in a large skillet until very hot, almost smoking. Add scallions and snow peas, tossing or stirring quickly to coat them with oil. Add stock, cover the skillet, and cook for 2 minutes. Meanwhile, mix the cornstarch with 2 tablespoons of cold water and the cilantro.

2. Stir the cornstarch mixture quickly into the peas, stirring constantly until the sauce thickens; season with soy sauce and sugar. Serve immediately. The entire cooking time for the peas should not exceed 5 minutes.

EGGPLANT PARMIGIANO

Note that to make these basic ingredients sing, the eggplant needs to be precooked.

Serves 8

Oil for frying

1 medium eggplant (about 1 pound), sliced thin

1 cup flour

3 eggs, beaten, mixed with ½ cup water or milk

3 cups bread crumbs

Four cups Basic Fresh Tomato Sauce (see Chapter 2) or 1 (28-ounce) jar store-bought sauce

1 pound part-skim mozzarella cheese, shredded

Chopped Italian parsley or whole fresh basil leaves

1. Heat the oil in a heavy skillet or fryer (about ½" deep) until a piece of vegetable sizzles when added. Dip a piece of eggplant in the flour and shake off excess; dip it in the egg mixture and shake off excess; then press it into the bread crumbs. Repeat with remaining slices of eggplant. Fry the slices until golden, about 3 minutes each; drain on a rack or on paper towels.

2. Heat oven to 350°F. Line the slices into a baking dish. Top each with a teaspoon of tomato sauce, and a small mound of shredded cheese. Bake until cheese is melted, browning and bubbly, about 15 minutes. Serve with additional tomato sauce on the side, garnished with chopped parsley or leaves of fresh basil.

PRESSURE COOKER RATATOUILLE

Ratatouille is sometimes served over potatoes. This version adds the potatoes to the dish. You can serve this ratatouille over whole grain pasta or topped with toasted garlic croutons.

Serves 4

2 tablespoons extra-virgin olive oil

2 zucchini, sliced

1 Japanese eggplant, peeled and sliced

1 small onion, thinly sliced

1 green bell pepper, diced

2 medium potatoes, peeled and diced

8 ounces fresh mushrooms, sliced

1 (28-ounce) can diced tomatoes

3 tablespoons tomato paste

3 tablespoons water

2 garlic cloves, minced

1 teaspoon oregano

1 teaspoon basil

⅛ teaspoon dried red pepper flakes

Salt and fresh black pepper, to taste

Parmigiano-Reggiano cheese, grated, or vegan mozzarella, such as Daiya Mozzarella Style Shreds

1. Coat the bottom and sides of the pressure cooker with oil. Add the remaining ingredients except cheese in layers in the order given. Lock the lid into place and bring to low pressure; maintain pressure for 6 minutes.

2. Remove from heat and quick-release the pressure. Remove the lid, stir, and taste for seasoning, adjusting if necessary. Serve topped with the grated cheese.

PC EGGPLANT CAPONATA

This versatile dish can be served hot, at room temperature, or cold.

Serves 8

¼ cup extra-virgin olive oil

¼ cup white wine

2 tablespoons red wine vinegar

1 teaspoon ground cinnamon

1 large eggplant, peeled and diced

1 medium onion, diced

1 medium green bell pepper, diced

1 medium red bell pepper, diced

2 cloves garlic, minced

1 (14½-ounce) can diced tomatoes

3 stalks celery, diced

½ cup oil-cured olives, pitted and chopped

½ cup golden raisins

2 tablespoons capers, rinsed and drained

Salt and freshly ground black pepper, to taste

1. Add all ingredients except salt and pepper to the pressure cooker. Stir well to mix. Lock the lid into place and bring to low pressure; maintain pressure for 8 minutes.

2. Remove from heat and quick-release the pressure. Remove the lid and stir the contents of the pressure cooker. Taste for seasoning and add salt and pepper, to taste.

Serving Suggestions

Caponata is often served as a salad but it has other uses as well. Try it as a sandwich spread on Italian bread, a dipping sauce for toasted baguette rounds, or relish.

PC MASHED EGGPLANT AND TOMATO SALAD

Serve this dish as a salad or as a dip with pita bread. It can be enjoyed hot or cold.

Serves 4–6

1 large eggplant, peeled and diced
½ cup water
3 tablespoons olive oil
3 cloves garlic, minced
2 cups tomatoes, chopped
2 teaspoons lemon juice
1 teaspoon paprika
1 teaspoon salt
2 tablespoons parsley

1. Add the eggplant and water to the pressure cooker. Lock on the lid. Bring to high pressure; maintain pressure for 4 minutes. Remove the pan from the heat, quick-release the pressure, and remove the lid. Drain and set aside.

2. Add the olive oil to the pressure cooker over medium heat. Add the garlic and sauté for 30 seconds. Add the cooked eggplant, tomatoes, lemon juice, paprika, and salt.

3. Lock on the lid. Bring to high pressure; maintain pressure for 2 minutes. Remove the pan from the heat, quick-release the pressure, and remove the lid.

4. Stir in the parsley, then serve.

Preparing Eggplant
Many cooks swear by salting eggplant before cooking with it to remove the bitter flavor. However, it's not necessary, and is up to the taste preferences of the cook.

STEAMED ASPARAGUS WITH HOLLANDAISE SAUCE

Hollandaise is what the French call a "mother sauce," meaning that it can be transformed into other sauces by adding just a few ingredients (tarragon, pepper, and shallots—béarnaise; mustard—Dijonnaise; orange concentrate—Maltaise, etc.).

Serves 6

- 3 egg yolks
- Juice of 1 lemon (about ¼ cup), divided
- 1 tablespoon plus a few drops of cold water
- 8 ounces (2 sticks) melted butter
- Pinch of cayenne
- ¼ teaspoon salt
- 1 bunch asparagus, woody bottoms trimmed off

1. In a large, steel mixing bowl over a pot of simmering water, or in a double boiler over a very low flame, whisk together the yolks, half of the lemon juice, and 1 tablespoon cold water. Whisk vigorously until the yolks attain a lemon-yellow color and become thick (about the consistency of creamy salad dressing). Be careful not to let the eggs cook into lumps—keep whisking all the time, and remove the bowl from the heat if it starts getting too hot. Once yolks are ready, set the bowl they are in onto a damp towel on a firm surface. Whisk in a few drops of cold water, then a few drops of the melted butter. Gradually whip in the melted butter in small increments, making sure that each addition is thoroughly incorporated before adding any more. Season with cayenne, salt, and remaining lemon juice.

2. Steam the asparagus for 5 minutes, until tender but still brightly colored. Divide onto plates; spoon hollandaise over the middle of the stalks.

PRESSURE COOKER ASPARAGUS WITH VEGAN HOLLANDAISE SAUCE

By making this recipe with tofu instead of eggs, you'll eliminate the cholesterol typically found in hollandaise sauce.

Serves 4

1½ pounds fresh asparagus
½ cup water
½ cup silken tofu
1 tablespoon lemon juice
1 teaspoon Dijon mustard
⅛ teaspoon cayenne pepper
⅛ teaspoon turmeric
1 tablespoon vegetable oil
Salt, to taste

1. Trim the end off each asparagus spear. Lay flat in the pressure cooker and add water. Lock lid into place and bring to high pressure; maintain for 3 minutes. Remove from heat and allow pressure to release naturally for 2 minutes.

2. Add the silken tofu to a food processor and purée until smooth. Add the lemon juice, mustard, cayenne, and turmeric. Blend until well combined. With the food processor still running, slowly add the oil and blend until combined. Season with salt, to taste, to complete the vegan hollandaise.

3. Pour the hollandaise into a small saucepan over low heat and cook until the sauce is warm.

4. Spoon the sauce over the asparagus spears to serve.

EGGPLANT AND TOMATO SAUTÉ

Serve this as an eggplant sauce with pasta or chilled as a summer salad with bulgur wheat pilaf or another grain salad.

Serves 8

1 medium eggplant (about 1 pound), cut lengthwise into 8 wedges

Kosher salt

3 tablespoons olive oil, divided

2 medium onions, sliced thickly (about ½")

¼ teaspoon crushed red pepper flakes

1 tablespoon chopped garlic (about 3 cloves)

2 cups chopped plum tomatoes

¼ cup chopped fresh oregano or parsley

1. Sprinkle the eggplant wedges liberally with kosher salt; set aside for 10–15 minutes, until water visibly pools under the wedges (this extracts some bitter juices, making the eggplant especially mellow for this recipe). Dry the eggplant off with a towel. Heat 2 tablespoons of olive oil in a large, heavy-bottomed skillet until a piece of vegetable sizzles when added. Fry the eggplant wedges until they are lightly browned and bubbling with juice. Transfer to a cutting board and cut into large (2") pieces.

2. Put remaining olive oil in the skillet, and heat 1 minute over medium heat. Add onions, crushed pepper, and garlic; cook, stirring occasionally, until onions are very soft, about 10 minutes. Add tomatoes, and cook just until they begin to break down into a chunky sauce. Add the eggplant and chopped oregano or parsley. Bring to a simmer; remove from heat. Season to taste.

SC MEATLESS MOUSSAKA

If you get your eggplant at the supermarket and suspect that it's been waxed, peel it before dicing it and adding it to the slow cooker.

Serves 8

- ¾ cup dry brown or yellow lentils, rinsed and drained
- 2 large potatoes, peeled and diced
- 1 cup water
- 1 stalk celery, diced fine
- 1 medium sweet onion, peeled and diced
- 3 cloves garlic, minced
- ½ teaspoon salt
- ¼ teaspoon ground cinnamon
- Pinch freshly ground nutmeg
- ¼ teaspoon freshly ground black pepper
- ¼ teaspoon dried basil
- ¼ teaspoon dried oregano
- ¼ teaspoon dried parsley
- 1 medium eggplant, diced
- 12 baby carrots, each cut into 3 pieces
- 1 (14½-ounce) can diced tomatoes
- 1 (8-ounce) package cream cheese or vegan cream cheese, softened

1. Add the lentils, potatoes, water, celery, onion, garlic, salt, cinnamon, nutmeg, pepper, basil, oregano, and parsley to a 4-quart slow cooker. Stir. Top with eggplant and carrots.
2. Cover and cook on low for 6 hours, or until the lentils are cooked through.
3. Stir in undrained tomatoes and add a dollop of cream cheese over lentil mixture. Cover, and cook on low for an additional 30 minutes.

SC SPICED "BAKED" EGGPLANT

Serve this as a main dish over rice or as a side dish as is.

Serves 4

1 pound eggplant, cubed

⅓ cup onion, sliced

½ teaspoon red pepper flakes

½ teaspoon crushed rosemary

¼ cup lemon juice

Place all ingredients in a 1½- to 2-quart slow cooker. Cook on low for 3 hours, or until the eggplant is tender.

Cold Snap

Take care not to put a cold ceramic slow cooker insert directly into the slow cooker. The sudden shift in temperature can cause it to crack. If you want to prepare your ingredients the night before use, refrigerate them in reusable containers, not in the insert.

SC | STUFFED EGGPLANT

This easy vegan dish is a complete meal in itself.

Serves 2

1 (1-pound) eggplant
½ teaspoon olive oil
2 tablespoons red onion, minced
1 clove garlic, minced
⅓ cup cooked rice
1 tablespoon fresh parsley
¼ cup corn kernels
¼ cup diced cremini mushrooms
1 (15-ounce) can diced tomatoes with onions and garlic
Tomato sauce, to taste

1. Preheat oven to 375°F.
2. Slice the eggplant in 2 equal halves, lengthwise. Use an ice cream scoop to take out the seeds. Place on a baking sheet, skin-side down. Bake for 8 minutes. Allow to cool slightly.
3. In a small skillet, heat the oil. Add the onion and garlic and sauté until softened, about 3 minutes.
4. In a medium bowl, stir the onion, garlic, rice, parsley, corn, and mushrooms. Divide evenly between the eggplant halves.
5. Pour the tomatoes onto the bottom of an oval 4- or 6-quart slow cooker. Place the eggplant halves side by side on top of the tomatoes. Cook on low for 3 hours.
6. Remove the eggplants and plate. Drizzle with tomato sauce, to taste.

SC ZUCCHINI RAGOUT

A ragout is either a main-dish stew or a sauce. This one can be served as either.

Serves 6

5 ounces fresh spinach

3 zucchini, diced

½ cup diced red onion

2 stalks celery, diced

2 carrots, diced

1 parsnip, diced

3 tablespoons tomato paste

¼ cup water

1 teaspoon freshly ground black pepper

¼ teaspoon kosher salt

1 tablespoon minced fresh basil

1 tablespoon minced fresh Italian parsley

1 tablespoon minced fresh oregano

Place all ingredients into a 4-quart slow cooker. Stir. Cook on low for 4 hours. Stir before serving.

Saving on Herbs

The cost of herbs can add up quickly, but you can save a little money by shopping at an international farmers' market or buying a blend of spices (an Italian blend would work well in this recipe) instead of buying each individually.

ASPARAGUS-SHALLOT SAUTÉ

Asparagus is loaded with beneficial insoluble fiber, which aids in digestion, sweeping unwanted potentially harmful items through the system before they can do damage.

Serves 6

1 bunch asparagus

Kosher salt

1 tablespoon olive oil (or butter; not vegan)

½ cup finely chopped shallots (about 4 shallots)

Pinch of roughly cracked black pepper

1 tablespoon dry white wine or sherry

Lemon wedges

1. Bring a large pot of water to a rolling boil, and cook the asparagus, shocking them in salted ice water when they are fully cooked but tender. Transfer to a cutting board and cut on a diagonal angle into 2" pieces.

2. Heat the olive oil in a large skillet; add the shallots and black pepper. Cook until translucent, about 3 minutes; add the wine and asparagus; cook until heated through. Season to taste. Serve with lemon wedges on the side.

ROASTED VEGETABLES

As an appetizer, main course, or as a spread with crackers, this mélange of roasted veggies, accented by sweet balsamic vinegar and mellow roasted garlic, is an easy comfort food. Cut everything into 1" cubes. You'll probably need two roasting pans or baking dishes for this recipe.

Serves 8

1 small eggplant (about 1 pound), cubed

1 small butternut squash (about 1½ pounds), peeled and cubed

1 pound red potatoes, cubed

3 large "horse" carrots, cut into 1" pieces, or approximately 1 pound of cello carrots

12 cloves garlic, peeled

2 large white onions, cut into 1" cubes

1 medium zucchini and 1 yellow squash, cubed

10 ounces mushrooms

3 tablespoons olive oil

1 teaspoon kosher salt

½ teaspoon freshly ground black pepper

½ cup mixed chopped herbs, such as rosemary, thyme, oregano, parsley, chives, or less than ¼ cup of dried mixed herbs

¼ cup good quality balsamic vinegar

1. Heat oven to 350°F. In a large bowl, combine eggplant, squash, potatoes, carrots, garlic, onions, zucchini, yellow squash, mushrooms, olive oil, salt, pepper, and mixed herbs; toss to coat.

2. Spread into a single layer onto 1 or 2 roasting pans, jelly-roll pans, or baking dishes. Cook 1–1½ hours, until vegetables are very tender and browned lightly. Sprinkle with balsamic vinegar, and set out to cool.

CHINESE WRINKLED STRING BEANS

This dish is delicious when seasoned with salt and sesame oil.

Serves 4

Oil for deep-frying

1 pound fresh green beans, stem ends snipped off

2 tablespoons peanut oil

½ cup chopped scallions

1 (1") piece fresh ginger, peeled and finely chopped

1 tablespoon chopped garlic

1 teaspoon sugar

1 teaspoon white vinegar

Salt

Asian sesame oil

1. Heat 2" of oil in a wok or deep skillet to 350°F (a piece of vegetable should sizzle vigorously, but the oil should not smoke). Carefully fry the green beans in 4 small batches. They will shrivel as they cook—they take about 5 minutes per batch. Leave time in between batches to let the oil come back up to temperature.

2. In a separate skillet, heat the peanut oil. Add the scallions, ginger, garlic, sugar, and vinegar. Cook 1 minute, until the garlic turns white. Add the green beans; toss to coat. Season with salt and Asian sesame oil.

GREEN BEANS AND PINE NUT SAUTÉ

The key to keeping this attractive dish vibrant is to select only exquisitely fresh, plump, unblemished green beans, and cook them in small batches just until tender, shocking them to lock in color, flavor, and nutrients.

Serves 6

2 tablespoons extra-virgin olive oil

½ cup finely chopped shallots or red onion

¼ cup pine nuts

1 pound fresh green beans, blanched in salted water and shocked

1 cup diced tomatoes

Salt and freshly ground black pepper

Heat the oil in a large skillet over medium heat; add the shallots and pine nuts. Cook until the pine nuts begin to brown lightly, 3–4 minutes. Add the green beans, tomatoes, salt, and pepper. Cook only enough to warm through and soften the tomatoes slightly. Serve hot or at room temperature.

PC FRESH GREEN BEANS WITH TOASTED SESAME

If fresh green beans are unavailable, you can use frozen beans instead.

Serves 4

2 cups water

1 pound fresh green beans

1 tablespoon olive oil

2 tablespoons toasted sesame seeds

Salt and pepper, to taste

1. Fill the bottom of the pressure cooker with water. Place the steamer basket in the pressure cooker.
2. Trim the ends off the green beans and place in the basket. Secure the lid; cook on high until pressure indicator rises. Lower heat and cook for 5 minutes.
3. Remove the green beans from the pressure cooker and toss in the olive oil. Sprinkle sesame seeds over green beans and season with salt and pepper, to taste.

SC ROSEMARY-THYME GREEN BEANS

In this recipe, the slow cooker acts like a steamer, resulting in tender, crisp green beans.

Serves 4

1 pound green beans

1 tablespoon fresh minced rosemary

1 teaspoon fresh minced thyme

2 tablespoons lemon juice

2 tablespoons water

1. Place all ingredients into a 2-quart slow cooker. Stir to distribute the spices evenly.
2. Cook on low for 1½ hours, or until the green beans are tender. Stir before serving.

PC FENNEL COOKED IN WHITE WINE

To make a fennel purée, use a slotted spoon to transfer it to a food processor after completing Step 2. Pulse until smooth, adding some of the cooking liquid if necessary.

Serves 4

4 fennel bulbs

1 tablespoon butter or vegan margarine, such as Earth Balance

1 tablespoon olive oil

1 small onion, diced

1 cup white wine

Salt and pepper, to taste

1. Cut off the tops and bottoms of the fennel bulbs and remove the two outer leaves. Thoroughly rinse under cold running water. Dice the bulbs. Set aside.

2. Bring the butter or margarine and oil to temperature in the pressure cooker over medium heat. Add the onion; sauté for 3 minutes. Stir in the diced fennel; sauté for 3 minutes. Stir in the wine. Lock the lid into place and bring to low pressure; maintain for 8 minutes. Quick-release the pressure and remove the lid. Simmer until fennel is soft. Add salt and pepper, to taste.

Fennel Facts

Fennel is in season during the fall, when you'll find this celery-like food in grocery stores. Like celery, you can enjoy fennel raw and in a salad, or gently cooked.

PC BUTTERNUT SQUASH

Winter is the peak season for this squash, which is loaded with vitamin A.

Serves 4–6

2 pounds butternut squash, peeled and cubed into 1" pieces

Water, as needed

2 tablespoons butter or vegan margarine such as Earth Balance

1 tablespoon brown sugar

1 teaspoon salt

1. Add the butternut squash, and enough water to cover the squash, to the pressure cooker. Lock the lid into place and bring to high pressure; maintain pressure for 4 minutes. Remove from heat and quick-release pressure.

2. Drain the liquid, then place the squash in a medium-size mixing bowl. Stir in the butter or margarine, brown sugar, and salt.

Butternut Squash Peak Season

Butternut squash is a type of winter squash. It is similar in flavor to pumpkin and can be steamed, baked, or puréed into a creamy soup.

SC STEWED SQUASH

Crisp and fresh, this is the perfect summer side dish to show off the season's bounty.

Serves 4

- 1 medium onion, cut into ¼" slices
- 3 cups sliced zucchini
- 1 tablespoon fresh dill
- 3 tablespoons lemon juice
- ¼ teaspoon salt
- ¼ teaspoon black pepper
- ¾ cup fresh corn kernels
- 1 teaspoon butter or vegan margarine

1. Place the onions on the bottom of a 1½- to 2-quart slow cooker. Top with zucchini, dill, lemon juice, salt, and pepper. Cook on low for 3½ hours.
2. Add the corn and butter or vegan margarine and stir. Cook for an additional 30 minutes on high.

PC SPAGHETTI SQUASH

Spaghetti squash looks like (and can be used like) strands of pasta. Top with marinara sauce or olive oil for a low-carb dish.

Serves 4

- 2 pound spaghetti squash, halved lengthwise
- ½ cup water
- 1 tablespoon olive oil
- 1 teaspoon salt

1. Scoop out the center of the squash, including the seeds, and discard. Place the squash face down in the steamer basket, then add water.
2. Lock the lid into place and bring to high pressure; maintain pressure for 10 minutes. Remove from heat and quick-release pressure.
3. When squash is cool enough to handle, use a fork to scoop the strands of "spaghetti" from the squash and place in a medium bowl. Drizzle the olive oil and sprinkle salt on top before serving.

PC WINTER VEGETABLE MEDLEY

Any earthy herbs, such as rosemary, thyme, or sage, will work well in this delicious recipe.

Serves 4–6

2 tablespoons olive oil

1 sprig rosemary

3 carrots, peeled and sliced

1 large sweet potato, diced and peeled

6 red potatoes, quartered

2½ cups butternut squash, peeled and cubed

1 cup water

Salt and pepper, to taste

1. Bring the olive oil and rosemary to medium heat in the pressure cooker. Add all of the vegetables, stirring until well coated, and cook for 5 minutes.

2. Add the water, then lock on the lid. Bring to high pressure; maintain pressure for 6 minutes. Remove the pan from the heat, slowly release the pressure, and remove the lid. Drain the water. Season with salt and pepper, to taste, and remove the rosemary sprig before serving.

PC CORN ON THE COB

"Shuck" means to peel off the husk and silk from the corn prior to cooking.

Serves 4

4 ears fresh sweet corn, shucked

½ cup water

1 tablespoon butter or vegan margarine, such as Earth Balance

Salt and black pepper, to taste

1. Place the rack in the pressure cooker and place the corn on the rack. Pour in the water.

2. Lock the lid into place and bring to low pressure; maintain pressure for 3 minutes. Remove the pressure cooker from heat, quick-release the pressure, and remove the lid.

3. Spread ¼ of the butter over each ear of corn and season with salt and pepper, to taste.

Corn's Peak Season

Corn is at its best during the peak season summer month of July. Whenever possible, use fresh fruits and vegetables for the biggest nutritional punch, but if fresh is not an option, frozen fruits and vegetables are a good alternative.

PC CILANTRO-LIME CORN ON THE COB

Dress up plain corn on the cob with seasoned butter. To add a little more kick, increase the amount of cayenne pepper.

Serves 4

4 ears fresh sweet corn, shucked

½ cup water

2 tablespoons butter or vegan margarine, such as Earth Balance

2 tablespoons cilantro, chopped

2 teaspoons fresh lime juice

½ teaspoon salt

½ teaspoon cayenne pepper

1. Place the rack in the pressure cooker and place the corn on the rack. Pour in the water.

2. Lock the lid into place and bring to low pressure; maintain pressure for 3 minutes. Remove the pressure cooker from heat, quick-release the pressure, and remove the lid.

3. In a small bowl, combine the butter or margarine, cilantro, lime juice, salt, and cayenne pepper until well blended.

4. When the corn is cool enough to handle, spread ¼ of the mixture on each ear of corn.

CREAMED CORN

Now that sweet corn of good quality is available for much of the year, celebrate with a rich, comforting dish of creamed corn accompanied by dark greens.

Serves 4

6 ears sweet corn, shucked

1 tablespoon butter

¼ cup finely chopped shallots or onions

½ cup heavy cream

Salt and freshly ground black pepper

Freshly chopped chives (optional)

Using a knife, cut the kernels from the cob with a tip-to-stem slicing motion. You should have about 3 cups. Melt the butter in a skillet; add the shallots and cook until soft, about 3 minutes. Add the corn and cream; cook until thickened, about 2 minutes; season with salt and pepper. Garnish with chives, if desired.

CORN AND PEPPER PUDDING

Serve this dish warm. It's perfect for any meal!

Serves 6

2 tablespoons unsalted butter, melted

3 cups cubed bread, about ½" dice

3 poblano or bell peppers, roasted and peeled, and then diced

6 ears sweet corn, shucked, kernels cut off with a knife (about 3 cups)

¼ cup chopped chives

1 teaspoon salt

½ teaspoon freshly ground black pepper

4 eggs

2 cups milk

¾ cup shredded jalapeño pepper jack cheese

1. Heat oven to 350°F. Combine the melted butter and bread cubes; bake in a single layer until lightly browned, about 10 minutes. In a mixing bowl, combine the roasted peppers, corn, chives, bread cubes, salt, and pepper. Transfer to a buttered 8" × 11" baking dish.

2. Whisk together the eggs and milk; pour over bread mixture. Allow to sit for 10 minutes, to let the bread absorb the custard; top with the shredded cheese. Bake until set in the center and lightly browned on top, about 1 hour.

PC PRESSURE COOKER CREAMED CORN

Creamed corn is an almost soupy vegetable side dish that is popular in the Midwest and South.

Serves 8

8 ears sweet corn, shucked

½ cup water

2 teaspoons butter or vegan margarine, such as Earth Balance

2 teaspoons flour

1 cup milk or unsweetened soymilk

2 teaspoons salt

1 teaspoon sugar

1. Place the rack in the pressure cooker and place the corn on the rack. Pour in the water.

2. Lock the lid into place and bring to low pressure; maintain pressure for 3 minutes. Remove the pressure cooker from heat, quick-release the pressure, and remove the lid.

3. When the corn is cool enough to handle, place each ear of corn over a large mixing bowl and remove the kernels from the corn with a knife, using long downward strokes and rotating the cob as you go.

4. Take half of the kernels and pulse in a food processor until just smooth.

5. In a small pan, melt the butter or margarine, then stir in the flour, being careful not to brown. Slowly stir the milk or soymilk into the roux, and stir until smooth.

6. Add all of the corn to the saucepan, bring to a boil, reduce heat, and simmer for 10 minutes. Add salt and sugar before removing from heat.

PC OKRA WITH CORN AND TOMATO

The "goo" that comes out of okra while cooking helps to thicken liquids.

Serves 8

4 ears fresh sweet corn, shucked

½ cup water

1 teaspoon olive oil

¼ cup red onion, diced

1 pound okra, tops removed and cut into ½" rounds

2 cups tomatoes, chopped

1 cup Pressure Cooker Vegetable Stock (see Chapter 5)

2 teaspoons salt

1 teaspoon cayenne pepper

1. Place the rack in the pressure cooker and place the corn on the rack. Pour in the water.

2. Lock the lid into place and bring to low pressure; maintain pressure for 3 minutes. Remove the pressure cooker from heat, quick-release the pressure, and remove the lid.

3. When the corn is cool enough to handle, place each ear of corn over a large mixing bowl and remove the kernels from the corn with a knife, using long downward strokes and rotating the cob as you go.

4. After cleaning the pressure cooker, add the olive oil over medium heat, then sauté the onion until just soft.

5. Add the okra, tomatoes, Vegetable Stock, salt, and cayenne, then stir.

6. Lock the lid into place and bring to high pressure; maintain pressure for 3 minutes. Remove the pressure cooker from heat, quick-release the pressure, and remove the lid. Stir in the corn before serving.

PC SUCCOTASH

Succotash can be made with a variety of beans, but the staple ingredients are lima beans and corn.

Serves 4

2 tablespoons butter or vegan margarine, such as Earth Balance

½ cup bell pepper, chopped

1 cup fresh lima beans

1 cup whole kernel corn

1 cup tomatoes, chopped

1 cup water

1 teaspoon salt

1. Bring the pressure cooker to medium heat; add the butter or margarine and bell pepper. Sauté for 3 minutes, or until the bell pepper begins to soften.

2. Add the lima beans, corn, tomatoes, water, and salt. Stir well.

3. Lock the lid into place and bring to high pressure; maintain pressure for 10 minutes. Remove from heat and quick-release the pressure.

Origin of Succotash

The word *succotash* derives from the Native American word *msickquatash*, which, according to Epicurious.com, means "boiled whole kernels of corn."

PC CORN MAQUE CHOUX

You can use drained canned corn, fresh corn cut from the cob, or thawed frozen corn in this recipe.

Serves 4

3 tablespoons butter or vegan margarine, such as Earth Balance

2 small onions, diced

1 small green bell pepper, diced

½ cup celery, diced

2 cloves garlic, minced

4 cups whole kernel corn

2 Roma tomatoes, peeled, seeded, and diced

½ cup cilantro leaves, chopped, plus additional for garnish

⅛ teaspoon cayenne pepper

½ cup tomato juice

Salt, to taste

Freshly ground black pepper, to taste

1. Melt the butter or margarine in the pressure cooker over medium heat. Add the onions, bell pepper, and celery; sauté for 3 minutes or until the vegetables are soft. Add the minced garlic and sauté an additional 30 seconds.

2. Stir in the corn, tomatoes, chopped cilantro, cayenne pepper, tomato juice, salt, and pepper. Lock the lid into place and bring to low pressure; maintain pressure for 5 minutes.

3. Remove from heat and quick-release the pressure. Use a slotted spoon to immediately transfer the corn and vegetables to a serving bowl. Taste for seasoning and add additional salt and pepper if needed. Garnish with cilantro and serve.

Cajun Cuisine

Maque choux is a Cajun dish, popular in southern Louisiana. Cajun food is known for being full flavored—heavy on seasoning and spice. It is similar to, and often confused with, Creole cuisine.

CHEESY POBLANO PEPPERS

Poblanos are a mild pepper often used in chile rellenos. Due to their thickness, these large, heart-shaped peppers are great for stuffing.

Serves 4

1 tablespoon olive oil

1 clove garlic, minced

¼ cup diced onion

4 poblano peppers, seeded and sliced into 1" rings

1 cup potatoes, peeled and diced into cubes

½ cup 2% milk or unsweetened soymilk

½ cup shredded Cheddar cheese or vegan Cheddar cheese

½ teaspoon salt

1. In a large sauté pan over medium heat, heat the olive oil. Add the garlic and onion and sauté for 2 minutes. Add the sliced poblano rings and sauté for 2 more minutes.

2. Pour the sautéed poblano mixture into a 4-quart slow cooker, then add the potato, milk or soymilk, cheese, and salt. Stir.

3. Cover and cook over low heat for 7–8 hours.

ROASTED RED BELL PEPPER PURÉE

Add sweet splashes of brilliant color to plates with this simple, delicious sauce.

Serves 8

4 roasted red bell peppers (see Roasted Peppers recipe in Chapter 3), chopped

1 tablespoon tomato paste

Zest and juice of 1 lemon

2 tablespoons extra-virgin olive oil

Salt and pepper to taste

Combine all ingredients in a food processor or blender. Purée until smooth. Heat in a saucepan before serving.

BRIE TIMBALES WITH ROASTED RED PEPPER SAUCE

Timbales are molded shapes that look especially dynamic as individual portions. Usually, they're made in custard molds, which are upended and served atop a sauce, such as the red bell pepper purée in this dish.

Serves 8

4 teaspoons butter, melted

7 ounces Brie

6 ounces cream cheese

4 ounces sour cream

3 eggs

Pinch of cayenne

Salt to taste

White pepper or hot pepper sauce to taste

1 teaspoon butter

1 recipe Roasted Red Bell Pepper Purée (see recipe in this chapter)

1. Heat oven to 350°F. Bring 2 quarts water to a boil. In a food processor or blender, combine the melted butter, Brie, cream cheese, sour cream, and eggs; process until very smooth. Season with cayenne, salt, and pepper or pepper sauce.

2. Butter 8 (4-ounce) ramekins or custard cups (small teacups will do fine also); fill with egg mixture. Place into a deep roasting pan or baking dish; put in the oven, and pour boiling water in until it reaches halfway up the sides of the cups. Bake until set, about 30 minutes. Allow the timbales to sit at room temperature for 10–15 minutes. Loosen timbales by running a knife around the inside of the cup, then inverting the cups onto small plates. Spoon red bell pepper sauce around.

CHAPTER 10

ONIONS, MUSHROOMS, AND TRUFFLES

RECIPE LIST

- JUMBO BEER-BATTERED ONION RINGS 540
- STUFFED ONIONS 541
- BRAISED LEEKS 542
- GRILLED LEEKS WITH TARRAGON AND LEMON 543
- SCALLION PANCAKES 544
- LEEK TART 545
- CARAMELIZED PEARL ONIONS 546
- SLOW COOKER CARAMELIZED ONIONS 547
- ONION TART 548
- ROASTED SWEET ONIONS 549
- ROASTED SHALLOTS 550
- GRILLED ONIONS WITH BALSAMIC GLAZE 551
- GRILLED SCALLIONS 552
- LEEK POTATO CAKES 553
- GARLIC BREAD 554
- BAKED PEPPERS AND ONIONS 555
- VIDALIA ONION SALAD 556
- CHIVE DUMPLINGS 557
- PISSALADIÈRE 558
- PICKLED RED ONIONS 559
- DUXELLES 560
- RISOTTO WITH PORTOBELLO MUSHROOMS, ONIONS, AND GARLIC 561
- CREAMED MORELS AND ASPARAGUS TIPS IN VOL-AU-VENTS 562
- FETTUCCINE WITH MORELS AND SPRING ONIONS 563
- POLENTA-STYLE GRITS WITH WILD MUSHROOM RAGOUT 564
- JOSH'S MUSHROOM DIP 565
- PORTOBELLO PITA WITH BUCKWHEAT AND BEANS 566
- GRILLED MARINATED PORTOBELLO MUSHROOMS 567
- MUSHROOM-SPELT SAUTÉ 568
- CHINESE THREE SLIVERS 569
- CHINESE BLACK MUSHROOMS WITH JADE BOK CHOY 570
- TAIWANESE MUSHROOM EGG 571
- SPRING MUSHROOM RISOTTO WITH MORELS AND ASPARAGUS 572
- MUSHROOM BRUSCHETTA 573
- MUSHROOM-BARLEY "RISOTTO" 574
- OVEN-ROASTED MUSHROOMS 575
- VEGETABLE-STUFFED PORTOBELLO MUSHROOMS 576
- CREAMED MUSHROOMS 577
- MUSHROOM-TOFU STIR-FRY 578

MUSHROOM TURNOVERS (EMPANADAS) **579**

PICKLED MUSHROOMS **580**

WARM OYSTER MUSHROOM SALAD **580**

MUSHROOM-LEEK TART **581**

MUSHROOM BARLEY **582**

MUSHROOM AND OLIVE BLEND **583**

JUMBO BEER-BATTERED ONION RINGS

This recipe is perfect to serve as an appetizer!

Serves 4

1 bottle (12 ounces) beer

2 extra-large eggs, beaten

½ cup peanut oil

2 cups cornstarch, plus extra for dredging

½ teaspoon salt

2 very large Spanish or Bermuda onions

Peanut oil for deep-frying

1. Whisk together the beer, eggs, ½ cup oil, cornstarch, and salt until it makes a thick batter. Cut the onions into 1" thick slices; separate into rings. Heat the fry oil to 360°F in a medium saucepan. Dredge the onion rings in cornstarch, dip into the batter, and fry. Do not overcrowd the pot. Add rings one by one to the pot, making sure the first has started to sizzle before adding the next (this prevents them from sticking together).

2. Drain on paper towels and sprinkle with salt before serving.

STUFFED ONIONS

French chef Georges Auguste Escoffier, founder of the Ritz Hotel in Paris, and one of the great chefs of all time, codified many of the classic recipes of France at the turn of the twentieth century. This is one of them, which is still taught to young chefs today.

Serves 4

4 medium Spanish onions
3 teaspoons butter, divided
1 chopped shallot
1 cup very finely chopped mushrooms
1 tablespoon dry white wine
1 tablespoon finely chopped parsley
Salt and freshly ground black pepper
2 cups strong vegetable stock

1. Heat oven to 375°F. Trim the tops from the onions, and cut the roots off, but leave the root core in to hold the onion together. Peel the skins. Blanch the onions in lightly salted boiling water for 10 minutes. Scoop out the insides, using a melon-ball scoop or spoon, leaving ⅓" walls. Chop the scooped insides, and sauté them in 1 teaspoon of the butter.

2. Melt the remaining 2 teaspoons of butter in a skillet; add the shallots. Cook over medium heat until they are translucent, about 5 minutes; add the mushrooms. Cook until mushrooms have wilted and most liquid has evaporated; add the wine and cook to almost dry. Remove from heat; add the chopped parsley. Season well with salt and pepper. Combine the mushroom mixture with the chopped onion insides and fill into the onion shells. Place in a small buttered baking dish with the vegetable stock. Cover with foil.

3. Bake for 1 hour, basting once. Remove the lid halfway through to allow the onions to brown.

BRAISED LEEKS

Silky, delicate braised leeks are juicy and light, making them an excellent foil for spicy dishes and fried foods. Broth from braising leeks is an excellent vegetable stock, so keep it for use in soups, stews, and risottos. Remember to wash leeks very well, twice even, as they often contain lots of sandy grit.

Serves 4

- 5 black peppercorns
- 5 parsley stems
- 1 bay leaf
- 1 onion, halved
- 2 carrots, thinly sliced
- 1 rib celery, sliced
- 3 quarts water
- 2 teaspoons salt
- 4 leeks, cleaned, halved lengthwise
- 1 tablespoon extra-virgin olive oil
- Chopped chives or parsley

1. Combine peppercorns, parsley stems, bay leaf, onion, carrots, and celery in a nonreactive pot with 3 quarts of water and 2 teaspoons salt. Bring to a boil; lower to a simmer. Add the leeks; simmer very gently for 15–20 minutes, until leeks are very tender.

2. Remove leeks from the broth; arrange them cut-side up on a platter. Drizzle with olive oil and sprinkle with chives or parsley.

GRILLED LEEKS WITH TARRAGON AND LEMON

Some vegetables are best grilled after a light blanching. Leeks achieve a tender, silky texture and mild vegetal sweetness on the grill when they've been steamed or blanched in boiling water before they hit the barbecue. Always leave the root core attached to hold cooking leeks together.

Serves 4

4 leeks, cleaned, split lengthwise

3 tablespoons extra-virgin olive oil, divided

Kosher salt and freshly ground black pepper

1 teaspoon Dijon mustard

2 teaspoons freshly squeezed lemon juice (about ½ of a lemon)

1 tablespoon freshly chopped tarragon, chervil, chives, or Italian parsley

1. Heat a grill or stovetop grill pan. Steam or blanch the leeks in boiling salted water for 5 minutes. Shock them by plunging them into ice-cold water; drain well. Lightly brush them with olive oil, top and bottom; lightly season them with salt and pepper. Grill the leeks on both sides until dark brown grill marks appear. Transfer to a platter.

2. Whisk together the mustard and lemon juice. Gradually whisk in the remaining olive oil; season the dressing with salt and pepper. Drizzle this dressing over the grilled leeks. Sprinkle with chopped tarragon (or other herb of your choice), and serve hot or at room temperature.

SCALLION PANCAKES

A Chinese takeout favorite, these delicious, crunchy pancakes are excellent with garlicky sautéed Asian greens and steamed jasmine rice.

Serves 4

2½ cups all-purpose flour

1½ teaspoons salt

1½ tablespoons peanut oil

1 cup water, boiling

4 teaspoons Asian toasted sesame oil

1 cup chopped scallion greens, plus extra for garnishing

½ cup corn oil for frying

1. In a large mixing bowl, combine 2 cups flour, salt, peanut oil, and 1 cup boiling water. Mix with a wooden spoon to form workable dough, adding more flour if necessary. Knead the dough on a lightly floured surface until smooth, about 5 minutes; wrap it in plastic film, and allow it to rest for 20 minutes.

2. Divide the dough into 4 parts. Roll out 1 part into a 6" × 8" rectangle. Brush with sesame oil and sprinkle with ¼ cup of scallions. Roll, jelly-roll style, into a cylinder; flatten the cylinder slightly, and crimp the ends. Coil the cylinder into a disk, and crimp or pinch to seal. Repeat with remaining dough. Roll the disks into 8" pancakes.

3. Heat a skillet over medium heat; add 3 tablespoons of corn oil. Fry the pancakes 1 at a time, adding more oil when necessary, and keeping finished cakes warm in the oven. Serve with a sprinkling of chopped scallions.

LEEK TART

In keeping with the tradition of pies at Thanksgiving, add this savory tart to your holiday table. Leeks are available year-round.

Serves 6

½ recipe Basic Pie Dough (see Chapter 6)

2 tablespoons unsalted butter

2 pounds leeks, sliced ¼", washed very thoroughly

½ teaspoon salt

Freshly ground black pepper

2 large eggs

½ cup cream or half-and-half

¼ teaspoon ground nutmeg

1. Heat oven to 400°F. Roll the dough to fit a 9" tart or pie pan. Set the dough in the pan; refrigerate until ready to use.

2. Melt the butter in a skillet and cook the leeks over low-medium heat until very soft, about 30 minutes, seasoning with ½ teaspoon salt and black pepper to taste. Do not brown. Whisk together the eggs, cream or half-and-half, and nutmeg; season with salt and pepper. Combine the leeks and the egg mixture, and pour into the pie shell. Bake until golden, about 25 minutes. Allow to rest 10 minutes before cutting.

CARAMELIZED PEARL ONIONS

You can use frozen pearl onions, which are already peeled, for this recipe. But the sweetness and crunch of fresh ones elevate the dish, so use them when you have the time and patience to peel for 20 minutes or so.

Serves 4

1 bag (2 cups) peeled pearl onions

2 teaspoons sugar or brown sugar

¼ teaspoon salt

1 tablespoon butter or olive oil

In a heavy-bottomed skillet over medium heat, combine onions, sugar, salt, and butter or olive oil with 1 cup cold water; bring to a simmer. Cook gently until all water is absorbed and onions are coated in a light glaze, about 5 minutes. Lower heat to low; cook slowly until glaze browns and onions attain golden brown appearance, about 5 minutes more. Alternative Method: Once liquid is reduced to a glaze, put the entire pan in a 350°F oven, and roast until browned.

SLOW COOKER CARAMELIZED ONIONS

Caramelized onions are a great addition to roasts, dips, and sandwiches.

Yields 1 quart

4 pounds Vidalia or other sweet onions

3 tablespoons butter or vegan margarine

1 tablespoon balsamic vinegar

1. Peel and slice the onions in ¼" slices. Separate them into rings. Thinly slice the butter or margarine.

2. Place the onions into a 4-quart slow cooker. Scatter butter or margarine slices over top of the onions and drizzle with balsamic vinegar. Cover and cook on low for 10 hours.

3. If after 10 hours the onions are wet, turn the slow cooker up to high and cook uncovered for an additional 30 minutes, or until the liquid evaporates.

Storing Caramelized Onions

Store the onions in an airtight container. They will keep up to 2 weeks refrigerated or up to 6 months frozen. If frozen, defrost overnight in the refrigerator before using.

ONION TART

With a lightly dressed salad, this makes an excellent lunch. Experiment with your own herb combinations to make this tart your own.

Serves 8

½ recipe Basic Pie Dough (see Chapter 6), or 1 (9") frozen pie crust

2 tablespoons unsalted butter

3 cups thinly sliced onions

3 teaspoons chopped fresh thyme leaves, or other herb, such as oregano or tarragon

1 tablespoon flour

¾ cup half-and-half

¼ cup sour cream

2 large eggs, beaten

¾ teaspoon salt

½ teaspoon freshly ground black pepper

1. Heat oven to 400°F. Roll the dough out to a 10" disk, and fit into a 9" tart pan or pie plate, cutting any excess from the edges or crimping in an attractive way; prick the bottom lightly with a fork in several places. Place a sheet of waxed paper on the pie shell; fill with pie beads or dried beans and "blind bake" until lightly browned, about 15 minutes; cool on a rack. If using a frozen pie crust, follow directions on the package to blind bake.

2. Lower oven to 350°F. Melt the butter in a skillet over medium heat. Add the onions and thyme or other herb; cook slowly until onions are soft and lightly browned, about 15 minutes. Stir in the flour and cook 1 minute more. Transfer to a mixing bowl; combine with the half-and-half, sour cream, eggs, salt, and pepper. Pour into parbaked pie shell; bake in center of oven until filling is set and lightly browned on top, about 35 minutes.

ROASTED SWEET ONIONS

The easiest recipes are sometimes the best. Choose sweet onions such as Vidalia or Texas Sweets for the most otherworldly experience.

Serves 4

4 large sweet onions, all the same size

1. Heat oven to 350°F. Trim the visible roots from the onions, but leave the skins on and the tops untrimmed. Place the onions root-end down in a baking dish. Roast in center of oven until onions are very soft and give easily to gentle pressure. They take between 60 and 90 minutes, depending on the size of the onions.

2. Peel the outer skin, but leave on the caramelized outer layers, which add extra flavor. Alternately, you could serve them in their skins and let guests unwrap them at the table.

ROASTED SHALLOTS

These sweet jewels pair surprisingly well with both Eastern and Western foods. The Thais actually use shallots as often as the French!

Serves 4

16 medium shallots, peeled, ends trimmed, root core left intact

1 teaspoon sugar

2 tablespoons olive oil

1. Heat oven to 350°F. Toss the shallots with the sugar to coat. Heat the oil in an oven-safe skillet over medium heat; add the shallots. Cook 1 minute, just to start the browning. Turn the shallots, and place the pan in the oven.

2. Roast for 30 minutes. Transfer to a plate to cool slightly. If necessary, peel off any leathery outer layers before serving.

GRILLED ONIONS WITH BALSAMIC GLAZE

The key to perfect, sweet grilled onions is slow, even cooking. They're custom-made for the outer edges of the grill, or a grill pan over a whisper of a flame.

Serves 4

4 large sweet onions (about the size of a baseball)

2 tablespoons extra-virgin olive oil

Kosher salt and freshly ground black pepper

1 cup good quality balsamic vinegar

1. Leaving the skin on, cut off the polar ends of the onions, about ½" from the root and sprout ends. Halve the onions laterally; a sharp knife will help keep the onion sections together, which makes flipping them on the grill easier. Brush them with olive oil and sprinkle them with kosher salt and black pepper to taste. In a saucepan over medium heat, simmer the balsamic vinegar until it has cooked down to syrup.

2. Heat a grill or stovetop grill pan to a low heat. Place the onion slices on the grill; cook slowly without moving them until dark grill marks appear, about 15 minutes. Turn once, using both tongs and a spatula to keep the rings together. Grill until the second side is well marked and juices begin to pool on the top, another 10 minutes. Brush with balsamic syrup 5 minutes before removing from the grill. Serve brushed with remaining syrup.

GRILLED SCALLIONS

Over brown rice, with a few Japanese pickles, this is an unconventionally flavored treat.

Serves 4

16 scallions

1 tablespoon pure maple syrup

2 teaspoons Asian toasted sesame oil

A few drops Tamari soy sauce

Assorted Japanese pickles, such as pickled daikon, baby carrots, or cabbage (Korean kimchi, fermented cabbage, is also a good choice)

Prepare a grill or stovetop grill pan over medium-high heat. Trim the root ends of the scallions, and cut off all but 5" of the green parts. Whisk together the syrup and the oil. Brush the scallions with the maple mixture. Place on the grill and cook, turning regularly, until they are golden brown and tender, about 5 minutes. Transfer to a platter; drizzle with soy sauce. Serve accompanied by Japanese pickles.

LEEK POTATO CAKES

With a dollop of crème fraîche, sour cream, or applesauce, these crisp disks are a texturally pleasing and comforting component of a complete meal. These are excellent with a small salad and a wedge of soft, ripened cheese such as Camembert.

Serves 4

2 cups finely chopped leeks, white part only

2 cups finely grated peeled potatoes

½ teaspoon dried sage

2 large eggs, beaten

2 tablespoons flour

1 teaspoon salt

¼ teaspoon freshly ground black pepper

Olive oil for frying

1. Wash the leeks very thoroughly to remove any grit. Combine the potatoes, leeks, sage, eggs, flour, salt, and pepper in a mixing bowl; mix well. Form into 8 (3") pancakes.

2. Heat ¼" of olive oil in a heavy skillet over medium heat until a piece of leek sizzles when added. Transfer 4 of the pancakes into the pan and cook gently, without moving them, until a crisp brown crust develops, about 5 minutes. Turn, and brown the other side; drain on paper towels, and repeat with remaining cakes.

GARLIC BREAD

It is always advisable to crisp loaves of crusty bread in the oven just before serving. This simple step improves the texture and flavor of breads by slightly more than 1,000 percent. By spreading some garlic and olive oil or butter on a split loaf, you can make the bread even more scrumptious at the same time.

Serves 6–8

- 1 loaf Italian bread, or other crusty loaf such as a baguette
- 3 tablespoons extra-virgin olive oil, softened unsalted butter, or margarine
- 2 cloves garlic, finely chopped (about 1 tablespoon)
- Pinch of crushed red pepper flakes (optional)

Heat oven to 375°F. Laterally split the loaf of bread. Whisk together the olive oil, butter, or margarine with the chopped garlic. Using a brush or a rubber spatula, generously slather both cut sides of the bread with garlic oil or butter. Sprinkle with some pepper flakes if desired. Place garlic bread halves on a sheet pan or baking dish and bake in center of oven until crisp and lightly browned, about 20 minutes.

Note: When crisping whole loaves in the oven, it is not necessary to cut them unless you're making them into garlic bread.

BAKED PEPPERS AND ONIONS

The fruity taste of good dark green olive oil pairs very well with the taste of peppers and onions, so don't skimp on this one—use only extra-virgin oil.

Serves 4

4 or 5 medium green and red bell peppers (about 1½ pounds)

1 pound small red potatoes

1 large yellow onion

¼ cup extra-virgin olive oil

Kosher salt and freshly ground black pepper

Heat the oven to 425°F. Wash the peppers and cut into 2" pieces. Scrub the potatoes and cut into 1" slices or chunks. Peel the onion and cut into chunks. Place everything into a shallow ovenproof dish; pour the olive oil over the vegetables; toss to coat. Sprinkle with the salt and lots of pepper. Bake for about 30 minutes, until the potatoes are tender.

VIDALIA ONION SALAD

Sweet onion varieties like Vidalia, Maui, Walla Walla, and Oso Sweet are so low in sulfur that they have more of a fruity taste than an "oniony" one. That makes them perfect for eating raw. Thin shavings have a pleasing crunch without the teary pungency of yellow onions.

Serves 4

1 large Vidalia or other sweet onion (about 8 ounces)

2 tablespoons extra-virgin olive oil

1 lemon

¼ teaspoon celery seeds

Kosher salt and freshly ground black pepper to taste

French bread, or other crusty bread, warmed in the oven to crisp

Slice the onion into very thin rings, almost shavings. Arrange them in an attractive mound at the center of a serving plate. Drizzle them well with olive oil and a squeeze of lemon. Shower them with celery seeds and season with salt and pepper. Allow them to rest for 30 minutes to an hour before serving with crusty bread.

CHIVE DUMPLINGS

Serve this recipe with a dumpling sauce.

Serves 6

1 cup finely diced firm tofu

1 cup finely chopped chives

1 teaspoon sugar

1 teaspoon Asian chili sauce or ½ teaspoon ground white pepper

1 egg white, beaten, divided

1 tablespoon soy sauce

1 teaspoon sesame oil

1 package wonton skins

1. Combine tofu, chives, sugar, chili sauce or pepper, all but 1 teaspoon of the egg white, soy sauce, and sesame oil.

2. Place 2 teaspoons of filling onto a wonton skin. Use your finger to moisten the edge of the wonton skin lightly with a bit of the remaining egg white. Fold 2 opposite corners of the skin together to form a triangle shape. Seal edges together by pinching tightly with your fingers. Repeat with remaining filling and wonton wrappers, making as many triangle-shaped dumplings as filling allows. Place them on a plate dusted with cornstarch.

3. Bring 3 quarts water to a rapid boil. Boil the dumplings in batches. Serve.

PISSALADIÈRE

This southern French version of pizza comes from Provence, the birthplace of tapenade, the olive and anchovy spread that is the flavor base for pissaladière. This recipe makes 6–8 individual pies, but you can just as easily make it as one large one, and cut pieces for your guests.

Serves 8

1 package active dry yeast

¾ cup hot tap water

2 tablespoons olive oil, divided

2 cups unbleached all-purpose flour

Salt

3 white onions, cut in half through root end, then sliced into thin strips

½ bunch thyme

¼ cup cornmeal

¼ cup tapenade or olive paste (available in specialty food stores)

3 tomatoes, seeds removed, cut into neat, fine dice (⅛")

½ bunch parsley, chopped separately

1. Dissolve yeast in water, then add 1 tablespoon olive oil; gradually add flour, stirring with a wooden spoon and incorporating a sprinkling of salt, until dough can be worked on a board. Knead on floured surface until smooth. Allow to rise in an oiled bowl in a warm place until double in size (about 1 hour).

2. Sauté the onions with the thyme in 1 tablespoon olive oil until evenly browned (caramelized). Roll out dough very thin (1/16" thick) on a floured surface. Using a 5"-diameter cookie cutter or a coffee can, cut 8 disks of dough and place them on a baking sheet generously dusted with cornmeal. Brush with olive oil. Spread about 2 teaspoons tapenade onto each disk, leaving a ½" border around the edge. Sprinkle on 2 tablespoons caramelized onions and a smattering of tomato dice.

3. Bake in very hot (450°F) oven until the crust is crisp and golden brown, about 20 minutes. Sprinkle with parsley and serve hot.

PICKLED RED ONIONS

Crunchy and beautifully pink, these pair as perfectly with summer grain salads, such as Succotash Salad (see Chapter 3), as they do with polenta and a wild mushroom sauté.

Serves 8

2 large red onions, thinly sliced

1 quart boiling water

½ cup white wine vinegar

½ cup cold water

½ cup honey

1 teaspoon salt

1 teaspoon black peppercorns

½ teaspoon whole allspice (optional)

Place the sliced onions in a bowl; pour the boiling water over them and allow them to steep for 5 minutes; drain. Whisk together the vinegar, cold water, honey, salt, peppercorns, and allspice, if desired. Add the onions, and allow them to marinate for 10 minutes. Transfer to a jar, cover tightly, and refrigerate until very cold. These pickled onions will keep for several months, and get better with age.

DUXELLES

This chopped mushroom spread is a classic French preparation. Chefs use it as a filling for turnovers, stuffed vegetables, savory strudels, and a zillion other things. It makes an excellent spread on crusts of baguette, and is fine in sandwiches.

Yields about 1 cup

1 (10-ounce) package mushrooms

1 tablespoon olive oil

3 shallots, chopped (about ½ cup)

½ teaspoon salt

¼ teaspoon freshly ground black pepper

¼ cup dry white wine

1 tablespoon finely chopped parsley

1. Chop the mushrooms finely (this is best done by hand, but may be done by pulsing them in batches of no more than 5 in a food processor until they're chopped, but not puréed).

2. Heat oil in a medium skillet over medium heat until a piece of shallot sizzles. Add the shallots and salt; cook until translucent, about 3 minutes. Add the mushrooms and black pepper; cook until the mushrooms have given up their liquid and the pan is almost dry, 5–7 minutes. Add the wine and cook until almost dry, about 3 minutes. Remove from heat; stir in chopped parsley.

RISOTTO WITH PORTOBELLO MUSHROOMS, ONIONS, AND GARLIC

This risotto is great as a main dish, but can also be served as a side.

Serves 4

4 large portobello mushrooms with stems

6 tablespoons unsalted butter, divided

4 large white onions, finely chopped

10 cloves garlic, finely chopped

Salt, to taste

1 cup arborio rice

5 cups vegetable stock or water

2 tablespoons grated imported Parmesan cheese, preferably Parmigiano-Reggiano

Freshly ground black pepper

1 bunch scallions, finely chopped

Scented olive oil, such as truffle oil, garlic oil, or herb oil (or very good extra-virgin olive oil)

1. Finely chop the stems of the mushrooms. Set the caps aside. In a large saucepan, melt 5 tablespoons of the butter, and sauté the onions and garlic over medium heat until translucent, about 2 minutes. Add the chopped mushroom stems, and sauté a minute longer. Season with salt.

2. Add the rice. Stir well to coat, then add 1 cup of stock or water and stir until the liquid is mostly absorbed. Add another cup of stock or water, stirring constantly, and allow the rice to absorb it. Continue adding liquid cup by cup, until all liquid is used and rice is tender, but still a little firm to the bite in the middle (about 25 minutes). Stir in remaining 1 tablespoon butter and cheese, and season to taste with salt and freshly ground black pepper. Set aside.

3. Slice the portobello caps paper-thin. Divide risotto into 4 bowls, immediately sprinkle with the shaved portobellos, and garnish with scallions and a drizzle (about 2 teaspoons) of truffle oil (or other flavored oil).

CREAMED MORELS AND ASPARAGUS TIPS IN VOL-AU-VENTS

Serve immediately so filling is hot.

Serves 6

1 (8-ounce) sheet puff pastry cut into 8 rectangular pieces, brushed with egg wash

2 tablespoons chopped shallots

1 tablespoon unsalted butter

14 fresh morels, cut into small pieces

¼ cup Madeira wine

½ cup strong vegetable stock

½ cup cream

Salt and freshly ground black pepper

1 teaspoon chopped fresh chives

24–30 cooked, pencil-thin asparagus tips

1. Arrange puff pastry rectangles on a baking sheet, spaced 1" apart. Bake at 400°F until highly puffed and the domed top is golden brown, about 20 minutes; set on a rack to cool. Halve the cooked vol-au-vents (the puffed pastries) laterally.

2. Sauté shallots in butter over medium heat until translucent (3 minutes). Add morels and cook for 5 minutes. Add Madeira. Simmer until volume is roughly halved, about 5 minutes more. Add stock and cook until almost dry. Add cream; simmer until sauce consistency thickens to coat the back of a spoon. Season with salt and pepper. Sprinkle in chives. Set the bottom halves of the puff pastry vol-au-vents onto serving plates. Spoon creamed morels over each bottom, allowing some to overflow. Top each with 4 asparagus tips, and cover with pastry tops.

FETTUCCINE WITH MORELS AND SPRING ONIONS

Long pieces of onion pair nicely with the shape of this pasta.

Serves 4

- 1 sprig fresh rosemary
- 8 ounces fresh morels, halved
- 2 teaspoons olive oil
- 6 spring onions or scallions cut into 1" pieces
- ½ pound imported fettuccine, cooked al dente, drained and tossed with a few drops of olive oil
- 1–2 cups strong vegetable stock
- 1 tablespoon unsalted butter
- 1 tablespoon chopped Italian (flat-leaf) parsley

1. In a skillet large enough to hold all ingredients, sauté the rosemary and morels in olive oil over medium heat for 5 minutes, until soft. Add the spring onions and sauté another 1 minute.

2. Add the cooked fettuccine, 1 cup of vegetable stock, and the butter, and simmer until sauce is creamy and adhering well to the pasta. Adjust consistency with remaining stock, season to taste, and serve sprinkled with chopped parsley, and Parmesan cheese if desired.

POLENTA-STYLE GRITS WITH WILD MUSHROOM RAGOUT

Cooked yellow cornmeal, known as polenta, is still poured directly onto the center of the wooden table (tavola) in some farmhouses in Italy. It is then topped with a stew or ragout, and family members draw whatever portion they want from the common "pot."

Serves 4

- 3½ cups Mushroom Vegetable Stock (see Chapter 5) or water
- 1 cup grits
- 1 pound assorted mushrooms
- 8 tablespoons (1 stick) butter, cut into small pieces
- 1½ teaspoons plus 2 pinches salt
- ¼ of a small lemon
- 2 teaspoons chopped fresh thyme (or ½ teaspoon dried)
- 2 teaspoons chopped fresh rosemary (or ½ teaspoon dried)
- 1 tablespoon cornstarch dissolved in ¼ cup cold water
- ¼ cup grated Parmesan cheese
- Freshly ground black pepper
- Roughly chopped Italian (flat-leaf) parsley

1. Bring 3 cups of the stock to a boil, then stir in the grits in a steady stream. Lower flame and set to simmer very slowly, stirring occasionally with a wooden spoon. Beware of splashing, since the stuff is molten lava at this point. Keep an eye on it while preparing the mushrooms. Cook for about 30 minutes.

2. Clean mushrooms as best you can without running under water, using a brush or paper towel. Heat a heavy skillet over a high flame until very hot, then add the mushrooms to the dry pan. Toss in ½ of the butter and allow it to melt under the mushrooms without shaking the pan (this helps them brown) for 2–3 minutes. Add 2 pinches of salt, a squeeze of lemon, the thyme and rosemary, and stir.

3. Add ½ cup stock to the mushrooms and swirl in the dissolved cornstarch. Simmer 1–2 minutes to cook out the starch, then set aside, covered.

4. Finish the grits by stirring in the remaining ½ stick of butter, grated cheese, and seasoning with 1½ teaspoons salt. A wooden spoon should stand up in the finished grits. To serve, portion grits onto 4 appetizer plates, make a depression on top of each portion, and spoon ¼ of the mushroom sauté onto each. Top with fresh ground black pepper and a sprinkling of chopped parsley.

JOSH'S MUSHROOM DIP

This dish is great when served with raw veggies or pita chips!

Serves 8

1 teaspoon olive oil

1 large portobello cap

1 (10-ounce) package white mushrooms

½ packet dried onion soup mix

1 pint sour cream

8 cups assorted raw vegetables, such as carrots, celery, mixed bell peppers, zucchini, and yellow squash, cut into sticks

1. Heat the olive oil in a small skillet over medium-high heat; cook the portobello until tender, about 5 minutes. Cool it and chop it finely. Chop the white mushrooms finely, either by hand or by pulsing in a food processor in batches of 5 at a time.

2. Stir the onion soup mix into the sour cream. Fold in the chopped mushrooms. Transfer to a bowl and serve surrounded by raw vegetables for dipping.

PORTOBELLO PITA WITH BUCKWHEAT AND BEANS

While buckwheat is actually a seed, not a grain, it has an earthy taste and pilaf-like texture that complete this earthy main-course sandwich.

Serves 4

4 medium-size portobello mushrooms, stems removed

Kosher salt and freshly ground black pepper

1 tablespoon olive oil

4 pita pocket breads, medium-size (about 8")

2 tablespoons mayonnaise or soy mayo

1 cup buckwheat groats or medium-granulation kasha, cooked according to directions on package

¼ pound cooked green beans

1. Brush the portobello caps clean (do not wash under water); season with salt and pepper. Heat oil in a large skillet until very hot, but not quite smoking. Cook the mushrooms top-side down over high heat until cooked through, about 4 minutes. Small pools of juice should appear where the stem was removed.

2. Cut an opening in a pita; slather the inside with mayonnaise. Spoon in a layer of cooked buckwheat groats or kasha, and add ¼ of the green beans. Stuff in 1 mushroom cap. Repeat with remaining pitas.

GRILLED MARINATED PORTOBELLO MUSHROOMS

Main-course mushrooms like these go with anything from summer salads to wintry wild rice dishes. They're one of the best vegetarian dinners to pair with red wine. If you don't have a grill, bake the mushrooms on a sheet pan in a 400°F oven for about 10 minutes.

Serves 4

4 large (4"–6" in diameter) portobello mushrooms, stems removed

1 cup extra-virgin olive oil

1 cup red wine vinegar

2 tablespoons soy sauce

1 tablespoon sugar

½ cup chopped fresh herbs (such as parsley, chives, tarragon, oregano) or 1 tablespoon dried herbs

1. Brush any dirt from the mushrooms, but do not wash them under water. Whisk together the olive oil, vinegar, soy sauce, sugar, and herbs. If using dried herbs, allow the mixture to steep for 15 minutes. In a shallow dish, pour the marinade over the mushrooms; marinate 10 minutes, turning occasionally.

2. Grill 2–3 minutes on each side. Serve whole or sliced. Sauce with leftover marinade, or save the marinade for another batch.

MUSHROOM-SPELT SAUTÉ

Spelt, wheat berries (sold in Hispanic markets as trigo), or barley make great whole-grain alternatives to rice.

Serves 4

2 tablespoons extra-virgin olive oil

1 large onion, diced

2 cloves garlic, chopped

Kosher salt and fresh ground black pepper

1 (10-ounce) package mushrooms, sliced

¼ cup dry sherry or white wine (optional)

2 cups cooked spelt (available at health food stores), wheat berries, or barley

Heat the olive oil in a skillet over high heat until it shimmers and a piece of onion sizzles in it. Add the onion and garlic; sprinkle with a little salt and pepper and cook for 5 minutes, until translucent. Add the mushrooms and cook, stirring occasionally, until some browning occurs, about 5 minutes; add the sherry, or white wine, if desired, and cook until it has almost all evaporated, 2–3 minutes. Add the spelt, wheat berries, or barley and cook until heated through; season to taste.

CHINESE THREE SLIVERS

The silky texture of slender, white enoki mushrooms contrasts here with crunchy bamboo and "meaty" bean curd. Advertising idea-man Tuan-Pu Wang, who introduced me to this dish, told me that the Chinese characters for it mean "three slivers." His creative touch was to serve the dish "taco style," wrapped in a crisp lettuce leaf.

Serves 4

2 tablespoons vegetable oil

1 can (4 ounces) sliced bamboo shoots, drained and rinsed

3 cakes (about 8 ounces) hard tofu, sliced into ¼" strips, patted dry with paper towel

1 package enoki mushrooms, roots trimmed, washed, and broken into individual strands

¼ cup Asian dumpling sauce (available in Asian markets) or other Asian dipping sauce

½ teaspoon sambal or other Asian chili paste (optional)

1 tablespoon cornstarch dissolved in 2 tablespoons cold water

1 head iceberg lettuce

1. Heat the oil in a skillet or wok until very hot but not smoky. Add the bamboo shoots and cook for 1 minute. Slide the tofu into the pan and cook over high heat without stirring until lightly browned. Add the enoki mushrooms, dumpling sauce, chili paste, and cornstarch solution. Cook until thick, about 2 minutes. Transfer to a serving bowl.

2. Select 4 unbroken leaves from the lettuce head; wash thoroughly and tear them in half. Place the bowl of cooked Chinese vegetables in the center of a large serving platter, and arrange the lettuce pieces around it. Guests spoon filling into the leaves and eat the lettuce wraps with their hands.

CHINESE BLACK MUSHROOMS WITH JADE BOK CHOY

The black mushrooms' smooth skin passes from soft to silky in the delicate sauce made from their soaking liquid, lending an almost sensual texture. Youthful, watery "jade," or "Shanghai," baby bok choy is increasingly available in produce markets, but plain old white bok choy is fine for its crunchy counterpoint.

Serves 4

- 20 dried black Chinese mushrooms, soaked overnight in 4 cups of water
- 1 tablespoon vegetable oil
- 3 cloves garlic, chopped (about 4 teaspoons)
- ¼ cup soy sauce
- 1 teaspoon sugar
- 1 pound baby jade bok choy heads, halved, or regular bok choy, cut into 1" chunks
- 2 tablespoons cornstarch dissolved in ½ cup cold water
- Few drops Asian toasted sesame oil (optional)

1. Pour the soaking liquid through a strainer or cheesecloth; set aside. Discard the stems from the mushrooms.

2. Heat the oil in a skillet or wok until a piece of vegetable sizzles in it. Add the garlic and the mushrooms; sauté for 5 minutes. Add 2 cups of the mushroom soaking liquid; bring to a simmer, and cook 15 minutes over low flame. Add the soy sauce, sugar, and bok choy; raise heat and cook until bok choy is tender, about 5 minutes. Stir in the cornstarch solution; cook until thick, about 2 minutes more. Remove from heat and sprinkle with a few drops of sesame oil, if desired.

TAIWANESE MUSHROOM EGG

This dish uses only the egg whites and a sweet "mayonnaise," also egg whites only.

Serves 4

6 hard-boiled eggs

2 teaspoons vegetable oil

12 shiitake mushrooms, stems removed, diced ¼"

1 egg white

1 teaspoon sugar

¼ teaspoon salt

½ teaspoon rice vinegar or white vinegar

⅓ cup peanut oil

1 tablespoon chopped fresh chives

1. Carefully halve the eggs lengthwise and discard the yolks; rinse out the whites. Heat the vegetable oil in a skillet and cook the mushrooms until well wilted, about 5 minutes; transfer to a plate to cool.

2. In a food processor on high speed, combine the egg white, sugar, salt, and vinegar. With the motor running, gradually incorporate the oil until a thick white mayonnaise is formed. Mix 2 tablespoons of this white mayonnaise with the cooked mushrooms. Spoon this mixture into the egg halves, allowing the filling to mound generously. Sprinkle the tops with chopped chives. Serve 3 per person.

SPRING MUSHROOM RISOTTO WITH MORELS AND ASPARAGUS

This woodsy risotto is perfect to serve on a crisp fall night.

Serves 6

½ pound medium-thick asparagus, woody lower parts removed, cut into 1" pieces

6 ounces fresh morels (or 2 ounces dried morels, soaked, liquid reserved), halved, and bottoms snipped

2 tablespoons butter, divided

Kosher salt and pepper to taste

1 medium onion, roughly chopped

6 ounces white mushrooms, sliced

2 cloves garlic, finely chopped

2 tablespoons olive oil

1½ cups arborio rice

½ cup dry white wine

5 cups hot Mushroom Vegetable Stock (see Chapter 5)

¼ cup freshly grated Parmesan cheese

1 lemon wedge

1 tablespoon chopped chives

1. Cook the asparagus pieces in boiling salted water until tender (about 4 minutes), drain, and set aside. Sauté morels in 1 tablespoon butter, seasoning liberally with kosher salt, until soft (about 5 minutes); set aside.

2. In a heavy-bottomed pot, gently sweat the onion, white mushrooms, and garlic in olive oil over medium heat until translucent, then stir in the rice with a wooden spoon until it is well coated with onion juices. Pour in the wine and stir constantly until it is absorbed.

3. Add 1 cup of the stock and stir constantly until it is absorbed. Repeat with the remaining stock, 1 cup at a time, until the rice is mostly tender, and has a saucy consistency (about 20 to 25 minutes).

4. Remove from heat, stir in the cheese and the remaining 1 tablespoon butter. Stir in the morels, asparagus, and a squeeze of lemon. Season to taste, and serve sprinkled with chives and extra Parmesan.

MUSHROOM BRUSCHETTA

This earthy bruschetta is great as an appetizer.

Serves 4

1 baguette or crusty country bread

4 teaspoons Aioli (see Chapter 2) or mayonnaise mixed with chopped garlic

8 ounces white mushrooms, plus ¼ pound mixed specialty mushrooms such as oyster, shiitake, enoki, or portobello (optional)

2 tablespoons olive oil (or butter; not vegan)

1 teaspoon mixed dried herbs, such as thyme, oregano, rosemary, and basil

Juice of ½ lemon

Kosher salt and freshly ground black pepper

Fresh chopped parsley or chives (optional)

1. Heat a stovetop grill (or an oven to 400°F). Slice the bread on a diagonal into 8 (1" thick) oblong slices; spread the Aioli onto both sides of each slice. Grill or bake the bread slices until dark brown marks decorate their faces, top and bottom. Transfer to a serving plate.

2. Cut the mushrooms into large, uneven chunks and slices, and mix all the varieties together. Warm a large, heavy skillet over high heat. Add the mushrooms to the dry pan all at once, then add the olive oil or butter; sprinkle the herbs on top. Cook without stirring for the first 4–5 minutes, allowing the mushrooms to get a brown crust. After 5 minutes, stir to mix in the herbs and cook until the accumulating liquid is mostly evaporated. Season well with lemon, salt, and pepper. Spoon onto the grilled bread and garnish with chopped parsley or chives if desired.

MUSHROOM-BARLEY "RISOTTO"

The saucy, resilient texture of risotto pairs with the nutty earthiness of barley when the barley is prepared risotto-style like this.

Serves 4

3 tablespoons olive oil

1 large onion, chopped (about 2 cups)

½ teaspoon garlic powder, or 4 cloves garlic, finely chopped

1 tablespoon chopped fresh rosemary, or 1 teaspoon dried

1 pound cremini or white mushrooms, sliced

1 teaspoon salt, and additional salt to taste

1 cup pearl barley

½ cup white wine

5 cups Mushroom Vegetable Stock (see Chapter 5) or other broth

Juice of 1 lemon

Pepper to taste

Chopped chives or Italian parsley

Parmesan cheese (optional)

1. Heat the oil in a large Dutch oven or saucepan over medium-high heat; add the onion, garlic, and rosemary. Cook 5 minutes, until onions are translucent; add the mushrooms and salt. Cook 5 minutes more, until the mushrooms have wilted a bit; add the barley.

2. Cook, stirring regularly, until the barley is well coated. Add the wine; cook until alcohol has evaporated, about 5 minutes. Stir in 1 cup of stock or broth; cook, stirring until it is absorbed. Repeat with remaining stock or broth, adding it in 1-cup increments and cooking until it's absorbed—about 20 minutes. Adjust seasoning with lemon, salt, and pepper. Transfer to wide soup plates. Garnish with chopped chives or parsley. Sprinkle with Parmesan cheese on the side, if desired.

OVEN-ROASTED MUSHROOMS

Roasting intensifies the flavor of these savory herbed mushrooms, making them an excellent topping for whole grains like brown rice, barley, or wheat berries.

Serves 4

1 pound white, cremini, or shiitake mushrooms

1 tablespoon extra-virgin olive oil

1 tablespoon chopped fresh thyme, or 1 teaspoon dried

½ teaspoon salt

Pinch of crushed red pepper flakes

Chopped Italian parsley

1 teaspoon balsamic vinegar or lemon juice

Heat oven to 400°F. If using shiitakes, remove stems. In a bowl, combine mushrooms, olive oil, thyme, salt, and red pepper flakes; toss to coat. Spread in a single layer in a roasting pan. Roast in center of oven for 30 minutes, until nicely browned. Toss with parsley and vinegar or lemon juice. Serve hot or room temperature.

VEGETABLE-STUFFED PORTOBELLO MUSHROOMS

Fork-and-knife mushrooms like portobellos are attractive and easy to serve. These can be made up to one day in advance and kept in the refrigerator before the final cooking step.

Serves 4

16 bite-size broccoli florets

2 tablespoons olive oil, divided

1 medium onion, chopped

10 ounces washed spinach leaves

Salt and pepper to taste

1 tablespoon heavy cream

1½ cups shredded Gruyère or Emmentaler cheese

4 large portobello mushrooms

1. Blanch the broccoli florets in boiling salted water and shock them in ice water. Heat 1 tablespoon olive oil over medium heat in a skillet and cook the onion until translucent, 5 minutes. Add the spinach, season with salt and pepper, and cook until spinach is wilted. Transfer to a plate to cool, and then squeeze any excess water from the spinach. In a food processor or with a knife, finely chop the spinach, and mix in the cream and ⅔ of the cheese. Taste for salt.

2. Remove the mushroom stems; scoop out some of the dark ribs in the center of the caps. Divide the spinach-cheese mixture into the mushroom caps. Arrange 4 broccoli florets into a tight bouquet in the center of the cap, planting the stem deep in the spinach filling. Mushrooms can be cooked now, or refrigerated for cooking later.

3. Heat the broiler. Heat remaining 1 tablespoon olive oil in a large skillet. Transfer the stuffed mushrooms to the pan, cover, and cook over medium heat for 10–15 minutes, or until cooked through. Uncover, sprinkle with remaining cheese, and broil until cheese is molten and bubbly.

CREAMED MUSHROOMS

For a decadent sense of luxury, nothing compares with the silky-rich taste of mushrooms in a mushroom-flavored cream sauce. This dish is delicious over polenta, poured over toasted bread for luscious open-faced sandwiches, or as part of a vegetarian sampler plate, with sweet glazed carrots, steamed snow peas, and crisp onion rings.

Serves 6–8

1 tablespoon finely chopped shallot or onion

2 tablespoons unsalted butter

10 ounces domestic or wild mushrooms (ceps, or porcinis, are exquisite prepared this way), sliced

½ teaspoon salt, and some pepper to taste

1 cup cream, plus 2 tablespoons

Lemon juice (optional)

1. In a heavy skillet, cook the shallot or onion in the butter for 1 minute; add the mushrooms, salt, and pepper. Cook until mushrooms have given up their water, and most of it has evaporated.

2. Add the cream; simmer until the cream has reduced almost to nothing. Remove pan from heat; stir in remaining 2 tablespoons of cream. A drop of lemon juice may be added to accentuate the flavor, if desired.

MUSHROOM-TOFU STIR-FRY

Dried Chinese black mushrooms make their own delicious stock when you soak them.

Serves 4

- 10 Chinese dried black mushrooms or ½ pound fresh shiitakes
- 2 tablespoons vegetable oil
- 1 medium onion, halved and sliced lengthwise
- 1 tablespoon chopped fresh ginger
- 1 bunch scallions, chopped
- 1 tablespoon chopped garlic
- ½ teaspoon salt
- 3 tablespoons hoisin sauce mixed with ½ teaspoon Asian sesame oil
- ½ teaspoon rice vinegar or white wine vinegar
- 1½ teaspoons cornstarch, dissolved in 1 tablespoon of mushroom soaking liquid or water
- 20 ounces of silken tofu, cut into cubes

1. Soak the mushrooms in 4 cups of hot water for at least 20 minutes, or overnight. Pour off and reserve the liquid. Remove the stems and slice the mushrooms thickly (¼"). Heat the oil in a large skillet; add the onions, ginger, scallions, and garlic. Cook until the onions are translucent, about 5 minutes; add 1 cup of mushroom soaking liquid. Add salt, hoisin mix, and vinegar; stir, and simmer 5 minutes. Stir in the cornstarch.

2. Spoon the tofu cubes onto the top of the cooking vegetables. Cover, and cook slowly until the tofu is hot, about 5 minutes. Serve with steaming hot brown rice.

MUSHROOM TURNOVERS (EMPANADAS)

Tailor these savory pastry pockets to your own taste. You may like to add cheese, or other sautéed vegetables—go ahead.

Serves 8

1 recipe Basic Pie Dough (see Chapter 6) or 1 package frozen puff pastry

1 recipe Creamed Mushrooms (see recipe in this chapter) or mushrooms from Step 2 of Polenta-Style Grits with Wild Mushroom Ragout (see recipe in this chapter)

1 egg, beaten

¼ cup milk

1. Heat oven to 350°F. Roll the dough to medium thickness (about the thickness of the cover of a hardcover book). Use an empty can or other cutter to stamp out 16 (5"-diameter) disks. Spoon 2 tablespoons mushroom filling onto the center of each disk. Moisten the edge of the disks very slightly, fold the disk to form a half-moon, and crimp shut with the tines of a fork. Combine the egg and milk, and brush this egg wash onto the tops of the turnovers. Transfer them to a baking sheet.

2. Bake for 25–30 minutes, until plump and golden brown.

PICKLED MUSHROOMS

As a snack or as part of a dinner buffet, pickled mushrooms bring an attractive piquancy to the table. They keep refrigerated for weeks.

Serves 8

1½ pounds small white mushrooms, halved

3 medium carrots, peeled and cut into julienne

1 tablespoon olive oil

½ cup canned pimento (red peppers), cut into 1" × ½" strips

½ teaspoon oregano

½ teaspoon garlic powder

¼ cup cider vinegar

½ teaspoon salt

¼ teaspoon freshly ground black pepper

Boil the mushrooms and the carrots separately; drain. Heat the oil in a medium skillet. Cook the carrots in the oil for 3 minutes; add the mushrooms. Cook 3 minutes more; add the pimento, oregano, garlic powder, cider vinegar, salt, and pepper. Cook until everything is heated through. Refrigerate for 24 hours before serving.

WARM OYSTER MUSHROOM SALAD

This variation on a popular salad from New York's Orso restaurant can be served warm or room temperature. If you can't grill or broil the mushrooms and onions, sauté them in very hot olive oil instead.

Serves 4

3 tablespoons extra-virgin olive oil, divided

1 tablespoon good quality balsamic vinegar

1 tablespoon finely chopped shallots

Kosher salt and freshly ground black pepper

2 medium red onions, peeled, cut into 12 (1") rings

½ pound oyster mushrooms, root ends trimmed, in small bunches

6 ounces frisée, chicory, or other resilient salad green

1. Whisk together 2 tablespoons olive oil, balsamic vinegar, and shallots; season with salt and pepper.

2. Heat a grill, stovetop grill pan, or broiler. Toss the onions and oyster mushrooms, separately, with the remaining 1 tablespoon olive oil. Season them with salt and pepper, and grill or broil separately. The mushrooms will cook quickly—in about 2 minutes. The onions will take longer—about 5 minutes. Spoon some of the dressing onto the hot mushrooms and onions, and use the rest to dress the greens. Arrange the hot vegetables atop the greens and serve.

MUSHROOM-LEEK TART

Savory pies are common in Italy and France, but with the exception of quiche, not too well known here. It's a shame, because they make beautiful presentations, and with the right ingredients they're unforgettable. This one is French in origin.

Serves 6

1 recipe Basic Pie Dough (see Chapter 6)

1 large egg

1 teaspoon milk

5 or 6 leeks, white parts only, chopped and washed twice

1 teaspoon sage

1 cup heavy cream

Kosher salt and freshly ground black pepper

1 package (10 ounces) white mushrooms, sliced

1. Roll out the pie bottom very thin, and press it into a 10" pie pan, leaving excess hanging over the rim of the pan. Roll out the pie top into an 11" round and place onto a floured sheet pan. Refrigerate both parts until needed. Whisk together the egg and milk.

2. Heat oven to 400°F. In a heavy skillet over medium heat, cook the leeks in a few drops of water until they're bright green, about 3 minutes; transfer to a plate to cool. In a bowl, combine the leeks with the sage, cream, salt, pepper, and mushrooms; mix well. Fill the pie bottom with the vegetable mixture. Brush the rim with egg wash and carefully place the top onto the pie (it's easiest if you fold it into quarters, then unfold it onto the pie). Brush the top well with egg wash, and cut a few vents with scissors or a knife. Bake in center of oven until golden and bubbly, about 35 minutes. Cool for 10–15 minutes before cutting into wedges.

MUSHROOM BARLEY

You'll be inspired by the amazing flavors in this dish!

Serves 8

1 mushroom-vegetable bouillon cube (Telma makes these—they're vegetarian, and usually sold with Jewish foods in the supermarket)

Kosher salt

1 (12-ounce) package barley-shaped egg noodle (both Goodman's and Manischewitz make this pasta, usually sold in the "Jewish Ingredients" section of the supermarket)

2 tablespoons olive oil

1 large onion, diced

1 teaspoon garlic powder

1 package (10 ounces) mushrooms, sliced

1. Bring 8 cups water to a boil; add the bouillon cube, 1 teaspoon salt, and the pasta. Cook until tender, about 10–15 minutes. Drain.

2. Heat the olive oil in a large heavy skillet for 1 minute over high heat; add the onion. Cook 5 minutes, until translucent. Add 1 teaspoon salt and the garlic powder; cook a minute more; add the mushrooms. Cook over high heat for 5–7 minutes more, until mushrooms have given up their liquid and most has evaporated. Toss the mushroom mixture with the cooked pasta.

SC MUSHROOM AND OLIVE BLEND

Try serving on top of toasted baguette slices or on pasta or as a savory side dish.

Serves 6

2 tablespoons butter or vegan margarine

1 clove garlic, minced

½ cup sliced shiitake mushrooms

½ cup sliced oyster mushrooms

½ cup chopped hen-of-the-woods mushrooms

¼ cup pitted and sliced Kalamata olives

½ teaspoon salt

¼ teaspoon pepper

Add all ingredients to a 2-quart slow cooker, cover and cook on low heat for 2 hours. Stir occasionally to make sure the butter or margarine is coating the mushrooms.

Mushroom Varieties

Hen-of-the-woods mushrooms are also called maitake mushrooms, and grow in clusters. If you can't find this variety, you can substitute ½ cup more shiitake or oyster mushrooms.

CHAPTER 11
PASTA DISHES

RECIPE LIST

BASIC PASTA **586**

GEMELLI WITH ASPARAGUS TIPS, LEMON, AND BUTTER **587**

PUMPKIN-SPINACH LASAGNA **588**

SWISS CHARD RAVIOLI **589**

WHITE LASAGNA WITH SPINACH AND MUSHROOMS **590**

FUSILLI (SPIRALS) WITH GRILLED EGGPLANT, GARLIC, AND SPICY TOMATO SAUCE **591**

FARFALLE (BOW-TIES) FRA DIAVOLO **592**

FIVE-MINUTE PASTA PESTO **592**

FETTUCCINE ALFREDO **593**

ZITI WITH PEPPERS AND MARINATED MOZZARELLA **594**

SPAGHETTI WITH ASPARAGUS, PARMESAN, AND CREAM **595**

ORECCHIETTE WITH ROASTED PEPPERS, GREEN BEANS, AND PESTO **596**

THE BEST PESTO **597**

LINGUINE WITH OLIVES, CAPERS, AND TOMATOES **598**

POLENTA WITH WILD MUSHROOMS **599**

FETTUCCINE WITH SHIITAKE MUSHROOMS AND BROWN BUTTER **600**

ANGEL HAIR WITH BROCCOLI RAAB, TOASTED GARLIC, FAVA BEANS, AND PECORINO CHEESE **601**

SPAGHETTI WITH SWEET CORN, TOMATOES, AND GOAT CHEESE **602**

BAKED ZITI **603**

SPINACH MANICOTTI **603**

RAW VEGGIE PASTA TOSS **604**

BASIC PASTA SALAD **605**

ROASTED VEGETABLE PASTA **606**

SMALL SHELLS WITH GRILLED VEGETABLES, OLIVES, OREGANO, AND TOMATOES **607**

LINGUINE WITH GORGONZOLA, ASPARAGUS, AND CREAM **608**

SPAGHETTI AI POMODORINI **609**

TAGLIATELLE AGLIO E OLIO **609**

MACARONI AND CHEESE **610**

PASTA PRIMAVERA WITH VEGETABLES **611**

PASTA SALAD WITH TOMATO, ARUGULA, AND FETA **612**

GNOCCHI AND MUSHROOMS IN ROSEMARY ALFREDO SAUCE **613**

VEGETABLE LINGUINE IN WHITE BEAN ALFREDO SAUCE **614**

ROTINI WITH RED WINE MARINARA **615**

PASTA FAGIOLE **615**

ORZO-STUFFED POBLANO PEPPERS **616**

ORZO-STUFFED TOMATOES **617**

PASTA PUTTANESCA **618**

WHOLE-WHEAT FETTUCCINE WITH MUSHROOM CREAM SAUCE **619**

BROCCOLI–PINE NUT PASTA SALAD **620**

FRESH SPINACH–WHITE WINE ANGEL HAIR PASTA **621**

PORTOBELLO STROGANOFF **622**

BOW-TIE PASTA IN A SAGE BEURRE BLANC SAUCE **623**

BASIC PASTA

Use this dough to make your own ravioli, fettuccine, tagliatelle, lasagna, etc.

Yields just under 2 pounds

3½ cups unbleached all-purpose flour

2 large eggs (egg substitute or ½ cup hot water will also work as a vegan alternative)

½ cup plus 2 teaspoons cold water

1 teaspoon salt

1 teaspoon olive oil

1. Pulse the flour, eggs, water, salt, and oil in a food processor until blended, being careful not to overheat the dough. Knead it for 10 minutes on a clean work surface, until the dough is smooth and highly elastic. The dough will be very stiff, and kneading will take a little elbow grease. Cut the dough into 4 pieces. It's best to let the dough rest 30 minutes before rolling it out.

2. If using a pasta-rolling machine (relatively inexpensive, around $20, and very liberating!), follow manufacturer's directions. If rolling by hand, proceed as follows: Flatten 1 of the dough pieces, place on a floured work surface, and roll from the center out, turning the circle ¼ turn every few moments. When the dough reaches a thickness of ⅛", wrap ⅓ around the rolling pin and draw it away from yourself, stretching it thin. Repeat this rolling and stretching process until the dough is thin enough to see your hand through. Repeat with remaining dough.

GEMELLI WITH ASPARAGUS TIPS, LEMON, AND BUTTER

Butter thickens this sauce and helps it adhere to these short, twisted pairs of macaroni, which have become one of the most popular shapes introduced in the last five years.

Serves 4

2 bunches medium asparagus, cut on bias into 1½" pieces

½ pound gemelli pasta

4 tablespoons unsalted butter, divided

Juice and zest of 2 lemons

½ cup vegetable stock or water

Salt and black pepper to taste

Grated Parmesan

1. Parcook the asparagus pieces in 3 batches; first in 6 quarts rapidly boiling salted water, then plunging them immediately into salted ice water as they are removed from cooking water (shock); then drain. Boil gemelli in the asparagus cooking water "al dente" (soft, but still slightly chewy in the center). Drain and rinse.

2. Melt 1 tablespoon butter in a skillet large enough to hold all ingredients (12" diameter), and add the lemon zest and asparagus pieces. Sauté on medium heat until asparagus is hot, then add the stock, toss in the pasta, and raise heat to high.

3. When pasta is steaming hot, swirl in the remaining butter, the lemon juice, and salt and pepper to taste. Serve in bowls, sprinkled with Parmesan.

PUMPKIN-SPINACH LASAGNA

Use either "sugar baby" pumpkins or butternut squash for this recipe. The larger kind, used for jack-o'-lanterns, are not very flavorful, and are intended mostly for decoration. If you find Mexican pumpkin, called calabaza (actually a large winter squash that resembles a pumpkin), use it.

Serves 8

1 pound lasagna

2 tablespoons olive oil, plus a drop

1 tablespoon salt

1 small pumpkin (2–3 pounds)

¼ teaspoon crushed red pepper flakes

¼ teaspoon ground nutmeg

3 cloves garlic, chopped

1 large bunch spinach (or cello bag), washed thoroughly

Freshly ground pepper

2 pounds ricotta

1 egg

4 ounces Parmesan, grated

4 ounces grated mozzarella or provolone cheese

2 cups tomato sauce

1. Cook lasagna according to directions on box (it's best to undercook a little). Rinse and drain. Toss with a drop of olive oil. Set aside. Refill pasta pot with 3 quarts water, add 1 tablespoon salt, and bring to a boil.

2. Peel pumpkin. (I cut off the top and bottom and shave the outside with a knife, always shaving downward, toward the cutting board. You may find a potato peeler easier.) Discard seeds and cube into bite-size pieces. Boil pumpkin pieces 15 minutes, until tender, in salted water. Drain, and toss with crushed pepper and nutmeg.

3. In a 10" skillet sauté half of the garlic in 1 tablespoon olive oil, adding half of the spinach when garlic starts to brown. Allow spinach to wilt, then turn out onto a plate, and repeat with remaining spinach and garlic. Season with salt and pepper. Mix the ricotta, egg, and Parmesan together. Set aside.

4. Assemble the lasagna in layers, starting with noodle, then cheese mixture, then spinach and pumpkin. Make 2 more layers, making sure to save unbroken lasagna for the top layer. Sprinkle grated mozzarella or provolone on top.

5. Bake 30 minutes at 400°F until brown and bubbling on top. Let rest 15 minutes before serving with tomato sauce on the side.

SWISS CHARD RAVIOLI

This Swiss Chard Ravioli is top of the line! Be prepared to serve it more than once a week to satisfy your hungry family!

Serves 8

2 tablespoons olive oil

1 medium onion, finely chopped

1 tablespoon chopped garlic (2–3 cloves)

Pinch of crushed red pepper flakes (optional)

1 large bunch (about 1½ pounds) red or green Swiss chard, stems removed

12 ounces (1½ cups) ricotta cheese

½ cup grated Parmigiano-Reggiano or Asiago cheese (use top quality here)

1 tablespoon bread crumbs

2 beaten eggs, divided

Salt and freshly ground black pepper

1 recipe Basic Pasta dough (see recipe in this chapter), rolled into 4 sheets, or 4 (9" × 14") sheets of any pasta dough

1. Heat the oil in a large skillet over medium-high flame. Add the onion, garlic, and red pepper if using; cook 5 minutes until onions are translucent. Add the chard; cook until just wilted. Transfer to a colander to cool and drain. Once the chard has cooled, squeeze out excess moisture with your hands. Transfer to a cutting board and give it a rough chopping.

2. In a large mixing bowl, combine the chopped chard, ricotta, Parmigiano-Reggiano, bread crumbs, and half the eggs. Season to taste with salt and black pepper (season it highly, as you'll only use a little in each ravioli).

3. Place 12 evenly spaced, tablespoon-size dabs of filling onto each of 2 pasta sheets. Using a pastry brush, paint in between the filling portions with the remaining egg. Loosely cover these pasta sheets with the remaining 2 sheets. Press down with your hands to squeeze out any air pockets, and press firmly to seal the filling in. Using a knife or fluted pastry cutter, cut between the ravioli, separating them, and pinch the edges extra tight between your fingers. Allow them to dry for 15–30 minutes before cooking in rapidly boiling salted water.

WHITE LASAGNA WITH SPINACH AND MUSHROOMS

This white lasagna doesn't use a marinara sauce, but with its delicious flavors, it doesn't need to!

Serves 12

5 cups milk

1 large onion, roughly chopped

2 bay leaves

4 whole cloves

Pinch of nutmeg

6 ounces (1½ sticks) unsalted butter

¾ cup flour

Salt and white pepper

1 package (1 pound) no-boil lasagna noodles (or parcooked regular lasagna)

1 pound ricotta

1 cup grated Parmigiano-Reggiano or other top-quality Parmesan cheese

1½ pounds shredded provolone, Monterey jack, or mozzarella cheese

1 pound mixed mushrooms (white, shiitake, cremini, portobello, etc.), sliced, seasoned, and sautéed

1½ pounds fresh spinach (or 1 pound frozen chopped spinach, thawed), cooked

1. Prepare the white sauce: Combine the milk, onion, bay leaves, cloves, and nutmeg in a small saucepan; simmer slowly for 10 minutes. In a medium saucepan, melt the butter, stir in the flour, and cook on medium-low until it smells slightly nutty and bubbles slightly, but has not darkened in color at all, about 3 minutes. Strain the milk; gradually whisk the strained milk into the bubbling flour mixture, whisking out any lumps that may form. Simmer 10 minutes; season with salt and white pepper.

2. Assemble the lasagna: Heat oven to 350°F. Spread 2 cups of white sauce on the bottom of a 9" × 13" baking dish. Arrange a layer of lasagna noodles onto the sauce; dot it with spoonfuls of ricotta (½ of total), and a sprinkling of each of the other cheeses (⅓ of each). Form another noodle layer on top of the cheese. Distribute all of the cooked mushrooms and spinach in a single layer, season with salt and pepper, and sprinkle with another third of the grated and shredded cheeses, and dot with the remaining ricotta. Top with a final layer of noodle, smooth on another 2 cups of white sauce, and sprinkle with remaining cheeses.

3. Bake until bubbly and browned on top, about 25 minutes. Rest at room temperature for 10 minutes before cutting into 12 servings. Serve the remaining white sauce on the side.

FUSILLI (SPIRALS) WITH GRILLED EGGPLANT, GARLIC, AND SPICY TOMATO SAUCE

Smoky, fruity flavors of grilled or roasted eggplant marry beautifully with tomatoes and garlic. Fusilli's deep crannies scoop up every drop of this complex-tasting sauce.

Serves 4

- 1 small eggplant (about ½ pound), cut lengthwise into 8 wedges
- 3 tablespoons olive oil, divided
- Kosher salt and freshly ground black pepper
- 3 cloves garlic, finely chopped (about 1 tablespoon)
- ¼ teaspoon crushed red pepper flakes
- ½ cup roughly chopped Italian parsley
- 4 cups tomato sauce (see various recipes in Chapter 2)
- ½ box (½ pound) fusilli or other pasta shape, cooked "al dente"
- 1 tablespoon butter (optional; not vegan)
- ¼ cup grated Parmesan cheese (optional; not vegan)

1. Heat grill, grill pan, or broiler. Toss the eggplant wedges with 1 tablespoon olive oil; season liberally with salt and pepper. Grill or broil it on the largest cut side for 4 minutes, until black marks show. Using tongs or a fork, turn to another side and cook 3 minutes more until it is bubbling with juices. Transfer to a cutting board to cool; cut into 1" pieces.

2. Mix remaining olive oil with garlic and red pepper flakes. Heat a large skillet over medium-high heat. Add the garlic mixture; allow to sizzle just 15 seconds, stirring with a wooden spoon, before adding the parsley. Cook 30 seconds; add the eggplant and tomato sauce. Bring to a simmer, add the cooked pasta, and cook until heated through; remove from heat. Finish by adding butter and cheese (if using), adjusting for seasoning and tossing well to combine. Serve in bowls, sprinkled with additional chopped parsley. Serve additional cheese on the side if desired.

FARFALLE (BOW-TIES) FRA DIAVOLO

This is a very quick, easy pasta.

Serves 8

2 tablespoons olive oil

1 tablespoon finely chopped garlic (about 3 cloves)

½ teaspoon crushed red pepper flakes

1 cup roughly chopped Italian parsley

4 cups Basic Fresh Tomato Sauce (see Chapter 2) or 1 (28-ounce) jar store-bought sauce

1 pound farfalle, cooked "al dente"

Kosher salt and freshly ground black pepper

1. Bring a pot of water to a boil for reheating the pasta. Heat a large skillet or heavy-bottomed pot large enough to hold all the ingredients over high heat. Add the oil, garlic, pepper flakes, and parsley; allow these ingredients to sizzle for 30 seconds. Add the tomato sauce; bring to a simmer.

2. Using a colander or China cap (a funnel-shaped strainer), dip the cooked pasta into the boiling water for 1 minute to reheat. Transfer the reheated pasta into the sauce, letting the water that adheres to the pasta drip into the sauce and thin it a little. Toss to coat; adjust consistency with additional pasta water, and season with salt and pepper to taste. Serve sprinkled with additional chopped parsley.

FIVE-MINUTE PASTA PESTO

This pesto is easy to make and even easier to love!

Serves 4

2 tablespoons olive oil

1 medium onion, sliced very thin

2 cups frozen peas

4 cups (about ½ box) parcooked ziti

3 quarts rapidly boiling water

Salt and pepper

⅓ cup pesto sauce

1 cup chopped tomatoes

Butter and grated Parmesan cheese (optional)

1. Heat the olive oil in a large skillet over very high heat; add the onions and peas. Place the parcooked ziti into the boiling water. When onions are translucent (3 minutes), use a slotted spoon or strainer to scoop the cooked pasta from the boiling water into the pan with the vegetables, allowing some of the pasta water to fall into the skillet along with it. Season well with salt and pepper.

2. Remove pan from the heat; add the pesto, chopped tomatoes, and butter and cheese if using. Toss to coat. Serve immediately.

FETTUCCINE ALFREDO

Rich enough to sate the hungriest guest, this creamy pasta was named for the famous Alfredo's restaurant in Rome.

Serves 4

8 ounces (½ box) fettuccine

½ cup butter

2 cloves garlic, minced

1 tablespoon flour

1½ cups whole milk

2 tablespoons cream cheese

1 cup grated Parmesan cheese, plus extra for garnish

Salt and freshly ground black pepper

1. Prepare the pasta according to package directions. Drain and keep warm.

2. In a large saucepan, melt the butter; add garlic and cook 2 minutes. Stir in the flour, then add the milk all at once, cooking and stirring over medium heat until thick and bubbly. Add the cream cheese; stir until blended. Add the Parmesan cheese; continue cooking until all cheese has melted. Toss with fettuccine; season with salt and pepper. Serve with extra Parmesan on the side.

ZITI WITH PEPPERS AND MARINATED MOZZARELLA

Certain peppers, like the very sweet red ones and the slightly bitter fresh green ones, are a must; from there you're on your own.

Serves 4

- 1 pound fresh mozzarella cheese or smoked fresh mozzarella, cut into ½" cubes
- 3 tablespoons olive oil, divided
- ½ cup mixed chopped fresh herbs, such as parsley, chives, oregano, mint, etc.
- Pinch of crushed red pepper flakes
- 1 teaspoon red or white wine vinegar
- Kosher salt and freshly ground black pepper
- 1 tablespoon chopped garlic (about 3 cloves)
- 2 cups sliced onions
- 3 cups sliced mixed bell peppers
- 2 cups Basic Fresh Tomato Sauce (see Chapter 2) or store-bought tomato sauce
- ½ box (½ pound) ziti, cooked al dente
- ¼ cup grated Parmesan cheese
- 1 tablespoon unsalted butter (optional)

1. Combine the mozzarella, 1 tablespoon of olive oil, the herbs, pepper flakes, vinegar, salt, and pepper. Marinate at room temperature for 30 minutes.

2. Combine remaining oil with chopped garlic. Heat a large skillet over high heat and bring a pot of water to a boil to reheat the pasta. Add the garlic oil to the pan, sizzle 10 seconds until the garlic turns white, and add the onions and peppers. Cook, stirring occasionally, until the onions are translucent. Add the tomato sauce and lower flame to a simmer. Dip the pasta in boiling water to reheat; transfer hot pasta to the sauce, allowing some of the pasta water to drip into the sauce and thin it. Season to taste with salt and pepper. Remove from heat.

3. Toss with marinated mozzarella, and Parmesan and butter if desired.

SPAGHETTI WITH ASPARAGUS, PARMESAN, AND CREAM

In the winter, asparagus is fatter and imported from the other side of the world. It's perfect for pastas like this, which rely on plump stems.

Serves 6

1 bunch asparagus (preferably chubby-stemmed)

2 teaspoons olive oil

2 medium shallots, sliced thin

¼ cup white wine

¼ cup vegetable stock or water

2 cups heavy cream

8 ounces (½ box) spaghetti, cooked al dente, drained, tossed with a drop of olive oil

¼ cup Parmigiano-Reggiano cheese or other top-quality Parmesan

Juice of 1 lemon, plus 6 lemon wedges

Kosher salt and freshly ground black pepper

1. Trim the bottoms of the asparagus, and use a vegetable peeler to peel off the skin from the bottom half of the stalks. Cut the asparagus into bite-size (about 1") pieces. Heat the oil in a large skillet over medium heat; add the shallots and cook 3 minutes to soften them. Add the asparagus and wine; cook until the wine is mostly evaporated, then add the stock or water.

2. When the asparagus is mostly cooked and the stock is mostly steamed out, stir in the cream and bring to a boil; add the spaghetti. Cook until the spaghetti is hot and the sauce is slightly thick; add the Parmigiano and remove from heat. Season with lemon juice, salt, and pepper. If necessary, adjust consistency with additional stock or water. Serve with lemon wedges on the side.

ORECCHIETTE WITH ROASTED PEPPERS, GREEN BEANS, AND PESTO

Orecchiette are "little ears" of pasta—dime-size concave disks that catch sauce very well, and have a substantial, hearty bite. If you can't find them, look for conchiglie (small shells), which are similar.

Serves 6

- ½ pound (½ box) orecchiette or other pasta shape
- 1 tablespoon olive oil
- 2 teaspoons chopped garlic
- 1 cup Roasted Peppers (see Chapter 3), sliced
- ¼ pound green beans, blanched
- ¼ cup dry white wine (optional)
- ¾ cup pesto
- ¼ cup roughly chopped Italian parsley
- Salt and pepper to taste
- 1 tablespoon unsalted butter
- Parmesan cheese
- Lemon wedges

1. Bring a pot of salted water to boil; cook the pasta until al dente (still a little chewy), drain it, but save a cup of the cooking water for later. Toss the pasta with a drop of olive oil; set aside.

2. Combine the olive oil and chopped garlic. Heat a large skillet for 1 minute over medium heat. Add the garlic oil; sizzle for 15 seconds, then add the Roasted Peppers and green beans. Sauté for 3 minutes; add the wine. Cook 1 minute until alcohol has evaporated. Add ½ cup pesto; stir. Add the cooked pasta, parsley, salt, pepper, and butter; simmer until heated through, adding a few drops of the reserved pasta water to make it saucy. Remove from heat; toss with Parmesan cheese. Serve with lemon wedges and a little extra pesto on the side.

THE BEST PESTO

It's true! This pesto really is the best.

Serves 8

5 cloves garlic, peeled

½ cup pine nuts, toasted to very light brown

1 large bunch basil, stems and veins removed, washed and dried thoroughly

2 cups extra-virgin olive oil

½ cup grated Parmigiano-Reggiano cheese

Coarse salt and freshly ground black pepper

1. Pulse garlic in food processor until finely chopped. Add nuts and pulse a few times just to break them into pieces. Scrape the bowl to loosen anything stuck to the sides.

2. Pile in all of the basil. Pour half of the oil over the leaves, and pulse until basil is medium chopped (pieces about the size of cooked rice). Transfer to a mixing bowl.

3. Using a plastic spatula or a wooden spoon, fold in the Parmigiano cheese; season with salt and pepper, and thin to sauce consistency with the remaining olive oil. It will keep in the refrigerator for 1 week, in the freezer for up to 2 months. When using frozen pesto, do not thaw, but break off what you need from a frozen block.

LINGUINE WITH OLIVES, CAPERS, AND TOMATOES

Remember to use a boxed variety of pasta when looking for a vegan pasta dish. Most fresh and many frozen pastas are made with eggs. You should also check the ingredients of any dry pasta you buy, just to be sure.

Serves 8

2 tablespoons olive oil

1 tablespoon chopped garlic

½ cup assorted olives, such as Picholine, Ligurian, Kalamata, or Niçoise, pitted

1 tablespoon small (nonpareil) capers

Pinch of crushed red pepper flakes

½ cup roughly chopped Italian parsley

2 cups chopped tomatoes

2 cups Basic Fresh Tomato Sauce (see Chapter 2) or other tomato sauce

Salt and pepper to taste

1 pound linguine, cooked al dente, drained, rinsed, and tossed with olive oil

2 tablespoons unsalted butter (optional; not vegan)

¼ cup grated Parmigiano-Reggiano cheese (optional; not vegan)

1. Heat the olive oil and garlic in a large, heavy-bottomed skillet or Dutch oven until it sizzles; add the olives, capers, red pepper flakes, and parsley. Cook 2 minutes; add the tomatoes. Cook until the tomatoes soften into a chunky sauce; add the tomato sauce, season to taste, and bring back to a simmer.

2. Add the cooked linguine; cook until heated through. Remove from heat, adjust seasoning, and toss with butter and cheese if desired. Serve sprinkled with additional chopped parsley.

POLENTA WITH WILD MUSHROOMS

Northern Italian comfort food like this was often placed directly onto the center of a wooden farmhouse table in Italy. Diners would draw portions from the center pile over to their plates. It's the perfect winter dinner.

Serves 4

1 recipe Polenta with Butter and Cheese (see Chapter 7)

1 tablespoon olive oil

1 pound assorted wild or exotic mushrooms, such as hedgehogs, shiitakes, oysters, and chanterelles (see "Fungus Among Us" in Chapter 4), sliced into large pieces

8 ounces white button mushrooms, sliced

2 tablespoons butter, divided

1 teaspoon salt

¼ cup chopped fresh herbs such as rosemary, thyme, oregano, and parsley, or 1 tablespoon dried

Juice of 1 lemon

Freshly ground black pepper

Grated cheese (optional)

1. Keep polenta warm over a very low flame on a back burner. Heat the olive oil until very hot, almost smoking, in a large skillet. Add the wild and white mushrooms and 1 tablespoon of butter; do not stir. Cook mushrooms undisturbed over a high flame for 5 minutes, to give them a nice browning. Season with salt; add the herbs, stir, and cook until the mushrooms are wilted and juicy. Remove from heat and swirl in a little lemon juice and remaining butter.

2. Pour the hot polenta into a deep serving dish or bowl—it should be thick but liquidy. In a minute, make an indentation in the center of the polenta, and spoon in the mushrooms. Serve with a few grinds of fresh black pepper, and grated cheese if desired.

FETTUCCINE WITH SHIITAKE MUSHROOMS AND BROWN BUTTER

This is an easy, elegant pasta dish.

Serves 4

- 4 ounces (1 stick) unsalted butter, divided
- ½ teaspoon kosher salt
- 3 leaves fresh sage or a pinch of dried
- 1 pound shiitake mushrooms, stems removed, sliced thin
- ¼ cup dry white wine
- ¼ cup vegetable stock or water
- 8 ounces (½ box) cooked fettuccine
- ¼ cup roughly chopped Italian parsley
- Juice of 1 lemon, plus 6 wedges

Place all but 1 tablespoon of the butter in a large skillet with the salt. Cook over medium heat until the butter turns brown and has a smoky, nutty aroma—it should not turn black or smell burnt. Add the salt and sage, and then the mushrooms. Cook without stirring for 5 minutes to brown the mushrooms. Stir; cook until the mushrooms are wilted and juicy; add the wine. Cook 1 minute to steam out the alcohol. Add the stock or water, cooked fettuccine, parsley, and lemon juice. Remove from heat, add remaining 1 tablespoon butter, and toss to coat. Serve with extra lemon wedges.

ANGEL HAIR WITH BROCCOLI RAAB, TOASTED GARLIC, FAVA BEANS, AND PECORINO CHEESE

Highlight one of spring's most delicious flavors by using fresh fava beans in this dish. If fresh favas are unavailable, use fresh or frozen green peas instead.

Serves 6

1 pound fresh fava beans, shelled (about 1 cup), or 1 cup fresh or frozen green peas

1 tablespoon olive oil

2 cloves garlic, finely chopped

Pinch of crushed red pepper flakes (optional)

¼ cup black olives, such as Niçoise or Kalamata, pitted

1 bunch broccoli raab, cut into bite-size pieces, blanched

1 box (1 pound) angel hair pasta (capellini—extra-thin spaghetti)

1 tablespoon butter

¼ cup grated Parmesan cheese

¼ pound block pecorino, feta, or other semihard cheese

Lemon wedges

1. Bring a large pot of salted water to a rolling boil. Drop the fava beans in for 2 minutes, then skim them out with a slotted spoon and shock them by plunging them into ice-cold water. Peel off the outer leathery skin. Set them aside. Keep the water at a rolling boil.

2. Heat the oil in a large skillet over medium heat. Add the garlic, pepper flakes, and olives, and cook, stirring, until the garlic begins to brown. Add the broccoli raab; cook until heated through, about 2 minutes. Turn off flame.

3. Put the angel hair pasta into the boiling water, stir well to separate, and cook until tender, about 5 minutes—it cooks very quickly; drain, and add to the skillet, allowing some of the water from the pasta to drip into the pan. Toss with butter and Parmesan; season to taste. Divide onto serving plates. Using a swivel vegetable peeler, shave pecorino cheese liberally over pasta. Serve with lemon wedges.

SPAGHETTI WITH SWEET CORN, TOMATOES, AND GOAT CHEESE

Late summer is the perfect time to scoop up sweet seasonal vegetables like scallions, corn, and tomatoes. When vegetables are ripe, they do all the work for you in a dish like this.

Serves 4

½ box (8 ounces) spaghetti

2 tablespoons butter or oil

4 scallions, chopped

2 cups fresh corn kernels (about 3 ears)

1 cup diced red bell pepper

1 jalapeño pepper, finely chopped

3 tomatoes, diced

¼ cup chopped cilantro

¼ cup water or stock

Salt and pepper to taste

2 ounces goat cheese, crumbled

1 lemon

1. Cook the pasta according to the package directions. Heat the butter or oil in a large skillet over medium heat. Add the scallions, corn, red bell pepper, and jalapeño. Cook 3 minutes; add the tomatoes, cilantro, and ¼ cup water or stock. Season to taste.

2. Add the pasta. Sprinkle in the crumbled cheese and toss to distribute. Divide into 4 portions, and garnish with additional chopped cilantro and lemon wedges.

BAKED ZITI

Italian-Americans have a cuisine that is distinctly their own, based on adaptation of ingredients available to their immigrant forefathers when they arrived in the United States. This is a staple of the Italian-American table.

Serves 10

1 box (1 pound) ziti

Olive oil

1 quart tomato sauce

1 pound whole-milk or part-skim ricotta cheese

1 pound whole-milk or part-skim mozzarella, shredded

Chopped Italian parsley

1. Prepare ziti al dente according to package directions; drain, rinse, and toss with a few drops of olive oil.

2. Heat oven to 350°F. Line the bottom of a 9" × 13" baking pan with half of the tomato sauce. Distribute half of the cooked ziti into the pan. Distribute the ricotta by the tablespoonful onto the ziti, and then sprinkle on half of the shredded cheese. Layer on the remaining ziti. Cover the top with most of the remaining sauce, saving about ½ cup for later—the top layer does not need to be even—or use all the remaining sauce to cover the pasta completely. Sprinkle on remaining shredded cheese. Bake 25 minutes until cheese is bubbly and starting to brown. Serve with additional tomato sauce on the side, garnished with chopped parsley.

SPINACH MANICOTTI

Everybody loves stuffed things, so give them some. Why not make it easy on yourself by making one of the easiest?

Serves 4–5

8–10 manicotti shells

5–6 ounces fresh spinach leaves, washed

1 pound ricotta cheese

½ cup grated Parmesan cheese

1 egg, beaten

½ teaspoon salt

¼ teaspoon pepper

2 cups tomato sauce

½ cup shredded mozzarella cheese

1. Cook the manicotti shells according to the package directions. Pick the stems from the spinach leaves. Steam or sauté spinach until just wilted. In a large bowl, combine the ricotta, Parmesan, egg, salt, and pepper; stir in the spinach.

2. Heat the oven to 350°F. Stuff the shells lightly (easy with a pastry bag or spoon); line them into a lightly greased 8" × 11" baking dish. Pour the sauce over all; sprinkle with mozzarella cheese. Bake uncovered 30–40 minutes, until bubbly in the middle.

Note: Use the same filling for jumbo stuffed shells, cannelloni, or other stuffed, baked pasta.

RAW VEGGIE PASTA TOSS

While cooking unlocks nutrients in some vegetables, such as the vitamin A in carrots, many vegetables are at their peak of healthful elements before cooking. So eating raw vegetables in dishes like this isn't just refreshing—it's smart.

Serves 4

1 small yellow squash, diced

1 small zucchini, diced

¼ cup extra-virgin olive oil

3 ripe Roma plum tomatoes, seeded and chopped

1 cup shredded broccoli (available at groceries as "broccoli slaw")

3 scallions, sliced

1 clove garlic, finely chopped

¼ cup chopped fresh basil

Salt and pepper to taste

8 ounces ziti or penne pasta

½ cup shredded mozzarella or provolone cheese

¼ cup shredded Parmigiano-Reggiano or other top quality Parmesan

1. In a large bowl, combine the yellow squash, zucchini, olive oil, tomatoes, broccoli, scallions, garlic, basil, salt, and pepper. Allow to stand while you prepare the pasta.

2. Cook the pasta according to the package directions. Immediately after draining, toss with the cheese until it melts, then toss with the vegetable mixture. Serve warm.

BASIC PASTA SALAD

If you decide to parcook the vegetables, simply throw them into the water with the pasta for 1 minute before draining.

Serves 6

8 ounces tricolor corkscrew (fusilli or spirali) pasta

1 cup or more Italian salad dressing

¼ cup sliced scallions

1 cup chopped broccoli (raw or parboiled)

1 cup chopped cauliflower (raw or parboiled)

1 cup shredded or chopped carrots

¼ cup sliced black olives

⅓ cup shredded Gouda or other cheese

⅓ cup cubed Cheddar cheese

⅓ cup shredded Parmigiano-Reggiano or other top-quality Parmesan

Salt and pepper

1. Cook the pasta according to package directions. While it's still warm, toss in a deep bowl with ¼ cup salad dressing; allow to cool to room temperature 30 minutes, stirring occasionally.

2. Meanwhile, combine all the vegetables in a deep, narrow bowl or container. Add about ½ cup of dressing and stir to coat; add up to ¼ cup more if necessary. Marinate 30 minutes at room temperature, stirring occasionally. Chill and marinate both bowls for at least 6 hours, or overnight. When ready to serve, combine the pasta and vegetables. Toss with cheeses and season to taste.

ROASTED VEGETABLE PASTA

Picnic-lovers: You've gotta try this one. Depending on your choice of vegetables, it's a combination barbecue and summer afternoon in northern Italy. And it's vegan! I like to cook my pasta all the way to soft (past "al dente") for this pasta salad.

Serves 12

- 1 recipe Roasted Vegetables (see Chapter 9) or Grilled Vegetable Antipasto (see Chapter 3) cut into 1" pieces
- 1 box (1 pound) good quality fusilli, penne, or other small pasta shape, cooked according to package directions (okay, a little softer than the box says)
- 2 tablespoons top-quality extra-virgin olive oil
- 2 teaspoons balsamic vinegar
- Pinch of sugar
- 1 teaspoon kosher salt
- ¼ teaspoon freshly ground black pepper
- ½ cup roughly chopped Italian parsley

Place roasted vegetables in a bowl and allow them to come to room temperature. Add the cooked pasta, olive oil, vinegar, and sugar. Toss to coat. Marinate 30 minutes. Season with salt and pepper; toss with parsley. Pack into picnic basket.

SMALL SHELLS WITH GRILLED VEGETABLES, OLIVES, OREGANO, AND TOMATOES

Make extra grilled vegetables next time you have the grill or the broiler on. See the recipe for Roasted Vegetables in Chapter 9 for a selection of veggies to use.

Serves 8

- 1 box (1 pound) shell-shaped pasta (conchiglie)
- 1 tablespoon olive oil or garlic oil
- ¼ cup pitted black olives, such as Kalamata, Gaeta, or Niçoise
- 4 cups Roasted Vegetables or store-bought grilled vegetables from a salad bar or deli counter
- ¼ cup chopped fresh oregano leaves, or 2 teaspoons dried
- 1 cup roughly chopped tomatoes
- 2 cups Basic Fresh Tomato Sauce (see Chapter 2) or other tomato sauce
- ¼ cup roughly chopped Italian parsley
- Salt and fresh ground black pepper to taste
- Vegetable stock or water
- 1 tablespoon unsalted butter (optional)
- ¼ cup grated Parmesan cheese (optional)

Cook pasta according to package directions; drain, rinse, and toss with a few drops of oil. Heat olive oil or garlic oil in a large (13") skillet or Dutch oven for 1 minute over a high heat; add olives and Roasted Vegetables. Cook 5 minutes, until hot; add oregano leaves. Cook 2 minutes more, until oregano is fragrant; stir in the tomatoes and the tomato sauce. Cook 1 minute more, then toss in the pasta, parsley, salt, pepper, and a splash of stock or water to keep it saucy. Cook until the pasta is hot. If desired, toss with butter and cheese.

LINGUINE WITH GORGONZOLA, ASPARAGUS, AND CREAM

Gorgonzola is a highly fragrant Italian blue cheese. You may prefer to make this dish using milder French Roquefort, English Stilton, or American Maytag blue cheese—all are delicious and work fine in this dish.

Serves 4

- ½ pound linguine, broken in half
- 1 tablespoon olive oil
- 1 teaspoon chopped garlic
- 1 pound cooked asparagus, cut into 1" pieces
- 1 cup heavy cream
- 1 cup crumbled Gorgonzola or other crumbly cheese
- 1 tablespoon finely chopped chives (optional)
- Lemon wedges (optional)

1. Cook linguine in a large pot of rapidly boiling, lightly salted water until it's soft but still slightly chewy; drain, retaining some of the cooking water, rinse under cold water, and toss with a few drops of olive oil. Set into a colander for later use. Put another pot of water on to boil for reheating the pasta.

2. Heat the oil for 1 minute over a medium heat; add the garlic and let it sizzle for 15 seconds, until it turns white. Add cooked asparagus. Sauté for 1 minute until heated through; add cream. Bring to a boil, then lower to a simmer and cook until cream is thick enough to coat the back of a spoon, about 3 minutes; stir in the blue cheese. Cook, stirring, until cheese is mostly melted, but a few lumps remain, about 2 minutes. Using a colander or strainer, dip the pasta into boiling water to reheat it, then add the hot pasta to the cream; toss to coat. If sauce is too thick, add a splash of the pasta cooking water. Serve with a sprinkling of freshly snipped chives and lemon wedges, if desired.

SPAGHETTI AI POMODORINI

The simplest pasta requires almost no cooking. Just toss the ingredients in a bowl with the cooked spaghetti.

Serves 4

½ pound spaghetti

2 cups diced plum tomatoes

2 tablespoons chopped fresh oregano leaves or Italian parsley

1 tablespoon extra-virgin olive oil

1 teaspoon finely chopped garlic

½ teaspoon salt

¼ teaspoon freshly ground black pepper

Cook the spaghetti according to the directions on the package; drain. Transfer the hot spaghetti to a large mixing bowl; add all other ingredients. Toss thoroughly.

TAGLIATELLE AGLIO E OLIO

The name means "cuttings with garlic and oil." Tagliatelle is similar to spaghetti, but is cut rather than extruded (terms that describe the method of manufacture), and is usually sold fresh, not dried. It's one of the easiest pastas to manufacture at home, using a home pasta-rolling machine (these inexpensive devices can enrich your food life).

Serves 4

½ recipe Basic Pasta (see recipe in this chapter), cut into thin strands, or 1 pound store-bought fresh tagliatelle, or ½ box dried linguine

2 tablespoons extra-virgin olive oil

2 teaspoons finely chopped garlic

Salt and freshly ground black pepper to taste

Butter and grated Parmesan cheese (optional; not vegan)

Italian parsley, chopped (optional)

Cook the pasta al dente; drain in a colander, reserving ½ cup of the hot cooking water. Combine the olive oil and garlic in a large skillet over high heat until the garlic sizzles and becomes fragrant, but does not brown. Add all the cooked pasta at once. Season to taste, add a few drops of cooking water, and toss to coat. If desired, toss with butter, cheese, and/or chopped parsley.

PC MACARONI AND CHEESE

You can speed up the process by cooking the milk, cream, and cheeses and stirring the mixture into the macaroni over very low heat until it's melted. Then follow the directions in Step 2, eliminating the need to preheat the broiler and brown the bread crumbs under the broiler.

Serves 6

1 tablespoon olive or vegetable oil

1 medium sweet onion, peeled and diced

1 clove garlic, peeled and minced

2 cups elbow macaroni

3 cups Pressure Cooker Vegetable Stock (see Chapter 5)

1 teaspoon salt

⅛ teaspoon freshly ground white pepper

½ cup whole milk or unsweetened soymilk

½ cup heavy cream or unsweetened soymilk

4 ounces Cheddar cheese, grated, or vegan Cheddar, such as Daiya Cheddar Style Shreds

4 ounces mozzarella cheese, grated, or vegan mozzarella (use vegan Cheddar if unavailable)

4 ounces Colby cheese, grated, or vegan Colby (use vegan Cheddar if unavailable)

¼ cup dried bread crumbs

2 tablespoons butter, melted, or vegan margarine, such as Earth Balance

1. Bring the oil to temperature in the pressure cooker over medium heat. Add the onion; sauté for 3 minutes or until the onion is soft. Add the garlic; sauté for 30 seconds. Add the macaroni and stir to coat it in the oil. Stir in the stock, salt, and pepper. Lock the lid into place and bring to high pressure; maintain pressure for 6 minutes. Quick-release the pressure and remove the lid.

2. Preheat the oven to 350°F. Drain the macaroni. Transfer to a 9" × 13" ovenproof baking dish. Stir in the milk and cream or soymilk, and cheeses. Mix the bread crumbs together with the melted butter or margarine and sprinkle over the top of the macaroni and cheese. Bake for 30 minutes or until the cheeses are melted and the bread crumbs are golden brown. Remove from the oven and let rest for 5 minutes. Serve.

PC PASTA PRIMAVERA WITH VEGETABLES

This light pasta dish is perfect for a mild spring day.

Serves 6–8

Water, as needed

1 pound dry bow-tie pasta

1 tablespoon extra-virgin olive oil

1½ cups squash, chopped

1½ cups zucchini, chopped

1 head broccoli, chopped

½ cup sun-dried tomatoes

2 cloves garlic

1 cup white wine

¾ cup cold butter or vegan margarine, such as Earth Balance

¼ cup basil, chopped

Salt and pepper, to taste

1. Fill the pressure cooker with enough water to cover the pasta. Bring the water to a boil. Add the pasta. Lock the lid into place and bring to high pressure; maintain pressure for 5 minutes. Use the natural-release method to release the pressure and then remove the lid. Drain and set the pasta aside.

2. While the pasta is cooking, add the olive oil to a pan over medium-low heat and sauté the squash, zucchini, broccoli, and sun-dried tomatoes until they begin to turn golden brown. Add the garlic and the white wine. Allow the white wine to reduce for about 2–3 minutes.

3. Add the butter to the pan, stirring constantly into the wine to create an emulsion.

4. Once the butter has melted, pour the sauce and veggies over the pasta and stir to coat. Garnish with the basil. Taste for seasoning, and add salt and pepper if necessary.

PASTA SALAD WITH TOMATO, ARUGULA, AND FETA

Serve this pasta salad at room temperature or after chilling in the refrigerator for at least 2 hours.

Serves 6–8

1 pound dry rotini pasta

Water, as needed

2 Roma tomatoes, diced

2 garlic cloves, minced

1 red bell pepper, diced

2 tablespoons white wine vinegar

⅓ cup extra-virgin olive oil

2 cups arugula or spinach, chopped

1 cup feta cheese or vegan feta cheese

Salt and pepper, to taste

1. Fill the pressure cooker with enough water to cover the pasta. Bring the water to a boil. Add the pasta. Lock the lid into place and bring to high pressure; maintain pressure for 7 minutes. Use the natural-release method to release the pressure and then remove the lid. Drain the pasta, then run cold water over the pasta until cooled. Set aside.

2. In a large bowl, mix the tomatoes, garlic, red bell pepper, vinegar, olive oil, arugula or spinach, and feta. Mix in the pasta and add salt and pepper to taste.

GNOCCHI AND MUSHROOMS IN ROSEMARY ALFREDO SAUCE

Gnocchi can be made from flour or potato but is typically treated like pasta in cooking, regardless of the main ingredient. Some stores carry vegetarian prepackaged gnocchi, such as DeLallo brand, or you can try making your own.

Serves 2–3

Water, as needed

16 ounces uncooked gnocchi

1 tablespoon extra-virgin olive oil

½ cup mushrooms, sliced

1 teaspoon fresh lemon juice

2 cups Béchamel Sauce (see Chapter 2), or vegan version of Béchamel Sauce

½ cup Parmesan cheese, or vegan Parmesan or mozzarella

½ cup tomatoes, diced

1 teaspoon rosemary, chopped

Salt and pepper, to taste

1. Fill the pressure cooker with enough water to cover the gnocchi. Bring the water to a boil. Add the gnocchi. Lock the lid into place and bring to high pressure; maintain pressure for 1 minute. Use the natural-release method to release the pressure and then remove the lid. Drain the gnocchi and set aside.

2. Add the olive oil to a pan over medium heat and sauté the mushrooms for about 1 minute. Add the gnocchi and sauté for 1 minute more.

3. Deglaze the pan with the lemon juice, then add the Béchamel Sauce and Parmesan cheese, and allow it to reduce until desired consistency is reached.

4. Stir in the tomatoes and rosemary. Taste for seasoning, and add salt and pepper, to taste, if necessary.

PC VEGETABLE LINGUINE IN WHITE BEAN ALFREDO SAUCE

Vegan white bean Alfredo mimics the taste of the dairy-based version but only contains a fraction of the fat!

Serves 6–8

Water, as needed

1 pound dry linguine

1 tablespoon olive oil

1 cup red bell pepper, diced

1 cup tomato, diced

3–4 cups White Bean Alfredo Sauce (see Chapter 2)

¼ cup basil, chopped

Salt and pepper, to taste

1. Fill the pressure cooker with enough water to cover the pasta. Bring the water to a boil. Add the pasta. Lock the lid into place and bring to high pressure; maintain pressure for 6 minutes. Use the natural-release method to release the pressure and then remove the lid. Drain the pasta, then set aside.

2. While the pasta is cooking, heat the olive oil in a pan over medium heat. Sauté the red bell pepper until it just begins to soften, about 3 minutes, then remove from heat.

3. In a large bowl, combine cooked pasta with the sautéed red pepper, fresh tomatoes, Alfredo Sauce, and basil.

4. Stir gently, and add salt and pepper to taste.

PC ROTINI WITH RED WINE MARINARA

When cooking pasta in a pressure cooker you only need to add the amount of water the pasta will absorb, which should be enough to just cover the dried pasta.

Serves 6–8

Water, as needed

1 pound dry rotini pasta

1 tablespoon extra-virgin olive oil

½ yellow onion, diced

3 cloves garlic, minced

1 (16-ounce) can crushed tomatoes

½ cup red wine

1 teaspoon sugar

⅛ cup basil, chopped

Salt and pepper, to taste

1. Fill the pressure cooker with enough water to cover the pasta. Bring to a boil. Add the pasta. Lock the lid into place and bring to high pressure; maintain pressure for 7 minutes. Use the natural-release method and then remove the lid. Drain and set aside.

2. Add the olive oil to a pan over medium heat and sauté the onion until it begins to caramelize. Add the garlic and sauté for an additional 30 seconds. Add the crushed tomatoes, red wine, and sugar, and simmer for about 10 minutes. Add the basil. Taste, and add salt and pepper.

PC PASTA FAGIOLE

This Italian dish is often served as a soup, but this less brothy version can be served as a main-course pasta dish, too.

Serves 6–8

Water, as needed

1 pound spaghetti pasta

4 cups cooked pinto beans

4 cups Basic Marinara Sauce (see Chapter 2)

1 cup mozzarella cheese or vegan mozzarella, such as Daiya Mozzarella Style Shreds

⅛ cup basil, chopped

1. Fill the pressure cooker with enough water to cover the pasta. Bring to a boil. Add the pasta. Lock the lid and bring to high; maintain pressure for 6 minutes. Use the natural-release method and then remove the lid. Set the pasta aside.

2. Preheat the oven to the broiler setting. Place one serving of pasta in a small bowl. Cover with the beans and sauce. Sprinkle cheese on top. Repeat with remaining servings. Place under the broiler until the cheese melts. Garnish with basil and serve.

PC ORZO-STUFFED POBLANO PEPPERS

Kick up the heat on these stuffed peppers by stirring cayenne pepper or minced pickled jalapeños into the orzo mixture.

Serves 4

Water, as needed

½ cup orzo pasta

¼ cup onions, diced

¼ cup tomatoes, diced

1 clove garlic, minced

2 tablespoons cilantro, chopped

1 tablespoon extra-virgin olive oil

Salt and pepper, to taste

4 large poblano peppers

1. Preheat the oven to 350°F. Fill the pressure cooker with enough water to cover the pasta. Bring the water to a boil. Add the pasta. Lock the lid into place and bring to high pressure; maintain pressure for 3 minutes. Use the natural-release method to release the pressure and then remove the lid.

2. In a medium bowl, combine the orzo, onions, tomatoes, garlic, cilantro, olive oil, salt, and pepper. Stir until combined.

3. Place the poblano peppers on a flat surface and cut out a long triangular portion from the top (stem to tip) to make room for the filling. Remove the seeds.

4. Fill each pepper with the orzo mixture and put the triangular piece of pepper back in place, covering the hole. Place on a baking sheet.

5. Bake for 45–50 minutes, or until tender.

Orzo Pasta

Orzo is a small rice-shaped pasta that is often used similarly to rice in cooking. It's a great alternative for chilled pasta salads, stuffing peppers or tomatoes, or tossed in a light sauce. Serving it with a heavy marinara or cream-based sauce is not recommended.

PC ORZO-STUFFED TOMATOES

Any type of larger tomato will work for this recipe. Use what is in season and available at a store near you.

Serves 4

Water, as needed

½ cup orzo pasta

4 beefsteak or large vine-ripe tomatoes

1 cup fresh mozzarella, chopped, or vegan mozzarella, such as Daiya Mozzarella Style Shreds

2 cloves garlic, minced

2 tablespoons fresh basil, minced

2 tablespoons fresh parsley, minced

Salt and pepper, to taste

2 tablespoons extra-virgin olive oil

1. Fill the pressure cooker with enough water to cover the pasta. Bring the water to a boil. Add the pasta. Lock the lid into place and bring to high pressure; maintain pressure for 3 minutes. Use the natural-release method to release the pressure and then remove the lid. Set the pasta aside.

2. Preheat the oven to 350°F. Cut the tops off the tomatoes and scoop out the pulp. Roughly chop the pulp with a knife and place it in a medium bowl. Add the orzo, mozzarella, garlic, basil, and parsley, and salt and pepper to taste.

3. Stuff the tomatoes with orzo mixture and place them on a baking sheet. Drizzle the olive oil over the tomatoes and bake them in the oven for 15–20 minutes.

PASTA PUTTANESCA

Rumor has it that this popular dish was invented by prostitutes, but depending on who is telling the story, the creator varies.

Serves 6–8

Water, as needed

1 pound linguine

2 teaspoons olive oil

2 garlic cloves, slivered

1 tablespoon fresh basil, chopped

2 tablespoons capers

¼ cup Kalamata olives, pitted and halved

1 teaspoon dried red pepper flakes

1 tablespoon brine (juice from the olives)

1 (14-ounce) can crushed tomatoes, drained

Salt and pepper, to taste

1. Fill the pressure cooker with enough water to cover the pasta. Bring the water to a boil. Add the pasta. Lock the lid into place and bring to high pressure; maintain pressure for 6 minutes. Use the natural-release method to release the pressure and then remove the lid. Drain with a colander and set the pasta aside.

2. In a sauté pan over medium heat, warm the oil. Add the garlic and cook for 2–3 minutes. Stir in the basil, capers, olives, and red pepper flakes and cook for 2 more minutes.

3. Stir in the brine and crushed tomatoes and simmer over low heat for 10–15 minutes. Season with salt and pepper to taste.

4. Combine the sauce with the linguine and serve.

WHOLE-WHEAT FETTUCCINE WITH MUSHROOM CREAM SAUCE

Whole-wheat pasta has a slightly different flavor and texture than regular pasta, and it pairs well with the earthy flavor of mushrooms.

Serves 6–8

Water, as needed

1 pound whole-wheat fettuccine

2 tablespoons butter or vegan margarine, such as Earth Balance

1 cup mushrooms, sliced (try button, shiitake, oyster, or portobello)

2 cloves garlic, minced

1 tablespoon all-purpose flour

1¼ cups milk or unsweetened soymilk

1 tablespoon fresh parsley, chopped

1 tablespoon fresh lemon juice

Salt and pepper, to taste

1. Fill the pressure cooker with enough water to cover the pasta. Bring the water to a boil. Add the pasta. Lock the lid into place and bring to high pressure; maintain pressure for 7 minutes. Use the natural-release method to release the pressure and then remove the lid. Set the pasta aside.

2. Melt 1 tablespoon of the butter in a sauté pan, then add the mushrooms and garlic. Sauté until the mushrooms are soft, about 4 minutes. Remove from the pan and set aside.

3. Melt the second tablespoon of butter, then stir in the flour and cook for about 1 minute to make a roux. Gradually stir in the milk, stirring continuously until smooth.

4. Add the cooked mushrooms, parsley, lemon juice, salt, and pepper and cook for 1–2 minutes.

5. Pour the sauce over warm pasta and serve immediately.

PC BROCCOLI–PINE NUT PASTA SALAD

Broccoli contains over 5 grams of protein per cup, making it a good staple ingredient in anyone's diet.

Serves 6–8

Water, as needed
1 pound rotini
⅓ cup pine nuts, toasted
1 head broccoli, blanched and chopped
1 red bell pepper, chopped
½ onion, diced
2 cloves garlic, minced
2 tablespoons red wine vinegar
⅓ cup extra-virgin olive oil
Salt and pepper, to taste

1. Fill the pressure cooker with enough water to cover the pasta. Bring the water to a boil. Add the pasta. Lock the lid into place and bring to high pressure; maintain pressure for 7 minutes. Use the natural-release method to release the pressure and then remove the lid. Pour the pasta and run cold water over it until cooled. Set the pasta aside.

2. In a sauté pan over low heat, toast the pine nuts until they are golden brown. Be careful not to burn them.

3. In a large bowl, combine the pine nuts, broccoli, red pepper, onion, garlic, vinegar, olive oil, and pasta. Taste for seasoning and add salt and pepper if needed.

Blanching

Boiling a vegetable for a very short period of time, then draining and plunging it into an ice-water bath is known as blanching. Cooks use this technique to soften vegetables or reduce cooking times so that a recipe will cook evenly.

PC FRESH SPINACH–WHITE WINE ANGEL HAIR PASTA

This light pasta dish can be made alcohol-free by substituting Pressure Cooker Vegetable Stock (see Chapter 5) and 1 teaspoon of vinegar for the white wine.

Serves 6–8

Water, as needed

1 pound angel hair pasta

1 tablespoon olive oil

¼ yellow onion, diced

2 cloves garlic, minced

½ cup white wine

¼ cup water, or as needed

1 tablespoon butter or vegan margarine, such as Earth Balance

1 tablespoon flour

Salt and pepper, to taste

1 cup steamed spinach

1. Fill the pressure cooker with enough water to cover the pasta. Bring the water to a boil. Add the pasta. Lock the lid into place and bring to high pressure; maintain pressure for 4 minutes. Use the natural-release method to release the pressure and then remove the lid. Set the pasta aside.

2. In a medium saucepan over low heat, add the olive oil, onion, and garlic. Cook until the onions are soft, about 5 minutes. Add the white wine and water, then bring to a low simmer. Continue simmering for about 10 minutes.

3. Add the butter and flour, stirring until completely combined and the sauce begins to thicken. If the sauce becomes too thick, add more water until you reach the desired consistency, then season with salt and pepper.

4. In a large mixing bowl, combine the spinach, pasta, and white-wine sauce, then toss until the pasta is completely coated.

PC PORTOBELLO STROGANOFF

Beef is commonly used in stroganoff recipes, but you can make a vegetarian or vegan version by using the "meaty" flavor of portobello mushrooms instead.

Serves 6–8

Water, as needed

1 pound linguine

1 tablespoon extra-virgin olive oil

1 yellow onion, diced

3 cups portobello mushrooms, roughly chopped

1 tablespoon all-purpose flour

4 cups Espagnole (see Chapter 2), or vegan version of Espagnole

½ cup sour cream or vegan sour cream, such as Tofutti Sour Supreme

1 tablespoon ground mustard

Salt and pepper, to taste

¼ cup chopped parsley

1. Fill the pressure cooker with enough water to cover the pasta. Bring the water to a boil. Add the pasta. Lock the lid into place and bring to high pressure; maintain pressure for 6 minutes. Use the natural-release method to release the pressure and then remove the lid. Set the pasta aside.

2. Heat the oil and sauté the onion and mushrooms. Sprinkle in the flour and cook to a paste. Add the Espagnole sauce and cook at a slow simmer for 20 minutes. Mix the sour cream and mustard together. Pour into the sauce and heat thoroughly. Taste for seasoning, and add salt and pepper if necessary.

3. Serve over the linguine and garnish with the parsley.

BOW-TIE PASTA IN A SAGE BEURRE BLANC SAUCE

Sage is an herb with an earthy and slightly minty flavor.

Serves 6–8

Water, as needed

1 pound bow-tie pasta

1 tablespoon extra-virgin olive oil

1 cup white mushrooms, sliced

1 small red onion, julienned

2 cloves garlic, minced

1 cup white wine

2 tablespoons white wine vinegar

¾ cup cold butter or vegan margarine, such as Earth Balance

1 cup tomatoes, diced

1 teaspoon dried sage

Salt and pepper, to taste

1. Fill the pressure cooker with enough water to cover the pasta. Bring the water to a boil. Add the pasta. Lock the lid into place and bring to high pressure; maintain pressure for 5 minutes. Use the natural-release method to release the pressure and then remove the lid. Set the pasta aside.

2. Add the olive oil to a pan and sauté the mushrooms and onion until golden brown. Add the garlic and sauté for an additional 30 seconds. Add the wine and vinegar, and let reduce for about 3 minutes. Add the cold butter to the pan, 1 tablespoon at a time, stirring the butter constantly into the wine to create an emulsion.

3. Once the butter has emulsified, add the tomatoes, sage, and salt and pepper, to taste. Toss with the pasta before serving.

CHAPTER 12
DESSERTS, BAKED GOODS, AND BEVERAGES

RECIPE LIST

PUMPKIN BREAD **626**

BANANA BREAD **627**

BANANA NUT BREAD **628**

TARTE TATIN **629**

SIMPLE CLOVERLEAF DINNER ROLLS **630**

CHOCOLATE MOUSSE **631**

NOODLE PUDDING **632**

OLD-FASHIONED BAKED APPLES **632**

"BAKED" APPLES **633**

EASY APPLESAUCE **634**

SPECIAL OCCASION CHUNKY APPLESAUCE **634**

CINNAMON-APPLE COBBLER WITH ROME BEAUTY APPLES **635**

CRANBERRY APPLESAUCE **636**

PINK MCINTOSH APPLESAUCE WITH CRANBERRY CHUTNEY **637**

CRANBERRY CHUTNEY **637**

GOLDEN DELICIOUS APPLE-STRAWBERRY CRISP **638**

APPLE-WALNUT UPSIDE-DOWN PIE **639**

SPICY SOUTHWESTERN CORNBREAD **640**

TIRAMISU **641**

CRÈME CARAMEL **642**

SAVORY SUN-DRIED TOMATO CHEESECAKE **643**

CARROT CAKE **644**

CHOCOLATE CAKE **645**

SPICED CHOCOLATE CAKE **646**

RED VELVET CAKE **647**

SOUR CREAM BUTTER CAKE **648**

FLOURLESS CHOCOLATE CAKE **649**

BANANA PUDDING CAKE **650**

GLAZED LEMON POPPY SEED CAKE **651**

CORNMEAL CAKE **652**

BASIC YELLOW CAKE **652**

BUTTER-CREAM FROSTING **653**

BLONDIES **654**

PEARS POACHED IN WHITE WINE WITH STRAWBERRY SAUCE **654**

SPICED PEACHES **655**

GINGER POACHED PEARS **656**

CINNAMON POACHED APPLES **656**

POACHED MIXED BERRIES **657**

PORT-POACHED FIGS **657**

DRIED FRUIT COMPOTE **658**

FRUIT COMPOTE **659**

CHOCOLATE CHIP COOKIES **660**

CREPES **660**

COTTAGE CHEESE BLINTZES **661**

PEANUT BUTTER CAKE **661**

COCONUT RICE PUDDING **662**

HOT FUDGE FONDUE **662**

CHOCOLATE-ALMOND FONDUE **663**

CHOCOLATE-CINNAMON FONDUE **663**

BANANAS FOSTER **664**

CARAMEL APPLES AND PEARS **664**

CHOCOLATE ALMOND BARS **665**

CHOCOLATE COCONUT BARS **665**

WHITE CHOCOLATE–MACADAMIA NUT BARS **666**

CHOCOLATE-COVERED PRETZELS **666**

CHOCOLATE-BERRY BREAD PUDDING **667**

LEMON CHEESECAKE **668**

CREAMY COCONUT RICE PUDDING **669**

MOLTEN FUDGE PUDDING CAKE **670**

PLUM PUDDING WITH BRANDY SAUCE **671**

PEANUT BUTTER AND FUDGE CHEESECAKE **672**

DATE PUDDING **673**

PIÑA COLADA BREAD PUDDING **674**

TAPIOCA PUDDING **675**

STEAMED DESSERT BREAD **676**

VEGAN FLAN **677**

HOT CRANBERRY-PINEAPPLE PUNCH **678**

GINGER-PEAR PUNCH **679**

WHITE TEA–BERRY FUSION **679**

VANILLA-LAVENDER TEA **680**

CHAI TEA **680**

CAFÉ MÖCHA **681**

PUMPKIN SPICE **681**

MINTY HOT CHOCOLATE **682**

HOT BUTTERED RUM **682**

HOT TODDY **683**

SPIKED APPLE CIDER **683**

SPICED WINE **684**

IRISH COFFEE **684**

MIXED BERRY PUNCH **685**

PEACH ICED TEA **685**

SOUTHERN-STYLE SWEET TEA **686**

MANGO-MINT ICED TEA **686**

SANGRIA **687**

HONEY-MINT GREEN TEA **687**

BLACKBERRY-MINT WHITE TEA **688**

CHERRY AND LIME PUNCH **688**

RASPBERRY LEMONADE **689**

CHERRY LEMONADE **689**

ORANGE AND LIME PUNCH **690**

PASSION FRUIT GREEN TEA **690**

PUMPKIN BREAD

Don't you dare use canned pumpkin for this bread! If you can't steal one of your kids' jack-o'-lanterns, use butternut squash instead!

Yields 1 loaf—about 10 slices

2 cups boiled and mashed pumpkin
1 cup sugar
1 cup brown sugar
½ cup oil
1 egg
2½ cups flour
½ teaspoon salt
½ teaspoon cinnamon
½ teaspoon cloves
¼ teaspoon nutmeg
2 teaspoons baking soda
1 cup chopped walnuts

1. Combine pumpkin, sugars, oil, and egg. Mix well.

2. Combine remaining ingredients, except nuts. Add to pumpkin mixture. Stir in nuts.

3. Bake in greased loaf pan at 350°F for 1 hour. Test periodically by inserting a toothpick into the center of the loaf; when the toothpick comes out clean, the bread is done.

SC BANANA BREAD

Oat bran adds extra fiber to this recipe, making it a heart-healthier bread.

Serves 8

- 1½ cups all-purpose flour
- ½ cup oat bran
- ¾ cup sugar
- ¼ teaspoon baking soda
- 2 teaspoons baking powder
- ½ teaspoon salt
- 3 ripe bananas, mashed
- 6 tablespoons butter or vegan margarine, softened
- 2 large eggs, beaten, or 2 teaspoons cornstarch mixed with 2 tablespoons warm water
- ¼ cup plain yogurt or vegan yogurt
- 1 teaspoon vanilla
- 1¼ cups walnuts

1. Add the flour, oat bran, sugar, baking soda, baking powder, and salt to a mixing bowl. Stir to mix.

2. In a food processor, add the bananas, butter or margarine, eggs or cornstarch mix, yogurt, and vanilla. Pulse to cream together.

3. Add the walnuts and flour mixture to the food processor. Pulse to combine and chop the walnuts. Scrape down the sides of the container with a spatula and pulse until mixed.

4. Treat a 4-quart slow cooker with nonstick spray. Add the batter to the slow cooker, using a spatula to spread it evenly across the bottom of the crock.

5. Cover and cook on high for 3 hours, or until a toothpick inserted in the center of the bread comes out clean.

6. Allow to cool uncovered before removing it from the slow cooker.

BANANA NUT BREAD

For fun, you can make this recipe into banana nut cupcakes or mini-muffins by baking them for half the time in muffin tins. It freezes well.

Yields 1 loaf

- 1¼ cups all-purpose flour
- 1 teaspoon baking soda
- ¼ teaspoon baking powder
- ½ teaspoon cinnamon
- ½ teaspoon salt
- 1 cup sugar
- 2 large eggs
- ½ cup oil
- 3 medium overripe bananas, mashed (1¼ cups)
- 1 teaspoon vanilla extract
- ¾ cup coarsely chopped walnuts, toasted lightly in a dry pan until fragrant

1. Heat oven to 350°F. Butter a 9" × 5" loaf pan. In a mixing bowl, whisk together the flour, baking soda, baking powder, cinnamon, and salt. In a separate bowl, whisk together the sugar, eggs, and oil; whip vigorously until creamy and light in color, about 5 minutes. Add mashed bananas and vanilla extract to the egg mixture. Add the flour mixture to the wet ingredients in 3 additions, mixing only as much as necessary to incorporate the ingredients, since overmixing will toughen the batter. Stir in the nuts and pour batter into prepared pan.

2. Bake in center of oven until the top is springy and a toothpick inserted in the center comes out clean, about 50–60 minutes. Allow to cool for 10 minutes; transfer to a rack to cool completely before slicing.

TARTE TATIN

This recipe is best served warm so if you make it ahead of time, be sure to reheat before serving.

Serves 8

8 tablespoons butter, room temperature

1 cup sugar

6 medium Gala or Golden Delicious apples, peeled, cored, and cut into quarters

1 thin (1/8") sheet store-bought puff pastry or Basic Pie Dough (see Chapter 6), cut into a circle 12" in diameter

1. Heat oven to 350°F. Spread the butter evenly into a 10" tarte tatin mold or heavy, 10" nonstick ovenproof skillet. Evenly spread sugar on sides and bottom of the pan. Starting at the edge of the pan, arrange apples, peeled side down, in concentric circles, fitting apples closely together.

2. Place pan over high heat, and cook without stirring until sugar caramelizes and turns dark golden brown, 15–20 minutes. Remove from heat and gently press the apples closer together with a wooden spoon, eliminating any gaps. Cover the apples with the puff pastry. The dough will overlap the rim of the pan. Bake until pastry is golden brown, about 30 minutes.

3. Remove from oven and rest it for 5 minutes. Place a large serving plate on top, and rapidly invert the tart; remove the pan. Serve warm.

SIMPLE CLOVERLEAF DINNER ROLLS

Nothing brings a more comforting aroma to the house than baking rolls. The dough can be made and rolled in advance, then frozen. Just thaw and rise before baking.

Serves 12

1 envelope active dry yeast
1 cup milk, lukewarm (about 110°F)
6 tablespoons butter, divided
3 tablespoons sugar
1 large egg
1 teaspoon salt
3½–4 cups all-purpose flour

1. In a large mixing bowl, combine yeast with 3 tablespoons of lukewarm water. Let stand 5 minutes. Add milk, 4 tablespoons butter, sugar, egg, and salt; mix well with a wooden spoon. Gradually add 2 cups of flour; mix 1 minute. Gradually mix in 1½–2 cups more flour, until dough is moist but not sticky. Knead 10 minutes, until it's smooth and elastic. Form into a ball and place in a mixing bowl with a few drops of oil; toss to coat. Cover bowl with plastic wrap; allow to rise in a warm place until double in size, about 1–1½ hours. Knead dough 1 minute; cover and refrigerate 30 minutes.

2. Form into 36 tight, round balls, rolling them against an unfloured surface. In a buttered muffin tin, place 3 balls in each muffin cup; cover loosely with greased plastic wrap. Allow to rise in a warm place until double in size, about 1–1½ hours.

3. Heat oven to 375°F. Melt remaining butter and brush it onto the rolls. Bake 25–30 minutes, until golden brown.

CHOCOLATE MOUSSE

While not exactly diet food, this mousse contains no egg yolks, making it lighter in both taste and fat than French chocolate mousse.

Serves 8

- 1½ tablespoons Kirschwasser or other cherry brandy
- 1½ tablespoons dark rum (such as Myer's)
- 1 tablespoon vanilla extract, plus a few drops
- 6 ounces dark chocolate (bittersweet)
- 1½ cups heavy cream
- 2½ tablespoons confectioners' sugar
- 6 egg whites, whipped to medium-soft peaks, refrigerated
- Additional whipped cream and chocolate shavings to garnish (optional)

1. Chill 8 (8-ounce) wineglasses. Combine cherry brandy, dark rum, 1 tablespoon vanilla extract, and chocolate in a double boiler or a steel mixing bowl set over a pot of simmering water. Warm, stirring occasionally, until melted and smooth. Whip together the cream, confectioners' sugar, and a few drops of vanilla until it forms soft peaks when the whisk is lifted from it.

2. Gently fold ⅓ of the whipped cream into the chocolate mixture. Fold the chocolate mixture back into the rest of the whipped cream, mixing only as much as is necessary to incorporate it most of the way (a few streaks of chocolate are okay). Fold the whipped egg whites very gently into the chocolate cream mixture, just barely enough to incorporate. Fill the mousse into a pastry bag with a star tip (or a plastic bag with a corner cut out), and pipe it into 8 chilled wineglasses. Cover the glasses individually with plastic wrap and chill for at least 6 hours, until set. Garnish with a spoonful of whipped cream and chocolate shavings if desired.

NOODLE PUDDING

Baked side-dish puddings, such as rice pudding, bread pudding, and noodle pudding, can do double duty as dessert, and are some of the old-fashioned comfort foods from my father's generation that are making a comeback.

Serves 6

2 large eggs

¼ cup sugar

1 cup cottage cheese

½ cup sour cream

¼ teaspoon salt

¼ cup raisins, soaked for 15 minutes in a cup of hot tap water

2 cups dried wide egg noodles

3 tablespoons butter, at room temperature

Ground cinnamon

1. Heat oven to 350°F. Combine eggs, sugar, cottage cheese, sour cream, salt, and raisins; stir well. Cook noodles according to package directions; drain and toss with butter. Add noodles to cottage cheese mixture; toss to coat. Transfer to a buttered 9" square baking dish. Cover with foil.

2. Bake until fully set in the middle, about 45 minutes, uncovering halfway through. Dust with cinnamon and allow to rest 10 minutes before cutting into portions.

OLD-FASHIONED BAKED APPLES

Serve these delicious apples warm after an autumn day outside. They'll warm you right up. .

Serves 4

4 baking apples (Romes or Cortlands are good)

8 whole cloves

2 ounces butter (½ stick)

⅓ cup light brown sugar

½ teaspoon ground cinnamon

1. Wash and dry apples thoroughly. Using a small knife, cut a divot from the top of the apples, leaving the stem intact. This "cover" will be replaced when baking. Scoop out the seeds and core with a melon-baller or small spoon. Drop 2 cloves into each apple.

2. Knead together the butter and brown sugar, along with the cinnamon, until it is a paste. Divide equally over the scooped apples, leaving enough space to replace the tops.

3. Place apples in a baking dish with ½ cup of water on the bottom. Bake 350°F for 1 hour. Sprinkle with cinnamon or powdered sugar before serving.

"BAKED" APPLES

Serve these lightly spiced apples as a simple dessert or a breakfast treat.

Serves 6

6 baking apples, cored and halved

½ cup water

1 cinnamon stick

1 knob peeled fresh ginger

1 vanilla bean

1. Place the apples in a single layer on the bottom of a 4- or 6-quart slow cooker. Add the water, cinnamon stick, ginger, and vanilla bean.

2. Cover and cook on low for 6–8 hours, or until the apples are tender and easily pierced with a fork.

3. Use a slotted spoon to remove the apples from the insert. Discard the cinnamon stick, ginger, vanilla bean, and water. Serve hot.

Baking with Apples

When baking or cooking, choose apples with firm flesh such as Granny Smith, Jonathan, McIntosh, Cortland, Pink Lady, Pippin, or Winesap. They will be able to hold up to long cooking times without turning to mush. Leaving the skin on adds fiber.

SC EASY APPLESAUCE

Homemade applesauce is easy to make and tastes much better than what you can get in the store. It freezes well, too, so you can make extra when apples are in season.

Yields about 4 cups

- 10 medium apples, peeled, cored, and sliced
- 2 tablespoons fresh lemon juice
- 2 tablespoons water
- 6" cinnamon stick (optional)
- Sugar, to taste (optional)

1. In a 4-quart slow cooker, add the apples, lemon juice, water, and cinnamon stick, if using. Stir to mix.
2. Cover and cook on low for 5 hours, or until the apples are soft and tender.
3. For chunky applesauce, mash the apples with a potato masher. For smooth applesauce, purée in a food processor or blender, use an immersion blender, or press through a food mill or large-mesh strainer.
4. While applesauce is still warm, add sugar to taste, if desired. Store covered in the refrigerator for up to 2 weeks, or freeze.

PC SPECIAL OCCASION CHUNKY APPLESAUCE

To sweeten the applesauce, stir in sugar or maple syrup, to taste, after you remove the lid from the pressure cooker.

Serves 6

- 8 Granny Smith apples
- 1 cup apple juice or cider
- 2 tablespoons fresh lemon juice
- ¼ cup sugar
- ⅓ cup light brown sugar, packed
- ½ teaspoon ground nutmeg
- ¼ teaspoon ground cinnamon
- ⅓ cup cinnamon hearts candy

1. Rinse, peel, core, and dice the apples. Add to the pressure cooker with apple juice or cider, lemon juice, sugar, brown sugar, nutmeg, and cinnamon. Stir well. Lock the lid into place and bring to low pressure; maintain for 4 minutes. Remove from heat and allow pressure to release naturally for 10 minutes.
2. Quick-release any remaining pressure. Stir in the candy until it's melted and blended, mashing the apples slightly as you do so. Serve warm or chilled. Can be stored for several days in the refrigerator.

CINNAMON-APPLE COBBLER WITH ROME BEAUTY APPLES

This dessert is an American favorite, and it makes a beautiful presentation at a picnic.

Serves 8

FILLING:

8 or 9 Rome Beauty apples, peeled, cored, and diced into 1" pieces

Pinch of salt

¼ teaspoon ground nutmeg

1 capful of vanilla extract

1½ teaspoons ground cinnamon

½ cup sugar

¼ cup flour

Juice of ½ lemon

BISCUIT TOPPING:

3 cups flour

½ teaspoon salt

2 teaspoons baking powder

2 eggs

½ cup sugar

⅔ cup milk

6 ounces melted butter

1. Make the filling: Preheat oven to 375°F. Mix together the apples, pinch of salt, nutmeg, vanilla, cinnamon, ½ cup sugar, ¼ cup flour, and lemon juice. Place in a 6" × 10" baking dish.

2. Make the topping: Sift together the flour, salt, and baking powder. In a separate bowl, combine the eggs, sugar, milk, and melted butter.

3. Add the wet ingredients to the dry, mixing only until they are well combined. Do not overmix. Batter should have consistency of thick oatmeal. Adjust with milk if necessary.

4. Spread batter over fruit filling as evenly as possible with your hands. Some holes are natural, and will make for a more attractive presentation.

5. Bake on bottom shelf of 375°F oven for 90 minutes, turning halfway through, and checking after 1 hour. Fruit should be bubbling thoroughly and biscuit topping should be nicely browned. Allow to cool at least 15 minutes before serving with vanilla ice cream and a sprig of fresh mint.

PC CRANBERRY APPLESAUCE

Make sure that the ingredients don't go above the halfway mark on the pressure cooker.

Serves 8

4 medium tart apples

4 medium sweet apples

1 cup cranberries

Zest and juice from 1 large orange

½ cup dark brown sugar

½ cup granulated cane sugar

1 tablespoon unsalted butter or vegan margarine, such as Earth Balance

2 teaspoons ground cinnamon

½ teaspoon ground cloves

¼ teaspoon freshly ground black pepper

⅛ teaspoon salt

1 tablespoon fresh lemon juice

1. Peel, core, and grate the apples. Wash the cranberries. Add the cranberries to the pressure cooker and top with grated apples. Add the remaining ingredients.

2. Lock the lid into place and bring to low pressure; maintain pressure for 5 minutes. Remove from heat and allow pressure to release naturally. Remove the lid; lightly mash the apples with a fork. Stir well. Serve warm or chilled.

PINK MCINTOSH APPLESAUCE WITH CRANBERRY CHUTNEY

Do not peel the apples before making Mac Applesauce. Cooking the Macs and Delicious apples with the skins on gives this sauce its distinctive pink color.

Serves 6

1 cinnamon stick, about 2" long

8 McIntosh and 2 Red Delicious apples, washed and quartered

¼ cup sugar

¼ cup water

1 recipe Cranberry Chutney (see recipe in this chapter)

1. Warm the cinnamon stick, dry, in a heavy-bottomed pot large enough to hold all the apples. Reduce flame to low and add the apples, sugar, and water. Cover tightly.

2. Simmer gently for 40 minutes, then uncover and simmer 10 minutes more.

3. Strain through a Foley food mill or push through a strainer with a flexible spatula. Cool and serve with a dollop of Cranberry Chutney.

CRANBERRY CHUTNEY

This recipe is great with applesauce or on its own.

Serves 2–3

2 cups fresh or frozen cranberries

¼ cup very finely diced red onion

1 cup sugar

6 whole cloves

¼ cup water

Combine all ingredients in a small, heavy-bottomed saucepot. Simmer 10–15 minutes, until all cranberries are broken and have a saucy consistency.

GOLDEN DELICIOUS APPLE-STRAWBERRY CRISP

Tailor this to suit your tastes and what's available—other berries, different nuts, etc.

Serves 8

8 or 9 Golden Delicious apples, peeled, cored, and cut into 1" cubes

3 tablespoons granulated sugar

¼ teaspoon ground cloves

½ teaspoon ground cinnamon

Juice of ½ lemon

1 cup plus 2 tablespoons all-purpose flour

1 cup almonds, roughly chopped

1 cup light brown sugar

⅛ teaspoon salt

4 ounces (1 stick) unsalted butter, cold, cut into pea-size pieces

1. Preheat oven to 350°F. Toss the apples with granulated sugar, spices, lemon juice, and 2 tablespoons flour. Fill into a 6" × 10" baking dish.

2. Toast almonds lightly in moderate oven at about 300°F. Cool.

3. Using your hands, rub together 1 cup flour, brown sugar, salt, and butter until mixture clumps. Add toasted nuts and cover the fruit evenly with this topping. Bake on bottom shelf of 350°F oven for 1 hour, until fruit is bubbling and topping is crisp. Serve with vanilla whipped cream or vanilla ice cream.

APPLE-WALNUT UPSIDE-DOWN PIE

Guaranteed: No one will ever forget this pie.

Serves 8

1 recipe Basic Pie Dough (see Chapter 6)

CARAMEL-WALNUT TOPPING:

1 cup light brown sugar

4 ounces (1 stick) unsalted butter

1 cup toasted walnut pieces, roughly chopped

Pinch of salt

APPLE FILLING:

8 or 9 Granny Smith apples, peeled, cored, and diced into 1" slices

½ cup sugar (give or take, depending on sweetness of apples)

1½ teaspoons ground cinnamon

½ teaspoon ground allspice

¼ teaspoon ground cloves

¼ cup flour

Pinch of salt

1. Melt brown sugar and butter together in a heavy-bottomed skillet, over medium-high heat, until smooth and bubbling. Cook 5 minutes. Stir in walnuts and salt, and remove from heat.

2. Spread into bottom of 9" pie pan.

3. Preheat oven to 375°F. Roll out bottom crust very thin (¼") and drape over caramel/walnut-lined pie pan. Mix filling ingredients and fill the pie, mounding somewhat in the center.

4. Roll out top crust (¼" thick). Brush rim of bottom crust with a little water to seal the crusts together, and cover the pie loosely with the top. Crimp the edges. Make several vents, using a fork or the tip of a knife.

5. Bake at 375°F for 1 hour, until filling is bubbling. Cool, then reheat quickly in a hot oven before inverting and unmolding. Serve with ice cream.

SPICY SOUTHWESTERN CORNBREAD

This smoky cornbread used to be a specialty at the Bright Food Shop, a Mexican/Southeast Asian "fusion" cuisine restaurant in New York City, before it closed.

Yields 2 loaves

4½ cups fine cornmeal

1 cup sugar

2 cups flour

4 tablespoons baking powder

1 tablespoon baking soda

4 teaspoons table salt

3½ cups buttermilk

1 cup oil

1 cup (2 sticks) melted butter

6 eggs

1½ tablespoons chopped jalapeño peppers

2 tablespoons puréed chipotle in adobo

1. Heat oven to 400°F. In a large mixing bowl, combine the cornmeal, sugar, flour, baking powder, baking soda, and salt. Mix thoroughly with a stiff wire whisk or spoon to combine well and break up any lumps. In a separate mixing bowl, mix the buttermilk, oil, melted butter, eggs, jalapeños, and chipotle; whisk well to combine. Fold the cornmeal mixture into the buttermilk mixture in 3 additions, mixing only as much as necessary to combine ingredients. Pour the batter into 2 (9" × 5") loaf pans or 1 (9" × 13") baking dish. It is not necessary to grease the pans.

2. Bake until the top springs back when pressed and a toothpick comes out clean when inserted into the center. Cook 10 minutes before turning onto a rack to cool completely.

TIRAMISU

Now that this adult dessert of espresso and Italian cream cheese (a.k.a. mascarpone) has become ubiquitous in restaurants, it's time to make the very best version at home.

Serves 12

9 egg yolks

1 cup quick-dissolving sugar

3 teaspoons vanilla extract

750 grams (a little more than 1½ pounds) mascarpone (Italian cream cheese)

1 tablespoon sweet Marsala wine

3 cups cream, whipped to medium-soft peaks

2 cups espresso or very strong brewed coffee

2 tablespoons dark rum (such as Myer's)

One package (about 60 pieces) lady fingers (a.k.a. savoiardi)

Cocoa powder

Mint sprigs, to garnish

1. Over a bath of warm water, stir together yolks, sugar, and vanilla until sugar dissolves. In an electric mixer or by hand, whip the yolks to medium-hard peaks; fold in the mascarpone and Marsala. Fold in the whipped cream.

2. Combine the coffee and rum. Quickly dip ¾ of the lady fingers into the coffee mixture, and use them to line the bottom and sides of a 10" springform pan or deep cake pan. Pour half of the cream mixture into the cookie-lined pan; dust thoroughly with cocoa powder. Dip remaining lady fingers in coffee mixture and layer them into the pan. Top that with the remaining cream.

3. Cover with plastic wrap and refrigerate overnight. Dust top with cocoa powder before cutting into 12 portions, with a hot, wet knife, and serving garnished with mint sprigs.

CRÈME CARAMEL

Silky smooth texture and complex flavor belie this classic French custard's simplicity. When unmolded, the caramel becomes its own natural sauce. Todd Snyder taught me this recipe.

Serves 8

1½ cups sugar, divided

3 cups heavy cream

6 egg yolks

1 teaspoon vanilla extract

1. Heat oven to 350°F. In a small, heavy-bottomed skillet, combine ¾ cup sugar with ½ cup water. Bring to a boil over medium-high heat and cook until sugar caramelizes into a deep orange brown. Watch the sugar closely when it begins to color, swirling the pan to keep it evenly colored. Pour immediately from the pan into the bottoms of 8 (6-ounce) custard cups or ramekins.

2. Bring cream and remaining ¾ cup sugar just to the boiling point, stirring to dissolve the sugar. Place egg yolks and vanilla extract in a bowl and pour the scalded cream mixture over them, whisking vigorously and constantly. Ladle this cream mixture into the caramel-lined molds. Set the molds into a deep roasting pan or casserole dish and place on the center rack of the oven. Carefully pour water into the roasting pan, filling just past the cream and egg mixture in the molds. Bake for exactly 50 minutes. Remove from oven to cool to room temperature, then refrigerate at least 8 hours or overnight.

3. Unmold the crème caramels by loosening the edges of the custard with a small knife, then inverting the molds onto a plate.

SAVORY SUN-DRIED TOMATO CHEESECAKE

You can freeze this cheesecake for up to 3 months, so it makes the perfect make-ahead addition for a cheese plate. Thaw a wedge of the cheesecake in the refrigerator and then serve at room temperature to spread on crackers or thin slices of crusty bread.

Yields 7" cheesecake

3 tablespoons butter, melted, or vegan margarine, such as Earth Balance

⅓ cup bread crumbs or savory cracker crumbs

½ cup sun-dried tomatoes in oil

6 cloves garlic, peeled and minced

1 teaspoon dried oregano

3 large eggs or 3 ounces silken soft tofu

3 tablespoons all-purpose flour

2 (8-ounce) packages cream cheese, or 18 ounces vegan cream cheese

¾ cup sour cream (optional)

½ cup scallion, diced

2 cups hot water

1. Coat the sides and bottom of a 7" springform pan with melted butter or margarine. Evenly distribute the crumbs over the bottom and sides. Place a 16" × 16" piece of plastic wrap on top of an equal-size piece of aluminum foil. Put the pan in the center of the plastic-wrap–topped foil; form and crimp the foil around the pan to seal the bottom.

2. Drain the tomatoes, leaving 1 tablespoon oil, and add to a food processor along with the garlic, oregano, eggs or tofu, flour, cream cheese, and ¼ cup sour cream, if desired. Purée until smooth. Stir in the scallion. Pour into the springform pan. Cover with foil; crimp to seal.

3. Place a trivet or rack on the bottom of the pressure cooker. Pour in the hot water. Use 2 (24") lengths of aluminum foil folded in half lengthwise twice to create 24" × 2" strips of foil. Crisscross the foil strips on the counter and place the springform pan in the center. Bring the ends of the foil strips up over the springform pan; hold on to the strips and use to lower the pan into the pressure cooker until it rests on the rack or trivet.

4. Lock the lid into place and bring to high pressure; maintain for 20 minutes. Remove from heat and let rest for 7 minutes before quick-releasing any remaining pressure. Remove the lid and cool in the pressure cooker until all of the steam has dissipated.

5. Use the foil strips to lift the pan from the pressure cooker. Remove the foil lid. Sop up any moisture with a paper towel. Cool. Spread the remaining ½ cup sour cream over the top.

SC CARROT CAKE

Ice this cake with cream cheese frosting, or for a vegan topping, glaze the cake while it's still warm (see "Carrot Cake Glaze" sidebar).

Serves 8

1½ cups all-purpose flour

½ teaspoon baking soda

1 teaspoon baking powder

¼ teaspoon salt

¾ teaspoon cinnamon

¼ teaspoon ground cloves

⅛ teaspoon freshly grated nutmeg

2 large eggs or 2 mashed bananas

¾ cup sugar

⅓ cup butter or vegan margarine

¼ cup water

1 cup carrots, grated

½ cup chopped walnuts

Cream cheese frosting

1. In a mixing bowl, add the flour, baking soda, baking powder, salt, cinnamon, cloves, and nutmeg. Stir to combine.
2. In a food processor, add the eggs or bananas, sugar, and butter or margarine. Process to cream together. Scrape into the flour mixture.
3. Pour in the water and add the grated carrots to the mixing bowl. Stir and fold to combine all ingredients. Fold in the nuts.
4. Treat a 4-quart slow cooker with nonstick spray. Add the carrot cake batter and use a spatula to spread it evenly in the crock.
5. Cover and cook on low for 2 hours, or until cake is firm in the center. Ice with cream cheese frosting.

Carrot Cake Glaze

Repeatedly pierce the top of the cake with a fork. Add ½ cup lemon, orange, or unsweetened pineapple juice; 1 teaspoon freshly grated lemon or orange zest; and 1½ cups of sifted powdered sugar to a microwave-safe measuring cup and stir to combine. Microwave on high for 30 seconds. Stir and repeat until sugar is dissolved. Pour evenly over the cake.

SC CHOCOLATE CAKE

This chocolate cake is a classic dessert prepared in a whole new way.

Serves 8

2 cups all-purpose flour

2 cups sugar

¾ cup unsweetened cocoa powder

1¾ teaspoons baking powder

1¾ teaspoons baking soda

1¼ cups 2% milk or soymilk

2 eggs or equivalent egg replacement

½ cup vegetable oil

1¼ cups water

1 cup vegan icing

1. In a medium bowl, mix all the dry ingredients.
2. In another medium bowl, mix all the wet ingredients except the icing.
3. Spray a 4-quart slow cooker with nonstick cooking oil.
4. Combine the dry and wet ingredients and pour into the slow cooker.
5. Cover and cook on medium-high heat for 1–2 hours.
6. Remove cake from slow cooker and cover with icing.

Vegan Icing

Finding vegan icing is a cinch because big-name companies sell it in grocery stores around the country. Duncan Hines and Betty Crocker both sell a variety of vegan icings.

SPICED CHOCOLATE CAKE

Serve with icing, powdered sugar, or ice cream on top.

Serves 10–12

1½ cups all-purpose flour

4 tablespoons cocoa powder

1 teaspoon cinnamon

1 teaspoon cayenne pepper

1 teaspoon sugar

¼ teaspoon salt

1 teaspoon baking powder

2 eggs, beaten, or 2 mashed bananas

4 tablespoons butter, melted, or vegan margarine, such as Earth Balance

1 cup milk or soymilk

2 cups hot water

1. In a medium bowl, mix the flour, cocoa powder, cinnamon, cayenne, sugar, salt, and baking powder. In a large bowl, beat the eggs, if using. Add the dry ingredients to the eggs or bananas. Slowly stir in the melted butter and the milk. Pour the cake mixture into an 8" round pan.

2. Add the steaming rack to the pressure cooker and pour in the hot water. Place the cake in the pressure cooker and lock the lid into place. Bring to high pressure, then reduce to low and cook for 30 minutes.

3. Remove the pressure cooker from the heat, quick-release the steam, and carefully remove the cake.

SC RED VELVET CAKE

Cream cheese or vegan cream cheese icing is the perfect topping for moist red velvet cake.

Serves 8

2 cups all-purpose flour
2 cups sugar
½ teaspoon salt
1¼ cups sugar
2 tablespoons cocoa powder
2 teaspoons red food coloring
½ cup vegetable oil
2 eggs or equivalent egg replacement
1 cup 2% milk or soymilk
1 tablespoon vinegar
1½ teaspoons vanilla extract
1 cup vegan icing

1. In a medium bowl, mix all the dry ingredients.
2. In another medium bowl, mix all the wet ingredients.
3. Spray slow cooker with nonstick cooking oil.
4. Combine all ingredients and pour into a 4-quart slow cooker. Cover and cook on medium-high heat for 1–2 hours.
5. Remove cake from slow cooker and cover with icing.

SOUR CREAM BUTTER CAKE

Frost this cake with homemade Butter-Cream Frosting (see recipe in this chapter) or a store-bought favorite. The cake is rich and moist, so serve it in very thin slices.

Serves 12

4 egg yolks

⅔ cup sour cream

1½ teaspoons vanilla

2 cups sifted cake flour

1 cup sugar

½ teaspoon baking powder

½ teaspoon baking soda

½ teaspoon salt

6 ounces (1½ sticks) unsalted butter, softened to room temperature

1. Heat oven to 350°F. Grease a 9" cake pan, dust it with flour, and line the bottom with waxed paper. In a bowl, whisk together the yolks, ¼ of the sour cream, and the vanilla. In a large, separate bowl, mix the flour, sugar, baking powder, baking soda, and salt; whisk vigorously to combine.

2. Add the butter and remaining sour cream to the flour mixture and mix well, until flour is completely moistened. Add the egg mixture to the flour mixture in 3 separate additions, mixing between each addition. Pour into prepared cake pan.

3. Bake in the middle of the oven until a toothpick inserted in the center comes out clean, usually about 35–40 minutes. Start checking at 25 minutes, since oven temperatures and ingredient characteristics vary, and it might be done quicker. Cool 10 minutes, then take out of pan and cool completely on a wire rack.

4. To frost, cut laterally in half and frost both sections, then stack smooth sides and refrigerate to set.

FLOURLESS CHOCOLATE CAKE

Luxury incarnate, this voluptuous chocolate cake is a vehicle for fine chocolate, so use the best you can get. Chocolate is high in heart-healthy antioxidants.

Serves 12

8 large eggs

1 pound semisweet chocolate

8 ounces (2 sticks) unsalted butter, cut into pieces the size of a hazelnut

¼ cup strongly brewed coffee (optional)

1. Heat oven to 325°F. Grease an 8" or 9" springform pan and line the bottom with waxed paper. Wrap the outside of the pan in foil to prevent leaks. Prepare a pot of boiling water.

2. Using a handheld or standing electric mixer, beat the eggs until double in volume (about 1 quart), about 5 minutes. Melt the chocolate and butter into the coffee in a double boiler or microwave until very smooth, stirring occasionally. Fold in the whipped eggs in 3 additions, mixing only enough as is necessary to incorporate them. Pour into prepared springform pan.

3. Place springform into a deep roasting pan and place on the lower middle rack of the oven. Pour enough boiling water into the roasting pan to come about halfway up on the sides of the cake. Bake about 25 minutes, until the cake rises slightly, has a thin, wispy crust, and reads 140°F on an instant-read thermometer inserted in the center. Transfer springform to a wire rack and cool to room temperature. Refrigerate overnight. Warm sides of springform with a hot, wet towel to loosen, then pop open, cut with a hot, wet knife, and serve dusted with confectioners' sugar and/or cocoa powder.

PC BANANA PUDDING CAKE

This is a delicious way to use up ripe bananas. You'll need to use a pressure cooker large enough to hold a 1-quart or 6-cup Bundt or angel food cake pan to make this recipe.

Serves 12

- 1 (18¼-ounce) package yellow cake mix or vegan cake mix
- 1 (3½-ounce) package instant banana pudding mix or vegan pudding mix
- 4 eggs or 4 ounces silken tofu
- 4 cups water
- ¼ cup vegetable oil
- 3 small ripe bananas, mashed
- 2 cups powdered sugar, sifted
- 2 tablespoons milk or soymilk
- 1 teaspoon vanilla extract
- ½ cup walnuts, toasted and chopped

1. Treat a 1-quart or 6-cup Bundt or angel food cake pan with nonstick spray. Set aside.

2. Add the cake mix and pudding mix to a large mixing bowl; stir to mix. Make a well in the center; add the eggs or tofu and pour in 1 cup water, oil, and mashed bananas.

3. Beat on low speed until blended. Scrape bowl and beat another 4 minutes on medium speed. Pour the batter into the prepared pan. Cover tightly with a piece of heavy-duty aluminum foil.

4. Pour 3 cups water into the pressure cooker and add the rack. Lower the cake pan onto the rack.

5. Lock the lid into place and bring to high pressure; maintain pressure for 35 minutes.

6. Remove the pressure cooker from the heat, quick-release the pressure, and remove the lid.

7. Lift the cake pan out of the pressure cooker and place on a wire rack to cool for 10 minutes, then turn the cake out onto the wire rack to finish cooling.

8. To make the glaze, mix together the powdered sugar, milk, and vanilla in a bowl. Drizzle over the top of the cooled cake. Sprinkle the walnuts over the glaze before the glaze dries.

PC GLAZED LEMON POPPY SEED CAKE

Make this cake ahead of time. The flavor improves if you wrap it in plastic wrap and store it for a day or two before you serve it.

Serves 8

½ cup butter, softened, or vegan margarine, such as Earth Balance
1 cup sugar
2 eggs, separated, or 2 ounces silken tofu
1 teaspoon vanilla
2 lemons
1¼ cups all-purpose flour
1 teaspoon baking soda
1 teaspoon baking powder
¼ teaspoon salt
⅔ cup whole milk or soymilk
⅓ cup poppy seeds
2 cups water
½ cup powdered sugar, sifted

1. Add the butter or margarine and sugar to a mixing bowl; beat until light and fluffy. Beat in the egg yolks or tofu, vanilla, grated zest from 1 lemon, and juice from 1 lemon.

2. Mix together the flour, baking soda, baking powder, and salt. Add the flour and milk in 3 batches to the butter mixture, mixing after each addition. Stir in the poppy seeds. If using eggs, add the egg whites to a chilled bowl. Whisk or beat until stiff. Fold the egg whites into the poppy seed batter.

3. Treat a 4-cup soufflé dish or Bundt pan with nonstick spray. Transfer the batter to the pan. Treat a 15" square of heavy-duty aluminum foil with nonstick spray. Place the foil, treated-side down, over the pan; crimp around the edges to seal.

4. Pour the water and place the rack into the pressure cooker. Crisscross long, doubled strips of foil over the rack to create handles to use later to remove the pan. Place the pan on the rack over the foil strips. Lock the lid into place and bring to low pressure; maintain pressure for 40 minutes.

5. Remove from heat and allow pressure to release naturally. Remove the lid. Lift the pan from the pressure cooker and place it on a cooling rack. Remove foil cover.

6. To make the glaze, whisk the juice and grated zest from the remaining lemon together with the powdered sugar. Transfer the cake to a serving platter and drizzle the glaze over the top.

PC CORNMEAL CAKE

Serve warm with maple syrup or make a maple-infused butter by whisking pats of chilled butter or vegan margarine into heated maple syrup.

Serves 6

- 2 cups milk or soymilk
- ¼ cup light brown sugar, packed
- 1 teaspoon orange zest, grated
- ½ cup fine yellow cornmeal
- 2 large eggs or 2 ounces silken tofu
- 2 tablespoons butter, melted, or vegan margarine, such as Earth Balance
- 2 tablespoons orange marmalade
- 1 cup water

1. Bring milk to a simmer over medium heat. Stir in the brown sugar; simmer and stir until the milk is at a low boil. Whisk in the orange zest and cornmeal. Simmer and stir for 2 minutes. Remove from heat. Whisk together the eggs or tofu, butter, and orange marmalade. Stir into the cornmeal mixture. Treat a 1-quart soufflé or heatproof glass dish with nonstick spray. Add batter.

2. Pour water into the pressure cooker and add rack. Place soufflé dish on the rack. Lock lid into place and bring to low pressure; maintain pressure for 12 minutes. Remove from heat and allow pressure to release naturally for 10 minutes. Quick-release any remaining pressure and remove the lid. Transfer to a wire rack.

PC BASIC YELLOW CAKE

Serve this staple dessert any way you'd like—topped with icing, a dollop of whipped cream or soy whip, or a sprinkling of powdered sugar.

Serves 10–12

- 1½ cups all-purpose flour
- 1 teaspoon baking powder
- 1 cup sugar
- ½ teaspoon salt
- 2 eggs, beaten, or 2 mashed bananas
- ½ cup butter, melted, or vegan margarine, such as Earth Balance
- 1 teaspoon vanilla extract
- 1 cup milk or soymilk

1. In a medium bowl, mix the flour, baking powder, sugar, and salt. In a large bowl, beat the eggs, if using. Add the dry ingredients to the eggs or bananas. Slowly stir in the melted butter, vanilla extract, and the milk.

2. Pour the cake mixture into an 8" round pan. Place the cake in the pressure cooker and lock the lid into place. Cook the cake for 30 minutes over a low flame without the weight in place.

3. Remove the pressure cooker from the heat and carefully remove the cake. Serve with whatever topping that you like.

BUTTER-CREAM FROSTING

For chocolate butter-cream, add 4 ounces of melted chocolate to this recipe at the end. It's excellent with milk chocolate.

Yields enough to frost 1 (9") cake

1½ cups sugar

½ cup water

2 large eggs plus 4 egg yolks

1 pound unsalted butter, softened to room temperature

2 teaspoons vanilla extract

1. Boil the sugar and water together without stirring until slightly thick and between 234–240°F on a candy thermometer (this is called the "soft ball" stage—a thin ribbon should fall with the last drops off a spoon). Whisk together eggs and yolks in a double boiler or steel bowl atop a pot of simmering water. Gradually whisk in the hot sugar syrup; heat, whisking constantly, until the mixture is hot to the touch, thick, and ribbony. Remove bowl from heat, and continue whisking until cool, about 5 minutes more.

2. In a mixer or bowl, beat the butter until it is fluffy and light. Gradually beat the whipped butter into the egg mixture, adding it in tablespoonfuls. Add the vanilla, and whisk to incorporate. If desired, flavor by adding melted chocolate, fruit liqueur, or espresso. Cool over an ice water bath until it reaches a comfortable consistency for spreading. Keeps in the refrigerator for up to 1 week.

BLONDIES

Chewy, butterscotch-flavored chocolate-chunk brownies are called blondies, and taste great out of the icebox.

Yields 36 pieces

1½ cups flour

½ teaspoon baking powder

½ teaspoon salt

6 ounces (1½ sticks) unsalted butter, at room temperature

Generous 1¾ cups brown sugar

2 teaspoons vanilla extract

3 large eggs

6 ounces (about 1 cup) semisweet chocolate chunks or chips

1. Heat oven to 350°F. Butter a 9" baking pan. In a medium bowl, using a stiff wire whisk, whisk together the flour, baking powder, and salt. Separately, combine the butter, brown sugar, and vanilla, and cream together using an electric mixer or by hand, until light and fluffy (about 2 minutes). Gradually beat in the eggs, working each in completely before adding the next. Scrape down mixing bowl; add the flour mixture. Beat just long enough to incorporate. Mix in chocolate chunks. Transfer the batter into the prepared baking pan and smooth with a spatula.

2. Bake until a toothpick inserted in the center comes out clean, about 30–35 minutes. Cool at room temperature at least 1 hour. Cut into 36 pieces. Will keep refrigerated for 1 week, or in freezer for up to 6 weeks.

PEARS POACHED IN WHITE WINE WITH STRAWBERRY SAUCE

This simply beautiful dessert is perfect in any season. It's light, contains no cholesterol, and finishes an elegant dinner or an everyday lunch with a touch of class.

Serves 8

1 bottle (750 ml) white wine (Chardonnay or Riesling are both excellent for this)

Zest of 1 lemon, shaved off with a vegetable peeler in strips

8 whole cloves

2 whole cinnamon sticks

1 cup sugar, divided

4 Bosc pears, peeled, halved lengthwise, seeds scooped out

1 pint strawberries, hulled and halved

1 teaspoon vanilla

8 sprigs fresh mint

1. Combine the wine, lemon zest, cloves, cinnamon sticks, and ½ cup sugar in a large (4–5 quart) pot; bring to a boil. Reduce heat to a simmer and add the pears, arranging them so they are mostly submerged. Cover tightly and cook slowly for 5 minutes; remove from heat and leave to steep 20 minutes. Chill.

2. In a blender, combine the strawberries, remaining ½ cup sugar, and vanilla. Purée until smooth, adding a few drops of water if necessary to get things started.

3. Spoon the sauce onto dessert plates to form small pools midplate. Serve the pears cut-side down atop the sauce, garnished with mint sprigs at the stem end.

PC SPICED PEACHES

To make spiced peach butter, after Step 2 process the peaches and liquid in a blender or food processor until smooth, and return to the pressure cooker. Simmer and stir over low heat for 30 minutes or until thickened enough to coat the back of a spoon.

Serves 6

2 (15-ounce) cans sliced peaches in syrup

¼ cup water

1 tablespoon white wine vinegar

⅛ teaspoon ground allspice

1 cinnamon stick

4 whole cloves

½ teaspoon ground ginger

Pinch cayenne pepper

1 tablespoon candied ginger, minced (optional)

3 whole black peppercorns (optional)

1. Add all of the ingredients to the pressure cooker. Stir to mix. Lock the lid into place and bring to low pressure; maintain pressure for 3 minutes. Remove the pressure cooker from the heat, quick-release the pressure, and remove the lid. Remove and discard the cinnamon stick, cloves, and peppercorns if used.

2. Return to medium heat. Simmer and stir for 5 minutes to thicken the syrup. Serve warm or chilled. To store, allow to cool and then refrigerate for up to a week.

SC GINGER POACHED PEARS

Fresh ginger best complements pear flavor, but if you only have ground, start by adding a smaller amount and then increasing after tasting.

Serves 8

5 pears, peeled, cored, and cut into wedges
3 cups water
1 cup white sugar
2 tablespoons fresh ginger, minced
1 teaspoon cinnamon

Add all ingredients to a 4-quart slow cooker. Cover and cook on low heat for 4 hours.

SC CINNAMON POACHED APPLES

Red apples, such as Gala or Red Delicious, complement the cinnamon and ground ginger in this recipe.

Serves 8

5 apples, peeled, cored, and cut into wedges
3 cups water
1 cup white sugar
1 teaspoon ground ginger
1 teaspoon cinnamon

Add all ingredients to a 4-quart slow cooker. Cover and cook on low heat for 4 hours.

SC POACHED MIXED BERRIES

Poached mixed berries are delicious on their own or served over a scoop of vanilla ice cream or soy ice cream.

Serves 8

½ cup blackberries

½ cup blueberries

½ cup strawberries, quartered

3 cups water

1 cup white sugar

1 lemon, juiced

Add all ingredients to a 4-quart slow cooker. Cover and cook on low heat for 3–4 hours.

Frozen Versus Fresh Berries

Frozen berries have a slightly different texture after they're defrosted than fresh berries do, but the texture works well in slow cooker recipes because of the long cooking time. Frozen berries allow you to use all types year-round, and they're usually cheaper than fresh berries, too.

PC PORT-POACHED FIGS

Serve the figs on top of soy ice cream—or simply on their own—with the syrup.

Serves 4

3 cups tawny port

1½ cups sugar

1 vanilla bean, split and scraped

½ teaspoon cinnamon

¼ cup orange juice

8 whole black peppercorns

12 dried black mission figs

1. Combine the port, sugar, vanilla pods and seeds, cinnamon, orange juice, and peppercorns in the pressure cooker over high heat. Bring to a boil and reduce the heat. Simmer for 20 minutes.

2. Add the figs. Lock the lid into place and bring to high pressure; maintain pressure for 6 minutes. Remove from heat and allow pressure to release naturally.

PC DRIED FRUIT COMPOTE

If you plan to add sugar to the dried fruit compote, do so before the fruit has cooled so that it can be stirred into the fruit mixture until it dissolves.

Serves 6

1 (8-ounce) package dried apricots

1 (8-ounce) package dried peaches

1 cup golden raisins

1½ cups orange juice

1 cinnamon stick

4 whole cloves

Sugar (optional)

1. Cut the dried apricots and peaches into quarters and add them to the pressure cooker along with the raisins, orange juice, cinnamon stick, and cloves. Lock the lid into place and bring to high pressure; maintain pressure for 3 minutes. Remove from heat and allow pressure to release naturally. Remove the lid.

2. Remove the cinnamon stick and cloves. Return to medium heat and simmer for several minutes. Serve warm or allow to cool, then add sugar to taste, if using. Cover and store in the refrigerator until needed, up to 1 week.

FRUIT COMPOTE

Serve as a topping for plain or soy yogurt.

Serves 6

1 cup apple juice

1 cup dry white wine

2 tablespoons sugar

1 cinnamon stick

¼ teaspoon ground nutmeg

Zest of 1 lemon

Zest of 1 orange

3 apples

3 pears

½ cup dried cherries, cranberries, or raisins

1. Add the apple juice and wine to the pressure cooker over medium-high heat. Bring to a boil. Stir in the sugar until dissolved. Add the cinnamon stick, nutmeg, lemon zest, and orange zest. Reduce heat to maintain a simmer.

2. Wash, peel, core, and chop the apples and pears. Add to the pressure cooker. Stir. Lock the lid into place and bring to high pressure; maintain pressure for 1 minute. Remove the pressure cooker from heat, quick-release the pressure, and remove the lid.

3. Use a slotted spoon to transfer the cooked fruit to a serving bowl. Return the pressure cooker to the heat and bring to a boil; boil and stir until reduced to a syrup that will coat the back of a spoon. Stir the dried cherries, cranberries, or raisins in with the cooked fruit in the bowl and pour the syrup over the fruit mixture. Stir to mix. Allow to cool slightly, then cover with plastic wrap and chill overnight in the refrigerator.

CHOCOLATE CHIP COOKIES

It's best to let these cookies cool completely before eating, but it takes a strong will to wait that long.

Serves about 12

2½ cups all-purpose flour

1 teaspoon baking soda

1 teaspoon salt

1 cup (2 sticks) unsalted butter, softened

¾ cup sugar

¾ cup (packed) light brown sugar

1 teaspoon vanilla extract

2 large eggs

2 cups (12-ounce package) semisweet chocolate chips

1. Heat oven to 375°F. In a mixing bowl, whisk together flour, baking soda, and salt. In a separate bowl, cream together the butter, granulated sugar, brown sugar, and vanilla using a wooden spoon. Add the eggs 1 at a time, mixing until incorporated before adding the next one.

2. Add the flour mix in 3 additions, mixing just enough to incorporate after each addition. Stir in the chocolate chips. Drop the dough in tablespoon-size drops onto ungreased baking sheets. Bake until golden, about 10 minutes. Cool the pans for a few minutes before transferring the cookies to a wire rack to cool completely.

CREPES

Sweet or savory, filled or simply sauced, crepes are delicate, elegant, delicious, and very easy to make. To make a dessert in a hurry, whisk together this batter, make some crepes, and slather them with Nutella, an Italian chocolate-hazelnut spread.

Yields about 8 crepes

½ cup flour

3 large eggs

1 cup milk

1 tablespoon olive oil

¼ teaspoon kosher salt

Butter

1. Whisk together the flour and eggs until they form a smooth paste. Gradually whisk in the milk, olive oil, and salt.

2. Heat a 10" nonstick skillet over medium heat. Add some butter and spread it around the pan with a brush or the corner of a towel. Add ¼ cup of batter to the pan. Swirl the pan around in a circular pattern to evenly distribute the batter.

3. Cook undisturbed until the edges become visibly brown. Using a wooden or rubber spatula, lift the edge of the crepe from the pan. Quickly flip the crepe using your fingers or a wooden spoon. Cook for 30 seconds on the second side, then slide onto a plate; keep warm while you repeat the procedure with remaining batter. Crepes can be stacked one atop the other for storage.

COTTAGE CHEESE BLINTZES

Tender, not chewy, and runny with fresh, milky-sweet filling, these blintzes are a simple luxury.

Serves 4

1 cup cottage cheese

½ cup ricotta

2 tablespoons sugar

1 large egg yolk

12 Crepes (see recipe in this chapter)

2 tablespoons unsalted butter, melted

Jams, jellies, and confectioners' sugar

1. In a food processor, pulse the cottage cheese, ricotta, and sugar until smooth. Transfer to a bowl; whisk in the yolk.

2. Heat oven to 325°F. Butter a 9" × 13" baking dish. On a clean work surface, spoon a generous tablespoon of cheese filling onto the bottom third of a crepe. Fold in the sides and fold the bottom up to envelop the filling; roll the crepe away from yourself. Repeat with remaining crepes; line them into the baking dish and brush them with the melted butter. Bake 10–15 minutes, until they have become visibly plump. Serve with a dusting of confectioners' sugar, and assorted jams and jellies on the side.

SC PEANUT BUTTER CAKE

Serve this cake with a drizzling of chocolate sauce on top to make it a peanut butter cup cake.

Serves 8

1 cup all-purpose flour

1 cup sugar

1 teaspoon baking powder

½ teaspoon baking soda

¾ cup water

½ cup peanut butter

⅛ cup vegetable oil

1 teaspoon vanilla extract

1. In a medium bowl, mix all the dry ingredients.

2. In another medium bowl, mix all the wet ingredients.

3. Spray slow cooker with nonstick cooking oil.

4. Combine the dry and wet ingredients and then pour into a 4-quart slow cooker. Cover and cook on medium-high heat for 1–2 hours.

SC COCONUT RICE PUDDING

Rice pudding, also referred to as porridge, is eaten around the world in many different forms.

Serves 8

1 cup white rice

1 quart soymilk

½ cup butter or vegan margarine

⅛ cup shredded coconut

1 cup sugar

1 teaspoon cinnamon

¼ teaspoon salt

Add all ingredients to a 4-quart slow cooker. Cover and cook on low heat for 6 hours.

SC HOT FUDGE FONDUE

Leftover Hot Fudge Fondue can be stored in a covered container in the refrigerator for up to 3 weeks. Reheat to serve, whisking in additional cream if needed.

Yields 4 cups

1 cup butter or vegan margarine

1 cup heavy cream or soymilk

½ cup light corn syrup

Pinch salt

16 ounces semisweet chocolate chips

1 tablespoon vanilla extract

1. Add the butter or margarine, cream or soymilk, corn syrup, and salt to a 4-quart slow cooker. Cover and cook on low for 1 hour.

2. Uncover and stir with a silicone-coated whisk or heatproof spatula; cover and cook for another hour. Uncover and stir or whisk until the sugar is completely dissolved.

3. Add the chocolate chips and vanilla. Stir or whisk until the chocolate is completely melted and incorporated into the fondue. Reduce the heat to warm until ready to serve directly from the slow cooker.

SC CHOCOLATE-ALMOND FONDUE

Fruit is often used for enjoying dessert fondue, but you can also try dipping pretzels or dense yellow cake for a different flavor.

Serves 16

2 (14-ounce) packages semisweet chocolate chips
2 cups plain soymilk
½ cup butter or vegan margarine
½ cup almond pieces

1. Add all ingredients to a 4-quart slow cooker. Cover and cook on low heat for 1 hour.
2. Serve the fondue warm with fruits such as strawberries, pineapples, apples, and bananas.

SC CHOCOLATE-CINNAMON FONDUE

Cinnamon is most often used in the ground form, but whole cinnamon sticks can be used, too. Just be sure to remove them from the fondue before serving.

Serves 16

2 (14-ounce) packages semisweet chocolate chips
2 cups plain soymilk
½ cup butter or vegan margarine
1 tablespoon ground cinnamon

1. Add all ingredients to a 4-quart slow cooker. Cover and cook on low heat for 1 hour.
2. Serve the fondue warm with fruits such as strawberries, pineapples, apples, and bananas.

SC BANANAS FOSTER

Bananas Foster is usually made from flambéed bananas served over vanilla ice cream, but as this recipe proves, the bananas can be made in a slow cooker, too.

Serves 8

- 1 cup dark corn syrup
- ⅛ cup rum
- ½ teaspoon vanilla extract
- 1 teaspoon cinnamon
- ¾ cup butter or vegan margarine
- ½ teaspoon salt
- 10 bananas, peeled and cut into bite-size pieces
- 4 cups vanilla ice cream or vegan vanilla ice cream

1. In a medium bowl, stir in the corn syrup, rum, vanilla extract, cinnamon, butter or margarine, and salt.
2. Add mixture and bananas to a 4-quart slow cooker. Cover and cook on low heat for 1–2 hours. Serve over a scoop of ice cream.

SC CARAMEL APPLES AND PEARS

Vegan caramels can be purchased online at AllisonsGourmet.com

Serves 8

- 2 green apples, cored, peeled, and cut into wedges
- 2 pears, cored, peeled, and cut into wedges
- 1 (14-ounce) package of caramels
- ⅛ cup butter or vegan margarine
- 1 teaspoon cinnamon
- ½ cup apple juice

Add all ingredients to a 4-quart slow cooker. Cover and cook on low heat for 1–2 hours.

SC CHOCOLATE ALMOND BARS

Save your dollar at the grocery store and make an entire batch of homemade candy bars.

Serves 16

2 (14-ounce) packages semisweet chocolate chips

2 cups almond pieces

1. Add all ingredients to a 4-quart slow cooker. Cover and cook on low heat for 1 hour, stirring every 15 minutes.

2. With a large spoon, scoop out the chocolate mixture and drop it onto wax paper. Allow to cool for 20–30 minutes.

Fun Shapes
Homemade candy bars make easy and budget-friendly holiday gifts, and making them in fun shapes is a festive touch. Spray the inside of a cookie cutter with nonstick spray, then lay it on top of the wax paper before dropping the chocolate on. Pour the chocolate into the cookie cutter and leave it in place until the chocolate is slightly firm.

SC CHOCOLATE COCONUT BARS

Shredded coconut sometimes comes sweetened, but if you'd like to cut the sugar in this treat, use unsweetened instead.

Serves 16

2 (14-ounce) packages semisweet chocolate chips

1 cup shredded coconut

1. Add all ingredients to a 4-quart slow cooker. Cover and cook on low heat for 1 hour, stirring every 15 minutes.

2. With a large spoon, scoop out the chocolate mixture and drop it onto wax paper. Allow to cool for 20–30 minutes.

WHITE CHOCOLATE–MACADAMIA NUT BARS

White chocolate is made from cocoa butter, not cocoa solids, which means it does not have the same nutritional benefits as dark chocolate.

Serves 16

2 (14-ounce) packages white chocolate chips

1 cup macadamia nut pieces

1. Add all ingredients to a 4-quart slow cooker. Cover and cook on low heat for 1 hour, stirring every 15 minutes.
2. With a large spoon, scoop out the white chocolate mixture and drop it onto wax paper. Allow to cool for 20–30 minutes.

CHOCOLATE-COVERED PRETZELS

To easily "dip" all of the pretzels at once, you can pour them all into the slow cooker, stir gently, and pour the entire mixture into a colander to strain the excess chocolate.

Serves 16

2 (14-ounce) packages semisweet chocolate chips

2 cups plain soymilk

½ cup butter or vegan margarine

4 cups miniature pretzels

1. Add all ingredients except pretzels to a 4-quart slow cooker. Cover, and cook on low heat for 1 hour.
2. Dip the pretzels in the chocolate and allow to cool on wax paper for 20–30 minutes.

PC CHOCOLATE-BERRY BREAD PUDDING

You can cut the fat a bit in Chocolate-Berry Bread Pudding by replacing the milk and cream with skim or 2% milk, but add one more egg to the batter if you do.

Serves 6

- 6 slices day-old challah or brioche, or vegan white bread
- ½ cup raspberry preserves
- ½ cup dried strawberries or prunes, diced
- ½ cup hazelnuts, chopped
- ½ cup cocoa powder
- ½ cup sugar
- Pinch salt
- 2 tablespoons butter, melted, or vegan margarine, such as Earth Balance
- 3 large eggs or 2 mashed bananas
- 2 cups whole milk or soymilk
- 2 cups heavy cream or soymilk
- 1 tablespoon vanilla
- 1 cup water

1. If the crusts on the bread are dark, remove them. If using fresh bread, lightly toast it. Spread raspberry preserves over the bread. Treat a 5-cup heatproof soufflé dish with nonstick spray.

2. Tear the bread into chunks. Layer half the bread in the bottom of the soufflé dish. Sprinkle with dried fruit and chopped hazelnuts. Add remaining bread with preserves.

3. Whisk the cocoa, sugar, and salt together. Add butter or margarine and eggs or bananas; whisk to mix. Whisk in milk and cream or soymilk, and vanilla. Pour half the cocoa mixture over the bread. Tap down the dish and wait several minutes for the bread to absorb the liquid. Pour in remaining cocoa mixture.

4. Tear off 2 large pieces of heavy-duty aluminum foil. Lay one piece of the foil over the top of the dish, crimping it slightly around the edges, and wrap it around the dish, folding it and tucking it under. Set the dish in the middle of the remaining piece of foil; bring it up and over the top of the dish and crimp to seal.

5. Pour water into the pressure cooker and add rack. Crisscross 2 long doubled pieces of foil over the rack. Place the covered soufflé dish over the crossed strips.

6. Lock lid into place and bring to high pressure; maintain for 15 minutes. Remove from heat and allow pressure to release naturally. Remove the dish from the pressure cooker, remove the foil, and place on a rack until ready to serve or until it's cool enough to cover and refrigerate.

PC LEMON CHEESECAKE

Serve this rich, popular dessert topped with cherry pie filling or sugared fresh blueberries, raspberries, or strawberries.

Serves 8

- 12 gingersnaps or vanilla wafers
- 1½ tablespoons almonds, toasted
- ½ tablespoon butter, melted, or vegan margarine, such as Earth Balance
- 2 (8-ounce) packages cream cheese, room temperature, or vegan cream cheese
- ½ cup sugar
- 2 large eggs, or 2 ounces silken tofu
- Zest of 1 lemon, grated
- 1 tablespoon fresh lemon juice
- ½ teaspoon natural lemon extract
- 1 teaspoon vanilla
- 2 cups water

1. Use a pressure cooker with a rack that's large enough to hold a 7" × 3" springform pan. Treat the inside of the pan with nonstick spray.
2. Add the cookies and almonds to a food processor. Pulse to create cookie crumbs and chop the nuts. Add the melted butter or margarine and pulse to mix.
3. Transfer the crumb mixture to the springform pan and press down into the pan. Wipe out the food processor bowl.
4. Cut the cream cheese into cubes and add it to the food processor along with the sugar; process until smooth. Add the eggs or tofu, lemon zest, lemon juice, lemon extract, and vanilla. Process for 10 seconds.
5. Scrape the bowl and then process for another 10 seconds or until the batter is well mixed and smooth.
6. Place the springform pan in the center of 2 (16" × 16") pieces of aluminum foil. Crimp the foil to seal the bottom of the pan.
7. Transfer the cheesecake batter into the springform pan. Treat one side of a 10" square of aluminum foil with nonstick spray; lay over the top of the springform pan and crimp around the edges.
8. Bring the bottom foil up the sides so that it can be grasped to raise and lower the pan into and out of the pressure cooker.
9. Pour the water into the pressure cooker. Insert the rack. Set the springform pan holding the cheesecake batter on the rack.
10. Lock the lid into place and bring to high pressure; maintain pressure for 8 minutes. Remove from heat and allow pressure to release naturally. Remove the lid.
11. Lift the covered springform pan out of the pressure cooker and place on a wire rack. Remove the top foil.
12. If any moisture has accumulated on top of the cheesecake, dab it with a piece of paper towel to remove it. Let cool to room temperature and then remove from the springform pan.

PC CREAMY COCONUT RICE PUDDING

Garnish this pudding with a sprinkling of ground cinnamon and serve with a dollop of whipped cream or soy whip.

Serves 6

1½ cups arborio rice, rinsed and drained

2 cups whole milk or soymilk

1 (14-ounce) can coconut milk

1 cup water

½ cup sugar

2 teaspoons ground cinnamon

½ teaspoon salt

1½ teaspoons vanilla

1 cup dried cherries, dried strawberries, or golden raisins

1. Add the rice, milk or soymilk, coconut milk, water, sugar, cinnamon, and salt to the pressure cooker. Cook and stir to dissolve the sugar over medium-high heat and bring to a boil. Lock the lid into place and bring to low pressure; maintain for 15 minutes.

2. Turn off the heat, quick-release the pressure, and remove the lid. Stir in the vanilla and dried fruit. Replace the cover, but do not lock into place. Let stand for 15 minutes. Stir and serve.

MOLTEN FUDGE PUDDING CAKE

Serve warm with a scoop of vanilla bean ice cream or soy ice cream and garnish with fresh fruit or dust with powdered sugar.

Serves 6

- 4 ounces semisweet chocolate chips
- ¼ cup cocoa powder
- ⅛ teaspoon salt
- 3 tablespoons butter or vegan margarine, such as Earth Balance, divided
- 2 large eggs, separated, or 2 ounces silken tofu
- ¼ cup sugar, plus extra for the pan
- 1 teaspoon vanilla
- ½ cup pecans, chopped
- ¼ cup plus 2 tablespoons all-purpose flour
- 2 teaspoons instant coffee granules
- 2 tablespoons coffee liqueur
- 1 cup water

1. Add the chocolate chips, cocoa, salt, and 2 tablespoons butter or margarine to a microwave-safe bowl. Microwave on high for 1 minute; stir well. Microwave in additional 20-second segments if necessary, until the butter or margarine and chocolate are melted. Set aside to cool.

2. Add the egg whites or tofu to a medium-size mixing bowl. Whisk until the egg whites are foamy. Gradually add ¼ cup of sugar, continuing to whisk until soft peaks form; set aside.

3. Add the egg yolks, if using, and vanilla to a mixing bowl; use a whisk or handheld mixer to beat until the yolks are light yellow and begin to stiffen. Stir in the cooled chocolate mixture, pecans, flour, instant coffee, and coffee liqueur.

4. Transfer a third of the beaten egg whites or tofu to the chocolate mixture; stir to loosen the batter. Gently fold in the remaining egg whites or tofu.

5. Treat the bottom and sides of a 1-quart metal pan with 2 teaspoons of the remaining butter. Add about a tablespoon of sugar to the pan; shake and roll to coat the buttered pan with the sugar.

6. Discard any extra sugar. Transfer the chocolate batter to the buttered pan.

7. Treat one side of a 15" piece of aluminum foil with the remaining teaspoon of butter. Place the foil butter-side down over the top of the pan; crimp around the edges of the pan to form a seal.

8. Pour the water into the pressure cooker. Place the rack in the cooker. Create handles to use later to remove the pan by crisscrossing long, doubled strips of foil over the rack.

9. Place the metal pan in the center of the rack over the foil strips. Lock the lid into place and bring to low pressure; maintain pressure for 20 minutes.

10. Remove pressure cooker from heat, quick-release pressure, and remove the lid. Lift the pan out of the pressure cooker and place on a wire rack. Remove foil cover.

11. Let rest for 10–15 minutes. To serve, spoon from the pan.

PC PLUM PUDDING WITH BRANDY SAUCE

This traditional steamed Christmas pudding can be made up to a month in advance if you refrigerate it in a brandy-soaked cheesecloth in a covered container. If made ahead, steam it or heat it gently in the microwave before serving it with the brandy sauce.

Serves 10

1 cup prunes, snipped

1 cup dried currants

1 cup dried cranberries

1 cup raisins

1 cup candied lemon peel, minced

½ cup dark rum

1 cup butter, partially frozen, or vegan margarine, such as Earth Balance

1½ cups all-purpose flour

1 cup dried bread crumbs

½ cup pecans, chopped

1 tablespoon candied ginger, minced

1 teaspoon baking soda

½ teaspoon salt

1 teaspoon ground cinnamon

¼ teaspoon ground nutmeg

¼ teaspoon ground cloves

3 eggs or 3 ounces silken tofu

2 cups light brown sugar, packed

3 cups water

1 cup heavy cream or soymilk

¼ cup brandy

1. Add the prunes, currants, cranberries, raisins, candied lemon peel, and rum to a bowl. Stir to mix. Cover and let stand at room temperature for 8 hours.

2. Partially freeze ¾ cup butter or margarine. Add the flour, bread crumbs, pecans, ginger, baking soda, salt, cinnamon, nutmeg, and cloves to a large mixing bowl. Stir to mix.

3. Grate the butter or margarine into the flour mixture. Add the marinated fruit. Toss grated butter or margarine and fruit into flour mixture. Add eggs or tofu and 1 cup of brown sugar to a separate bowl; whisk to mix. Pour into the flour-butter or margarine-fruit mixture. Combine the two mixtures together.

4. Wrap the base of a 7" or 8" springform pan with heavy-duty aluminum foil. Transfer the batter to the springform pan.

5. Tear off a 25"-long piece of heavy-duty aluminum foil and treat one side of one 8" end of the foil with nonstick spray. Place the nonstick spray-treated side of the foil over the top of the springform pan and then wrap the remaining foil under and over the pan again; crimp to seal.

6. Pour the water and place the rack into the pressure cooker. Crisscross long doubled strips of foil over the rack to create handles to use later to remove the pan.

7. Place springform pan on rack, over foil strips. Lock lid into place and bring to high pressure; maintain for 1 hour.

8. Remove from heat and allow pressure to release . Remove lid. Lift pan from the pressure cooker and cool. Remove foil cover.

9. Let rest and cool for 15 minutes, then run a knife around the edge of the pudding to loosen it from the sides of the pan. Unmold the pudding and transfer it to a plate.

10. To make the brandy sauce, add remaining cup of brown sugar, cream or soymilk, and remaining ¼ cup butter or margarine to a saucepan placed over medium-high heat. Simmer and stir until sugar dissolves; stir in the brandy. Simmer and stir for 10 minutes. Serve over the warm pudding.

PC PEANUT BUTTER AND FUDGE CHEESECAKE

Adults and kids alike love peanut butter and chocolate, so this dessert will be a hit with everyone.

Serves 8

1 cup toasted, unsalted peanuts

½ cup vanilla wafers

1 tablespoon cocoa powder

3 tablespoons butter, melted, or vegan margarine, such as Earth Balance

1 cup peanut butter

2 (8-ounce) packages cream cheese, softened, or vegan cream cheese

½ cup light brown sugar, packed

½ cup powdered sugar, sifted

2 tablespoons cornstarch

2 large eggs or 2 ounces silken tofu

¼ cup sour cream or soy sour cream

1 (12-ounce) package semisweet chocolate chips

2 cups water

1. Add the peanuts, vanilla wafers, and cocoa to a food processor. Pulse to grind the peanuts and turn the vanilla wafers into crumbs. Add the butter or margarine. Pulse to mix. Press into the bottom of a 7" springform pan. Set aside. Wipe out the food processor.

2. Add the peanut butter, cream cheese, and brown sugar to the food processor. Process until smooth. Add the powdered sugar and cornstarch to a small bowl; stir to mix well. Add to the food processor with the eggs or tofu and sour cream. Process until smooth. Remove the lid and stir in the chocolate chips. Transfer the batter to the springform pan.

3. Wrap the base of the pan with heavy-duty aluminum foil. Tear off a 25"-long piece of heavy-duty aluminum foil and treat one side of one 8" end of the foil with nonstick spray. Place the spray-treated side of the foil over the top of the pan and then wrap the remaining foil under and then over the pan again; crimp to seal.

4. Pour the water and place the rack into the pressure cooker. Crisscross long, doubled strips of foil over the rack to create handles to use later to remove the pan. Place the springform pan on the rack over the foil strips. Lock the lid into place and bring to high pressure; maintain pressure for 22 minutes.

5. Remove from heat and allow pressure to release naturally. Remove the lid. Lift the pan from the pressure cooker and place it on a wire rack. Allow to cool slightly. Refrigerate at least 4 hours before serving.

PC DATE PUDDING

This is a rich, decadent dessert in the tradition of an English sticky toffee pudding.

Serves 8

2½ cups dates, pitted and snipped

1½ teaspoons baking soda

1⅔ cups boiling water

2 cups dark brown sugar, packed

½ cup butter, softened, or vegan margarine, such as Earth Balance

3 large eggs or 3 ounces firm tofu

2 teaspoons vanilla

3½ cups all-purpose or cake flour

4 teaspoons baking powder

Pinch salt

2 cups water

1. Add the dates to a mixing bowl and toss them together with the baking soda. Pour the boiling water over the dates. Set aside.

2. Add the brown sugar and butter or margarine to a food processor. Process to cream them together, and then continue to process while you add the eggs or tofu and vanilla. Use a spatula to scrape the brown sugar mixture into the bowl with the dates. Stir to mix.

3. Add the flour, baking powder, and salt to a bowl; stir to mix. Fold into the date and brown sugar mixture.

4. Wrap the base of a 7" or 8" springform pan with heavy-duty aluminum foil. Treat the pan with nonstick spray.

5. Press the batter into the springform pan. Tear off a 25"-long piece of heavy-duty aluminum foil and treat one side of one 8" end of the foil with nonstick spray. Place the treated side of the foil over the top of the springform pan and then wrap the remaining foil under and then over the pan again; crimp to seal.

6. Pour the water and place the rack into the pressure cooker. Crisscross long, doubled strips of foil over the rack to create handles to use later to remove the pan. Place the springform pan on the rack over the foil strips. Lock the lid into place and bring to low pressure; maintain pressure for 50 minutes.

7. Remove from heat and allow pressure to release naturally. Remove the lid. Lift the pan from the pressure cooker and place it on a cooling rack.

PIÑA COLADA BREAD PUDDING

If desired, you can add 1 tablespoon butter and 2 tablespoons brown sugar to the juice drained from the pineapple. Simmer and stir over medium-low heat until it thickens, and then serve over the bread pudding.

Serves 8

1 (16-ounce) can cream of coconut

1 cup heavy cream or soymilk

3 large eggs or 3 ounces silken tofu

½ cup butter, melted, or vegan margarine, such as Earth Balance

¾ cup sugar

1½ teaspoons rum flavoring

¼ teaspoon ground nutmeg

1 (20-ounce) can pineapple chunks, drained

1¼ cups coconut

8 cups French bread, torn into 2" cubes

1½ cups water

1. Add the cream of coconut, cream or soymilk, eggs or tofu, butter or margarine, sugar, rum flavoring, and nutmeg to a large bowl. Whisk to mix thoroughly. Stir in the drained pineapple and coconut. Fold in the bread cubes.

2. Treat a 5-cup soufflé dish with nonstick spray. Transfer the bread pudding mixture into the dish. Pour in the water and place the rack into the pressure cooker.

3. Crisscross long, doubled strips of foil over the rack to create handles to use later to remove the pan.

4. Treat one side of a 15"-square piece of heavy-duty aluminum foil with nonstick spray. Lay the foil, treated-side down, over the soufflé dish and crimp the edges to seal.

5. Tear off another piece of heavy-duty foil to completely wrap the soufflé dish to ensure the seal. Place over the crisscrossed pieces of foil.

6. Lock the lid into place and bring to high pressure; maintain pressure for 12 minutes. Remove pressure cooker from heat, quick-release pressure, and remove lid.

7. Remove pan from the pressure cooker, uncover, and place on a wire rack to cool. Serve warm, at room temperature, or chilled.

PC TAPIOCA PUDDING

Add another dimension to this dish by combining it with other flavors. You can stir in some toasted pecans, chocolate chips, or coconut.

Serves 4

½ cup small pearl tapioca

1¾ cups water

⅓ cup sugar

1 tablespoon butter, or vegan margarine, such as Earth Balance

2 large eggs or 2 ounces firm tofu

⅛ teaspoon salt

1½ cups milk or soymilk

1 cup heavy cream or soymilk

1 teaspoon vanilla

1. Combine the tapioca and ¾ cup water in a small bowl; cover and let soak overnight.

2. Add the sugar, butter or margarine, eggs or tofu, and salt to a bowl; beat until smooth. Stir in the milk and cream or soymilk, and vanilla. Drain the tapioca and stir into the milk mixture.

3. Treat a 1-quart stainless steel bowl with nonstick spray. Pour the tapioca mixture into the bowl. Cover the bowl tightly with heavy-duty aluminum foil.

4. Pour the remaining cup of water into the pressure cooker and add the rack. Crisscross long, doubled strips of foil over the rack to create handles to use later to remove the pan. Center the covered pan holding the tapioca mixture on the foil strips on the rack.

5. Lock the lid into place and bring to low pressure; maintain pressure for 12 minutes. Remove the pressure cooker from the heat, quick-release the pressure, and remove the lid.

6. Lift the pudding out of the pressure cooker. Let rest for 15 minutes and then remove the foil cover. Stir. Taste for flavor and add more vanilla if desired. Chill until ready to serve.

PC STEAMED DESSERT BREAD

Toast leftovers by placing slices on the oven rack or a cookie sheet in a 350°F oven for 5 minutes.

Serves 8

½ cup unbleached all-purpose flour

½ cup stone-ground cornmeal

½ cup whole-wheat flour

½ teaspoon baking powder

¼ teaspoon fine salt

¼ teaspoon baking soda

½ cup maple syrup

½ cup buttermilk, or ½ cup soymilk plus 1 tablespoon vinegar

1 large egg or 1 ounce silken tofu

Butter, as needed, or vegan margarine, such as Earth Balance

2 cups water

1. Add the flour, cornmeal, whole-wheat flour, baking powder, salt, and baking soda to a mixing bowl. Stir to combine.

2. Add the maple syrup, buttermilk or soymilk/vinegar, and egg or tofu to another mixing bowl. Whisk to mix, then pour into the flour mixture. Mix until a thick batter is formed.

3. Butter the inside of a 6-cup heatproof pudding mold or baking pan. Add enough batter to fill ¾ full.

4. Butter one side of a piece of heavy-duty aluminum foil large enough to cover the top of the baking dish. Place butter-side down over the pan and crimp to seal.

5. Pour the water and place the rack into the pressure cooker. Crisscross long, doubled strips of foil over the rack to create handles to use later to remove the pan. Place the pan on the rack over the foil strips. Lock the lid into place and bring to low pressure; maintain pressure for 1 hour.

6. Remove from heat and allow pressure to release naturally. Remove lid. Lift pan from pressure cooker and place on a cooling rack. Remove foil.

7. Test the bread with a toothpick; if the toothpick comes out wet, place the foil over the pan and return it to the pressure cooker for 5 more minutes, repeating if necessary. If the bread is done, use a knife to loosen the bread and invert it onto the cooling rack. Serve the bread warm.

PC VEGAN FLAN

To remove flan from the ramekins, dip the bottom in hot water for about 15 seconds, then turn over onto a plate.

Serves 6

½ cup plus 1½ tablespoons sugar, divided

2 cups plain soymilk

1 tablespoon agar-agar flakes

½ cup extra-firm silken tofu

1 tablespoon vanilla extract

¼ teaspoon salt

1. Place ½ cup sugar in a saucepan over medium-low heat. Stir and melt until golden. Pour into the bottom of ramekins.

2. Pour the soymilk into the pressure cooker and sprinkle with the agar-agar flakes. Let sit for 10 minutes. Bring to a boil over high heat, then reduce the heat to low. Lock the lid into place and maintain pressure for 3 minutes. Remove from heat and allow pressure to release naturally.

3. Blend the tofu, remaining sugar, vanilla, salt, and soymilk mixture in a blender or large food processor until very smooth.

4. Pour the tofu mixture into the ramekins over the syrup, then cover with plastic wrap and refrigerate for at least 2 hours.

HOT CRANBERRY-PINEAPPLE PUNCH

If you prefer, you can omit the brown sugar and water called for in this recipe and sweeten it with 2 cups of apple juice instead.

Serves 20

8 cups cranberry juice

8 cups unsweetened pineapple juice

2 cups brown sugar, packed

2 cups water

2 (3") cinnamon sticks

2 teaspoons whole cloves

1. In a 4-quart slow cooker, add the cranberry juice, pineapple juice, brown sugar, and water.

2. Break the cinnamon sticks into smaller pieces and add them along with the whole cloves to a muslin spice bag or wrap them in cheesecloth tied shut with cotton string or kitchen twine. Add to the slow cooker.

3. Cover and cook on low for 1 hour.

4. Uncover and stir until the brown sugar is dissolved into the juice.

5. Cover and cook for another 7–8 hours.

6. Uncover the cooker and remove the spice bag or cheesecloth; holding over the slow cooker, squeeze to extract the seasoned juice. To serve, ladle into heatproof mugs.

SC GINGER-PEAR PUNCH

Adding a touch of sparkling water at the end will make this punch even more refreshing.

Serves 6

6 cups water

½ cup sugar

1" piece fresh ginger, peeled and grated

6 pears, peeled and diced

Ice

24 ounces sparkling water

1. In a 4-quart slow cooker, add the water, sugar, and ginger.
2. Place the pear in a cheesecloth and twist to close, then add to the slow cooker.
3. Cover and cook on low heat for 3 hours.
4. Allow the punch to cool completely, then fill each glass with ice, ¾ full with the punch, then top it off with a splash of plain sparkling water.

SC WHITE TEA–BERRY FUSION

Fruit-filled teas are delicious served warm or chilled and served over ice.

Serves 8

8 white tea bags

½ cup blackberries, halved

½ cup raspberries, halved

2 tablespoons sugar

8 cups water

1. Add all ingredients to a 4-quart slow cooker. Cover and cook on low heat for 2 hours.
2. Remove the tea bags and strain the fruit before serving.

White Tea

White tea is harvested mainly in China. It is made from immature tea leaves plucked just before the buds fully open. The leaves go through even less processing than green tea leaves (they are steamed rather than air-dried). Because of this, they remain close to their natural state, meaning they contain more cancer-fighting polyphenols than other teas. White tea has also been found to bolster the immune system and prevent plaque.

SC VANILLA-LAVENDER TEA

Black tea, green tea, or white tea will all work well in this recipe. The choice is yours!

Serves 8

8 black tea bags

8 cups water

½ teaspoon vanilla extract

1 tablespoon sugar

2 sprigs lavender

1. Place the tea bags, water, vanilla extract, and sugar in a 4-quart slow cooker.
2. Place the lavender in a cheesecloth and twist to close, then add to the slow cooker.
3. Cover and cook on low heat for 2 hours.
4. Remove the tea bags and lavender before serving the tea warm.

SC CHAI TEA

Chai tea typically refers to tea that has been brewed with Indian spices and herbs.

Serves 8

8 bags Darjeeling tea

2 quarts water

1 cinnamon stick

8 whole cloves

1 cup soymilk

2 tablespoons sugar

5 cardamom pods

1 tablespoon fresh ginger, sliced

1. Place the tea bags, water, cinnamon, cloves, soymilk, sugar, cardamom, and ginger in a 4-quart slow cooker. Cover and cook on low heat for 2 hours.
2. Pour the tea through a strainer and serve warm.

Iced Chai

Chai tea can be enjoyed warm during the winter or cold in the summer. Simply pour the chai over ice or combine a glass of tea with a ½–1 cup of ice in the blender.

SC CAFÉ MOCHA

With many drinks at specialty coffee shops coming in around $5, you can save big money by making a budget-friendly version at home.

Serves 12

8 cups fresh-brewed coffee

2 cups 2% milk or soymilk

4 tablespoons chocolate sauce

2 ounces dark chocolate, finely chopped

1. Add all the ingredients to a 4-quart slow cooker. Cover and cook on low heat for 2 hours.
2. Serve warm or chilled and top with whipped cream if desired.

Coffee in America

Coffee consumption is on the rise in the United States. Studies show that Americans now drink a whopping 336 million cups of coffee each year!

SC PUMPKIN SPICE

Canned pumpkin works in this recipe as long as the texture is very smooth.

Serves 8

1 cup puréed pumpkin

8 cups 2% milk or soymilk

2 tablespoons sugar

½ teaspoon ground cloves

½ teaspoon allspice

½ teaspoon ground cinnamon

Add all ingredients to a 4-quart slow cooker and stir until very well combined. Cover and cook on low heat for 2 hours.

SC MINTY HOT CHOCOLATE

Several brands of chocolate syrup such as Hershey's are "accidentally vegan." Just be sure to read the label before purchasing.

Serves 8

8 cups 2% milk or soymilk
8 tablespoons chocolate syrup
¼ cup fresh mint, chopped

1. Pour the milk or soymilk and chocolate syrup into a 4-quart slow cooker and stir well.
2. Place the fresh mint in a cheesecloth and twist until closed, then add to the slow cooker.
3. Cover and cook on low heat for 1 hour.
4. Remove the mint before serving warm.

Many Uses of Mint
Besides being a refreshing herb, mint has had many medicinal uses throughout history. It has been used to relieve headaches, cure indigestion and heartburn, and help people fall asleep.

SC HOT BUTTERED RUM

Time the cooking of this drink so that you can stir in the rum and let it mull for 20 minutes before serving.

Serves 12

½ cup unsalted butter or vegan margarine
8 cups water
2 cups firmly packed light brown sugar
Pinch salt
½ teaspoon freshly ground nutmeg
⅛ teaspoon ground cloves
⅛ teaspoon ground cinnamon
1 cup dark rum

1. Add the butter or margarine and 2 cups of the water to a 4-quart slow cooker. Cover and cook on high for ½ hour, or until the butter is melted.
2. Stir in the brown sugar, and then add the remaining water, salt, nutmeg, cloves, and cinnamon. Cover and cook on low for 2–4 hours.
3. Twenty minutes before serving, stir in the rum; cover, and cook for 20 minutes. To serve, ladle into small heatproof mugs.

SC HOT TODDY

Hot Toddies have been used for many years as an alternative remedy for congestion and colds.

Serves 8

½ cup bourbon

¼ cup honey

2 lemons, juiced

2 cups water

1 stick cinnamon

1. Add all ingredients to a 4-quart slow cooker and stir until very well combined. Cover and cook on low heat for 2 hours.
2. Remove the cinnamon stick and serve warm.

Origins of the Hot Toddy

The Hot Toddy originated in Scotland. Interestingly, the original version did not contain alcohol; that was added later for the medicinal value.

SC SPIKED APPLE CIDER

The dark rum adds a delicious complexity to this cider.

Serves 6

6 cups apple cider

6 ounces dark rum

1 apple, cored and thinly sliced

Add all ingredients to a 4-quart slow cooker. Cover and cook on low heat for 2 hours.

SC SPICED WINE

This is a great wine to make for winter holiday parties.

Serves 6

1 (750-ml) bottle red wine

½ teaspoon ground cinnamon

½ teaspoon ground cloves

½ teaspoon ground nutmeg

1 tablespoon orange zest

Add all ingredients to a 4-quart slow cooker. Cover and cook on low heat for 2 hours.

Garnishments

After zesting your orange peel for the spiced wine, cut the orange into thin circles and add to each drink as a garnish. Alternatively, you may cut each orange wedge into 3 pieces and add to the slow cooker for increased fruity flavor.

SC IRISH COFFEE

The coffee, which is best made using medium-roast beans, can be made ahead and added to the slow cooker 2 hours before you plan to serve dessert.

Serves 16

16 cups brewed coffee

½ cup sugar

1 cup Irish whiskey

1. If you are using chilled coffee, add it to a 4-quart slow cooker; cover and cook on low for 1 hour. If you're using fresh-brewed coffee, you can skip this step.

2. Stir in the sugar until it's dissolved. Cover and cook on low for 1 hour.

3. To serve, ladle into heatproof mugs. Add whiskey and garnish with a dollop of whipped cream, if desired.

Origins of Irish Coffee

Joseph Sheridan, a chef in Ireland, is said to be the first to ever serve Irish coffee. The drink was created to cheer up a group of American travelers on a gloomy winter night in the 1940s.

SC MIXED BERRY PUNCH

Feel free to use whatever berries happen to be in season to create this refreshing punch.

Serves 8

1 cup blackberries
1 cup blueberries
1 cup strawberries
1 lemon, juiced
½ cup sugar
2 quarts water

1. Add all ingredients to a 4-quart slow cooker. Cover and cook on low heat for 2 hours.
2. Pour punch through a strainer and serve chilled.

SC PEACH ICED TEA

If fresh peaches are not in season, use canned peaches instead.

Serves 8

8 bags black tea
2 quarts water
2 peaches, thinly sliced
½ cup sugar
4 whole cloves

1. Add all ingredients to a 4-quart slow cooker. Cover and cook on low heat for 2 hours.
2. Pour tea through a strainer and serve chilled.

SC SOUTHERN-STYLE SWEET TEA

Mix 4 ounces of sweet tea with 4 ounces of lemonade to create the famous Arnold Palmer drink.

Serves 8

8 bags black tea

2 quarts water

¾ cup sugar

Add all ingredients to a 4-quart slow cooker. Cover and cook on low heat for 2 hours.

Sweet Tea History

Most sweet tea consumed in America before World War II was made with green tea. During the war, green tea sources were cut off, causing the United States to switch to black.

SC MANGO-MINT ICED TEA

The sweetness of the mango combined with the refreshing bite of mint makes this a must-have summer drink.

Serves 8

1 (15-ounce) can mangos, chopped

8 bags black tea

2 quarts water

¾ cup sugar

¼ cup mint leaves, whole

1. Add all ingredients to a 4-quart slow cooker. Cover and cook on low heat for 2 hours.
2. Pour tea through a strainer and serve chilled.

SC SANGRIA

Sangria is a very common wine punch that originated in Spain.

Serves 8

1 (750-milliliter) bottle red wine
1 orange, halved
1 lime, halved
1 cup cherries
1 cup diced pineapples
½ cup brandy
1 quart ginger ale

1. Add all ingredients except for the ginger ale to a 4-quart slow cooker. Cover and cook on low heat for 2 hours.
2. Allow sangria to cool in the refrigerator for at least 1 hour. Add the ginger ale just before serving.

SC HONEY-MINT GREEN TEA

Make this tea vegan by simply using sugar or agave nectar instead of honey.

Serves 8

8 bags green tea
2 quarts water
½ cup sugar
¼ cup honey
¼ cup mint leaves, whole

1. Add all ingredients to a 4-quart slow cooker. Cover and cook on low heat for 2 hours.
2. Pour tea through a strainer and serve warm or chilled.

SC BLACKBERRY-MINT WHITE TEA

The blackberries in this recipe can easily be exchanged for raspberries or blueberries.

Serves 8

8 bags white or green tea

2 quarts water

2 cups blackberries

¼ cup mint leaves, whole

¾ cup sugar

1. Add all ingredients to a 4-quart slow cooker. Cover and cook on low heat for 2 hours.
2. Pour tea through a strainer and serve warm or chilled.

SC CHERRY AND LIME PUNCH

Create a cherry and lime slushy by adding this punch and 3 cups ice to a blender.

Serves 8

2 cups frozen cherries

5 limes, halved

2 quarts water

½ cup sugar

1. Add all ingredients to a 4-quart slow cooker. Cover and cook on low heat for 2 hours.
2. Pour punch through a strainer and serve chilled.

SC RASPBERRY LEMONADE

Raspberries are usually in season June through August, making this a great summer drink.

Serves 8

1 cup raspberries

10 lemons, juiced

½ cup sugar

2 quarts water

1. Add all ingredients to a 4-quart slow cooker. Cover and cook on low heat for 2 hours.

2. Pour lemonade through a strainer and serve chilled.

SC CHERRY LEMONADE

Cherries are very high in disease-fighting antioxidants.

Serves 8

2 cups frozen cherries

10 lemons, juiced

½ cup sugar

2 quarts water

1. Add all ingredients to a 4-quart slow cooker. Cover and cook on low heat for 2 hours.

2. Pour lemonade through a strainer and serve chilled.

SC ORANGE AND LIME PUNCH

Use fresh-squeezed orange juice for an even tastier punch.

Serves 6

2 cups orange juice
5 limes, halved
½ cup sugar
2 quarts water

1. Add all ingredients to a 4-quart slow cooker. Cover and cook on low heat for 2 hours.
2. Pour punch through a strainer and serve chilled.

SC PASSION FRUIT GREEN TEA

The passion fruit is native to Brazil and Argentina.

Serves 8

8 bags green tea
2 quarts water
½ cup sugar
½ passion fruit juice or nectar

1. Add all ingredients to a 4-quart slow cooker. Cover and cook on low heat for 2 hours.
2. Pour tea through a strainer and serve chilled.

APPENDIX:

STANDARD U.S./METRIC MEASUREMENT CONVERSIONS

VOLUME CONVERSIONS

U.S. Volume Measure	Metric Equivalent
⅛ teaspoon	0.5 milliliter
¼ teaspoon	1 milliliter
½ teaspoon	2 milliliters
1 teaspoon	5 milliliters
½ tablespoon	7 milliliters
1 tablespoon (3 teaspoons)	15 milliliters
2 tablespoons (1 fluid ounce)	30 milliliters
¼ cup (4 tablespoons)	60 milliliters
⅓ cup	90 milliliters
½ cup (4 fluid ounces)	125 milliliters
⅔ cup	160 milliliters
¾ cup (6 fluid ounces)	180 milliliters
1 cup (16 tablespoons)	250 milliliters
1 pint (2 cups)	500 milliliters
1 quart (4 cups)	1 liter (about)

WEIGHT CONVERSIONS

U.S. Weight Measure	Metric Equivalent
½ ounce	15 grams
1 ounce	30 grams
2 ounces	60 grams
3 ounces	85 grams
¼ pound (4 ounces)	115 grams
½ pound (8 ounces)	225 grams
¾ pound (12 ounces)	340 grams
1 pound (16 ounces)	454 grams

OVEN TEMPERATURE CONVERSIONS

Degrees Fahrenheit	Degrees Celsius
200 degrees F	95 degrees C
250 degrees F	120 degrees C
275 degrees F	135 degrees C
300 degrees F	150 degrees C
325 degrees F	160 degrees C
350 degrees F	180 degrees C
375 degrees F	190 degrees C
400 degrees F	205 degrees C
425 degrees F	220 degrees C
450 degrees F	230 degrees C

BAKING PAN SIZES

U.S.	Metric
8 × 1½ inch round baking pan	20 × 4 cm cake tin
9 × 1½ inch round baking pan	23 × 3.5 cm cake tin
11 × 7 × 1½ inch baking pan	28 × 18 × 4 cm baking tin
13 × 9 × 2 inch baking pan	30 × 20 × 5 cm baking tin
2 quart rectangular baking dish	30 × 20 × 3 cm baking tin
15 × 10 × 2 inch baking pan	30 × 25 × 2 cm baking tin (Swiss roll tin)
9 inch pie plate	22 × 4 or 23 × 4 cm pie plate
7 or 8 inch springform pan	18 or 20 cm springform or loose bottom cake tin
9 × 5 × 3 inch loaf pan	23 × 13 × 7 cm or 2 lb narrow loaf or pâté tin
1½ quart casserole	1.5 liter casserole
2 quart casserole	2 liter casserole

INDEX

Note: Page numbers in **bold** indicate recipes that can be fixed in **slow cookers**. Page numbers in *italics* indicate recipes that can be fixed in *pressure cookers*.

Alcohol. *See* Beverages; Wine
Almonds. *See* Nuts and seeds
Appetizers. *See* Hors d'oeuvres and snacks
Apples
   about: baking with, 633
   Apple Butter, 67
   Apple Streusel Oatmeal, 53
   Apple-Walnut Upside-Down Pie, 639
   "Baked" Apples, **633**
   Caramel Apples and Pears, **664**
   Cinnamon-Apple Cobbler with Rome Beauty Apples, 635
   Cranberry-Apple Chutney, 94
   Cranberry Applesauce, *636*
   Easy Applesauce, **634**
   Fruit Compote, *659*
   Golden Delicious Apple-Strawberry Crisp, 638
   Mincemeat, *103*
   Old-Fashioned Baked Apples, 632
   Pink McIntosh Applesauce with Cranberry Chutney, 637
   Special Occasion Chunky Applesauce, *634*
   Spiked Apple Cider, **683**
   Tarte Tatin, 629
   Wild Rice with Apples and Almonds, 374
Apricots
   Dried Apricot Preserves, 99
   Dried Fruit Compote, *658*
Artichokes
   Artichoke and Cheese Squares, 203
   Artichoke Dip, 153
   Artichokes in Court Bouillon with Lemon Butter, 454
   Celery Root, Artichoke, and Potato Gratin, 309
   Mediterranean Vegetable Stew, **258**
   Quinoa Artichoke Hearts Salad, *146*
   "Steamed" Artichokes, **308**
   Vegan Spinach and Artichoke Dip, **156**
Asparagus
   Asparagus-Shallot Sauté, 518
   Creamed Morels and Asparagus Tips in Vol-au-Vents, 562
   Cream of Asparagus Soup, 215
   Gemelli with Asparagus Tips, Lemon, and Butter, 587
   Linguine with Gorgonzola, Asparagus, and Cream, 608
   Pressure Cooker Asparagus with Vegan Hollandaise Sauce, *512*
   Spaghetti with Asparagus, Parmesan, and Cream, 595
   Spring Mushroom Risotto with Morels and Asparagus, 572
   Steamed Asparagus with Hollandaise Sauce, 511
Avocados
   Avocado-Beet Wraps with Succotash, 367
   Avocado Kappa Maki Sushi Rolls, 364
   Avocado Sashimi with Miso Dressing, 501
   California Garden Salad with Avocado and Sprouts, 135
   Guacamole, 176

Baba Ghanoush, 161, **162**
Bamboo shoots
   Chinese Three Slivers, 569
   Steamed Spring Rolls, *186*
Bananas and plantains
   Banana Bread, **627**
   Banana Nut Bread, 628
   Banana Nut Bread Oatmeal, *51*
   Banana Pudding Cake, *650*
   Bananas Foster, **664**
   Red Beans with Plantains, *438*
Barbecue sauces, **79**, *80*
Barbecue seasoning, 80
Barley
   Barley and Corn Salad, 132
   Barley Risotto, *378*
   Mushroom, Barley, and Collard Greens Soup, 234
   Mushroom Barley, 582
   Mushroom-Barley "Risotto," 574
   Mushroom Barley Soup, **246**
   Portobello Barley, **404**
   Stuffed Cabbage, 473
   White Bean and Barley Soup, **212**
Basil
   Basil Pesto, 62
   The Best Pesto, 597
   Garlic and Basil Butter, 65
   Minestrone with Basil Pesto, 229
   Stuffed Cabbage, 473
   Sun-Dried Tomato Pesto Dip, *172*
   Tomato Basil Soup, **216**
Beans and legumes. *See also* Chickpeas; Green beans; Lentils
   about: prepping black-eyed peas, 416; using/prepping dried beans, 268, 409; white beans, 435
   Acorn Squash Chili, **288**
   Adzuki Beans, **422**
   Angel Hair with Broccoli Raab, Toasted Garlic, Fava Beans, and Pecorino Cheese, 601
   Avocado-Beet Wraps with Succotash, 367
   Beer-Lime Black Beans, *418*
   Black Bean, Corn, and Fresh Tomato Chili, **283**
   Black Bean and "Sausage" Chili, **287**
   Black Bean Burritos, 377
   Black Bean–Cilantro Fritters, *419*
   Black Bean Dip, *196*
   Black Beans, **425**
   Black Bean Salsa, **436**
   Black Bean Soup, **214**
   Black-Eyed Peas, **427**
   Boston-Style Baked Beans, *420*
   Bourbon Baked Beans, **421**
   Brunswick Stew, **254**
   Caribbean Relish, *105*
   Cheesy Peasy Potatoes, **333**
   Chipotle Black Bean Salad, **409**
   Chipotle-Thyme Black Beans, *417*
   Cuban Black Beans, **413**
   Cuban Black Beans and Rice (Moros y Cristianos), 376
   Cuban Black Bean Soup with Coriander Tofu Sour Cream, 232
   Dhal, *187*
   Dinner Loaf, *451*
   Fajita Chili, **282**
   Fried Rice with Green Peas and Egg, 370
   Frijole Dip, **168**
   Garden Vegetable Chili, **286**
   Hoppin' John, **416**, *445*
   Huevos Rancheros, 47
   Jamaican Red Bean Stew, **255**
   Lima Beans, *423*
   Lima Beans and Dumplings, **424**
   Mexican Beer Black Beans, **429**
   Mexican Frijoles Refritos (Refried Beans), 389
   Minestrone Soup, **228**
   Minestrone with Basil Pesto, 229
   Minted Sweet Peas, 362
   New Orleans Red Beans and Rice, **359**
   Open-Faced Bean Burrito, **411**
   Pasta Fagiole, *615*
   Pinto Beans, **422**
   Pinto Bean Soup with Salsa Fresca, 235
   Pressure Cooker Cuban Black Beans and Rice, *414*
   Pressure Cooker Hoppin' John, *445*
   Pressure Cooker Paella, *401*
   Puerto Rican Gandules (Pigeon Peas), 361
   Quick Three Bean Salad, 124
   Red Bean and Pasta Soup, 211
   Red Bean Chili, **284**
   Red Bean Fritters, *439*
   Red Beans and Rice, **360**
   Red Beans and Rice Pie with Oregano and Tomatoes, 358
   Red Beans and Yellow Rice, 357

Red Beans with Plantains, *438*
Shredded "Chicken" Chili, **278**
Simple Split Pea Soup, **248**
Slow Cooker Refried Beans, **412**
Slow Cooker Tofu Ranchero, **46**
Smoky Black-Eyed Pea Soup with Sweet Potatoes and Mustard Greens, 220
Southwestern Casserole, **332**
Southwest Vegetable Chili, **275**
Spicy Black-Eyed Peas and Kale, **437**
Spicy Breakfast Burrito, **45**
Spicy White Bean–Citrus Dip, 195
Stir-Fried Snow Peas with Cilantro, 506
Succotash, *533*
Succotash Salad, 121
Summer Chili, **289**
Summer Vegetable Bean Salad, **435**
Sweet Potato Chili, **280**
Texas Caviar, *174*
Texas Stew, **272**
Three Bean Chili, **281**
Three Bean Salad, *113*
Tuscan White Bean Ragout, 371
Tuscan White Bean Soup, 231
Vegan Chili, **274**
White Bean Alfredo Sauce, *75*
White Bean and Barley Soup, **212**
White Bean and Tomato Stew, **259**
White Bean Cassoulet, **268**
White Bean–Leek Purée, *442*
White Beans, **426**
White Beans and Rice, *441*
White Beans with Garlic and Fresh Tomato, *440*
White Beans with Rosemary and Fresh Tomato, **430**
Yellow Split Pea Soup with Cactus and Hominy, 226
Beer-Cheese Soup, **243**
Beer-Lime Black Beans, *418*
Beets
    about: nutritional value, 247; peak season, 304
    Avocado-Beet Wraps with Succotash, 367
    Beet Risotto Cakes, 384
    Braised Beet Greens, *317*
    Buttered Beets, *304*
    Citrusy Beets, **300**
    Honey-Orange Beets, 303
    Marinated Beet Salad, 136
    Roasted Beets, 299
    Summer Borscht, **247**
Berries
    Blackberry Jam, *106*
    Blackberry-Mint White Tea, **688**
    Blueberry Jam, *102*
    Chocolate-Berry Bread Pudding, *667*
    Cranberry-Apple Chutney, *94*

Cranberry Applesauce, *636*
Cranberry Chutney, 637
Cranberry-Pecan Pilaf, *396*
Cranberry Sauce, 69
Cranberry-Walnut Brussels Sprouts, **466**
Creamy Coconut Rice Pudding, *669*
Fruit Compote, *659*
Golden Delicious Apple-Strawberry Crisp, 638
Hot Cranberry-Pineapple Punch, **678**
Mixed Berry Punch, **685**
Pink McIntosh Applesauce with Cranberry Chutney, 637
Poached Mixed Berries, *657*
Raspberry Coulis, **83**
Raspberry Lemonade, **689**
Strawberry Jam, *98*
Strawberry Sauce, 654
Summer Fruit Dip, **171**
White Tea–Berry Fusion, **679**
Beverages
    about: white tea, 679
    Blackberry-Mint White Tea, **688**
    Café Mocha, **681**
    Chai Tea (hot or iced), **680**
    Cherry and Lime Punch, **688**
    Cherry Lemonade, **689**
    Ginger-Pear Punch, **679**
    Honey-Mint Green Tea, **687**
    Hot Buttered Rum, **682**
    Hot Cranberry-Pineapple Punch, **678**
    Hot Toddy, **683**
    Irish Coffee, **684**
    Mango-Mint Iced Tea, **686**
    Minty Hot Chocolate, **682**
    Mixed Berry Punch, **685**
    Orange and Lime Punch, **690**
    Passion Fruit Green Tea, **690**
    Pumpkin Spice, **681**
    Raspberry Lemonade, **689**
    Sangria, **687**
    Southern-Style Sweet Tea, **686**
    Spiced Wine, **684**
    Spiked Apple Cider, **683**
    Vanilla-Lavender Tea, **680**
    White Tea–Berry Fusion, **679**
Black beans. *See* Beans and legumes
Blackberries. *See* Berries
Black-eyed peas. *See* Beans and legumes
Blanching, 620
Blintzes, cottage cheese, 661
Blondies, 654
Blueberries. *See* Berries
Bok choy
    Baby Bok Choy, **488**
    Chinese Black Mushrooms with Jade Bok Choy, 570
    Korean-Style Hot Pot, **269**

    Shanghai Bok Choy with Garlic and Black Bean Sauce, 460
    Soy-Glazed Bok Choy, **487**
Brandy Sauce, *671*
Breads
    Banana Bread, **627**
    Banana Nut Bread, 628
    Fried Green Tomato Bruschetta, 175
    Garlic Bread, 554
    Indian Chapati Pan Bread, 366
    Mushroom Bruschetta, 573
    Pumpkin Bread, 626
    Scones, 31
    Simple Cloverleaf Dinner Rolls, 630
    Spicy Southwestern Cornbread, 640
    Steamed Dessert Bread, *676*
    Tomato and Black Olive Bruschetta, 194
    Tomato and Bread Salad (Panzanella), 114
Breakfast and brunch, 23–59
    Almond and Dried Cherry Granola, **37**
    Apple Streusel Oatmeal, *53*
    Banana Nut Bread Oatmeal, *51*
    Boursin Omelet, 27
    Breakfast Casserole, **44**
    Breakfast Quinoa with Fruit, **38**
    Breakfast Tofu and Veggies, **43**
    Challah French Toast, 29
    Cheese Grits, **36**
    Corny Polenta Breakfast Pancakes, 30
    Country Grits, **36**
    Easy Tofu "Eggs," **43**
    French Toast Casserole, **38**
    Garden Tofu Scramble, *34*
    Grandma's Cornmeal Mush, **44**
    Granola, 24
    Hash Browns, **39**
    Home Fries, 24
    Huevos Rancheros, 47
    Irish Oatmeal with Fruit, *54*
    Maple-Pecan Oatmeal, *55*
    Miso Eggs Benedict, 26
    Onion, Pepper, and Potato Hash Browns, **39**
    Pear Oatmeal, *51*
    Poblano Hash Browns, *42*
    Pressure Cooker Hash Browns, *40*
    Pressure Cooker Tofu Ranchero, *58*
    Red Pepper Grits, *37*
    Roasted Vegetable Frittata, 48
    Rosemary Home Fries, **50**
    Scones, 31
    Scrambled Egg Burritos, 25
    Scrambled Eggs Masala, 28
    Slow Cooker Spicy Tofu Scramble, *35*, **41**
    Slow Cooker Tofu Ranchero, **46**
    Spicy Breakfast Burrito, **45**
    Spinach and Portobello Benedict, *59*

Spinach Quiche, 49
Steel-Cut Oats, *52*
Stuffed Eggs, 25
Sunrise Tofu Scramble, **33**
Tempeh Sausage Crumbles, **42**
Three Pepper Vegan Frittata/Scramble, *56*
Tofu Frittata/Scramble, *32*
White Gravy, **50**
Yeasty Tofu and Veggies, *57*
Broccoli
    Broccoli Dip, **167**
    Broccoli Florets with Lemon Butter Sauce, 469
    Broccoli in Lemon Butter Sauce, *471*
    Broccoli–Pine Nut Pasta Salad, *620*
    Bulgur with Broccoli and Carrot, **405**
    Crudités with Three Dips, 158
    Gai Lan (Chinese Broccoli) with Toasted Garlic, 475
    Garden Tofu Scramble, *34*
    Pasta Primavera with Vegetables, *611*
    Potato-Broccoli Casserole, **349**
    Raw Veggie Pasta Toss, 604
    Sunrise Tofu Scramble, **33**
    Vegetable Fried Rice, **399**
    Vegetable-Stuffed Portobello Mushrooms, 576
    Yeasty Tofu and Veggies, *57*
Broccoli raab
    Angel Hair with Broccoli Raab, Toasted Garlic, Fava Beans, and Pecorino Cheese, 601
    Garlicky Broccoli Raab, 484
    Sautéed Broccoli Raab, *470*
Brussels sprouts
    Basic Buttered Brussels Sprouts, 464
    Cranberry-Walnut Brussels Sprouts, **466**
    Pan-Seared Brussels Sprouts, 465
Bulgur
    Bulgur Stuffing, *392*
    Bulgur with Broccoli and Carrot, **405**
    Tabbouleh, 129
Burritos, 25, **45**, *377*, **411**
Butters. *See* Sauces and spreads

Cabbage
    Braised Red Cabbage (Chou Rouge à la Flamande), 467
    Cabbage Stewed in Tomato Sauce, 462
    Homemade Sauerkraut, **489**
    Kimchi-Style Cabbage, *474*
    Seitan and Cabbage Stew, **264**
    Southeast Asian Slaw, 110
    Steamed Spring Rolls, *186*
    Stir-Fried Asian Greens, 459
    Stuffed Cabbage, 473
    Summer Vegetable Slaw, 122
    Szechuan Stir-Fried Cabbage with Hot Peppers, 483
Cactus, 226
Cajun cuisine, 534
Cakes. *See* Chocolate; Desserts
Caponata, eggplant, *509*
Carrots
    Bulgur with Broccoli and Carrot, **405**
    Carrot and Mushroom Terrine, 313
    Carrot Cake, **644**
    Carrot Cake Glaze, 644
    Carrot Purée with Nutmeg, 219
    Carrots and Ginger, *314*
    Carrot Timbales, 302
    Creamed Carrots, 315
    Crudités with Three Dips, 158
    Meatless Moussaka, **514**
    Moroccan Root Vegetables, **324**
    Old-Fashioned Glazed Carrots, 351
    Parsnip and Carrot Bake, 312
    Swiss Chard Rolls with Root Vegetables, 476
    Turnip and Carrot Purée, *318*
    Vegetable Fried Rice, **399**
    Vegetable Gado-Gado, 190
    Winter Vegetable Medley, *526*
Cauliflower
    Aloo Gobi (Cauliflower and Potato Curry), 456, *457*
    Cauliflower Chowder, **267**
    Cauliflower Soup, **240**
    Crudités with Three Dips, 158
    Curried Cauliflower, **458**
    Pressure Cooker Aloo Gobi, *457*
    Smooth Cauliflower Soup with Coriander, 224
    Vegetable Rice Pilaf, *395*
Celery root
    about, 253
    Celery Root, Artichoke, and Potato Gratin, 309
    Celery Root Mash, 310
    Celery Root Soup, *253*
    Salad of Celery Root and Pears, 115
Chai Tea (hot or iced), **680**
Cheese
    about: Fontina, 379; Italian, 379; mozzarella (and buffalo mozzarella), 125, 379; Tofu ricotta, 403
    Artichoke and Cheese Squares, 203
    Beer-Cheese Soup, **243**
    Breakfast Casserole, **44**
    Brie Timbales with Roasted Red Pepper Sauce, 537
    Cheese Fondue, 154
    Cheese Grits, **36**
    Cheese Soufflé, 202
    Cheesy Peasy Potatoes, **333**
    Cheesy Poblano Peppers, **535**
    Chili-Cheese Dip, **166**
    Cottage Cheese Blintzes, 661
    Eggplant "Lasagna," **403**
    Eggplant Parmigiano, 507
    eggs with. *See* Eggs
    Fricos (Cheese Crisps), 205
    Garlic-Parmesan Mashed Potatoes, **348**
    Insalata Caprese (Tomato-Mozzarella Salad), 125
    Jalapeño Cheese Dip, *165*
    Lemon Cheesecake, *668*
    Mini Goat Cheese Pizzas, 181
    Open-Faced Bean Burrito, **411**
    pasta with.. *See* Pasta
    Peanut Butter and Fudge Cheesecake, *672*
    Polenta with Butter and Cheese, 385
    Potatoes Au Gratin, **336**
    Ricotta and Goat Cheese Crespelle, 149
    Roquefort Vinaigrette, 116
    Savory Sun-Dried Tomato Cheesecake, *643*
    Spinach and Feta Pie, 479
    Sweet White Salad with Shaved Asiago, 131
    Tomato and Cheese Tart, 492
    Zucchini "Lasagna," 504
Cherries
    Almond and Dried Cherry Granola, **37**
    Cherry and Lime Punch, **688**
    Cherry Lemonade, **689**
    Creamy Coconut Rice Pudding, *669*
    Fruit Compote, *659*
Chicken, vegetarian
    Creole Jambalaya, *388*
    Fajita Chili, **282**
    Mock Chicken and Rice, **406**
    Posole, **265**
    Shredded "Chicken" Chili, **278**
    Spicy Buffalo Strips, **182**
    Teriyaki "Chicken" Strips, **183**
Chickpeas
    Chana Masala, **433**, *449*
    Chickpea-Parsley-Dill Dip, *164*
    Chickpeas in Potato-Onion Curry, 365
    Chickpea "Tuna" Salad Sandwich, *444*
    Creamy Chickpea Soup, **245**
    Hummus, 177
    Hummus bi Tahini with Sprouts and Cherry Tomatoes in a Pita Pocket, 390
    Mediterranean Chickpeas, **410**
    Pressure Cooker Chana Masala, **449**
    Pressure Cooker Wasabi-Barbecue Chickpeas, *443*
    Raj's Chickpeas in Tomato Sauce, 372
    Warm Chickpea Salad, *111*
    Wasabi-Barbecue Chickpeas, **431**
    Zesty Lemon Hummus, **178**

Chilaquiles (Tortilla Stew), 500
Chili
    about: canned vegetarian chili, 166
    Acorn Squash Chili, **288**
    Black Bean, Corn, and Fresh Tomato Chili, **283**
    Black Bean and "Sausage" Chili, **287**
    Chili-Cheese Dip, **166**
    Chili con "Carne," **277**
    Cincinnati Chili, **276**
    Fajita Chili, **282**
    Five Pepper Chili, **279**
    Garden Vegetable Chili, **286**
    Lentil Chili, **285**
    Red Bean Chili, **284**
    Shredded "Chicken" Chili, **278**
    Southwest Vegetable Chili, **275**
    Summer Chili, **289**
    Sweet Potato Chili, **280**
    Three Bean Chili, **281**
    Vegan Chili, **274**
Chipotle powder, 249
Chive Dumplings, 557
Chocolate
    about: vegan icing, 645
    Café Mocha, **681**
    Chocolate Almond Bars, **665**
    Chocolate-Almond Fondue, **663**
    Chocolate-Berry Bread Pudding, *667*
    Chocolate Cake, **645**
    Chocolate Chip Cookies, 660
    Chocolate-Cinnamon Fondue, **663**
    Chocolate Coconut Bars, **665**
    Chocolate-Covered Pretzels, **666**
    Chocolate Mousse, 631
    Flourless Chocolate Cake, 649
    Hot Fudge Fondue, **662**
    Minty Hot Chocolate, **682**
    Molten Fudge Pudding Cake, *670*
    Peanut Butter and Fudge Cheesecake, *672*
    Spiced Chocolate Cake, *646*
    Tiramisu, 641
    White Chocolate–Macadamia Nut Bars, **666**
Chorizo. *See* Sausage
Chutneys. *See* Sauces and spreads
Cinnamon
    Chocolate-Cinnamon Fondue, **663**
    Cinnamon and Sugar Peanuts, **199**
    Cinnamon-Apple Cobbler with Rome Beauty Apples, 635
    Cinnamon Poached Apples, **656**
Citrus
    about: freezing leftovers, 265; zest vs. juice, 240
    Cherry and Lime Punch, **688**
    Cherry Lemonade, **689**

Chili-Orange Butter for Grilled Bread, 66
Citrusy Beets, **300**
Glazed Lemon Poppy Seed Cake, *651*
Honey-Orange Beets, 303
Lemon Butter Sauce, 469, 471
Lemon Cheesecake, *668*
Lemon Dill Sauce, **76**
Mixed Citrus Marmalade, *100*
Orange and Lime Punch, **690**
Orange-Sesame Vinaigrette, 118
Raspberry Lemonade, **689**
Rosemary-Lemon Butter, 66
Spicy White Bean–Citrus Dip, 195
Coconut
    Chocolate Coconut Bars, **665**
    Coconut Curry Sauce, **83**
    Coconut Rice Pudding, **662**
    Creamy Coconut Rice Pudding, *669*
    Piña Colada Bread Pudding, *674*
Coffee and espresso
    Café Mocha, **681**
    Irish Coffee, **684**
    Peach Iced Tea, **685**
    Tiramisu, 641
Collard greens. *See* Greens
Cookies and bars. *See* Desserts
Corn. *See also* Polenta
Corn and cornmeal. *See also* Polenta
    about: peak season, 527
    Avocado-Beet Wraps with Succotash, 367
    Barley and Corn Salad, 132
    Black Bean, Corn, and Fresh Tomato Chili, **283**
    Brunswick Stew, **254**
    Cilantro-Lime Corn on the Cob, *528*
    Corn and Pepper Pudding, 530
    Corn and Potato Chowder, 233
    Corn Maque Choux, *534*
    Cornmeal Cake, *652*
    Corn on the Cob, *527*
    Creamed Corn, 529
    Garden Vegetable Soup, **242**
    Grandma's Cornmeal Mush, *44*
    Okra with Corn and Tomato, *532*
    Pressure Cooker Creamed Corn, *531*
    Southwest Corn Chowder, **256**
    Spaghetti with Sweet Corn, Tomatoes, and Goat Cheese, 602
    Spicy Southwestern Cornbread, 640
    Succotash, *533*
    Succotash Salad, 121
    Texas Caviar, *174*
    Texas Stew, **272**
    Vegetable Dumpling Stew, **262**
    Wheat and Corn Wraps with Tofu, 369
Couscous, *356*
    Couscous-Stuffed Red Peppers, *391*
    Olive and Pepper Couscous Salad, *147*

Cranberries. *See* Berries
Creole cuisine, 388
Crepes, 660
    Cottage Cheese Blintzes, 661
    Ricotta and Goat Cheese Crespelle, 149
Cruciferous vegetables. *See specific vegetables*
Cucumbers
    Asian Cucumber Salad, 120
    Avocado Kappa Maki Sushi Rolls, 364
Curry
    Chickpeas in Potato-Onion Curry, 365
    Chilled Curry Potato-Fennel Soup, 223
    Coconut Curry Sauce, **83**
    Curried Cauliflower, **458**
    Curried Lentils, **415**
    Curried New Potato Salad, 139
    Curried Parsnips, 307
    Curried Rice, **408**
    Curried Seitan Stew, **261**
    Curry Dip, 159
    Lentil-Spinach Curry, *446*
    Madras Curry Dressing, 119
    Red Lentil Curry, **448**

Date Pudding, *673*
Desserts, 624–77. *See also* Breads; Chocolate
    about: vegan icing, 645
    Apple-Walnut Upside-Down Pie, 639
    "Baked" Apples, **633**
    Banana Pudding Cake, *650*
    Bananas Foster, **664**
    Basic Pie Dough, 293
    Basic Yellow Cake, *652*
    Blondies, 654
    Butter-Cream Frosting, 653
    Caramel Apples and Pears, **664**
    Carrot Cake, **644**
    Carrot Cake Glaze, 644
    Cinnamon-Apple Cobbler with Rome Beauty Apples, 635
    Cinnamon Poached Apples, **656**
    Coconut Rice Pudding, **662**
    Cornmeal Cake, *652*
    Cottage Cheese Blintzes, 661
    Cranberry Applesauce, *636*
    Cranberry Chutney, 637
    Creamy Coconut Rice Pudding, *669*
    Crème Caramel, *642*
    Crepes, 660
    Date Pudding, *673*
    Dried Fruit Compote, *658*
    Easy Applesauce, **634**
    Fruit Compote, *659*
    Ginger Poached Pears, **656**
    Glazed Lemon Poppy Seed Cake, *651*
    Golden Delicious Apple-Strawberry Crisp, 638

Lemon Cheesecake, *668*
Noodle Pudding, *632*
Old-Fashioned Baked Apples, *632*
Peanut Butter and Fudge Cheesecake, *672*
Peanut Butter Cake, **661**
Pears Poached in White Wine with Strawberry Sauce, *654*
Piña Colada Bread Pudding, *674*
Pink McIntosh Applesauce with Cranberry Chutney, *637*
Plum Pudding with Brandy Sauce, *671*
Poached Mixed Berries, **657**
Port-Poached Figs, *657*
Red Velvet Cake, **647**
Savory Sun-Dried Tomato Cheesecake, *643*
Sour Cream Butter Cake, *648*
Special Occasion Chunky Applesauce, *634*
Spiced Chocolate Cake, *646*
Spiced Peaches, *655*
Steamed Dessert Bread, *676*
Tapioca Pudding, *675*
Tarte Tatin, *629*
Tiramisu, *641*
Vegan Flan, *677*
Dhal, *187*
Dill
   Chickpea-Parsley-Dill Dip, *164*
   Dill Potato Salad, *139*
   Dill Red Potatoes, **339**
   Lemon Dill Sauce, **76**
Dips. *See* Hors d'oeuvres and snacks
Dolmades, *163*
Dough, for pies, *293*
Drinks. *See* Beverages
Dumplings, lima beans and, **424**
Dumpling stew, vegetable, **262**

Edamame
   Easy Edamame, **434**
   Edamame-Seaweed Salad, *112*
   Sea Salt Edamame, *450*
Eggplant
   about: preparing, 258, 510
   Baba Ghanoush, 161
   Eggplant and Tomato Sauté, 513
   Eggplant Caponata, *509*
   Eggplant Caviar, *173*
   Eggplant "Lasagna," **403**
   Eggplant Parmigiano, 507
   Eggplant Rolatine, 505
   Fusilli (Spirals) with Grilled Eggplant, Garlic, and Spicy Tomato Sauce, 591
   Grilled Vegetable Antipasto, 126
   Mashed Eggplant and Tomato Salad, *510*
   Meatless Moussaka, **514**

Mediterranean Vegetable Stew, **258**
Pressure Cooker Ratatouille, *508*
Ratatouille, 502, *508*
Roasted Vegetables, 519
Slow Cooker Baba Ghanoush, **162**
Spiced "Baked" Eggplant, **515**
Stuffed Eggplant, **516**
Eggs
   about: replacers for, 419
   Basic Egg Salad, 137
   Boursin Omelet, 27
   Breakfast Casserole, **44**
   Challah French Toast, 29
   Chinese Soy Sauce Eggs, 155
   French Toast Casserole, **38**
   Fried Rice with Green Peas and Egg, 370
   Huevos Rancheros, 47
   Miso Eggs Benedict, 26
   Roasted Vegetable Frittata, 48
   Scrambled Egg Burritos, 25
   Scrambled Eggs Masala, 28
   Spinach Quiche, 49
   Stuffed Eggs, 25
   Taiwanese Mushroom Egg, 571
   Two Cheese Strata, 204
Empanadas, 579
Escarole
   Scented Escarole with Fennel, 468
   Tuscan White Bean Ragout, 371
Étouffée, **263**

Farfalle. *See* Pasta
Fennel
   about, 523
   Chilled Curry Potato-Fennel Soup, 223
   Fennel Cooked in White Wine, *523*
   Scented Escarole with Fennel, 468
   Sweet Fennel with Lemon and Shaved Parmigiano, 192
Figs, port-poached, *657*
Filé powder, 257
Fish and seafood, vegetarian
   Avocado Sashimi with Miso Dressing, 501
   Chickpea "Tuna" Salad Sandwich, 444
   Étouffée, **263**
Flan, vegan, *677*
Fondue, 154, **662–63**
French Fries, 301
French toast, 29
French Toast Casserole, **38**
Fritters, black bean–cilantro, *419*
Fritters, red bean, *439*
Frostings. *See* Desserts
Fruit. *See also specific fruit*
   Dried Fruit Compote, *658*
   Fruit Compote, *659*
   Summer Fruit Dip, **171**

Gai Lan (Chinese Broccoli) with Toasted Garlic, 475
Garlic
   about: roasting, 69
   Aioli (Garlic Mayonnaise), 64
   Garlic and Basil Butter, 65
   Garlic Bread, 554
   Garlicky Broccoli Raab, 484
   Garlic-Parmesan Mashed Potatoes, **348**
   Garlic Parsley Mashed Potatoes, *325*
   Garlic-Parsley Potatoes, **350**
   Red Garlic Mayonnaise (Rouille), 62
   Risotto with Portobello Mushrooms, Onions, and Garlic, 561
   Roasted Garlic Mashed Potatoes, 323
   Roasted Garlic Spread, *185*
   Rosemary-Garlic Mashed Potatoes, **331**
   Slow-Roasted Garlic and Tomato Sauce, 69
   Tomato, Garlic, and Parsley Quinoa Salad, *144*
   White Wine–Garlic Sauce, **84**
Gazpacho, 225
Ginger
   about: fresh vs. ground, 314
   Carrots and Ginger, *314*
   Ginger-Pear Punch, **679**
   Ginger Poached Pears, **656**
Grains. *See specific grains*
Grape jelly, *107*
Grape leaves, stuffed, *163*
Gravy. *See* Sauces and spreads
Green beans
   Chinese Wrinkled String Beans, 520
   Crudités with Three Dips, 158
   Fresh Green Beans with Toasted Sesame, 522
   Garden Vegetable Soup, 242
   Green Beans and Pine Nut Sauté, 521
   Orecchiette with Roasted Peppers, Green Beans, and Pesto, 596
   Rosemary-Thyme Green Beans, **522**
   Summer Vegetable Slaw, 122
   Vegetable Gado-Gado, 190
   Vegetable Rice Pilaf, *395*
   Winter Greens Salad with Green Beans and Roquefort Vinaigrette, 116
Greens. *See also* Kale; Spinach; Swiss chard
   Braised Beet Greens, *317*
   Collard Greens with Tomatoes and Cheddar, 485
   Hoppin' John, **416**
   Mushroom, Barley, and Collard Greens Soup, 234
   Savory Turnip Greens, *319*
   Smoky Black-Eyed Pea Soup with Sweet Potatoes and Mustard Greens, 220
   Smoky Spicy Collard Greens with Turnip,

466
Southern-Style Collards, *486*
Stir-Fried Asian Greens, 459
Super Greens Stew, **271**
Grills, stovetop, 127
Grits, **36–37**, 564
Guacamole, 176

Herbed Potatoes, **342**
Herbed Red and Yellow Tomatoes on Honey-Nut Bread, 496
Herb-Mixed Turnips, 306
Herbs, saving on, 517
Herb-Stuffed Tomatoes, **495**
Hominy, 226, **265**
Honey-Mint Green Tea, **687**
Hors d'oeuvres and snacks, 150–205
Artichoke and Cheese Squares, 203
Artichoke Dip, 153
Baba Ghanoush, 161
Barbecue "Meatballs," **189**
Black Bean Dip, *196*
Black Bean Salsa, **436**
Boiled Peanuts, *200*
Broccoli Dip, **167**
Cajun Peanuts, **198**
Caramelized Onion Dip, **169**
Cheese Fondue, 154
Cheese Soufflé, 202
Chickpea-Parsley-Dill Dip, *164*
Chili-Cheese Dip, **166**
Chinese Soy Sauce Eggs, 155
Cinnamon and Sugar Peanuts, **199**
Crudités with Three Dips, 158
Curry Dip, 159
Dhal, *187*
Eggplant Caviar, 173
Fricos (Cheese Crisps), 205
Fried Green Tomato Bruschetta, 175
Frijole Dip, **168**
Guacamole, 176
Hummus, 177
Jalapeño Cheese Dip, *165*
Josh's Mushroom Dip, 565
Manchego-Potato Tacos with Pickled Jalapeños, 179
Mini Goat Cheese Pizzas, 181
Mini Lentil-Scallion Pancakes with Cumin Cream, 180
Mixed Veggie Dip, **170**
Potato Pakoras (Fritters), 157
Rancheros Salsa, 152
Roasted Garlic Spread, *185*
Salsa Fresca (Pico de Gallo), *198*
Simple Salsa, 506
Slow Cooker Baba Ghanoush, **162**
Spiced Pecans, 201
Spicy Buffalo Strips, **182**
Spicy White Bean–Citrus Dip, 195
Steamed Spring Rolls, *186*
Stuffed Grape Leaves, *163*
Stuffed Mushrooms, 191
Summer Fruit Dip, **171**
Sun-Dried Tomato Pesto Dip, **172**
Sweet and Sour "Meatballs," *188*
Sweet Fennel with Lemon and Shaved Parmigiano, 192
Sweet Potato and Rosemary Pizza, 193
Teriyaki "Chicken" Strips, **183**
Texas Caviar, *174*
Tomatillo Salsa, *184*
Tomato and Black Olive Bruschetta, 194
Two Cheese Strata, 204
Vegan Spinach and Artichoke Dip, **156**
Vegetable Gado-Gado, 190
Watercress Dip, 160
Wild Mushroom Ragout in Puff Pastry Shells, 197
Zesty Lemon Hummus, **178**
Hummus, 177, 178, 390

Ingredients, overview of, 21–22. *See also specific main ingredients*

Jambalaya, *388*
Jams and preserves. *See* Sauces and spreads

Kale
Kale with Garlic and Thyme, 481
Kale with Red Pepper Flakes and Cumin, *482*
Spicy Black-Eyed Peas and Kale, **437**
Super Greens Stew, **271**
Kasha
Kasha Varnishkes, 368
Portobello Pita with Buckwheat and Beans, 566
Kimchi-Style Cabbage, *474*
Kombu, 237, *444*

Lavender, in Vanilla-Lavender Tea, **680**
Leeks
Braised Leeks, 542
Grilled Leeks with Tarragon and Lemon, 543
Leek Potato Cakes, 553
Leek Tart, 545
Mushroom-Leek Tart, 581
Peppery Brown Rice Risotto, *379*
Potato-Leek Soup, **242**
Potato Risotto, **334**
Vichyssoise (Potato and Leek Soup), 227
White Bean–Leek Purée, *442*
Lemon. *See* Citrus
Lentils, **428**
Curried Lentils, **415**
Egyptian Lentils and Rice, 375
Lentil Chili, **285**
Lentil Pâté, *447*
Lentil Salad, 134
Lentil Soup with Cumin, 230
Lentil-Spinach Curry, *446*
Lentils with Sautéed Spinach, White Wine, and Garlic, **432**
Meatless Moussaka, **514**
Mini Lentil-Scallion Pancakes with Cumin Cream, 180
Red Lentil Curry, *448*
Red Lentil Soup, **213**

Mango-Mint Iced Tea, **686**
Maple-Glazed Sweet Potatoes, **341**, *346*
Meat, vegetarian. *See also* Chicken, vegetarian; Sausage; Tempeh
about: mock meatloaf, *451*
Barbecue "Meatballs," **189**
Chili con "Carne," **277**
Cincinnati Chili, **276**
Dinner Loaf, *451*
Mock Meatball Stew, **273**
Sweet and Sour "Meatballs," *188*
Metric conversion charts, 691
Millet, in Three Grain Pilaf, *393*
Mincemeat and mincemeat seasoning, *103*
Mint
Blackberry-Mint White Tea, **688**
Honey-Mint Green Tea, **687**
Mango-Mint Iced Tea, **686**
Minted Sweet Peas, 362
Minty Hot Chocolate, **682**
Miso
Miso Dressing, 501
Miso Eggs Benedict, 26
Miso Soup, 237
Moussaka, meatless, **514**
Mushrooms
about: varieties of, 583; wild, 197
Carrot and Mushroom Terrine, 313
Chinese Black Mushrooms with Jade Bok Choy, 570
Chinese Three Slivers, 569
Creamed Morels and Asparagus Tips in Vol-au-Vents, 562
Creamed Mushrooms, 577
Duxelles, 560
Fettuccine with Morels and Spring Onions, 563
Fettuccine with Shiitake Mushrooms and Brown Butter, 600
Garden Tofu Scramble, *34*
Gnocchi and Mushrooms in Rosemary Alfredo Sauce, *613*
Grilled Marinated Portobello Mushrooms, 567

Josh's Mushroom Dip, 565
Korean-Style Hot Pot, **269**
Mushroom, Barley, and Collard Greens
    Soup, 234
Mushroom and Olive Blend, 583
Mushroom Barley, 582
Mushroom-Barley "Risotto," 574
Mushroom Barley Soup, **246**
Mushroom Bruschetta, 573
Mushroom Cream Sauce, *619*
Mushroom-Leek Tart, 581
Mushroom-Spelt Sauté, 568
Mushroom-Stuffed Tomatoes, 494
Mushroom-Tofu Stir-Fry, 578
Mushroom Turnovers (Empanadas), 579
Mushroom Vegetable Stock, 218
Oven-Roasted Mushrooms, 575
Pickled Mushrooms, 580
Polenta-Style Grits with Wild Mushroom
    Ragout, 564
Polenta with Wild Mushrooms, 599
Portobello Barley, **404**
Portobello Pita with Buckwheat and
    Beans, 566
Portobello Stroganoff, *622*
Risotto with Portobello Mushrooms,
    Onions, and Garlic, 561
Roasted Vegetables, 519
Seitan and Mushroom Stew, **260**
Spinach and Portobello Benedict, *59*
Spinach-Stuffed Vegetables, 478
Spring Mushroom Risotto with Morels
    and Asparagus, 572
Stuffed Mushrooms, 191
Stuffed Onions, 541
Sunrise Tofu Scramble, **33**
Taiwanese Mushroom Egg, 571
Vegetable-Stuffed Portobello Mushrooms,
    576
Warm Oyster Mushroom Salad, 580
White Lasagna with Spinach and
    Mushrooms, 590
Wild Mushroom Ragout in Puff Pastry
    Shells, 197
Wild Mushroom Risotto, **382**
Wild Mushroom Risotto with Truffles, 383
Wild Mushroom Soup with Thyme, 217
Wild Rice and Portobello Soup, **252**
Wild Rice Salad with Mushrooms and
    Almonds, 128
Zucchini "Lasagna," 504
Mustard. *See* Sauces and spreads

Nuts and seeds. *See also* Peanuts and peanut
butter
    about: cashew cream uses, 92; cooking
        with cashews, 74; toasting nuts, 104;
        toasting pine nuts, 172
    Almond and Dried Cherry Granola, **37**
    Apple-Walnut Upside-Down Pie, 639
    Banana Nut Bread, 628
    Banana Nut Bread Oatmeal, *51*
    Broccoli–Pine Nut Pasta Salad, *620*
    Cashew Cream Sauce, *92*
    Chocolate Almond Bars, **665**
    Chocolate-Almond Fondue, **663**
    Cranberry-Pecan Pilaf, *396*
    Cranberry-Walnut Brussels Sprouts, **466**
    Glazed Lemon Poppy Seed Cake, *651*
    Granola, 24
    Green Beans and Pine Nut Sauté, *521*
    Peach and Toasted Almond Preserves,
        104
    Spiced Pecans, 201
    Spinach with Pine Nuts (Pignoli) and
        Garlic, 462
    Vegan Alfredo, **74**
    White Chocolate–Macadamia Nut Bars,
        666
    Wild Rice Salad with Mushrooms and
        Almonds, 128
    Wild Rice with Apples and Almonds, 374

Oats
    Almond and Dried Cherry Granola, **37**
    Apple Streusel Oatmeal, *53*
    Banana Nut Bread Oatmeal, *51*
    Granola, 24
    Irish Oatmeal with Fruit, *54*
    Maple-Pecan Oatmeal, *55*
    Pear Oatmeal, **51**
    Steel-Cut Oats, *52*
Okra
    Brunswick Stew, **254**
    Garden Vegetable Soup, **242**
    Okra Gumbo, **257**
    Okra with Corn and Tomato, *532*
    Vegetable Dumpling Stew, **262**
Olives
    Black Olive Butter, 65
    Greek Salad Tacos, 148
    Linguine with Olives, Capers, and
        Tomatoes, 598
    Mediterranean Vegetable Stew, **258**
    Mushroom and Olive Blend, 583
    Olive and Pepper Couscous Salad, *147*
    Small Shells with Grilled Vegetables,
        Olives, Oregano, and Tomatoes, 607
    Tomato and Black Olive Bruschetta, 194
    Warm Spinach Salad with Potatoes, Red
        Onions, and Kalamata Olives, 143
Onions. *See also* Leeks
    about: choosing varieties, 335; storing
        caramelized, 547
    Baked Peppers and Onions, 555
    Caramelized Onion Dip, **169**
    Caramelized Pearl Onions, 546
    Chickpeas in Potato-Onion Curry, 365
    Fettuccine with Morels and Spring
        Onions, 563
    French Onion Soup, **241**
    Grilled Onions with Balsamic Glaze, 551
    Grilled Scallions, 552
    Jumbo Beer-Battered Onion Rings, 540
    Onion Jam, 63
    Onion Tart, 548
    Pickled Red Onions, 559
    Pissaladière, 558
    Risotto with Portobello Mushrooms,
        Onions, and Garlic, 561
    Roasted Shallots, 550
    Roasted Sweet Onions, 549
    Scallion Pancakes, 544
    Slow Cooker Caramelized Onions, **547**
    Stuffed Cabbage, 473
    Stuffed Onions, 541
    Sweet Onion Relish, *97*
    Swiss Chard Rolls with Root Vegetables,
        476
    Vidalia Onion Salad, 556
Orzo. *See* Pasta

Pancakes, 30, 180, 321, 373, 477, 544
Pantry items, 21
Parsley
    Chickpea-Parsley-Dill Dip, *164*
    Garlic Parsley Mashed Potatoes, *325*
    Garlic-Parsley Potatoes, **350**
Parsnips
    about, 320
    Curried Parsnips, 307
    Moroccan Root Vegetables, **324**
    Parsnip and Carrot Bake, 312
    Parsnip Purée, 296, *320*
    Slow Cooker Parsnip Purée, **297**
    Swiss Chard Rolls with Root Vegetables,
        476
Passion Fruit Green Tea, **690**
Pasta, 584–623. *See also* Polenta
    about: orzo, 616; shapes for soup, 228
    Angel Hair with Broccoli Raab, Toasted
        Garlic, Fava Beans, and Pecorino
        Cheese, 601
    Baked Ziti, 603
    Basic Pasta, 586
    Basic Pasta Salad, 605
    The Best Pesto, 597
    Bow-Tie Pasta in a Sage Beurre Blanc
        Sauce, *623*
    Broccoli–Pine Nut Pasta Salad, *620*
    Cincinnati Chili, **276**
    Farfalle (Bow-Ties) Fra Diavolo, 592
    Fettuccine Alfredo, 593
    Fettuccine with Morels and Spring

Onions, 563
Fettuccine with Shiitake Mushrooms and Brown Butter, 600
Five-Minute Pasta Pesto, 592
Fresh Spinach–White Wine Angel Hair Pasta, 621
Fusilli (Spirals) with Grilled Eggplant, Garlic, and Spicy Tomato Sauce, 591
Gemelli with Asparagus Tips, Lemon, and Butter, 587
Gnocchi and Mushrooms in Rosemary Alfredo Sauce, 613
Greek-Style Orzo and Spinach Soup, **250**
Linguine with Gorgonzola, Asparagus, and Cream, 608
Linguine with Olives, Capers, and Tomatoes, 598
Macaroni and Cheese, 610
Minestrone Soup, **228**
Minestrone with Basil Pesto, 229
Mock Meatball Stew, **273**
Noodle Pudding, 632
Orecchiette with Roasted Peppers, Green Beans, and Pesto, 596
Orzo-Stuffed Poblano Peppers, 616
Orzo-Stuffed Tomatoes, 617
Pasta Fagiole, 615
Pasta Primavera with Vegetables, 611
Pasta Puttanesca, 618
Pasta Salad with Tomato, Arugula, and Feta, 612
Pho, **251**
Portobello Stroganoff, 622
Pumpkin-Spinach Lasagna, 588
Raw Veggie Pasta Toss, 604
Red Bean and Pasta Soup, 211
Roasted Vegetable Pasta, 606
Rotini with Red Wine Marinara, 615
Small Shells with Grilled Vegetables, Olives, Oregano, and Tomatoes, 607
Spaghetti Ai Pomodorini, 609
Spaghetti with Asparagus, Parmesan, and Cream, 595
Spaghetti with Sweet Corn, Tomatoes, and Goat Cheese, 602
Spinach Manicotti, 603
Swiss Chard Ravioli, 589
Tagliatelle Aglio e Olio, 609
Tofu Noodle Soup, **238**
Vegetable Linguine in White Bean Alfredo Sauce, 614
White Lasagna with Spinach and Mushrooms, 590
Whole-Wheat Fettuccine with Mushroom Cream Sauce, 619
Ziti with Peppers and Marinated Mozzarella, 594
Peaches

Dried Fruit Compote, 658
Peach and Toasted Almond Preserves, *104*
Peach Iced Tea, **685**
Peach Jam, *107*
Spiced Peaches, 655
Peanuts and peanut butter
about: Cajun peanuts, 200
Boiled Peanuts, *200*
Cajun Peanuts, **198**
Cinnamon and Sugar Peanuts, **199**
Easy Peanut Sauce, **85**
Peanut Butter and Fudge Cheesecake, *672*
Peanut Butter Cake, **661**
Spicy Peanut Sauce, *86*
Pears
Caramel Apples and Pears, **664**
Cinnamon Poached Apples, **656**
Fruit Compote, *659*
Ginger-Pear Punch, **679**
Ginger Poached Pears, **656**
Mincemeat, *103*
Pear Oatmeal, **51**
Pears Poached in White Wine with Strawberry Sauce, 654
Salad of Celery Root and Pears, 115
Vanilla-Spice Pear Butter, *68*
Peas. *See* Beans and legumes
Pecans. *See* Nuts and seeds
Peppers
Baked Peppers and Onions, 555
Brie Timbales with Roasted Red Pepper Sauce, 537
Cheesy Poblano Peppers, **535**
Corn and Pepper Pudding, 530
Couscous-Stuffed Red Peppers, *391*
Five Pepper Chili, **279**
Grilled Vegetable Antipasto, 126
Jalapeño Cheese Dip, *165*
Jalapeño-Tomatillo Sauce, **76**
Manchego-Potato Tacos with Pickled Jalapeños, 179
New Mexico Chili Sauce, 81
Olive and Pepper Couscous Salad, *147*
Orecchiette with Roasted Peppers, Green Beans, and Pesto, 596
Orzo-Stuffed Poblano Peppers, 616
Rainbow Bell Pepper Marmalade, *101*
Rancheros Salsa, 152
Red Pepper Grits, *37*
Roasted Peppers, 127
Roasted Red Bell Pepper Purée, 536
Roasted Red Pepper Sauce, *85*
Southwest Vegetable Chili, **275**
Stuffed Peppers, **398**
Summer Vegetable Bean Salad, **435**
Summer Vegetable Slaw, 122

Three Pepper Sauce, **84**
Three Pepper Vegan Frittata/Scramble, **56**
Vegan Chili, **274**
Vegetable Gado-Gado, 190
Yellow Pepper Coulis, *91*
Ziti with Peppers and Marinated Mozzarella, 594
Pickled Mushrooms, 580
Pickled Red Onions, 559
Pie dough, 293
Pineapple
Hot Cranberry-Pineapple Punch, **678**
Piña Colada Bread Pudding, *674*
Pissaladière, 558
Pizzas, 181, 193, 558
Plantains. *See* Bananas and plantains
Plums
Plum Pudding with Brandy Sauce, *671*
Plum Sauce, *93*
Polenta
Corny Polenta Breakfast Pancakes, 30
Creamy Thyme Polenta, *387*
Pan-Fried Polenta with Marinara, *386*
Polenta-Style Grits with Wild Mushroom Ragout, 564
Polenta with Butter and Cheese, 385
Polenta with Wild Mushrooms, 599
Posole, **265**
Potatoes. *See also* Sweet potatoes
about: ricer for smoothing, 327
Aloo Gobi (Cauliflower and Potato Curry), 456, *457*
Braised Fingerling Potatoes, *338*
Breakfast Casserole, **44**
Celery Root, Artichoke, and Potato Gratin, 309
Cheesy Peasy Potatoes, **333**
Chickpeas in Potato-Onion Curry, 365
Chilled Curry Potato-Fennel Soup, 223
Classic American Potato Salad, 120
Corn and Potato Chowder, 233
Crisp Potato Pancakes, 321
Curried New Potato Salad, 139
Dill Potato Salad, *139*
Dill Red Potatoes, **339**
French Fries, 301
Garden Vegetable Soup, **242**
Garlic-Parmesan Mashed Potatoes, **348**
Garlic Parsley Mashed Potatoes, *325*
Garlic-Parsley Potatoes, **350**
German Potato Salad, *140*
Hash Browns, **39**
Herbed Potatoes, **342**
Home Fries, 24
Leek Potato Cakes, 553
Manchego-Potato Tacos with Pickled Jalapeños, 179
Meatless Moussaka, **514**

INDEX 699

Mexican Spice Potatoes, **347**
Onion, Pepper, and Potato Hash Browns, **39**
Poblano Hash Browns, *42*
Potato-Broccoli Casserole, **349**
Potatoes Au Gratin, **336**
Potatoes Paprikash, **330**
Potato-Leek Soup, **242**
Potato Messaround, **328**
Potato Pakoras (Fritters), 157
Potato Piccata, **343**
Potato Risotto, **334**
Pressure Cooker Aloo Gobi, *457*
Pressure Cooker Hash Browns, *40*
Pumpkin Stew, **266**
Roasted Garlic Mashed Potatoes, 323
Roasted Vegetables, 519
Roasted Yukon Gold Potatoes, 294
Rosemary Fingerling Potatoes, **337**
Rosemary-Garlic Mashed Potatoes, **331**
Rosemary Home Fries, **50**
Rosemary Mashed Potatoes, *326*
Rosemary New Potatoes, 322
Scalloped Potatoes, **335**
Southwestern Casserole, **332**
Swiss Chard Rolls with Root Vegetables, 476
Turnip and Potato Gratin, 295
Twice-Baked Potatoes, 327
Vichyssoise (Potato and Leek Soup), 227
Warm Potato Salad with Balsamic Vinegar and Onions, 138
Warm Spinach Salad with Potatoes, Red Onions, and Kalamata Olives, 143
White Potato Pie, 292
Winter Vegetable Medley, *526*
Pretzels, chocolate-covered, **666**
Pumpkin
Pumpkin-Ale Soup, **222**
Pumpkin Bread, 626
Pumpkin Soup with Caraway Seeds, 221
Pumpkin Spice (beverage), **681**
Pumpkin-Spinach Lasagna, 588
Pumpkin Stew, **266**

Quinoa, *355*
about, 38
Breakfast Quinoa with Fruit, **38**
Quinoa Artichoke Hearts Salad, *146*
Quinoa Salad with Tomatoes and Cilantro, 362
Three Grain Pilaf, *393*
Tomato, Garlic, and Parsley Quinoa Salad, *144*

Radicchio
Grilled Radicchio, 480
Grilled Vegetable Antipasto, 126

Raisins
Creamy Coconut Rice Pudding, *669*
Dried Fruit Compote, *658*
Fruit Compote, *659*
Raspberries. *See* Berries
Ratatouille, 502, *508*
Rice and wild rice
about: brown rice nutritional benefits, 354; paella staples, 401; white rice, 394; wild rice, 355
Beet Risotto Cakes, 384
Brown Rice, *354*
Brown Rice and Vegetables, **408**
Chinese Black Rice, *387*
Coconut Rice Pudding, **662**
Cranberry-Pecan Pilaf, **396**
Creamy Coconut Rice Pudding, *669*
Creole Jambalaya, *388*
Cuban Black Beans and Rice (Moros y Cristianos), 376
Curried Rice, **408**
Easy Saffron Vegetable Risotto, 381
Egyptian Lentils and Rice, 375
Fried Rice with Green Peas and Egg, 370
Green Rice Pilaf, 396
Mexican Rice, 375
Mock Chicken and Rice, **406**
New Orleans Red Beans and Rice, **359**
Paella, **400**–*402*
Peppery Brown Rice Risotto, *379*
Potato Risotto, **334**
Pressure Cooker Cuban Black Beans and Rice, *414*
Pressure Cooker Hoppin' John, *445*
Pressure Cooker Paella, **401**
Pumpkin Risotto, *380*
Red Beans and Rice, **360**
Red Beans and Rice Pie with Oregano and Tomatoes, 358
Red Beans and Yellow Rice, 357
Rice Pilaf, *394*
Risotto with Portobello Mushrooms, Onions, and Garlic, 561
Saffron Rice, **405**
Spanish Rice, **407**
Spring Mushroom Risotto with Morels and Asparagus, 572
Stuffed Eggplant, **516**
Stuffed Grape Leaves, *163*
Stuffed Peppers, **398**
Sushi Rice, 363
Three Grain Pilaf, *393*
Tomatillo Rice, **397**
Vegan Chorizo Paella, *402*
Vegetable Fried Rice, **399**
Vegetable Rice Pilaf, *395*
White Beans and Rice, *441*
White Rice, *354*

Wild Mushroom Risotto, **382**
Wild Mushroom Risotto with Truffles, 383
Wild Rice, *355*
Wild Rice and Portobello Soup, **252**
Wild Rice Salad with Mushrooms and Almonds, 128
Wild Rice Vegetable Pancakes, 373
Wild Rice with Apples and Almonds, 374
Wild Rice with Mixed Vegetables, **374**
Root vegetables, 290–351. *See also specific root vegetables*
Rosemary
about: growing, 326
Gnocchi and Mushrooms in Rosemary Alfredo Sauce, *613*
Rosemary Alfredo Sauce, *613*
Rosemary Fingerling Potatoes, **337**
Rosemary-Garlic Mashed Potatoes, **331**
Rosemary-Lemon Butter, 66
Rosemary Mashed Potatoes, *326*
Rosemary New Potatoes, 322
Rosemary-Thyme Green Beans, **522**
Sweet Potato and Rosemary Pizza, 193
Roux, 87
Rutabagas
Herb-Mixed Turnips, 306
Rutabaga Oven Fries, 305
Turnip and Potato Gratin, 295

Saffron Rice, **405**
Saffron vegetable risotto, 381
Salad dressings
Balsamic Vinaigrette, 133
Caesar Salad Dressing, 123
Madras Curry Dressing, 119
Orange-Sesame Vinaigrette, 118
Roquefort Vinaigrette, 116
Salads, 108–49
Asian Cucumber Salad, 120
Barley and Corn Salad, 132
Basic Egg Salad, 137
Basic Pasta Salad, 605
Broccoli–Pine Nut Pasta Salad, *620*
Caesar Salad, 123
California Garden Salad with Avocado and Sprouts, 135
Chipotle Black Bean Salad, **409**
Classic American Potato Salad, 120
Curried New Potato Salad, 139
Dill Potato Salad, *139*
Edamame-Seaweed Salad, *112*
German Potato Salad, *140*
Greek Salad Tacos, 148
Grilled Vegetable Antipasto, 126
Insalata Caprese (Tomato-Mozzarella Salad), 125
Lentil Salad, 134
Marinated Beet Salad, 136

Mashed Eggplant and Tomato Salad, *510*
Mediterranean Sweet Potato Salad, *142*
Mixed Baby Greens with Balsamic Vinaigrette, 133
Olive and Pepper Couscous Salad, *147*
Pasta Salad with Tomato, Arugula, and Feta, *612*
Quick Three Bean Salad, 124
Quinoa Artichoke Hearts Salad, *146*
Ricotta and Goat Cheese Crespelle, 149
Roasted Peppers, 127
Salad of Celery Root and Pears, 115
Southeast Asian Slaw, 110
Succotash Salad, 121
Summer Vegetable Bean Salad, **435**
Summer Vegetable Slaw, 122
Sweet Potato Salad, **141**
Sweet White Salad with Shaved Asiago, 131
Tabbouleh, 129
Tatsoi Salad, 117
Three Bean Salad, *113*
Tofu Salad, 130
Tomato, Garlic, and Parsley Quinoa Salad, *144*
Tomato and Bread Salad (Panzanella), 114
Vidalia Onion Salad, 556
Warm Chickpea Salad, *111*
Warm Oyster Mushroom Salad, 580
Warm Potato Salad with Balsamic Vinegar and Onions, 138
Warm Spinach Salad with Potatoes, Red Onions, and Kalamata Olives, 143
Wheat Berry Salad, *145*
Wild Rice Salad with Mushrooms and Almonds, 128
Winter Greens Salad with Green Beans and Roquefort Vinaigrette, 116
Salsas. *See* Hors d'oeuvres and snacks
Salt, kosher, 177
Sandwiches and wraps
　Avocado-Beet Wraps with Succotash, 367
　Black Bean Burritos, 377
　Chinese Three Slivers, 569
　Greek Salad Tacos, 148
　Herbed Red and Yellow Tomatoes on Honey-Nut Bread, 496
　Manchego-Potato Tacos with Pickled Jalapeños, 179
　Open-Faced Bean Burrito, **411**
　Portobello Pita with Buckwheat and Beans, 566
　Scrambled Egg Burritos, 25
　Spicy Breakfast Burrito, **45**
　Wheat and Corn Wraps with Tofu, 369
Sangria, **687**
Sauces and spreads, 60–107. *See also* Salad dressings

about: balancing acidity of tomatoes, 72; butter and char, 66; gel point for preserves, 99; roux, 87; sugar crystals and gelling process, 100
Aioli (Garlic Mayonnaise), 64
Apple Butter, *67*
Au Jus, *88*
Barbecue Sauce, **79**
Basic Fresh Tomato Sauce, 70
Basic Marinara Sauce, **74**
Basil Pesto, 62
Béchamel Sauce, *88*
The Best Pesto, 597
Beurre Blanc, *89*
Blackberry Jam, *106*
Black Olive Butter, 65
Blueberry Jam, *102*
Brandy Sauce, *671*
Caribbean Relish, *105*
Cashew Cream Sauce, *92*
Chili-Orange Butter for Grilled Bread, 66
Coconut Curry Sauce, *83*
Country Barbecue Sauce, *80*
Country White Gravy, **77**
Cranberry-Apple Chutney, *94*
Cranberry Chutney, 637
Cranberry Sauce, *69*
Creamy Dijon Sauce, **77**
Dried Apricot Preserves, *99*
Easy Grape Jelly, *107*
Easy Peanut Sauce, **85**
Espagnole, *87*
Fresh Tomato Chutney, *95*
Fresh Tomato Sauce, *72*
Garden Marinara Sauce, *73*
Garlic and Basil Butter, 65
Green Tomato Chutney, *96*
Hollandaise Sauce, 511, 512
Homemade Ketchup, *82*
Jalapeño-Tomatillo Sauce, **76**
Lemon Butter Sauce, 469, 471
Lemon Dill Sauce, **76**
Maître d' Butter, 64
Mincemeat, *103*
Miso Dressing, 501
Mixed Citrus Marmalade, *100*
Mole, **81**
Mushroom Cream Sauce, *619*
New Mexico Chili Sauce, 81
Onion Jam, *63*
Peach and Toasted Almond Preserves, *104*
Peach Jam, *107*
Plum Sauce, *93*
Puttanesca Sauce, **78**
Quick Tomato Sauce, 71
Rainbow Bell Pepper Marmalade, *101*
Raspberry Coulis, **83**
Red and Yellow Plum Tomato Chutney, 499

Red Garlic Mayonnaise (Rouille), 62
Red Wine Marinara, 615
Rémoulade Sauce, 497
Roasted Red Pepper Sauce, *85*, 537
Rosemary-Lemon Butter, 66
Sage Beurre Blanc Sauce, 623
Slow-Roasted Garlic and Tomato Sauce, 69
Spicy Peanut Sauce, *86*
Strawberry Jam, *98*
Strawberry Sauce, 654
Sweet Onion Relish, *97*
Three Pepper Sauce, **84**
Tofu Sour Cream, 63
Vanilla-Spice Pear Butter, *68*
Vegan Alfredo, **74**
Vegan Hollandaise Sauce, 512
Vodka Sauce, *90*
White Bean Alfredo Sauce, **75**
White Gravy, **50**
White Wine–Garlic Sauce, **84**
Yellow Pepper Coulis, *91*
Sauerkraut, homemade, **489**
Sausage
　Black Bean and "Sausage" Chili, **287**
　Breakfast Casserole, **44**
　Creole Jambalaya, *388*
　New Orleans Red Beans and Rice, **259**
　Tempeh Sausage Crumbles, **42**
　Vegan Chorizo Paella, *402*
Scallions. *See* Onions
Seafood, vegetarian. *See* Fish and seafood, vegetarian
Seitan
　Curried Seitan Stew, **261**
　Seitan and Cabbage Stew, **264**
　Seitan and Mushroom Stew, **260**
　Seitan Bourguignonne, **270**
Shallots, 518
Shallots, roasted, 550
Slow cooker, using, 515
Snacks. *See* Hors d'oeuvres and snacks
Soups and stews, 206–89. *See also* Chili
　about: choosing right broth, 242; pasta shapes for soup, 228; storing broth, 210
　Acorn Squash Soup with Anise and Carrots, 236
　Beer-Cheese Soup, **243**
　Black Bean Soup, **214**
　Brunswick Stew, **254**
　Butternut Squash Soup, **244**
　Carrot Purée with Nutmeg, 219
　Cauliflower Chowder, **267**
　Cauliflower Soup, **240**
　Celery Root Soup, **253**
　Chilaquiles (Tortilla Stew), 500
　Chilled Curry Potato-Fennel Soup, 223
　Corn and Potato Chowder, 233

Cream of Asparagus Soup, 215
Creamy Chickpea Soup, **245**
Cuban Black Bean Soup with Coriander Tofu Sour Cream, 232
Curried Seitan Stew, **261**
Étouffée, **263**
French Onion Soup, **241**
Garden Vegetable Soup, **242**
Gazpacho, 225
Greek-Style Orzo and Spinach Soup, **250**
Hot and Sour Soup, **239**
Jamaican Red Bean Stew, **255**
Korean-Style Hot Pot, **269**
Lentil Soup with Cumin, 230
Mediterranean Vegetable Stew, **258**
Minestrone Soup, **228**
Minestrone with Basil Pesto, 229
Miso Soup, 237
Mock Meatball Stew, **273**
Mushroom, Barley, and Collard Greens Soup, 234
Mushroom Barley Soup, **246**
Mushroom Vegetable Stock, 218
No-Beef Broth, **210**
Okra Gumbo, **257**
Pho, **251**
Pinto Bean Soup with Salsa Fresca, 235
Posole, **265**
Potato-Leek Soup, **242**
Pressure Cooker Vegetable Stock, *209*
Pumpkin-Ale Soup, **222**
Pumpkin Soup with Caraway Seeds, 221
Pumpkin Stew, **266**
Red Bean and Pasta Soup, 211
Red Lentil Soup, **213**
Seitan and Cabbage Stew, **264**
Seitan and Mushroom Stew, **260**
Seitan Bourguignonne, **270**
Simple Split Pea Soup, **248**
Smoky Black-Eyed Pea Soup with Sweet Potatoes and Mustard Greens, 220
Smooth Cauliflower Soup with Coriander, 224
Southwest Corn Chowder, **256**
Summer Borscht, **247**
Super Greens Stew, **271**
Texas Stew, **272**
Tofu Noodle Soup, **238**
Tomato Basil Soup, **216**
Tomato Soup, 216
Tortilla Soup, **249**
Tuscan White Bean Ragout, 371
Tuscan White Bean Soup, 231
Vegetable Broth, **210**
Vegetable Dumpling Stew, **262**
Vegetable Stock, 208
Vichyssoise (Potato and Leek Soup), 227
White Bean and Barley Soup, **212**
White Bean and Tomato Stew, **259**
White Bean Cassoulet, **268**
Wild Mushroom Soup with Thyme, 217
Wild Rice and Portobello Soup, **252**
Yellow Split Pea Soup with Cactus and Hominy, 226
Zucchini Ragout, **517**
Sour Cream Butter Cake, 648
Soymilk, unsweetened, 243
Spelt, in Mushroom-Spelt Sauté, 568
Spices, toasting, 133
Spinach
 Creamed Spinach, 472
 Fresh Spinach–White Wine Angel Hair Pasta, *621*
 Greek-Style Orzo and Spinach Soup, **250**
 Lentil-Spinach Curry, *446*
 Lentils with Sautéed Spinach, White Wine, and Garlic, *432*
 Potato Risotto, **334**
 Pumpkin-Spinach Lasagna, 588
 Spinach and Feta Pie, 479
 Spinach and Portobello Benedict, *59*
 Spinach and Tomato Sauté, 455
 Spinach Manicotti, 603
 Spinach Pancakes with Cardamom, 477
 Spinach Quiche, 49
 Spinach-Stuffed Vegetables, 478
 Spinach with Pine Nuts (Pignoli) and Garlic, 462
 Tatsoi Salad, 117
 Vegan Creamed Spinach, **463**
 Vegan Spinach and Artichoke Dip, **156**
 Warm Spinach Salad with Potatoes, Red Onions, and Kalamata Olives, 143
 White Lasagna with Spinach and Mushrooms, 590
Spring rolls, *186*
Sprouts
 California Garden Salad with Avocado and Sprouts, 135
 Hummus bi Tahini with Sprouts and Cherry Tomatoes in a Pita Pocket, 390
 Pho, **251**
Squash
 about: butternut peak season, 524
 Acorn Squash Chili, **288**
 Acorn Squash Soup with Anise and Carrots, 236
 Breakfast Tofu and Veggies, **43**
 Butternut Squash, *524*
 Butternut Squash Soup, **244**
 Crudités with Three Dips, 158
 Cumin-Roasted Butternut Squash, 493
 Grilled Vegetable Antipasto, 126
 Pasta Primavera with Vegetables, *611*
 Ratatouille, 502
 Raw Veggie Pasta Toss, 604
 Roasted Vegetables, 519
 Spaghetti Squash, *525*
 Spinach-Stuffed Vegetables, 478
 Stewed Squash, *525*
 Vegetable Gado-Gado, 190
 Winter Vegetable Medley, *526*
Stocks. *See* Soups and stews
Strawberries. *See* Berries
Stuffing, bulgur, *392*
Sushi
 Avocado Kappa Maki Sushi Rolls, 364
 Sushi Rice, 363
Sweet potatoes
 Chipotle and Thyme Mashed Sweet Potatoes, *344*
 Chipotle and Thyme Sweet Potatoes, **340**
 Gingered Mashed Sweet Potatoes, 311
 Maple-Glazed Sweet Potatoes, **341**
 Mashed Sweet Potatoes, *345*
 Mediterranean Sweet Potato Salad, *142*
 Pressure Cooker Maple-Glazed Sweet Potatoes, *346*
 Sweet Potato and Rosemary Pizza, 193
 Sweet Potato Casserole, **329**
 Sweet Potato Chili, **280**
 Sweet Potato Salad, **141**
 Winter Vegetable Medley, *526*
Swiss chard
 Braised Swiss Chard, 461
 Super Greens Stew, **271**
 Swiss Chard Ravioli, 589
 Swiss Chard Rolls with Root Vegetables, 476

Tabbouleh, 129
Tacos, 148, 179
Tapioca Pudding, *675*
Teas. *See* Beverages
Tempeh
 Breakfast Casserole, **44**
 Tempeh Sausage Crumbles, **42**
Toasting
 nuts, 104
 pine nuts, 172
 spices, 133
Tofu
 about: Tofu ricotta, 403
 Breakfast Tofu and Veggies, **43**
 Chinese Three Slivers, 569
 Chive Dumplings, 557
 Cuban Black Bean Soup with Coriander Tofu Sour Cream, 232
 Easy Tofu "Eggs," **43**
 Eggplant "Lasagna," **403**
 Garden Tofu Scramble, *34*
 Hot and Sour Soup, **239**
 Korean-Style Hot Pot, **269**
 Miso Soup, 237
 Mushroom-Tofu Stir-Fry, 578

Pressure Cooker Tofu Ranchero, 58
Slow Cooker Spicy Tofu Scramble, 35, **41**
Slow Cooker Tofu Ranchero, **46**
Spicy Breakfast Burrito, **45**
Spinach and Portobello Benedict, 59
Sunrise Tofu Scramble, 33
Three Pepper Vegan Frittata/Scramble, 56
Tofu Frittata/Scramble, **32**
Tofu Noodle Soup, **238**
Tofu Salad, 130
Tofu Sour Cream, 63
Tortilla Soup, **249**
Wheat and Corn Wraps with Tofu, 369
Yeasty Tofu and Veggies, 57

Tomatillos
about, 184
Jalapeño-Tomatillo Sauce, **76**
Tomatillo Rice, **397**
Tomatillo Salsa, 184

Tomatoes
about: balancing acidity of, 72; campari, 289; peeling, 95
Basic Fresh Tomato Sauce, 70
Basic Marinara Sauce, **74**
Cabbage Stewed in Tomato Sauce, 462
Collard Greens with Tomatoes and Cheddar, 485
Eggplant and Tomato Sauté, 513
Fresh Tomato Chutney, 95
Fresh Tomato Sauce, 72
Fried Green Tomato Bruschetta, 175
Fried Green Tomatoes with Rémoulade Sauce, 497
Garden Marinara Sauce, 73
Green Tomato Chutney, 96
Grilled Vegetable Antipasto, 126
Herbed Red and Yellow Tomatoes on Honey-Nut Bread, 496
Herb-Stuffed Tomatoes, **495**
Homemade Ketchup, **82**
Insalata Caprese (Tomato-Mozzarella Salad), 125
Mashed Eggplant and Tomato Salad, 510
Mushroom-Stuffed Tomatoes, 494
Okra with Corn and Tomato, 532
pasta with. See Pasta
Puttanesca Sauce, **78**
Quick Tomato and Oregano Sauté, 503
Quick Tomato Sauce, 71
Raj's Chickpeas in Tomato Sauce, 372
Red and Yellow Plum Tomato Chutney, 499
Red Wine Marinara, 615
Salsa Fresca (Pico de Gallo), 198
Savory Sun-Dried Tomato Cheesecake, 643
Simple Salsa, 506
Slow-Roasted Garlic and Tomato Sauce, 69
soups and stews with. See Chili; Soups and stews

Spinach and Tomato Sauté, 455
Stewed Tomatoes, **495**
Succotash, 533
Sun-Dried Tomato Pesto Dip, **172**
Tomato, Garlic, and Parsley Quinoa Salad, 144
Tomato and Black Olive Bruschetta, 194
Tomato and Bread Salad (Panzanella), 114
Tomato and Cheese Tart, 492
Tomato Confit with Fine Herbs, 498
White Beans with Rosemary and Fresh Tomato, **430**

Tortillas
about: steaming, 45
Avocado-Beet Wraps with Succotash, 367
Black Bean Burritos, 377
Chilaquiles (Tortilla Stew), 500
Greek Salad Tacos, 148
Huevos Rancheros, 47
Manchego-Potato Tacos with Pickled Jalapeños, 179
Open-Faced Bean Burrito, **411**
Pressure Cooker Tofu Ranchero, 58
Scrambled Egg Burritos, 25
Slow Cooker Tofu Ranchero, **46**
Spicy Breakfast Burrito, **45**
Tortilla Soup, **249**
Wheat and Corn Wraps with Tofu, 369

Turnips
Herb-Mixed Turnips, 306
Mashed Turnips, 316
Moroccan Root Vegetables, **324**
Savory Turnip Greens, 319
Smoky Spicy Collard Greens with Turnip, 466
Swiss Chard Rolls with Root Vegetables, 476
Turnip and Carrot Purée, 318
Turnip and Potato Gratin, 295

Vanilla-Lavender Tea, **680**
Vanilla-Spice Pear Butter, 68
Vegetables. See also specific vegetables
about: blanching, 620; steaming, 167
Brown Rice and Vegetables, **408**
Crudités with Three Dips, 158
Easy Saffron Vegetable Risotto, 381
Mixed Veggie Dip, **170**
Pasta Primavera with Vegetables, 611
Raw Veggie Pasta Toss, 604
Roasted Vegetable Frittata, 48
Roasted Vegetable Pasta, 606
Roasted Vegetables, 519
Small Shells with Grilled Vegetables, Olives, Oregano, and Tomatoes, 607
soups and stocks with. See Chili; Soups and stews
Spinach-Stuffed Vegetables, 478

Summer Vegetable Bean Salad, **435**
Vegetable Fried Rice, **399**
Vegetable Gado-Gado, 190
Vegetable Linguine in White Bean Alfredo Sauce, 614
Wild Rice Vegetable Pancakes, 373
Wild Rice with Mixed Vegetables, **374**
Winter Vegetable Medley, **526**
Yeasty Tofu and Veggies, 57
Zucchini "Lasagna," 504
Veggie dogs, topping for, 489
Vodka Sauce, 90

Wasabi
about, 431
Avocado Kappa Maki Sushi Rolls, 364
Pressure Cooker Wasabi-Barbecue Chickpeas, 443
Wasabi-Barbecue Chickpeas, **431**
Watercress
Stir-Fried Asian Greens, 459
Watercress Dip, 160
Winter Greens Salad with Green Beans and Roquefort Vinaigrette, 116
Wheat berries
Mushroom-Spelt Sauté, 568
Wheat and Corn Wraps with Tofu, 369
Wheat Berry Salad, 145
White beans. See Beans and legumes
White Chocolate–Macadamia Nut Bars, **666**
Wild rice. See Rice and wild rice
Wine
about: selecting for cooking, 84
Au Jus, **88**
Beurre Blanc, 89
Pears Poached in White Wine with Strawberry Sauce, 654
Red Wine Marinara, 615
Sangria, **687**
Spiced Wine, **684**
White Wine–Garlic Sauce, **84**
Yellow Pepper Coulis, **91**
Wraps. See Sandwiches and wraps

Yuca con Mojo (Yuca with Garlic and Lime), 298

Zucchini
Breakfast Tofu and Veggies, **43**
Crudités with Three Dips, 158
Garden Vegetable Chili, **286**
Grilled Vegetable Antipasto, 126
Pasta Primavera with Vegetables, 611
Ratatouille, 502
Raw Veggie Pasta Toss, 604
Spinach-Stuffed Vegetables, 478
Zucchini "Lasagna," 504
Zucchini Ragout, **517**

INDEX 703

ABOUT THE AUTHOR

Rachel Rappaport is a recipe creator, cooking teacher, and blogger. Her blog, *Coconut & Lime* (CoconutAndLime.com), was named one of the top fifty food blogs in the world by MSN's Delish.com. Rappaport writes a column for *Taste of the Bay* magazine about using local seasonal ingredients, and her recipes (as well as her thoughts on food) have been featured in such diverse outlets as NPR.org, the *Baltimore Sun*, the *L.A. Times*, WashingtonPost.com, and the *New York Sun*.